# PARIS 1924

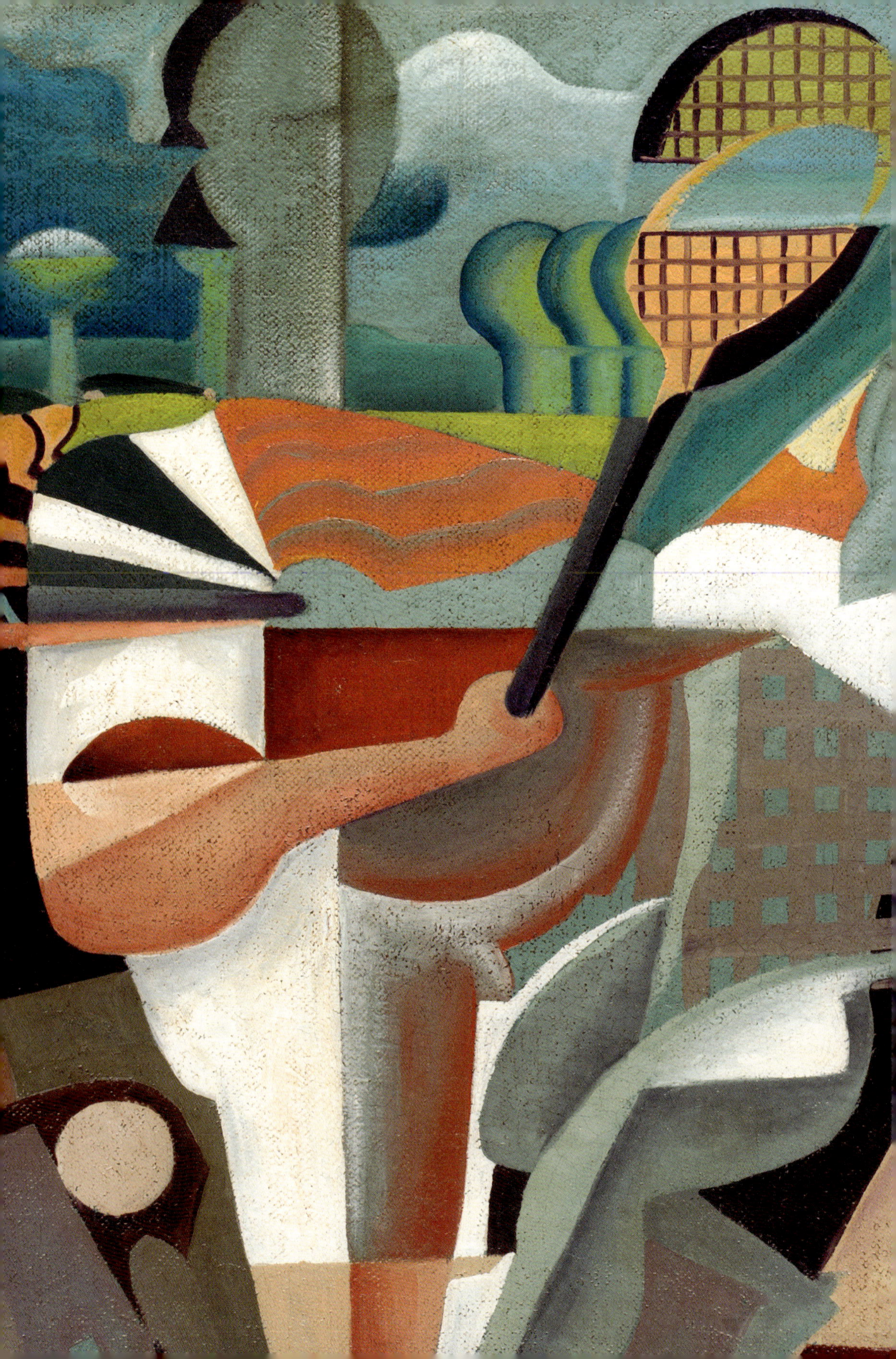

# PARIS 1924

## SPORT, ART AND THE BODY

*edited by*

Caroline Vout and Christopher Young

THE FITZWILLIAM MUSEUM, UNIVERSITY OF CAMBRIDGE

IN ASSOCIATION WITH PAUL HOLBERTON PUBLISHING

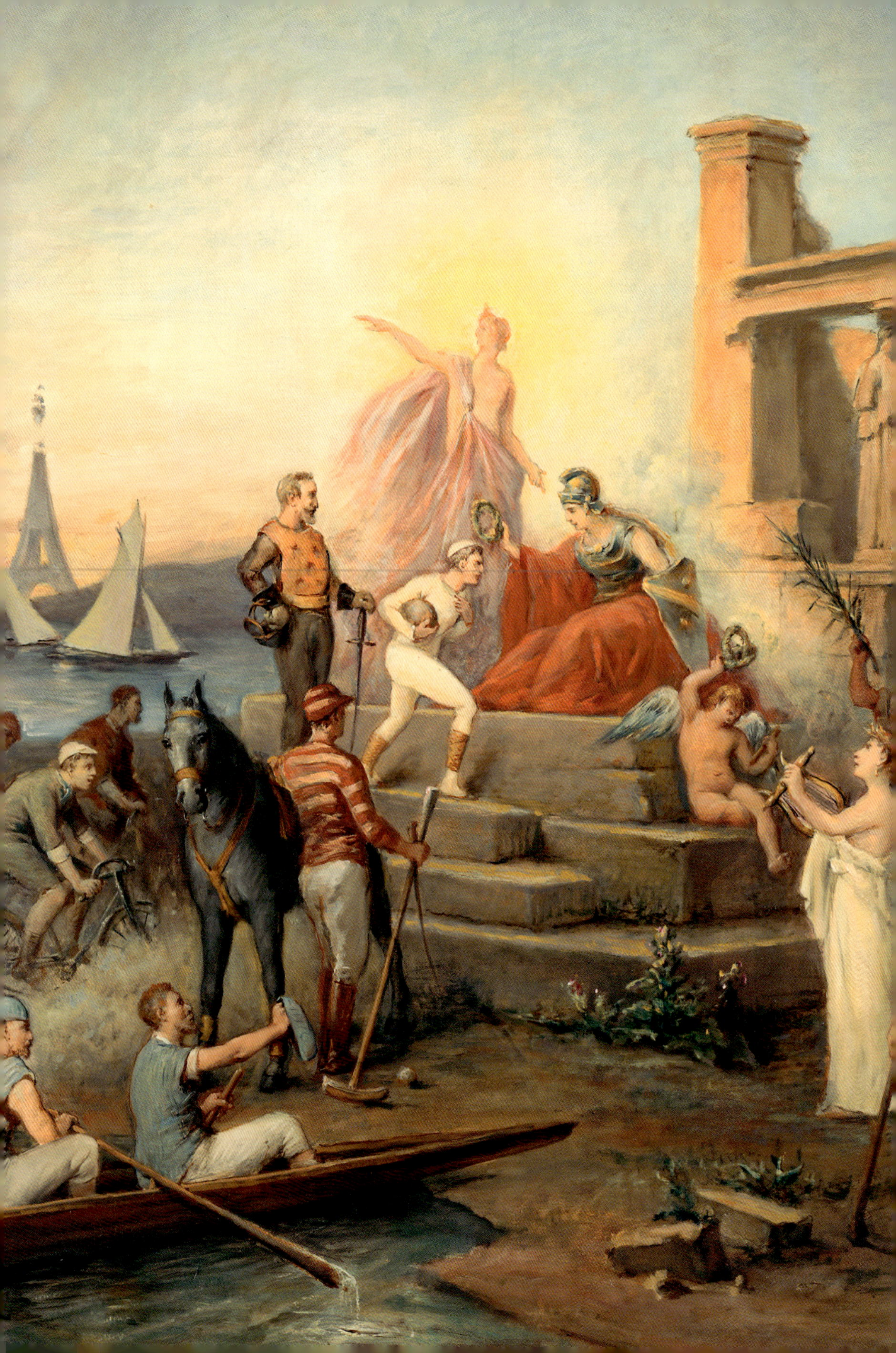

# INTRODUCTION:
## PIERRE DE COUBERTIN, THE OLYMPICS AND PARIS 1924

CAROLINE VOUT AND CHRISTOPHER YOUNG

In spring 1886, the French educator and soon-to-be founder of the modern Olympics, Pierre de Coubertin, visited the Fitzwilliam Museum in Cambridge. Amidst the conviviality of the colleges and excursions to the environs, the Museum was a highlight, as was meeting the Museum's Director, Charles Walston, who shared his passion not only for art but for the ancient world and sport. Coubertin was impressed by the marble entrance hall and the collections (J.M.W. Turner's watercolours in particular) but was taken most by his host's devotion to physical pursuits. For Walston was not only a fine classical archaeologist (whose works already included *The Influence of Athletics Upon Greek Art*, 1883), but a keen equestrian who hunted and rode cross country. He could not wait to show off his horse, prompting his guest to declare that his colleagues in France had a thing or two to learn from 'ce sportsman, aussi aimable que savant' (this sportsman of equal charm and knowledge).[1]

Walston remained a useful contact for Coubertin. When the Frenchman arranged an international congress at the Sorbonne in 1894 to re-found the Olympics, Walston ensured that the King of Greece and the Duke of Sparta, whom he had met while excavating in Argos, attended, thus providing a critical link to the country best placed to make a success of the venture.[2] Two years later, the inaugural Games took place in Athens. Walston did not just attend, but competed in the shooting and helped organise the athletics, gymnastics, cycling and tennis. He was to become 'a distinctive cultural

**1.** Charles de Coubertin (1822–1908)
*Allegory of Sports*, 1896 (detail)
*(Allégorie aux sports)*
Oil on canvas, 800 × 975 cm
Olympic Museum Collections, Lausanne (4134)

No image better captures Pierre de Coubertin's vision for the Olympics than this painting by his father Charles from 1896. With Paris on the left and Athens on the right, the modern and classical worlds turn towards each other. A range of new sports pay homage and are lauded simultaneously by an ancient lyre. In the founder's lifetime, the painting appeared on the cover of the *Revue Olympique*, the IOC's official bulletin. It is now on permanent display at the Olympic Museum in Lausanne.

influence on Coubertin throughout the critical years of development of the Olympic movement' and in 1924 chaired the British committee responsible for entries to the Arts Competition that accompanied the sport.[3]

Paris 1924 was the eighth Olympiad and Coubertin's last as President of the International Olympic Committee (IOC). It was at his special request that the 1924 Games were awarded to the French capital, making it the first city to host twice, having succeeded Athens in 1900. There was a notable Cambridge presence (see Holt's chapter). Not only did Walston exert an influence, but the University's students excelled in the sporting arena, contributing 11 of Britain's 35 medals. Had they been entered as a separate nation, they would have come ninth in the overall rankings. On the track alone, Cambridge won the blue-riband 100m (Harold Abrahams) and 800m (Douglas Lowe); Lowe's roommate, Edinburgh University student Eric Liddell, took gold in the 400m. Some of these feats were recorded in *Chariots of Fire*, which won the Academy Award in 1981 for Best Motion Picture.

But this catalogue, like the exhibition it accompanies, is not about Cambridge. It is about the moment when the world's leading sports event came of age: Paris 1924 were the largest Games to date, with the broadest international participation and the widest media following. And it is about how that sporting event was conceived – and received – as a cultural enterprise. The Olympics are often remembered for their political entanglements – Berlin 1936 being the prominent example before World War II – but the return of the Games to Paris in 2024 gives occasion to reflect on what made the Games 'The Games'. What they were meant to be, what they had become over their founder's lifetime and how a wide variety of people – from athletes and functionaries through writers and artists – reacted to them a hundred years ago are questions that still resonate today.

Those interested in sport would do well to take these reactions seriously. What the Games were is inextricable from how they were framed by the city, its topography and architecture, and by its posters, stamps and postcards; inextricable too from how they were then represented in the press and in art, through films, photographs, sculptures, drawings and paintings. Looking at these genres, we find a Games that eluded the founder's tight control; and we begin to forge a new methodology for studying Olympic history. We appreciate how the Games were seen in France and across the globe, and how they transcended their period and place to enter the cultural imaginary.

Their influence on the cultural imaginary was indeed considerable. Not only did they have a major impact on attitudes to health and to the questions of fitness and nationalism made so urgent by World War I; but in a European city famed for avant-garde artists exploring new ways of representing the strength and frailty of the human form, and on a world stage eager to look to a new future, the Games also challenged, and contributed to, ideas about body image, gender, race, celebrity and fashion. Today, sporting culture and visual culture are often seen as separate spheres. This exhibition, like the Cultural Olympiad of Paris 2024, seeks to fulfil Coubertin's vision by bringing them together and inviting us to see both sport and art in a new light.

## COUBERTIN'S OLYMPIC VISION

The modern Olympics are based on the ancient Greek Games, which were held every four years from (traditionally) 776 BCE until the fourth or fifth century CE in the Sanctuary of Zeus at Olympia. Some said they had been founded long before that, in the mists of time, by Zeus's son, Herakles, whose statues were even more muscular than those erected to the winners. The original Games evolved to include horse racing, pentathlon, running, wrestling and boxing. Largely forgotten in the Middle Ages and early modern period, the Games resurfaced in the mid-eighteenth century through the work of German art historian Johann Joachim Winckelmann, whose study of Greek sculpture was influential among European elites educated in Greek and Latin literature and culture (fig. 2). This legacy, especially its 'classical' visual language, soon defined what fitness looked like. Already in the nineteenth century, there were various attempts to revive the Games – in Britain, Sweden and Greece – but these were small events, confined to their local environments. The organiser of the British version reached out to the

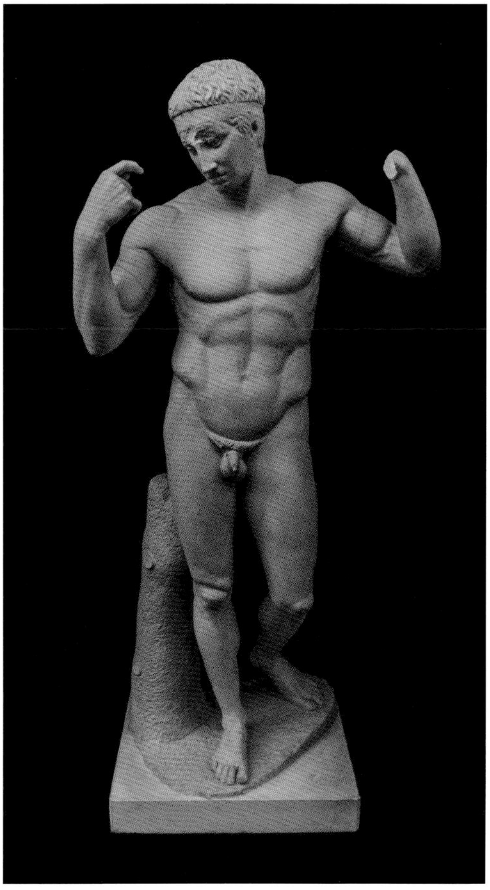

**2.** (cat.2) Domenico Brucciani and Co., London (1841–1900s); after unrecorded Roman maker (British Museum, London, 117–38 CE, marble); after Polykleitos (bronze, now lost, *c.* 440 BCE)
Plaster cast of *Ribbon Binder* (*Diadoumenos*), *c.* 1880

Plaster, metal, paint, 197.7 × 98.4 × 61.8 cm
Museum of Classical Archaeology, Cambridge (185)

This muscular athlete ties a winner's ribbon around his forehead. His body is originally attributed to Polykleitos, one of ancient Greece's most influential sculptors. Polykleitos was renowned for rendering the human body as beautiful, balanced, symmetrical and ideal. For Coubertin, too, there could be no beauty 'without poise and proportion'. As the statue avoids our gaze, it asks for admiration.

Greeks, but the idea of a recurring international event in the Games' original homeland was slow to catch on.

Why did Coubertin succeed where others had not? For one, he was driven by powerful motives: first, to promote sport as a means of strengthening his home country France after its humiliating defeat in the Franco-Prussian War (1870–71); and second, when that project reached its limits, to further sport internationally and contribute to greater dialogue between countries. More importantly, in the late nineteenth century Coubertin stood at a confluence of factors from which none of his predecessors had benefited.

The first of these factors was sport itself. Physical culture was not, of course, unknown in the nineteenth century. Activities such as horse racing and cycling, put on for entertainment and often pursued by professionals, were as popular in France (see Dine's chapter) as elsewhere in Europe. Gymnastics – a broad umbrella that covered apparatus exercises, massed calisthenics, running and jumping (akin to modern athletics) – were practised by hundreds of thousands in their free time across the Continent and beyond. Coubertin was interested in neither. He had little regard for the Mammon of commercial concerns, and much less still for gymnastics. The former he could hardly influence, setting financial gain aside and restricting the Games to amateurs. The latter he sought to supplant. Gymnastics was non-competitive, and, weighed down as it was by national traditions, seemed to him outdated. By contrast, organised athletics and team sports such as football, rugby, hockey and tennis, which had emerged in recent decades in Britain, were newly popular in Europe. They were attractive to the urban middle classes, allowed for competition and international comparison, and imbued forward-looking values. These were the sports that Coubertin's Olympic movement sought to foster and steward through their formative years. The Olympics were a pledge to the future, inspired less by ancient history than by an ideal. As Coubertin wrote in the year of their founding: 'Modern, very modern, will be these restored Olympian Games ... There will be no tripods, no incense; those things are dead, and dead things do not revive.'[4]

The second factor that Coubertin harnessed was the rise of world fairs. The Olympics would be unimaginable without their growth and impact. Started in London in 1851, when the wares of 25 nations were admired by six million visitors, the fairs encapsulated modernity and promoted the development of global networks. Sponsored and controlled by national governments and international NGOs, they produced '"official" versions of public culture'.[5] They displayed cutting-edge technology (e.g. the colt revolver, the elevator, refrigeration and the electric lightbulb) and brought pageant, parades, choirs and drama. Paris hosted three – in 1878, 1889 and 1900 – as part of a programme of cultural policies conceived by the new Third Republic to rebuild national pride after the Franco-Prussian War.[6] In 1889, the city was abuzz. Thirty million attended, and when President Sadi Carnot processed to the Expo site under the Eiffel Tower, specially built for the occasion, half a million people lined the streets to greet him. Many of the rites and symbols witnessed at the opening – the entry procession, raising of flags, national anthems and the presence of the head of state – would soon translate into Olympic tradition.[7] Coubertin was so enamoured of the Chicago Expo of 1893 that he is believed to have immediately offered the city a future Games.

The final factor that aided Coubertin was the undiminished presence of the ancient world. Not only were the Classics a staple of European education, but archaeological discoveries kept these interests fresh and brought life to the literature – none more so than the excavation of the Olympics' original site by German archaeologist Ernst Curtius. Curtius (a lithe, committed gymnast) had called for work on Olympia as early as 1851, but was not granted funding until some 20 years later, ironically in celebration of the German victory over the French.[8] By the late 1880s, parts of the stadium and the temples of Zeus and Hera had been uncovered, to great acclaim. Coubertin, who was helping with the 1889 Paris Expo, proposed Olympia as one of its major themes. Although his suggestion was not taken up, the fair did include a reconstruction of the ancient site on the basis of Curtius's dig and a few modest sports events, entitled 'Olympic Games', on the Champs de Mars. Coubertin, and others, were captivated. In the years immediately before the founding of the modern Olympics, the rediscovery of the ancient site gave momentum to the new endeavour. From the founding onwards, the classical world was constantly and confidently cited – France's 1924 Official Report opens with an account of the ancient Games[9] – but not slavishly followed. For early Olympians, that world was always there as they shaped their own, to be acknowledged and drawn upon whenever needed.

Conducive circumstances did not, however, make for an easy start. The IOC, although retaining ultimate sanction, was beholden to what local organisers, working under specific local conditions, could and would do; there was never much learning from one Games to the next. Being embedded in trade fairs, as they were in 1900 (Paris), 1904 (St. Louis) and 1908 (London), did not help either. It was not until Stockholm 1912 that the Games, standing independent, finally settled. The Swedes gave the Games a centredness, compactness and coherence that they had lacked until that point. From the Opening to the Closing Ceremony, they exuded a sense of sport as a cultural phenomenon like none before them.[10] In 1920 the ceremonials were augmented with an oath for athletes and the now famous five-ring flag, which Coubertin had designed in 1914 to symbolise the earth's five continents. The IOC Session in 1921 adopted the motto 'Citius, Altius, Fortius' (Faster, Higher, Stronger). However, these inventions took time to catch on. The now famous rings appeared at the Opening in Paris and on the tickets (fig. 3), but were absent from official posters, stamps and from the city's Olympic emblem (fig. 4).

1924 was a crucial moment in the history of the Olympics. By the time Paris was awarded the Games (on the basis of a simple letter of support from the city), only Stockholm had come close to matching the founder's vision, and that lay twelve years in the past. War had intervened. What had been an impressive bid to host the previous Games by Antwerp had – post hostilities, in 1920 – resulted in a meagre affair. Much was riding on Paris. Could its Olympics capture the public's imagination after the horrors of war? Could they attract the media's interest? And could their values flourish?

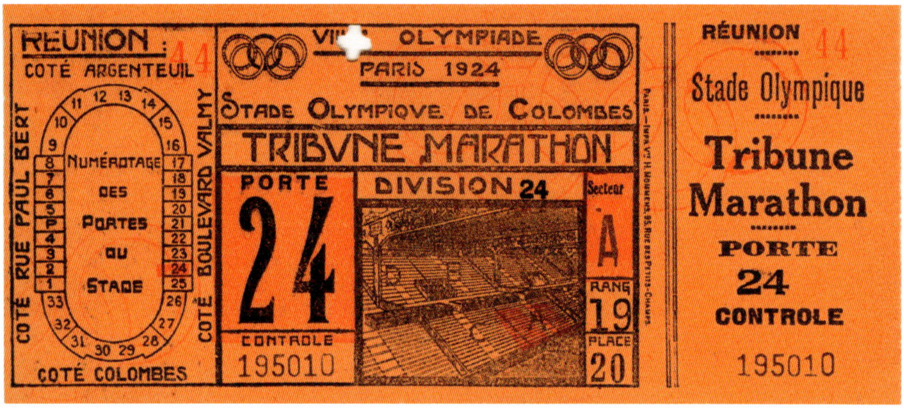


**3.** (cat. 15) Unrecorded maker
Used admission ticket to the Olympic stadium at Colombes, Paris, 1924

Colour printing on orange-coloured paper, 17.6 × 7.9 cm
Markus Osterwalder, Switzerland, Olympic historian and collector

Tickets for the main stadium of the Paris 1924 summer Olympics have more to them than those from the Winter Games in the Alps earlier that year: practical information about the stand, gate, block and row is balanced by the Olympic rings and by representations of the stadium with the gate number highlighted in colour.

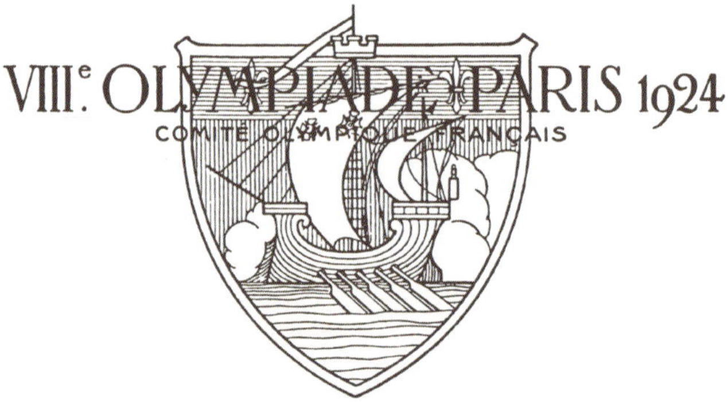


**4.** Unrecorded designer
Emblem of the Paris 1924 Summer Olympics, *c.* 1924

This image shows the design printed on a white background

The Organising Committee chose the traditional coat of arms of Paris as its emblem, a majestic single-masted ship commemorating the city's founding in the Middle Ages on the Île de la Cité. Emblazoned across it are the time and place of the Games. The Olympic rings, introduced in Antwerp four years earlier, are absent. The emblem, which could be adapted to fit different contexts, appeared on mastheads, stamps, envelopes and the rule books for individual sports.

## PARIS 1924

The festivities with which the Games commenced gave immediate visual expression to what the Olympics stood for, connected Paris to Antwerp and Stockholm, and distinguished Olympic competition from other sporting events. The splendour of Paris's Opening Ceremony – modest by later standards but unsurpassed at the time – did not only leave a lasting impression on those who saw it in the stadium, it was also conveyed to millions more in images and words. The British Olympic Association's (BOA) Report, for example, contained an advert for Woodland Fullwood, sports photographer, whose panorama of the Ceremony was available to buy for 12 shillings and sixpence. Encouraging potential purchasers, the notice cited one of England's best-known sports writers, who described the 'impelling spectacle' (fig. 5) as follows: 'An epic in colour, in life, in animation, in all that makes for manliness, and for chivalry it was. It burned itself onto one's very being'.[11]

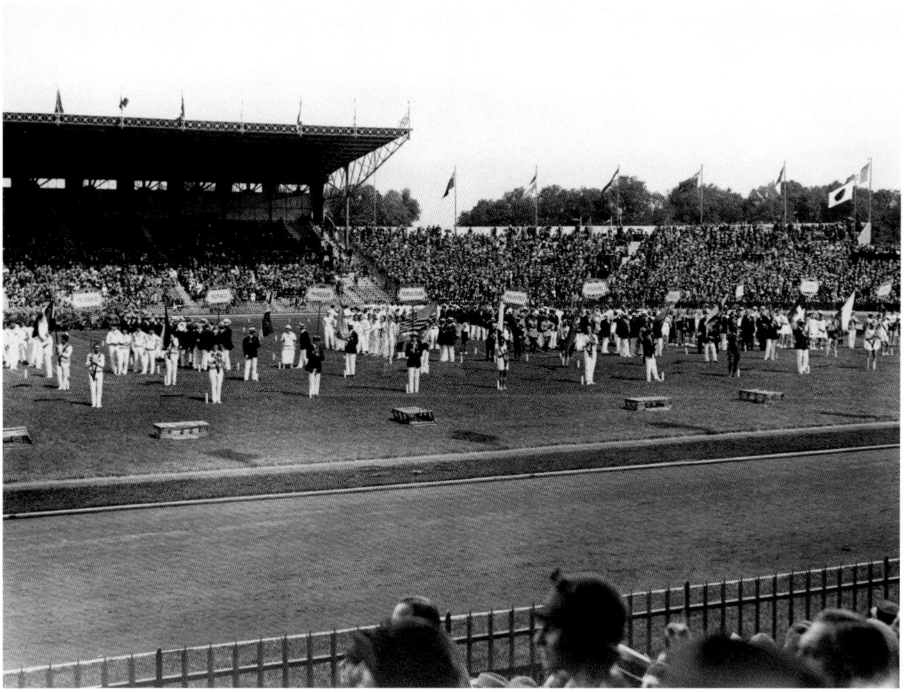

**5.** (cat. 22) Unrecorded photographer
Paris 1924 Olympic Games, Opening Ceremony, parade of athletes, the delegation in the middle of the Olympic stadium, 5 July 1924
Black and white photograph
Comité International Olympique (CIO)
(PHO11072460)

The ceremony every athlete dreamed of taking part in. The black and white image cannot capture what struck observers most: the blaze of colour. 'Under a perfect blue sky', the BOA Report wrote, 'and without the smallest hitch to mar the very imposing spectacle ... the many-coloured uniforms of the athletes of various nations, set off by the bright sunshine, gave an appearance of carnival to the Stadium.'

In a world of black and white media, the quote is a reminder of the picturesque polychromy of the event, with its flags and uniforms – the Australians in green blazers, the Canadians in white trimmed with salmon pink, India in white trimmed with red, and the British, like the Americans, 'fine and smart' in blue and white in the 'bright sunshine' – not to mention the choirs, brass and pipes of the bands and whoops of the crowd. There was fascination too in the 'hard and fit' bodies of the Scandinavians, the 'imposing' Americans and small Haitians, and in the fact that the Japanese were there at all, only months after the Great Kanto Earthquake and tsunami had killed an estimated 140,000.[12] Also there, World War I notwithstanding, were Turkey, Bulgaria, Hungary and Austria. Only Germany was not invited. While the Soviet government spurned the Games to host its own international Games in Moscow, China (competing for the first time) sent four tennis players, although they withdrew before playing any matches.

Some events had already happened by the time of the Opening Ceremony on 5 July. But its bringing together of competitors, officials and dignitaries, the pomp and the pageantry, was crucial for painting a picture of international unity and for instilling in spectators a shared sense that each sporting performance was greater than itself, a spectacle of awe and beauty akin to the ritual and religiosity of the original Games at Olympia. There would be no Olympic flame until Amsterdam four years later and no torch relay bringing it from Olympia to the host city until Berlin 1936, but the parade of athletes and the solemn oath sworn by a single athlete on behalf of his fellow participants from a dais decorated with the Olympic rings, his right arm raised in what would become known as the Olympic salute, was as moving as it was symbolic. The debate, both in the French Olympic Committee and in the press, about who this athlete should be added to the drama (tennis star Suzanne Lenglen was in the frame only, in the end, for the honour to go to all-round athlete Georges 'Géo' André). No wonder 'enterprising photographers were at work leaning dangerously from encircling aeroplanes',[13] taking images like the one for sale in the advert.

Paris was in thrall to new media (the expansion of tabloids, the advent of radio, the networking of film and newsreel companies). And the Games delivered sensational content, not just because of the record-breaking performances on display but because of the star athletes, many of them never seen before on French soil. The Uruguayan football team was a case in point, the first from Latin America (see Huddleston's chapter). In front of the largest crowds of the Games, they came from nowhere to win the tournament, startling opponents and dazzling spectators, with Black midfielder José Andrade hailed as a marvel.

Paavo Nurmi, the Games' other major star, *had* been seen before but, since winning the 10,000m in Antwerp, not outside his native Finland. In Paris, he won everything but the 10,000m (for which he was not selected), claiming five golds in the distance races (see Young's chapter). In the 1500m final his blistering first lap destroyed the field: none of his rivals had seen him use the same tactics in the Finnish trials. To the rest of the world, the Finns were a glorious mystery. 'Finland hailed as nation of athletes: likened to ancient Greece', trumpeted the *New York Times* on 20 July 1924. It continued, 'Homer's bloomin' lyre never vibrated to stories of such feats of endurance as were displayed by Paavo Nurmi and his teammates'.[14] What was the Finns' secret? Was it their DNA, their character, the fact that 80% of them lived in the countryside? Or was it diet, saunas or their own athletic clubs? Crucially, could it be replicated?

This was a particularly burning question in light of the reawakening of rivalries between Britain and the USA (see Cronin's chapter). The world's oldest international track and field fixture – Oxford and Cambridge versus Harvard and Yale – predated the Olympics by two years. From the off, the differences between the two countries were apparent. At the inaugural meet in 1894, Montague Shearman, co-founder of the British Amateur Athletics Association, was open-mouthed at the Americans' club and college system, well-paid instructors and scientific manner. 'Englishmen will be very foolish', he warned, 'if they neglect the lesson which has been taught them by America ... Sport is an amusement and not a business: but what is worth doing is worth doing well.'[15] Foolish or not, the British stuck to their ways. At the 1908 Olympics in London, the widely held view that the Americans, though amateurs, had adopted an overly professional approach caused rancour. But 1924 was different. The British were still less specialised and more moderate in their regimes than the Americans. This much is clear from the training manual that Harold Abrahams wrote with his brother (fig. 61), and its advice to prepare scientifically without 'torture' and to eat a mixed diet rather than a 'freak', 'vegetarian' (as Nurmi did from age 15 to 21), 'a fruitarian, a nutarian' diet, not to mention its equivocation about whether drinking and smoking should be avoided (see Heggie's chapter).[16] But in their own way, they were sharpening up. Under Alec Nelson, the University of Cambridge had a modern, progressive trainer; Abrahams engaged the services of professional coach Sam Mussabini (fig. 62); and Eric Liddell was guided by the astute Tom McKerchar.[17] In Paris, the British 'ran the [Americans] off their feet', as *Chariots of Fire* put it six decades later – something they have yet to do again.

Less obvious at the time, but more significant in the long run, was the participation of women. Numbers had been growing steadily since 1908 (36 in London, 57 in Stockholm, 78 in Antwerp) but took a leap in Paris (136). These, of course, were perishingly small (men's participation through the 1920s averaged 2750), and the growth thereafter was glacial (it was not until Barcelona 1992 that women would reach the men's 1920s average).[18] The situation in the interwar period is striking because women were excelling, on a par with men, in what would now be termed extreme sports. In flying, open-water swimming and motor rallying women produced feats of skill, endurance and bravery over colossal distances.

In more traditional sports, however, which had started as male activities, women had to fight their way in. At the IOC, Coubertin's attitude did not help. Calling on ancient Greece to confirm his prejudices, he saw the Olympics as a male-only domain and, until the end of his life, regretted admitting women at all. Three Women's Olympiads were organised from 1921–23 in Monte Carlo in protest; another was held in London in August

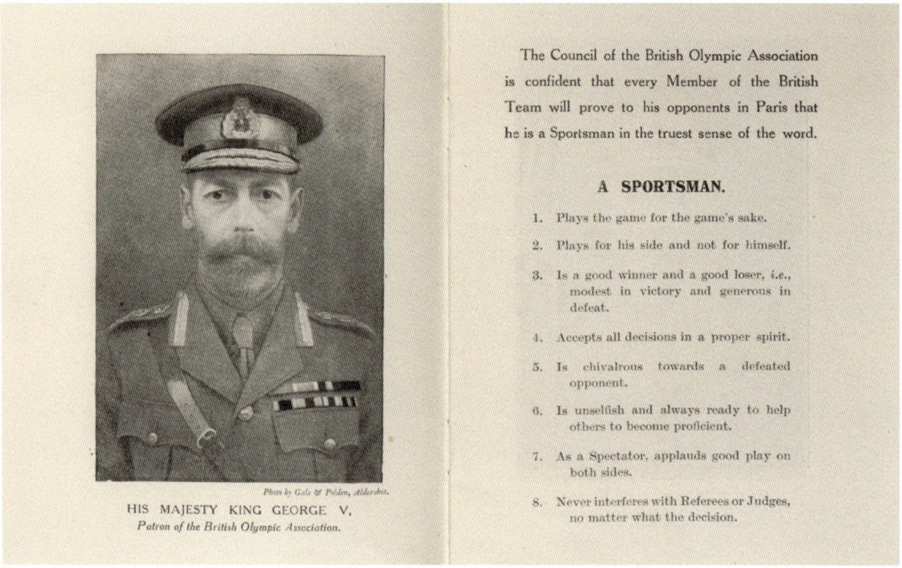

Photo by Gale & Polden, Aldershot.

HIS MAJESTY KING GEORGE V,
*Patron of the British Olympic Association.*

The Council of the British Olympic Association is confident that every Member of the British Team will prove to his opponents in Paris that he is a Sportsman in the truest sense of the word.

**A SPORTSMAN.**

1. Plays the game for the game's sake.
2. Plays for his side and not for himself.
3. Is a good winner and a good loser, *i.e.*, modest in victory and generous in defeat.
4. Accepts all decisions in a proper spirit.
5. Is chivalrous towards a defeated opponent.
6. Is unselfish and always ready to help others to become proficient.
7. As a Spectator, applauds good play on both sides.
8. Never interferes with Referees or Judges, no matter what the decision.

**6.** (cat. 17) The British Olympic Association (founded 1905)
'A Sportsman' from *The Eighth Olympiad Paris 1924*, booklet, 1924
Printing on paper, 14 × 22.4 cm
Churchill Archives Centre, Papers of Sir Arthur Marshall, Cambridge (MSHL Acc 2082)

Members of the 1924 British Olympic team, officials and competitors, men and women, were given a booklet on how to be a 'sportsman'. It educated them in winning, losing, dressing and travel – vouchers were issued for economy fares via Dieppe, returning within 30 days from arrival.

1924.[19] The national associations, run by men of a certain age, were hardly moved. When the Prince of Wales addressed the 'gentlemen' at the BOA's Banquet in Paris, he noted that the athletes at the Opening Ceremony were 'a world of sportsmen, a world of men', representing a movement that had introduced 'manly sport and manly exercises' into their countries.[20] Each had received a 'sportsman's' instructions on how to behave (fig. 6), advising them on the wearing of Association ties and white flannel trousers. But times were changing, and gold medallists like British swimmer Lucy Morton and US tennis player Helen Wills Moody would refuse to conform to a marginal role.

## IMAGE

No amount of levelling up could make every competitor equal. In their different ways, the two official posters of the 1924 Games reference the ideal Greek body, the first in its decision to give its athletes bare chests (fig. 7) and strategically placed palm branches, and the second (though its javelin thrower wears contemporary kit), in a colour and pose that conjure ancient bronze statues of the kind that were erected at Olympia in the fifth

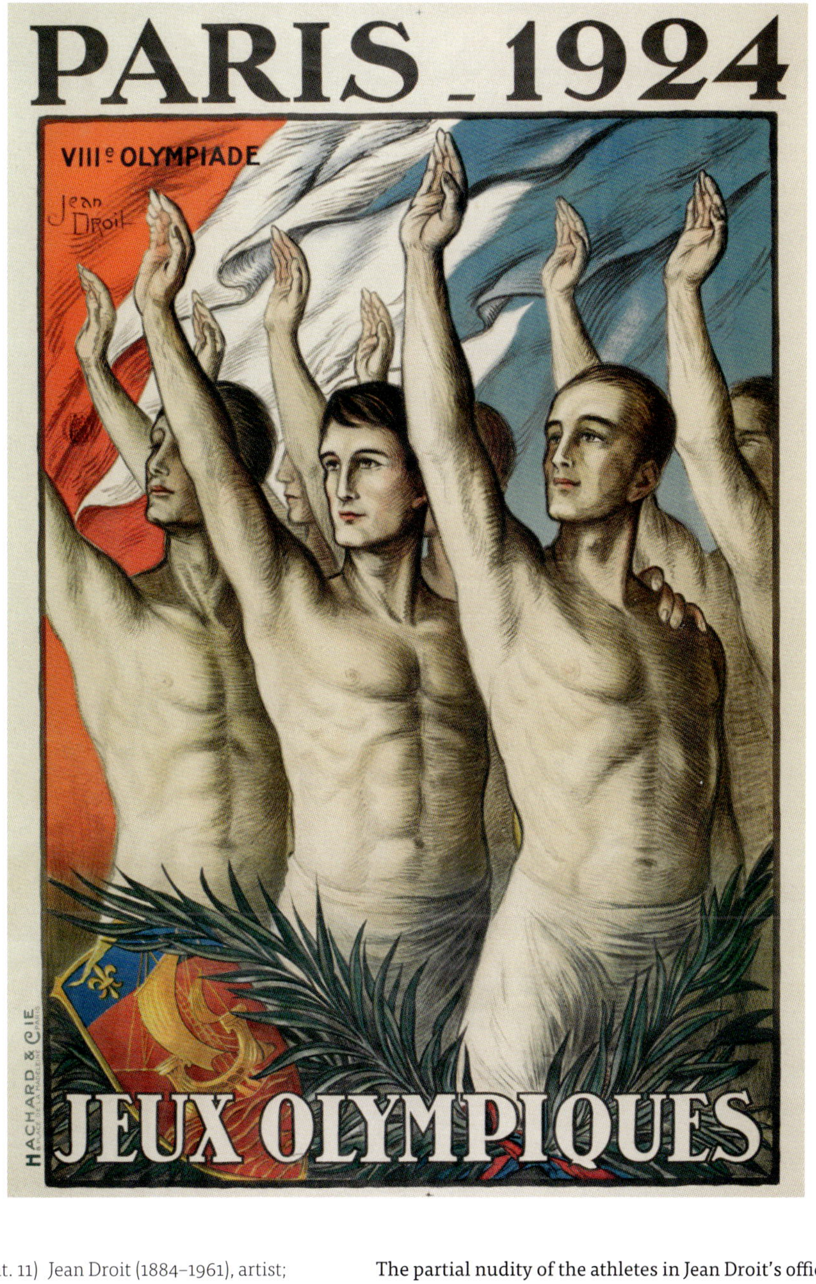


**7.** (cat. 11) Jean Droit (1884–1961), artist; Hachard & Co., Paris (active 1920s), printer
Official poster for the Paris 1924 Olympic Games, 1924
Colour lithography on paper, 116 × 79.6 cm
Victoria and Albert Museum, London (E.329-2006)

The partial nudity of the athletes in Jean Droit's official poster for the 1924 Paris Games gives them an ancient ancestry and homosociality. The combination of their Olympic salute and bare breasts with the French flag is reminiscent of Eugène Delacroix's 1830 painting *Liberty Leading the People*, which the Louvre acquired in 1874 – a large-scale work that has been described as 'the most important French painting'.

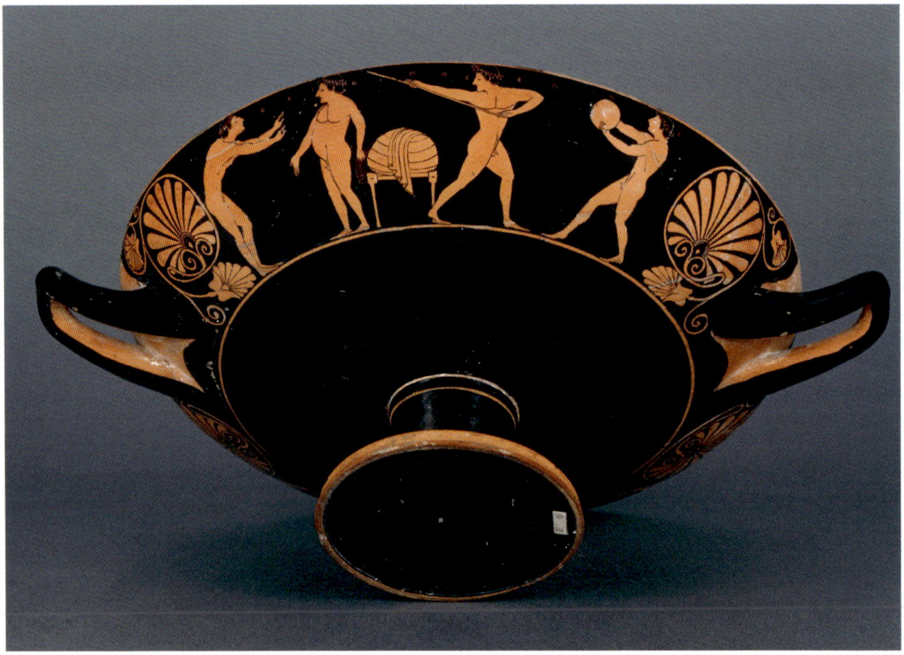

**8.** (cat. 5) Pheidippos
(active 525–510 BCE), painter
Kylix (cup), *c.* 510 BCE
Red-figure pottery, 13.9 × 42 × 33.6 cm
British Museum, London (1846,0512.2)

This Athenian red-figure drinking cup shows that there was no single athletic ideal, even among Greek men. The sprinter's body (far left) is different from the boxer's body, which is different again from that of the javelin or discus thrower. On the other side, another male figure, nude except for a helmet, shield and greaves, runs to the left. Perhaps he is a competitor in an armed foot-race of a kind held at the ancient Olympics.

century BCE (cat. 13). But even the ancients recognised that different sports asked for different things. One just has to look at a late sixth-century Greek drinking cup to see that the discus and javelin throwers are depicted as slimmer than the paunchy boxer, who holds the thongs with which he bound his hands, but not as slight as the runner, bending as if on the start line (fig. 8).

This tension between the real and ideal became particularly intense in the wake of World War I, when artists responded to the fragmentation and annihilation of millions of bodies in works that aimed at redefining what it meant to be human. Futurism, Abstractionism, Cubism and the stylisation of Art Deco survived the atrocities to be joined in 1924 by the publication in Paris of the Surrealist Manifesto (see Vere's chapter). The intuitive, automatic, dynamic ways of seeing that these movements promoted competed with calls to return to the order of classicism. But, for many, classicism stood for an order that had failed. German artist George Grosz's *Gymnast* of around 1922 (fig. 9)

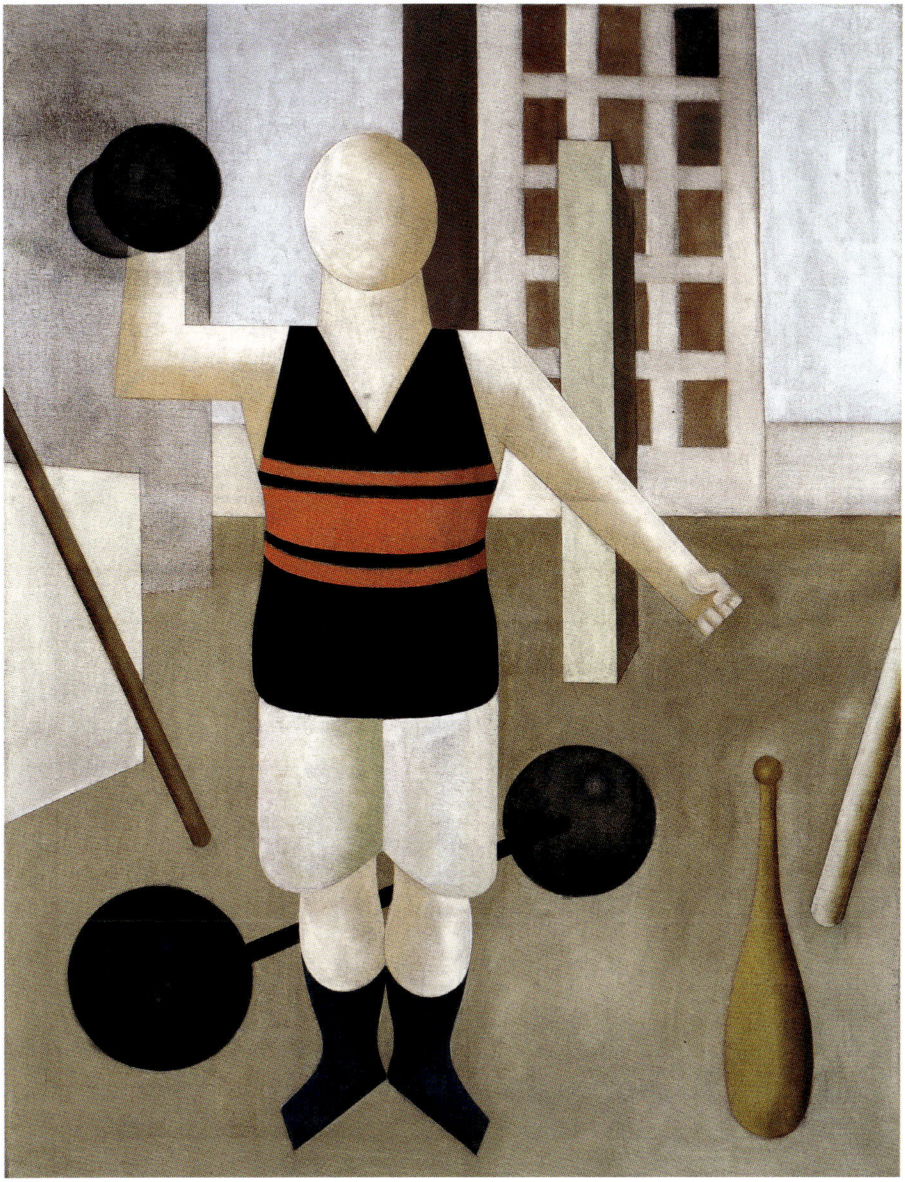

**9.** (cat. 82) George Grosz (1893–1959)
*The Gymnast*, *c*. 1922
Oil on canvas, 104.1 × 80 cm
McNay Art Museum, San Antonio, Texas (1974.26)

Man and his gym equipment merge as they assume a similar shape in Grosz's painting of a gymnast. At the root of 'gymnastics' is the ancient Greek word *gymnos*, 'naked'. There is nothing naked about this gymnast; he is enigmatic, abstract, automaton-like.

has no truck with classical contours. Skittle-shaped, with pole-like limbs and a head as round as his dumbbell, he stares blankly at the viewer as he morphs into his equipment – man as machine. As well as responding to war, artists were also responding to a technological revolution that saw planes, trains and automobiles collapse space and time to challenge traditional ways of being in the world.

At the same time, women's success in sports presented its own challenges as far as figurative art was concerned. In contrast to their male counterparts, *active* women found few models in ancient Greece and Rome, the legacy of which had turned centuries of women into Venuses. Willi Baumeister's *Female Runner II* of 1925 is a different species (fig. 64): its small head and elongated limbs are closer to the Mannerist style of the sixteenth century, which itself responded to Renaissance love of classical proportion. As the figure takes the bend, its sleek form asks women everywhere to imagine a freer future.

Grosz and Baumeister would compete in the 1928 summer Olympics – not in sport, but in the Olympic Arts Competition (see Osgood's essay). From 1912 to 1948, an Olympic competition in architecture, literature, music, painting and sculpture added to Coubertin's vision of the Games as a perfect package, as sublime as the ancient Greek games, which took place in sanctuaries during religious and cultural festivals. Coubertin's father, Charles, had been a successful painter (fig. 1) and much of Stockholm's success, in Coubertin's eyes, depended on these (then inaugural) events, in which – under a pseudonym – he had himself taken gold in the literature. Paris's illustrious juries heaped on the prestige but Walston, responsible for Britain's arts entries, found it hard to drum up interest. Four years later, Grosz and Baumeister failed to win medals. Perhaps their work was too cutting-edge. Victorious in Paris was sports illustrator Jean Jacoby, and his documentary-like paintings of football and rugby (figs 87 and 88).

## IMPACT

On the ground in Paris, the Games were a mixed success. The host nation might have expected to lose to the USA, but – with the largest delegation in the competition – not to tiny Finland. The French looked on in envy, bemoaning their country's lack of tradition and miserable investment in sport, the poor discipline and work ethic of their athletes. The fact that the organisers failed to secure public funding for a state-of-the-art new stadium only emphasised the point. Compared to today, the Games look poorly attended. Ten million tickets were set to go on sale for Paris 2024, with sessions sold out over a year in advance; a century earlier, sales hit only around 600,000.[21] But these numbers were in line with the historic trend. Paris doubled the spectatorship of the previous three Games; Los Angeles doubled that figure again in 1932 to what became the norm until Tokyo exceeded two million in 1964. The trouble was that Paris 1924 did not break even.[22] Not only was there the recognisable problem of prohibitive pricing, but many events were in the suburbs, the main stadium and Olympic Village (the first in Olympic history) on 'the extreme west side of Paris' and the swimming 'on the extreme east side', a 'ruinous' taxi ride from the centre.[23] The Parisian sporting paper *L'Auto* went so far as to suggest that bit by bit the Games had ended in 'general indifference'; that they were 'too long and too confused' – and this despite its front page trumpeting that they had roused 'a great interest not only in Paris and in France but in every country of the world'.[24]

Coubertin's assessment of his farewell Olympics was equally downbeat. His memoirs, published in 1931, gave 1924 a less than glowing report. The founder was aggrieved that his home city made so little of the Games, either for their own purposes or to further the Olympic movement. As his retirement wore on, he became strapped for cash and his resentment towards France for never honouring him personally drove him into the arms of the Germans, who flattered him and won his favour before the 1936 Olympics.[25] He had little to say about 1924 as a sporting event, except to lash out at the press for what he perceived as its ill-treatment of the athletes. He reproached them for their inability to grasp the strength, self-determination and sporting spirit of the competitors, and begrudged the fact, more generally, that they declared each Olympics the last.[26] Doubtless, there was some truth in his criticism, but he was doing an injustice to the high-calibre journalists writing at the time – Grantland Rice in the US, Ben Bennison in Britain, Willy Meisl in Germany and Gabriel Hanot in France. Sport would continue to need both types of coverage, high and low, and fortunately for the Olympics both would gather pace irrespective of what the founder – and others – thought. Sport was becoming everyone's, the Olympics too.

The assorted impact of any Games is not limited to the host nation. For the rest of the world, Paris proved less of a disappointment. Compared to the 29 nations in Antwerp in 1920, the 44 that participated in 1924, from five continents, made the Paris Games truly global. As if this was not enough, the broadcasting (for the first time in Olympic history) of radio commentary in streets, shops and so on, combined with the pictures and caricatures of the competitors and the reportage, commentary, debate and satire in a recently expanded culture of print and photographic media, turned the 1924 Games into a sporting event like never before and gave its athletes a forum for influence. This post-Olympic influence played out in a myriad of different ways – from Lucy Morton's star-billing at Blackpool Tower Circus on the same programme as a female lion tamer, through American swimmer Johnny Weissmuller's transition from Olympic superstar to Hollywood idol (see Michelakis's chapter), to rower Benjamin Spock, who would train as a paediatrician and write a best-selling book on childcare. Uruguay exploited their stunning performances on the pitch to stage a charm offensive off it and improve the country's international standing; in 1930 they would stage FIFA's first breakaway World Cup. Andrade and American long jumper William DeHart Hubbard challenged ideas of beauty and privilege long tied to whiteness, and female Olympians – though few in number – subverted rigid notions of how women should look and behave (see Vout's chapter). The uncorseted dresses and leisurewear advertised off the back of the Games revolutionised fashion forever (fig. 10).

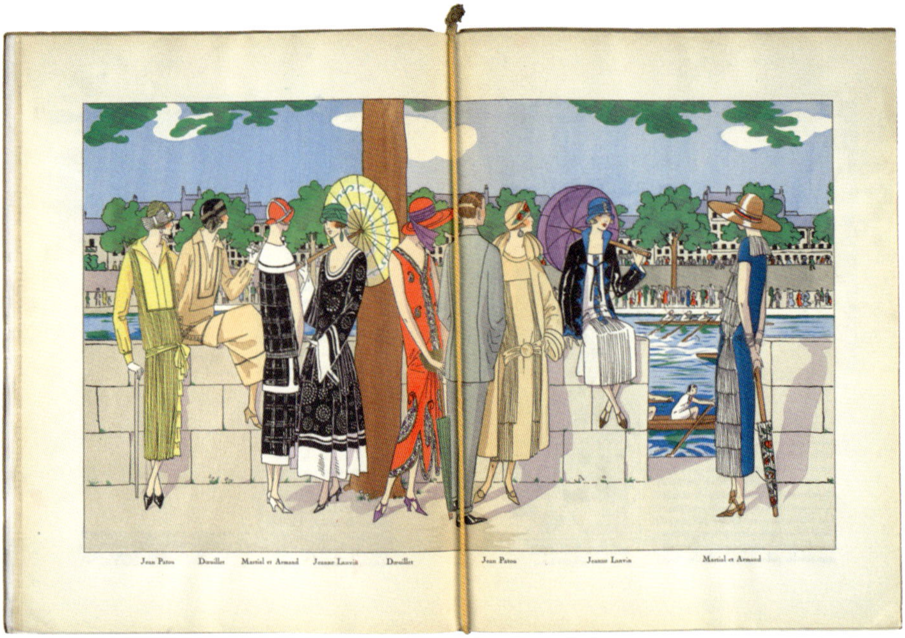

**10.** (cat. 152) Unrecorded artist;
Éditions d'art: Paris, publisher
*Art-Taste-Beauty: Pages of Feminine Elegance*,
no. 46 (15 June 1924), centre spread
*(Art-goût-beauté: feuillets d'élégance féminine)*
Lithography with hand-coloured *pochoir* on
paper, paper covers, 33 × 24 cm
Private collection

This exquisitely illustrated centre spread of the June 1924 issue of French magazine *Art-goût-beauté*, bound with a silk cord, imagines women watching the Olympic rowing in the latest drop-waisted haute couture designs by Lanvin, Doeuillet, Martial et Armand and Patou.

Rarely has there been a greater demonstration of sport's sway on society. This might not have been what the French thought they were paying for, or what Coubertin envisaged for his presidential swan song. But Paris 1924 represents a new point of departure in Olympic history. Stockholm might have put on the first and long-unsurpassed 'perfect' Games in 1912, but Paris, twelve years later, marks the moment when individual athletes from a range of sports and nations could, through the course of a single sporting event, have impact around the world.

## 1924 AND 2024

There was a darker side to Paris too. Barely six years after the end of World War I, the 1924 Olympics still stood in the shadow of the conflict. A quarter of 20- to 27-year-olds in France had been killed and over a million were permanently disabled. Many of them were to be seen on the streets of the capital. As well as attending banquets, the Prince of Wales and the British team were photographed visiting Paris's Tomb of the Unknown Soldier; the Uruguayans visited it too (fig. 51). But commemoration, though obligatory and heartfelt, had limited effect. Throughout the 1920s, there were few moments when Europeans did not fear another war. Paris 1924 gave hope, but it also sounded a note of caution. The fencing competitions were marred by disagreements between the Italian and Hungarian teams, which threatened diplomatic relations between France and Benito Mussolini's Italy. And there were violent scenes on and off the pitch at the ill-tempered rugby final between the USA and France (see Bolz's chapter). In July 1924 already *The Times* was citing the thuggery at the rugby among other 'disgraceful scenes' to claim that the Games exacerbated 'international bitternesses instead of soothing them'.[27] Other writers disagreed. But in 15 years, the world would be again at war. Oath-taker and French flag-bearer Géo André, who had been wounded in World War I, would be killed in action by German forces.

Paris 2024 stands at an unexpectedly difficult juncture. Much has happened since the award of the Games to France in September 2017: a global pandemic that rendered the delayed 2020 Olympics in Tokyo a pale and mournful imitation, and wars in Ukraine and Gaza that dominate news headlines. As the Games unfurl to their fullest grandeur again, in the city of their founder, they do so at a time when world events pose questions about the meaning and appropriateness of sporting contest. Global bodies have weighed in to mitigate. In November 2023, the UN General Assembly continued its now 30-year tradition of calling for an 'Olympic Truce' (i.e. a pause in violence world-wide immediately before, during and after the Games). Weeks later, the IOC paved the way for Russians and Belarusians to compete in Paris as 'Individual Neutral Athletes', provided that they had not actively supported the war in Ukraine. At the time of writing, it would be folly to offer a prediction of what will happen on either front. Less risky, perhaps, is to imagine what Coubertin's opinion might have been. Although no pacifist (he took part, despite his advanced age, in World War I), he would have wished to see the Games preserved under the best possible conditions. Disturbed by the continued exclusion of Germany in 1924, he is likely to have approved of any measure to lift a ban on athletes too.

Coubertin's legacy is his unwavering faith in sport's potential to change lives. Not only did he believe that it made people healthier but also that it made them better, more internationally-minded and cultured people. Sport for Coubertin transcended race, class and time. For all his faults and the many greater flaws of some who followed, it is worth remembering, debating and celebrating these facts. It is also worth remembering the multifarious ways in which sport inspired, and continues to inspire, art; and that it shapes ideas about the body and bodies' relationships with other bodies, not only through physical exercise but well beyond the swimming pool or running track.

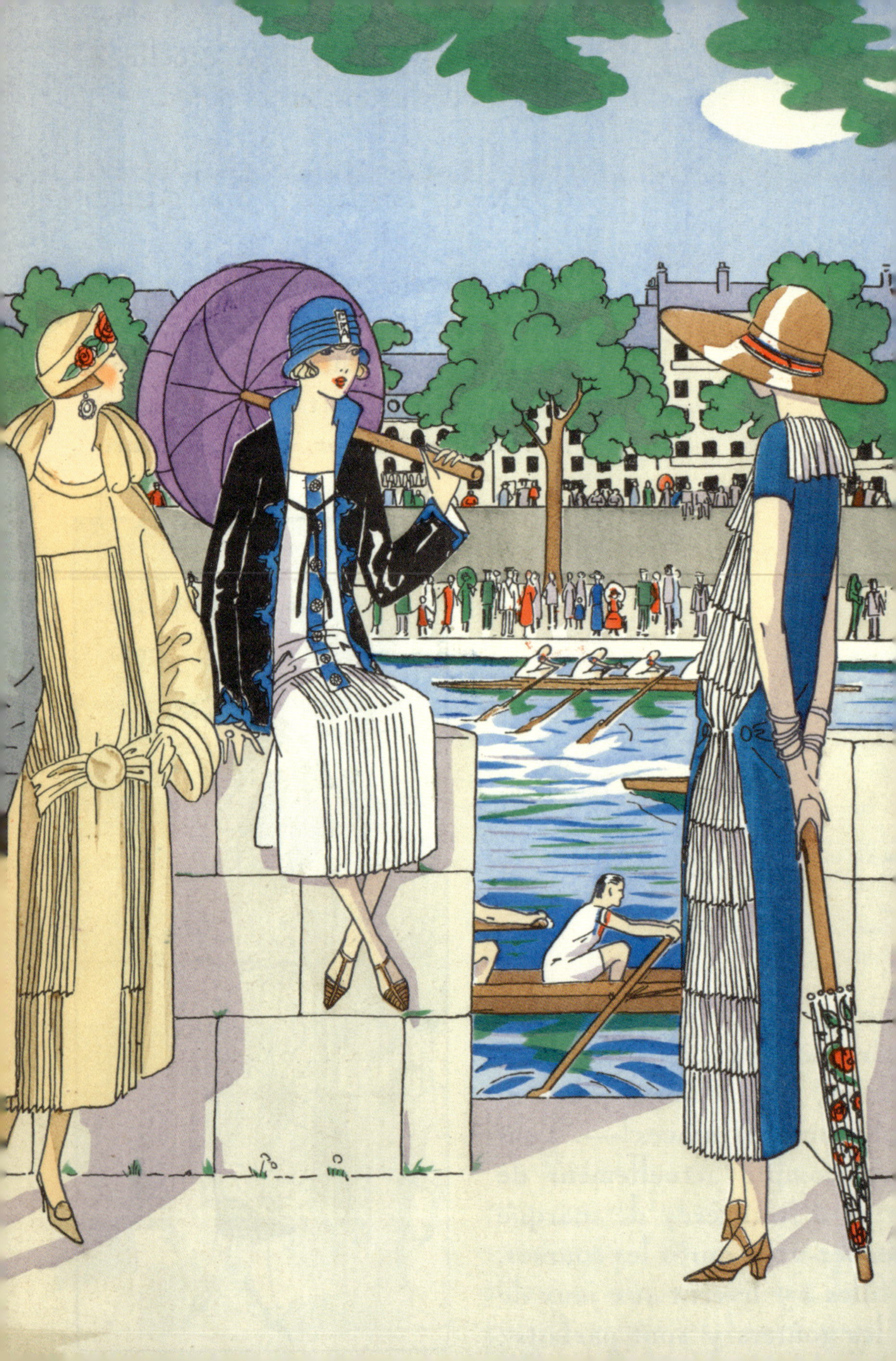

# PARIS

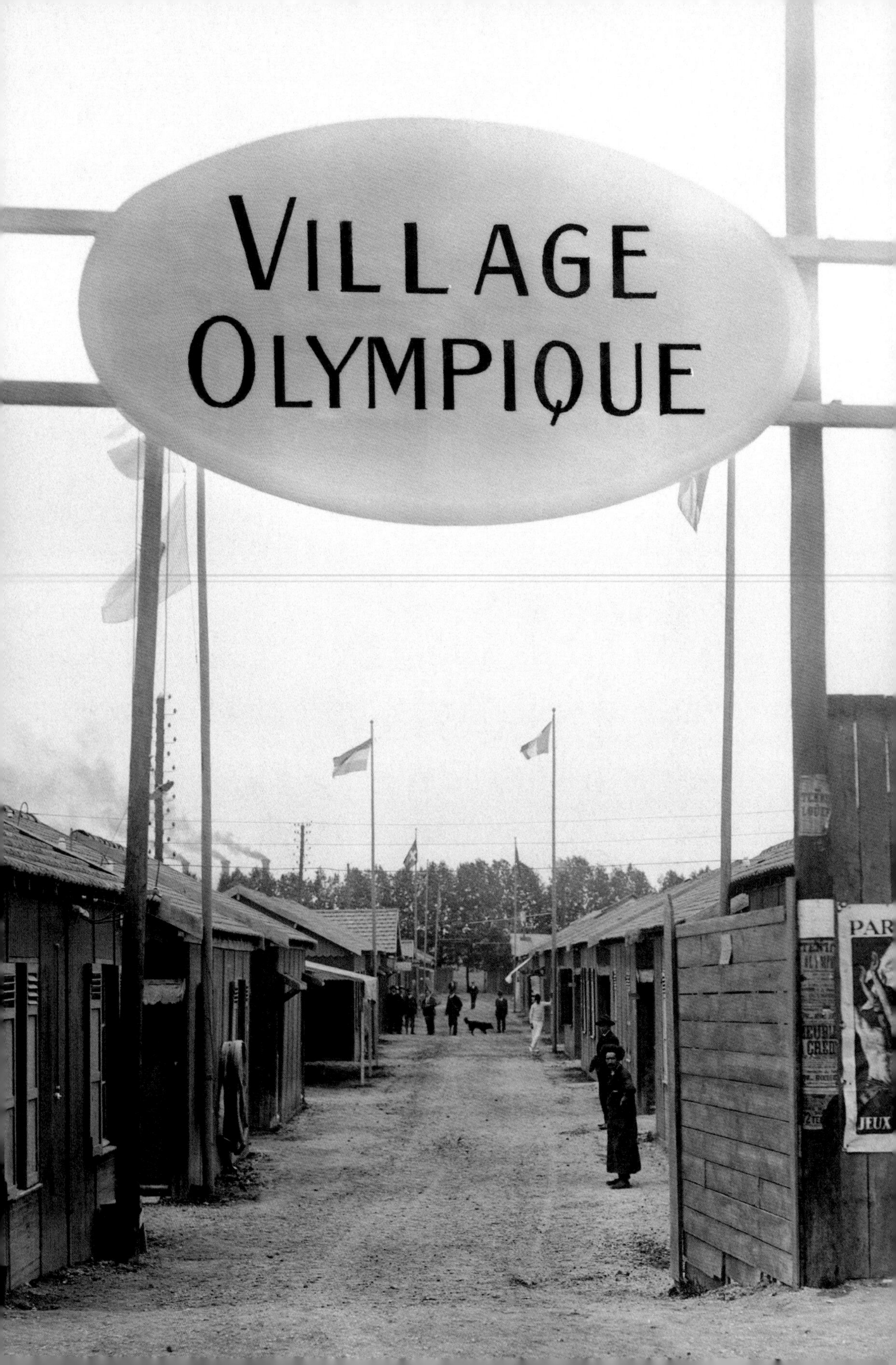
VILLAGE
OLYMPIQUE

# 1

# CITY OF SPORT

PHILIP DINE

The organisers of the 2024 Paris Olympics have shown considerable ambition in the 'venue concept' for the return of the Games to the city. A century on from the 1924 Olympiad, the sporting mega-event will mobilise the capital's historic core, expanding to take in stadiums variously located within the Île-de-France region before spreading out to major cities in other parts of the country. Provincial venues include the Marseille marina on the Mediterranean coast, while surfing and related disciplines will take place nearly 10,000 miles away at Teahupo'o, in Tahiti, French Polynesia. It is in central Paris, however, that the infrastructural demands of this grand project will be most apparent. As the organisers explain, the city's landmarks 'are being transformed into sporting arenas to offer spectators an unparalleled experience and provide an outstanding backdrop for sporting prowess'.[1]

The contrast to 1924 could not be starker. Parisians who attended the Olympics a hundred years ago were offered an altogether more modest and grittily suburban spectacle (fig. 12). On one level, this was only fitting, given that it was on the city's fringes that modern French sport had emerged in the later nineteenth and early twentieth centuries, durably establishing itself in locations such as Colombes, the north-western municipality chosen as the primary venue for that year's Olympic Games. The historically peripheral location assigned to sport in the French capital is one of the three interlocking strands addressed in this chapter, which explores the specificity of Paris as a city of sport. The others are the growth of commercial sports, in particular horse racing, cycling

**11.** (cat. 20) Unrecorded photographer
Paris 1924 Olympic Games,
Olympic Village, the entrance
(A.N. Paris postcard series, no. 1), 1924
Black and white photograph
Comité International Olympique (CIO)
(PHO11106719)

The first ever Olympic Village offered spartan accommodation to male competitors in rows of wooden huts flying national flags. Facilities included a laundry, a barber shop and a post office, while the on-site restaurant offered typically French fare, including wine with meals. Note how part of one of the official Olympics posters (fig. 7) is visible on the right.

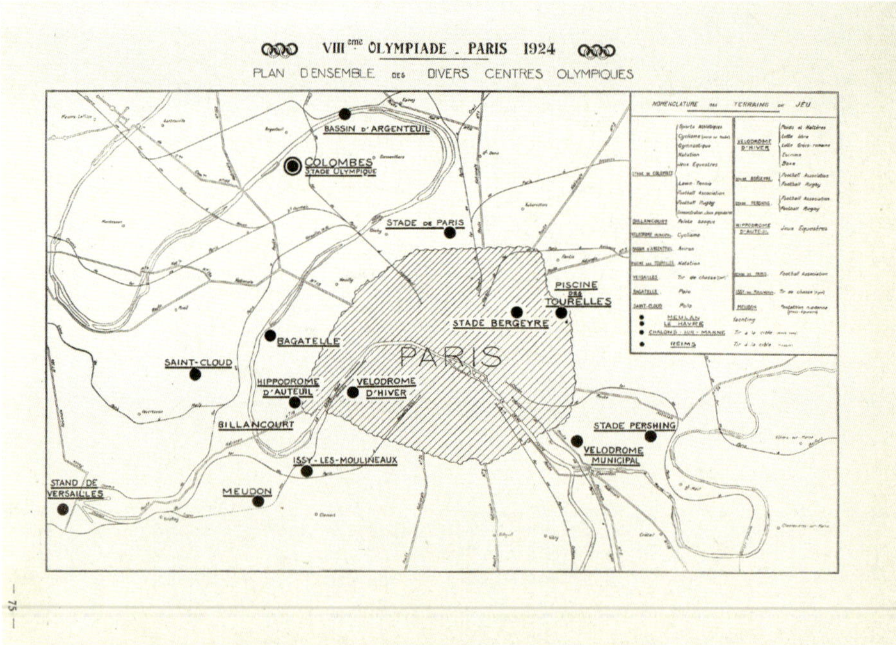


**12.** Map of event locations, reproduced in *Games of the Eighth Olympiad Paris 1924: Official Report of the French Olympic Committee*, Paris 1924 (*Jeux de la VIIIe Olympiade Paris 1924: Rapport Officiel du Comité Olympique Français*)

In contrast to the 2024 Paris Olympics, the 1924 Olympic competitions took place predominantly outside the city's boundaries. Only aquatic events at the new Tourelles pool on its eastern margin, combat sports and weightlifting at the Vélodrome d'Hiver, and football at the ephemeral Stade Bergeyre (1918–26) were available to residents within the city limits.

and boxing, and the fact that the larger plans of the 1924 organisers had to be drastically scaled back. These complementary themes will be set against the rise of athletic sports in France, in which a leading role was famously played by Baron Pierre de Coubertin.

Modern sports came late to France, specifically in the wake of the country's defeat in the Franco-Prussian War of 1870. One expression of the resulting crisis of masculinity was the popular vogue for gymnastics following the German model, in preparation for military service and as an expression of revanchist nationalism. This working-class physical engagement was followed in the 1880s and 1890s by the enthusiasm of more privileged sections of Parisian society for rugby union, association football, rowing and track and field athletics. Imported from Great Britain by an anglophile elite, such pursuits encouraged new modes of sociability centred on an extensive network of sports clubs, the development of which was made significantly easier by the state's liberalisation of its laws on public association in 1901. However, both the amateur ethos and the spirit of pacific internationalism championed by the new athletic sports had to compete for public recognition not only with the performative patriotism of military gymnastics, but also with a range of novel commercial spectacles.

The first of these was horse racing, which exploited the open spaces available in the former royal hunting preserves of the Bois de Boulogne to the west of the city and the Bois de Vincennes to the east. These parks – later municipalised – would become privileged sites of ludic innovation. The Longchamp course for flat racing opened on the city's affluent western outskirts in 1856 and would be joined by neighbouring Auteuil in 1873 as a venue for jump races, while Vincennes, in the less-favoured eastern suburbs, was opened in 1863 and substantially redeveloped in 1879 as the hub of the country's distinctive trotting industry. Horse racing, along with the green spaces in which it took place, was straightforwardly incorporated into the project of comprehensive urban renewal overseen between 1852 and 1870 by Emperor Louis-Napoléon Bonaparte (who reigned as Napoleon III) and his highly inventive architect, Baron Georges-Eugène Haussmann. In common with the Grands Boulevards and the Opéra, the racecourse proved enduringly appealing to fashionable Parisian society and provided inspiration for leading painters, including Édouard Manet and Edgar Degas, as well as for literary chroniclers such as Émile Zola and Marcel Proust. Such artistic interest is indicative of the broader contribution that racing made to the emergence at this time of an authentically modern 'society of the spectacle'.[2]

Moreover, the combined administrative and representational innovations of horse racing served to lay the ground for the practical organisation and cultural reception of the socially prestigious athletic sports that followed. These new sports, which were largely invented in England, would be enthusiastically championed by the founder of the modern Olympics, Coubertin, acting through his umbrella organising body, the Union des Sociétés Françaises des Sports Athlétiques (Union of French Athletic Sports Societies, or USFSA), ably assisted by his fellow sporting evangelisers within the nascent Olympic movement. The overlap between the two organisations is highlighted by the adoption of the USFSA's maxim – 'Citius, Altius, Fortius' (Faster, Higher, Stronger) – as the Olympic motto for Paris 1924 and all subsequent Games.

Following the 'revival' of the Olympics in Athens in 1896,[3] Coubertin ensured that Paris would host in 1900, albeit in a poorly managed form that betrayed the event's limited social standing as a late addition to that year's Universal Exhibition. When the city hosted again in 1924 (the penultimate year of Coubertin's presidency), it was determined to avoid the mistakes of the past. The French capital was promoted as a beacon of innovation in the sporting sphere, with particular attention given to 'the great open-air theatre that constitutes a modern stadium'.[4] The not dissimilar aims of the managers of Paris 2024 are predicated on the temporary transformation of the city into an appropriate setting for world-class competition. Paradoxically, this unseats Paris's annual global sporting event, the Tour de France, first run in 1903. In a wholly exceptional modification of the race's annually varied but still broadly traditional route, the organisers of the

2024 edition decided to bypass the capital and its historic landmarks, finishing instead in Nice to leave the stage clear for the Olympic Games. In any other year, the concluding stage of the three-week-long event transforms the city into the world's most prestigious cycle track, in a spectacular reassertion of competitive and cultural centrality.[5]

## PARIS'S SPORTING INFRASTRUCTURE

Professional cycling in France had its origins in track racing at a network of suburban velodromes built in the 1890s, the success of which encouraged the rise of cycle road racing; together, these sporting innovations would have a lasting impact on the capital and the country, producing France's major sporting spectacle (fig. 13). Two substantial arenas, the Parc des Princes in the west and the Vélodrome de Vincennes in the east,

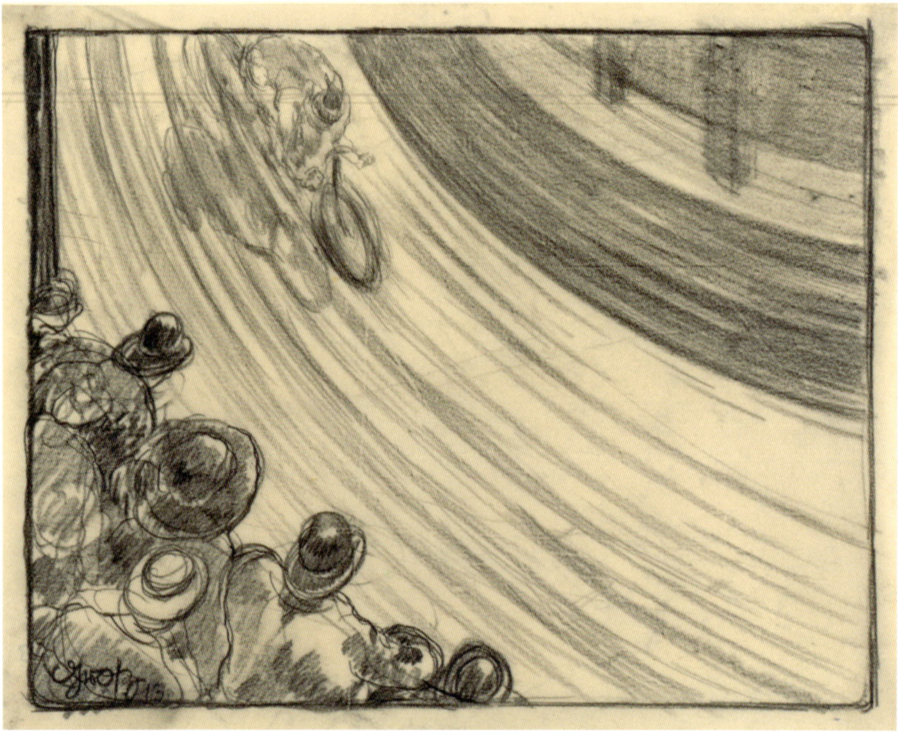

**13.** (cat. 87) George Grosz (1893–1959)
*The Cycle Race*, 1913

Chalk on tracing paper, 22 × 27.9 cm
The Fitzwilliam Museum, Cambridge
(PD.12-1969)

German artist George Grosz's drawing of a cycle race is all about speed and the excitement of seeing competitors whizz past. Although we cannot see the spectators' faces, we appreciate the tension as one of them at least leans forward to get a better view. The roundness of their hats echoes the spinning of the cycle's wheels.

were constructed in 1894 and 1897 respectively. The former stadium would go on to become a major venue for rugby and football matches, as well as continuing to host important cycling competitions. However, both locations are primarily noteworthy as illustrations of the commercial vitality of Parisian cycling, as energetically marketed to working-class spectators. Together with the established spectacle of horse racing and the emerging phenomenon of professional boxing (fig. 14), cycling would consistently generate the capital's largest paying audiences, with all three sports attracting sustained entrepreneurial and cultural investment.

Cycling's broad appeal is best exemplified by the Six Jours de Paris (Six Days of Paris) endurance race, launched in 1913 and traditionally held at the Vélodrome d'Hiver, the 'winter' or indoor stadium constructed on the site of the former Machine Room of the 1900 Universal Exhibition. This project was the brainchild of Henri Desgrange, editor of the country's leading sports daily, *L'Auto*, and a pivotal figure in cycling history. Desgrange opened the new venue in 1903, the same year in which his even more celebrated creation, the Tour de France, first took to the country's roads. The Vélodrome d'Hiver would quickly achieve huge popularity, making it one of the very few proven arenas within the city's boundaries available to the organisers of the 1924 Olympics.

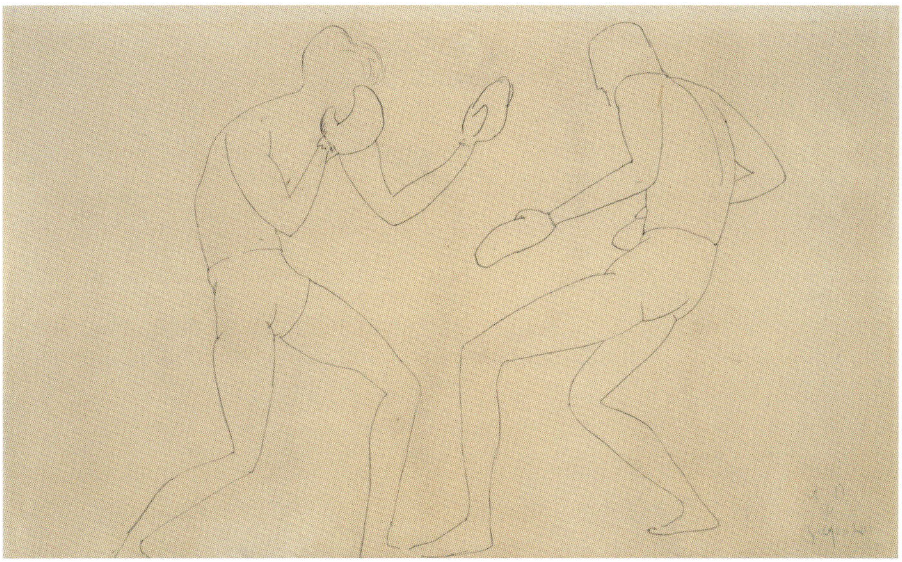

**14.** (cat. 127) André Dunoyer de Segonzac (1884–1974)
*The Boxers*, *c.* 1910–14
(*Les Boxeurs*)
Pen and ink on paper, 26 × 42.7 cm
The Fitzwilliam Museum, Cambridge
(PD.104-1961)

Segonzac's drawing captures something of the drama of boxing in Paris in the 1910s. Its angle puts the viewer ringside, looking up, close to the sweat and sawdust.

They would use it for the boxing, wrestling, fencing and weightlifting competitions.[6] Among those drawn to the Vélodrome were figures from both the city's homegrown and expatriate literary communities, including Paul Morand and Ernest Hemingway. In *A Moveable Feast*, posthumously published in 1964, Hemingway would chronicle the horse racing, track cycling and boxing cultures of the Paris that he had known in the 1920s.[7]

The most recent of these spectacles, professional boxing, had come to prominence in the early twentieth century, thanks to an outstanding group of African American fighters, the most famous of whom was Jack Johnson, the first black heavyweight champion of the world, who retained the title from 1908 to 1915. One look at the leading boxing venues at this time highlights the paucity of the capital's broader sporting infrastructure: the Folies Bergères cabaret, the Élysée Montmartre theatre and the Nouveau Cirque de Paris were all adapted to the new craze.[8] Nevertheless, as with horse racing and cycling before it, public enthusiasm for the sport was enormous, its visceral appeal drawing very profitably for match promoters on a racially inflected 'violent fantasy' (see Vout's chapter).[9] Working-class spectators who flocked to the new spectacle were joined by cultural luminaries such as the writers Guillaume Apollinaire, Blaise Cendrars and Colette, together with painters including Francis Picabia and the Paris-based Dutch artist Kees van Dongen, who produced a full-length nude study of Jack Johnson.[10] In a watershed moment for mass broadcasting in France, coverage of the July 1921 world title bout in Jersey City between decorated war veteran Georges Carpentier and the reigning heavyweight champion Jack Dempsey made use of the trans-Atlantic telegraph to relay match commentary in what was the country's first radio transmission of a sporting event.[11] The young Simone de Beauvoir was a notable observer as news of the French challenger's defeat brought tears to the eyes of men and women alike in the streets of Paris.[12]

## PARIS 1924 AND ITS VENUES

The commercial success of these new professional sports owed much to extensive media coverage, as well as to imaginatively repurposed venues such as the Vélodrome d'Hiver, which would host boxing matches as well as cycling competitions for six decades. As an established urban arena, the Vélodrome naturally appealed to the organisers of the 1924 Games. However, their designated main Olympic stadium was significantly more peripheral, being in the factory district of Colombes, some ten kilometres from the city centre. This site was chosen not for logistical reasons, but rather because its sitting tenants, the Racing Club de France, offered to make it available. This elite association was founded in 1882 as the country's first indigenous sports club. Its athletics facilities at the Croix-Catelan sports grounds in the Bois de Boulogne were used for the 1900 Paris Olympics, while its tennis courts would host the French national championships until the construction of the Roland-Garros Stadium, in the neighbouring 16th arrondissement, in 1927. It was against this backdrop that Suzanne Lenglen, Paris born and bred and her country's first international sports star, would put French tennis and French sporting fashion on the map either side of World War I. As for the Racing Club's most prestigious – and, until 2021 at least,[13] conspicuously male-dominated – sport, the Croix-Catelan site was also the historical home of its celebrated rugby team. The club became France's first national champions in 1892, beating city rivals Stade Français in a match refereed by no less than Coubertin himself.[14] The Racing Club would continue to be based primarily at the Croix-Catelan facilities until 1907, when the opening of the new Colombes stadium enabled it to switch its playing headquarters. Originally a racecourse, opened in 1883, the municipally-owned venue was rented and minimally converted for athletic sports by the newspaper *Le Matin*, which retained the lease until 1920, when it was ceded to the Racing Club.

When, with Coubertin's instrumental support, Paris was selected in May 1921 as the host city for the 1924 Games, its sporting infrastructure was deemed inadequate by the French Olympic Committee. The city's objective inadequacies had been underlined when a sports festival for servicemen was proposed as part of the allied victory celebrations at the end of World War I. No suitable venue being available, the US Army's Corps of Engineers rapidly converted a former racecourse in the Bois de Vincennes into a stadium with space for some 25,000 seated and 10,000 standing spectators, thereby making possible the 1919 Interallied Games. However, as 'the handiwork of foreigners',[15] what became known as the 'Stade Pershing' did not appeal to the Paris 1924 organisers as their principal venue and was used for just a few matches in the Olympic football tournament. Instead, the French Olympic Committee launched an architectural competition for a wholly new stadium, able to accommodate 100,000 spectators, with an adjoining swimming pool, tennis courts and an arena for combat sports and weightlifting (fig. 15).[16] The winning entry was submitted by experienced stadium designer Louis Faure-Dujarric, a figure closely associated with the Racing Club, as was the organising committee's general-secretary, Frantz Reichel. A member of France's victorious 1900 Olympic rugby team, Reichel went on to become a shrewd sports administrator and an influential journalist on the daily *Le Figaro*. However, the refusal of the municipal authorities in March 1922 to fund the grandiose scheme proposed by Faure-Dujarric and promoted energetically by Reichel meant that, instead of creating what would have been the biggest sports complex in Europe, the 1924 organisers had to seek an altogether more modest solution. What is more, it had to be one that could be implemented in short order. As a result, the organisers were faced with a fragmentation of the 1924 Games, with venues scattered across the metropolitan area and little attention paid to the provision of adequate public transport or the affordability of tickets for the optimistically anticipated mass audience. In the end, it was only thanks to the timely – but by no means selfless – intervention of the Racing Club that its Colombes site was made available for the substantial redevelopment required to enable Paris to host the Games at all (fig. 16).

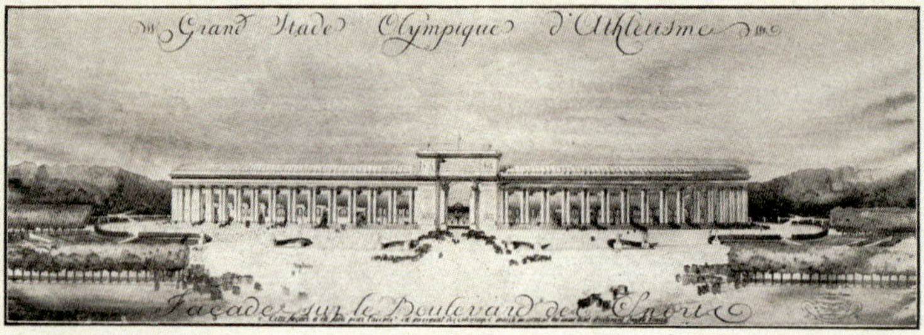


Projet de M. Louis FAURE-DUJARRIC, classé premier. — Vue extérieure du Grand Stade.

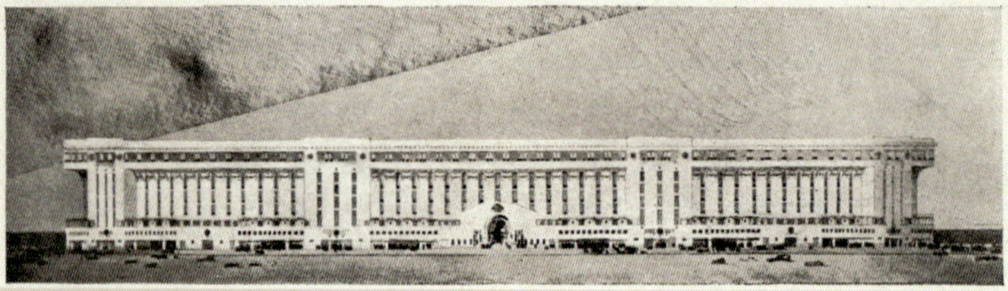

Projet de MM. BRANDON, BARD et G. DE SAINT-CYR, classé deuxième.
Façade du Stade Olympique. (Cette façade mesure une longueur de 300 mètres).

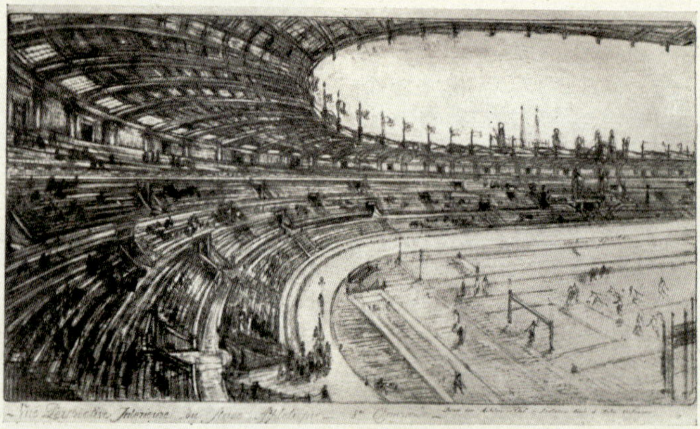

Projet de M. TRONCHET, classé troisième.
Vue perspective intérieure du Stade Athlétique.

— 44 —

**15.** Designs entered for the Olympic stadium architecture competition, reproduced in *Games of the Eighth Olympiad Paris 1924: Official Report of the French Olympic Committee*, 1924, Paris 1924 (*Jeux de la VIIIe Olympiade Paris 1924: Rapport Officiel du Comité Olympique Français*)

The Paris 1924 organisers invited submissions for a new 100,000-capacity stadium, with accommodation for 2,000 athletes, an adjoining swimming pool, tennis courts and other dedicated competition spaces. While his winning entry was never funded, Louis Faure-Dujarric did oversee the more modest but still extensive renovation of the Colombes stadium.

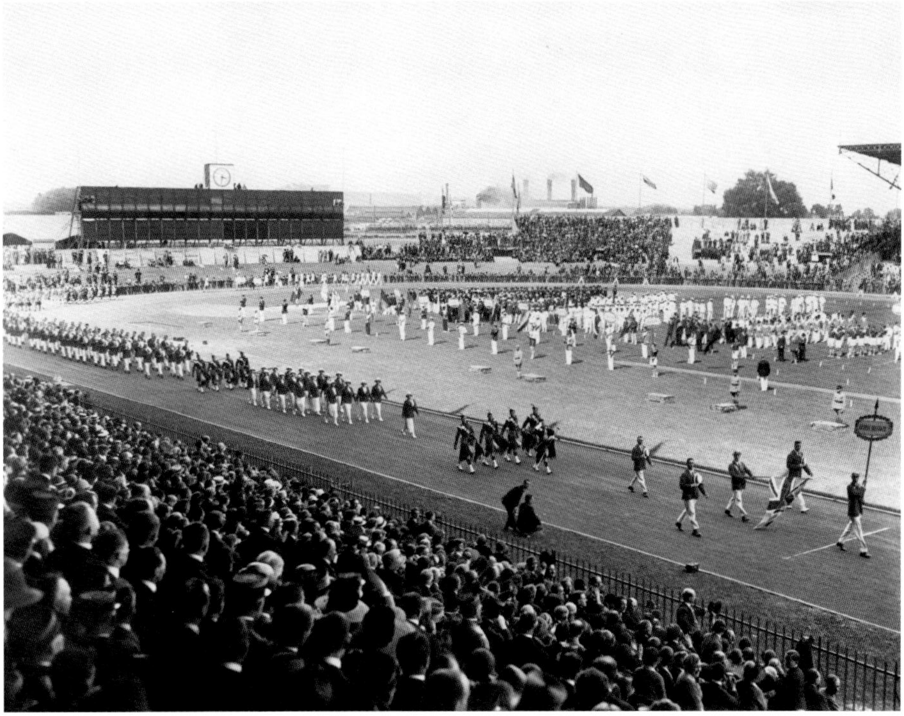

**16.** (cat. 21) Unrecorded photographer
Paris 1924 Olympic Games, Opening Ceremony, parade of athletes, Great Britain (GBR), 5 July 1924
Black and white photograph
Comité International Olympique (CIO) (PHO11072465)

The Colombes venue for Paris 1924 resulted from the extensive refurbishment of an existing suburban facility, unpropitiously located near a pumping station for the Paris wastewater system. The latter building's towering chimneys are clearly visible here and are also regularly glimpsed in Jean de Rovéra's film record of the Games.

## THE STADIUM AT COLOMBES

Redevelopment at Colombes brought to the surface conflicting conceptions of sport and its social role. While the city's (albeit scaled-back) financial support made it possible for the Games to take place, work on the stadium drew on the available public funding in such a way as significantly to reinforce the existing private monopoly on Parisian sporting spaces. Automobile access for affluent spectators was thus a priority for the organisers, while rail, tram and bus connections for the less well-off were not.[17] Nevertheless, the wholesale redevelopment of Colombes was capably overseen by Faure-Dujarric as the Olympic competition-winning architect. The transformed site provided the city with a spacious modern stadium, durably built of reinforced concrete, which would have a significant legacy as a multisport venue.[18] More immediately, the substantially refurbished

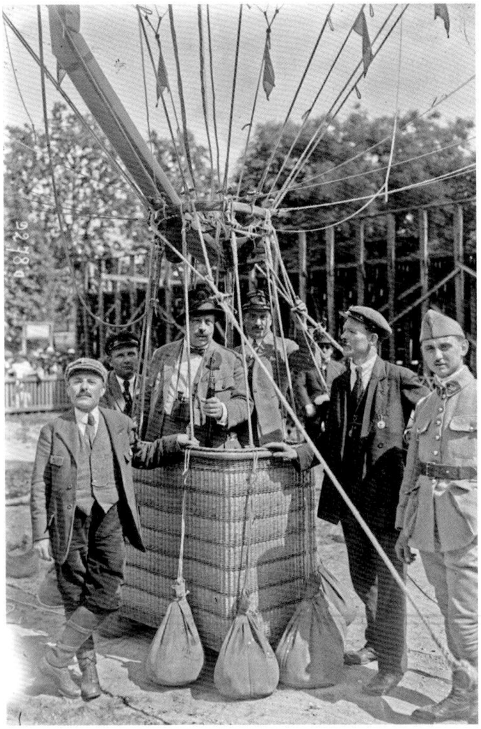

**17.** (cat. 85) Agence Rol photographic agency (founded 1904)
Edmond Dehorter (1877–1965) prepares to broadcast at Colombes stadium from a tethered hot-air balloon, 9 June 1924
Glass-plate negative
Bibliothèque nationale de France, Paris (Rol, 92780)

With microphone and binoculars at the ready, Dehorter prepares to take to the air for live radio coverage of the Olympic football final. This pioneering broadcaster challenged the existing monopoly of the written press on sports commentary by operating as an inventive and audacious 'wireless' reporter.

venue offered a fitting backdrop to the many outstanding performances recorded in 1924, not least those of Paavo Nurmi and his fellow Finns (see Young's chapter).

Notwithstanding such notable exploits, the stadium's suburban location would result in disappointing attendances and the consequent commercial failure of the Paris Games, with only the Olympic football final being a genuinely popular attraction. This flagship event's broad appeal was underlined by the ingenious reporting of balloon-mounted wireless commentator Edmond Dehorter, a pioneer of sports broadcasting in France (fig. 17). The Olympic football tournament may be regarded as a precursor of the World Cup, another great French sporting invention, and specifically the creation of Jules Rimet, the then president of the Fédération Internationale de Football Association (FIFA), the game's world governing body, founded in Paris in 1904. Intriguingly, Uruguay, the winners of the 1924 Olympic tournament (see Huddleston's chapter), would again emerge victorious at the inaugural World Cup in 1930. For its part, association football, which would not be professionalised in France until 1932, was a characteristic component of the sporting culture of the capital and especially its suburbs, as exemplified by Rimet's own Red Star club, which was based in the northern district of Saint-Ouen-sur-Seine.[19]

In his assessment of the eighth Olympiad, historian Robert Lewis comments that 'While Paris still hosted the Olympics in 1924 after the private Racing Club de France

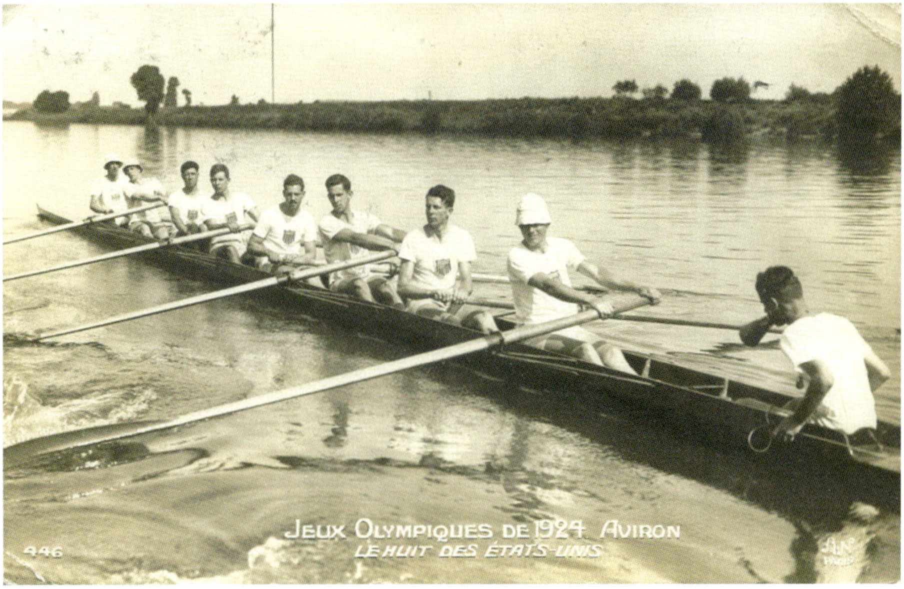


**18.** (cat. 44) Unrecorded photographer
*Olympic Games of 1924, Rowing, the eight of the United States of America* (A.N. Paris postcard series, no. 446), 1924
*(Jeux Olympiques de 1924, Aviron, Le Huit des États-Unis)*
Gelatin silver print on paper, 8.9 × 14 cm
Courtesy of Thomas E. Weil (publication only)

The Bassin d'Argenteuil offered the Olympic regatta a natural setting conveniently close to the Colombes stadium. The feature race was won by the Yale University eight representing the United States. The winning crew included James Rockefeller, of the celebrated banking dynasty, and Benjamin Spock, the future best-selling paediatrician.

rescued the COF [Comité Olympique Français] by expanding its own stadium in time for the Games, the entire Olympic experience was stamped by thwarted expectations.' Lewis goes on to note the reduced capacity of the final version of the Olympic stadium, at around 60,000 places, as well as what was widely perceived by the organisers as its unappealing site. As he explains:

> Nor was the location of the Olympic stadium in the industrial suburb of Colombes, north-west of Paris, reminiscent of the Olympia of antiquity. The ... *Manchester Guardian* called Colombes 'one of the least attractive of the suburbs' around Paris, 'a township of many factory chimneys, gravelled empty spaces, and unkempt trees'.[20]

On the positive side, ample space was available in the vicinity of the Colombes stadium to build the Olympic Village required to house competitors, a stipulation included for the first time in the International Olympic Committee's contract with the host city for the 1924 Games (fig. 11). This peripheral site also lent itself admirably to those events able

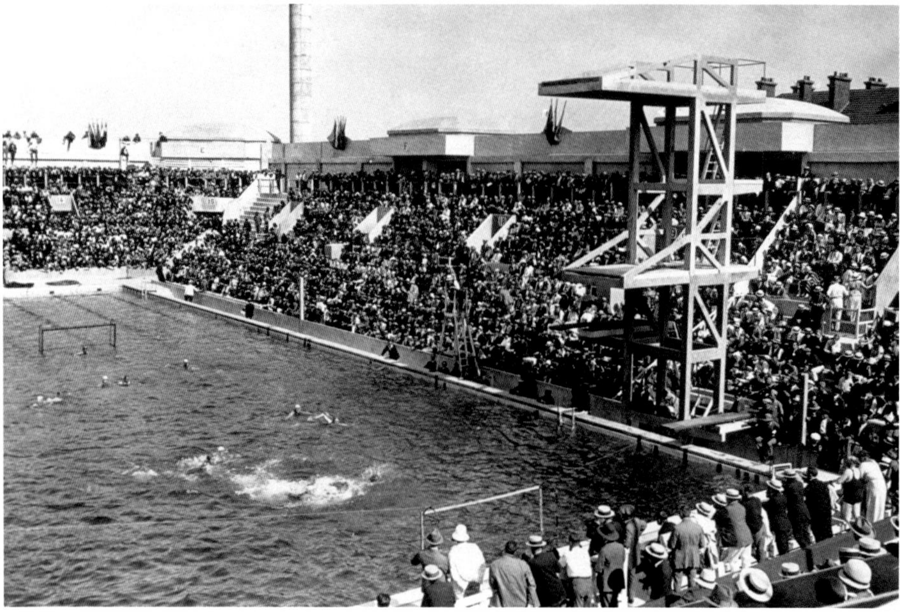

**19.** (cat. 23) Unrecorded photographer
Paris 1924 Olympic Games, men's water polo, general view at the Tourelles Olympic swimming pool, 4 May 1924
Black and white photograph
Comité International Olympique (CIO) (PHO10483875)

The Piscine des Tourelles was the outstanding new construction of Paris 1924. The country's first Olympic-size pool was characterised by its grand scale and harmonious proportions, while its eight monumental stairways and steep terraces offered ready access and an excellent view to 10,000 spectators.

to exploit the stadium's proximity to semi-rural countryside, a network of local roads and the River Seine (fig. 18). These included the cross country (fig. 98) and marathon, cycle road racing, and the rowing regatta held at Argenteuil, a location made famous a half-century earlier by the Impressionists, including the district's most celebrated resident, Claude Monet.

Elsewhere, while the swimming pool initially planned for the Colombes site failed to materialise, the municipal and departmental authorities did provide the funding required for the construction in 1923 of a combined 50-metre swimming and 5.5-metre diving pool at the Porte des Lilas, on the city's eastern boundary (fig. 19). This 10,000-capacity aquatic arena was the work of Léopold Bévières, like Faure-Dujarric a graduate of the École des Beaux-Arts, who combined a reinforced concrete core with brick and ceramic cladding in an inventive expression of Art Deco monumentality.[21] In addition to its length, the new venue's design included marked lanes for competitors, thereby establishing a template for all future Olympic pools. It was here that the American stars Johnny Weissmuller, Duke Kahanamoku and Gertrude Ederle (see Cronin's chapter) would enthral Parisian audiences, before translating their talents, with varying degrees of success, to the Hollywood screen. It may consequently be argued that it was in the purpose-built Piscine des Tourelles that the aspirations of the Games' organisers found their most complete expression, combining sport and spectacle in an authentically innovative urban space.[22]

*

More broadly, the peripheral locations of Paris 1924 point to ideological tensions as well as infrastructural weaknesses within the French capital's 'sportscape'. Rival conceptions of sport's social significance meant that it was perceived either as an extension of the education system or as a branch of the entertainment industry, but rarely as both. This divergence was most sharply expressed in the relative importance attributed to amateurs and professionals within any given sport. For the administrators, if not always the practitioners, of the athletic pursuits showcased at the Olympic Games, amateurism was sacrosanct. However, it was in the professionalised arenas of horse racing, cycling and boxing that the demands of the paying public had historically been met most effectively. Planning for Paris 1924 was undermined by this ambiguity, colouring the organisers' opinions as regards public and private spaces, urban and suburban sites, and the competing needs of players and spectators. Such frictions also help to explain the French Olympic Committee's inability to attract funding for the new stadium complex conceived as the focal point of the event. The consequent dispersion of the Games and their associated failure as a commercial undertaking did not, for all that, prevent their lasting cultural legacy. A combination of architectural and organisational innovations, memorable sporting performances and intensive media coverage meant that the Paris 1924 Olympiad would come to be regarded as the first authentically modern incarnation of this global mega-event. Only time will tell how Paris 2024 will be judged against this historical backdrop.

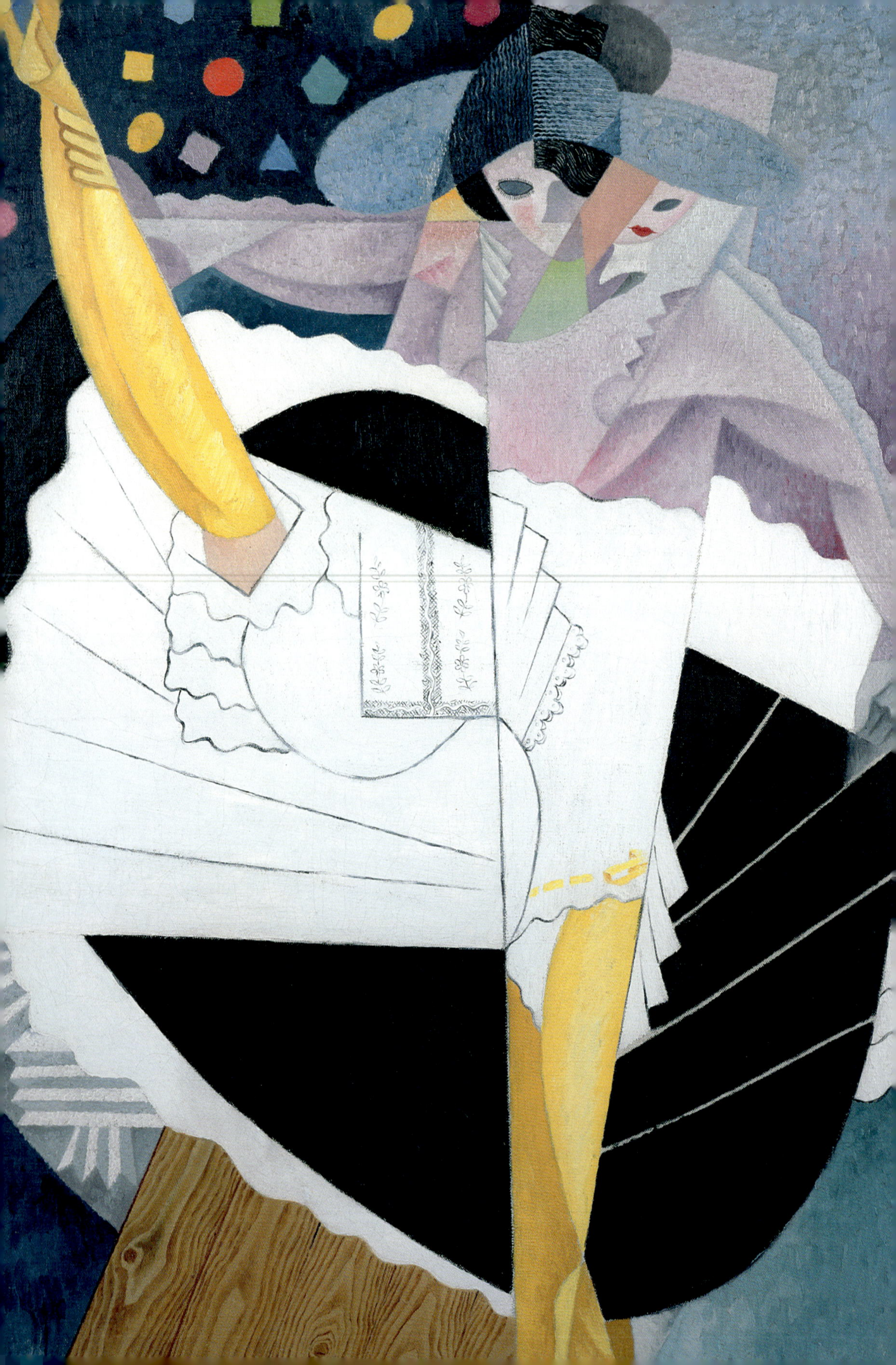

# 2

# CITY OF ART

BERNARD VERE

The Paris that hosted the Olympics in 1924 was the undisputed capital of the art world, a title it had retained since the Games were last staged there in 1900. Of course, the Olympics themselves had connections to that world through their founder Pierre de Coubertin, whose father Charles was an academic painter, who regularly participated in the official Paris Salons of the late nineteenth century (fig. 1). The Sorbonne was deliberately chosen in 1894 as the venue for the 'Congress' to decide whether to revive the Olympic Games, in part because of its newly completed murals by French neoclassicist Pierre Puvis de Chavannes. In time, the younger Coubertin's vision for these modern Olympics included prizes for art and architecture (see Osgood's chapter).

## CHANGING VISIONS

But if Paris was still the undisputed capital of the art world, a lot had changed in the first quarter of the twentieth century. Old artistic certainties, already under attack from the Impressionists, had crumbled completely with major exhibitions held on the deaths of Paul Cézanne and Paul Gauguin. The self-taught Henri Rousseau had established a career as what we would now term an unconventional, naïve even, 'outsider', managing to show work and build a reputation beyond the orthodox art world. Then the waves of radical groupings – Henri Matisse and the Fauves, the Cubists, the Italian Futurists – had caused consternation, gathering notoriety and column inches in the decade before

**20.** (cat. 83) Gino Severini (1883–1966)
*Dancer no. 5*, 1915/16 (detail)
(*Danseuse no. 5*)
Oil on canvas, 93.3 × 74 cm
Pallant House Gallery, Chichester
(CHCPH 0594)

Montmartre's network of nightclubs was integral to the social scene of the Parisian avant-garde, and Italian Futurist Gino Severini was an enthusiastic participant. He recalled that the can-can dancers there seemed 'dressed like all the other women until they raised their skirts during their dance. When caught under bright spotlights, all you could see was a blur of contrasting blacks and whites, a splendour of greys in a whole range of purples, greens, and blues.'

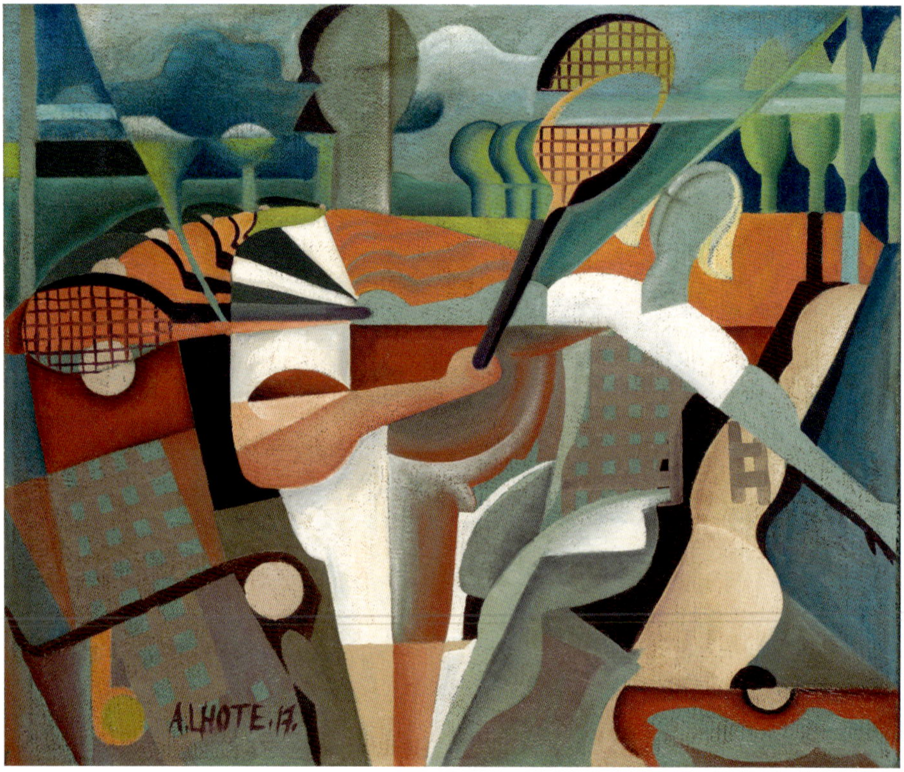

**21.** (cat. 94) André Lhote (1885–1962)
*Tennis Players*, 1917
(*Joueurs de Tennis*)
Oil on canvas, 45.7 × 54.6 cm
Wimbledon Lawn Tennis Museum, London (WTM:1994/176)

André Lhote had risen to prominence in the Cubist movement before World War I. Unable to fight on medical grounds, Lhote returned to his native Gascony and began to paint sporting subjects. Here he shows two bob-haired women playing the game, which was becoming increasingly fashionable in France.

World War I. Questions had been asked by politicians about whether this was really art and, more importantly, whether it was really French art, a worry fuelled both by rising tensions with Germany and by the fact that many of Cubism's leading practitioners, most notably the Spaniard Pablo Picasso, were not themselves French. In fact, this was a symptom of the success of Paris, which became a magnet for artists not just from elsewhere in Europe but from around the world, thanks in part to the burgeoning number of private art schools that also provided income for the artists who taught at them.

World War I and the ensuing Spanish Flu pandemic had interrupted much of this. The former had driven even French artists out of Paris, while others joined up or returned to their native countries. The latter had claimed the life of Guillaume Apollinaire, not simply a poet but one of the main champions of the artistic avant-garde. It also produced a reconsideration of Paris's visual culture. What were now viewed as the wilder excesses of Cubism were reined in, although there were still Cubists aplenty at the end of the war, such as André Lhote (fig. 21) or Henri Laurens (fig. 80). One such response came from the architect Le Corbusier and his painter friend Amédée Ozenfant, who likened Cubism to visiting the North Pole: it was important to go there once, but since 'today we know that it is only a frozen desert, to want to return there would be a vain fantasy'.[1] Le Corbusier and Ozenfant's movement was called Purism, which they viewed as an improvement on Cubism and promoted in their journal, tellingly called *L'Esprit Nouveau* (The New Spirit). But there were also those, like Picasso, who turned more obviously back to the classical for inspiration. Harlequins and Pulcinellas, characters from the theatrical genre known as commedia dell'arte, were also suddenly in vogue, thanks to artists such as Juan Gris and Gino Severini, who had only a decade or so earlier joined the founder of the Futurists, Filippo Tommaso Marinetti, in proclaiming the modern city and machinery as inspirations for twentieth-century art (fig. 20). A pre-war Cubist like Auguste Herbin vacillated between total abstraction and social realist paintings of men playing boules in provincial France. Other, newer trends were emerging. Dada had come to Paris at the end of the war and Surrealism was beginning to be discussed and would be officially launched in the autumn. In short, there was not a dominant style and a lot of things were up for grabs.

The Olympics themselves had also undergone developments in their growing pains to find their identity. They had expanded rapidly and, to some extent, softened their emphasis on classical antecedents as well as having broken the link to the international trade fairs that saw the first Parisian Games held in parallel with the 1900 Universal Exhibition (see Introduction). Now there were film crews, radio broadcasts, cameras trained on the action to produce photographs for the daily press, which reported on the events in the same papers that covered the artistic scandals of the day. Notional amateur and gold medallist at the Antwerp Olympics of 1920, Suzanne Lenglen (fig. 70) was at least as famous as her French professional contemporaries, such as the boxer Georges Charpentier or the cyclist Henri Pélissier. It was on the front page of the newspaper *Excelsior*, celebrating Pélissier's victory in the 1923 Tour de France, that Picasso altered a picture of the rider, turning him and his wife into a pair of classical figures (fig. 22). Picasso gives Pélissier a cloak and armoured breastplate, with the suggestion of victor's laurels. The laurel wreath was awarded to winners in the ancient Olympics and continued to be an important part of Olympic iconography in the 1924 Games, appearing on medals and stamps. In Picasso's sketch, however, this classicism is undercut by the preservation of Pélissier's team logos. Still visible through his new breastplate, his racing jersey bears the names of his trade team sponsors, bicycle manufacturer Automoto and the tyre maker Hutchinson, reminding us that although the first Tour de France had been organised but three years after the 1900 Olympics, it had been founded on very different principles – as a commercial race with professional riders designed to sell newspapers. The intervening twenty years had seen these differences narrow. Pélissier's professional

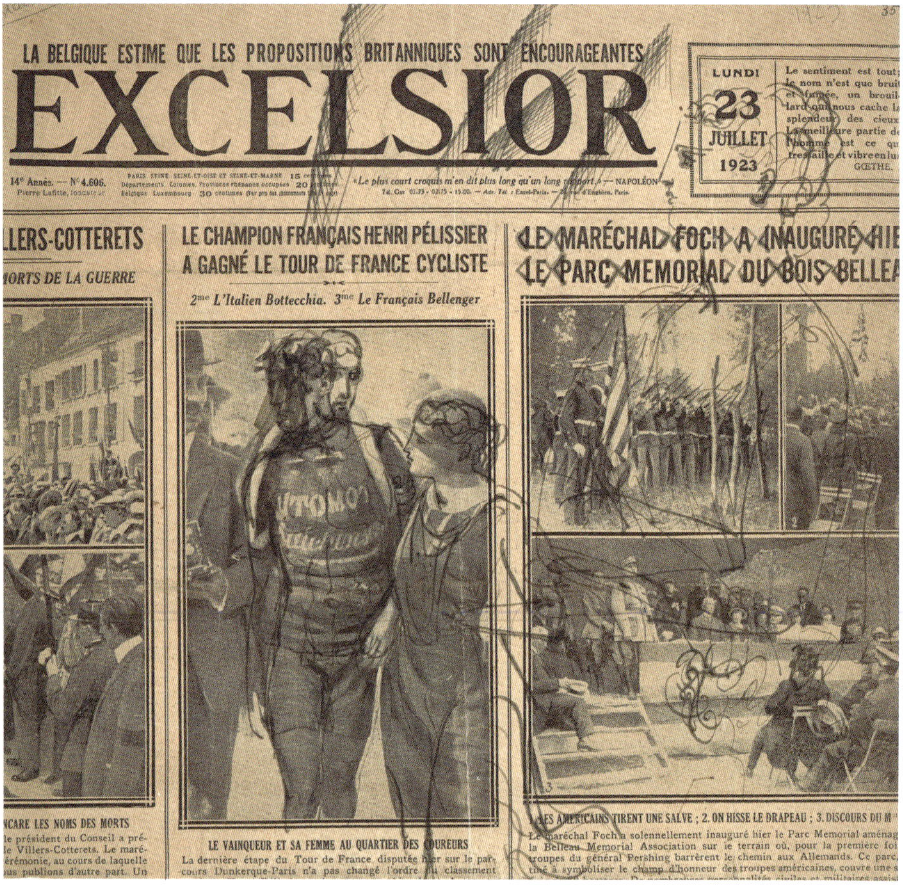


**22.** (cat.115) Pablo Picasso (1881–1973)
*Antique figures in profile*, Antibes, summer 1923
(*Personnages à l'antique de profil*)
Ink on paper, *Excelsior*,
Monday, 23 July 1923
33 × 35.5 cm
Musée national Picasso-Paris (MP984)

Pablo Picasso's doodle onto the front page of French newspaper *Excelsior* turns the winner of the 1923 Tour de France, Henri Péllisier, and his wife into a pair of classical figures. The move is both ennobling and jarring, because cycling was France's most popular sport and also its most commercialised. As a professional on the Automoto team, Pélissier was ineligible to ride in the following year's Olympics. The road race was won by his French compatriot Amand Blanchonnet, who would himself later turn professional.

status may have made him ineligible to ride at the Olympics, but in the summer of 1924 the Olympics would rival the Tour for French press coverage (see Dine's chapter).

Two direct manifestations of artistic engagement with the Paris Games will now be my focus, and it seems fitting that their very different natures exemplify two extremes of this engagement. One is the Bal Olympique (Olympic Ball), organised by the Union des

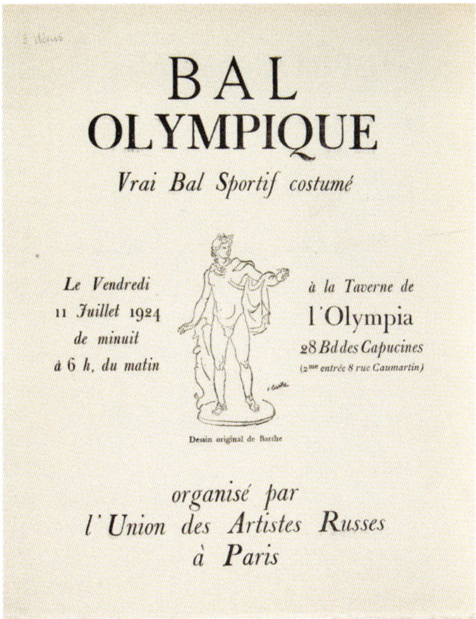


**23.** (cat. 113) After Pablo Picasso (1881–1973), Marie Vassilieff (1884–1957), Victor Barthe (1887–1954) and others; L'Union des Artistes Russes & François Bernouard: Paris, publisher
*Olympic Ball, Real Sports Costume Ball*, programme, 1924
(*Bal Olympique, Vrai Bal Sportif Costumé*)
Printed text on heavy paper with illustrations of original drawings, 29 × 24.5 cm
McNay Art Museum, San Antonio, Texas (TL1999.18.2)

Artists can find any excuse for a party. The Bal Olympique took place during the course of the Games, on Friday 11 July from midnight until 6.00am, and was organised by an expatriate association that served Russian artists based in Paris. A drawing of the ancient Apollo Belvedere statue graces the programme's cover. Apollo was the handsome god of music, song and poetry.

Artistes Russes à Paris (Union of Russian Artists in Paris), a ball that took place on 11 July 1924, with Natalia Gontcharova (cat. 118) and her partner Mikhail Larionov prominently involved, but of which we have little tangible record other than the programme and flyers that were produced (fig. 23). The other is a series of paintings by the avant-garde artist Robert Delaunay. Titled *Coureurs* (Runners), there are at least eight canvases now scattered across museums and private collections. All are based on athletics events that took place on Thursday 10 July 1924, which leads to the intriguing – although admittedly unproven – possibility that Delaunay watched the track events in the stadium at Colombes before heading to the Bal Olympique with his Ukrainian-born wife, artist Sonia Delaunay-Terk, the following night.

## THE BAL OLYMPIQUE

The Bal Olympique brought together an intriguing roster of participants and organisers for an event that started at midnight and concluded at six in the morning, taking place at the appropriately named Taverne Olympique on Boulevard des Capucines. The names of its organising committee, listed on the flyer (fig. 24), make clear that it encompassed several strands of avant-garde Parisian society. Among them are the filmmaker Dudley Murphy and his wife Katherine Hawley, in town to make the pioneering *Ballet Mécanique* with Fernand Léger (Hawley appears as the woman on the swing in the film's opening shot). There is the art critic and collector of Cubism Maurice Raynal, and Marcel Hiver, editor of the new arts magazine *CAP: Critique – Art – Philosophie*. Rolf de Maré is among

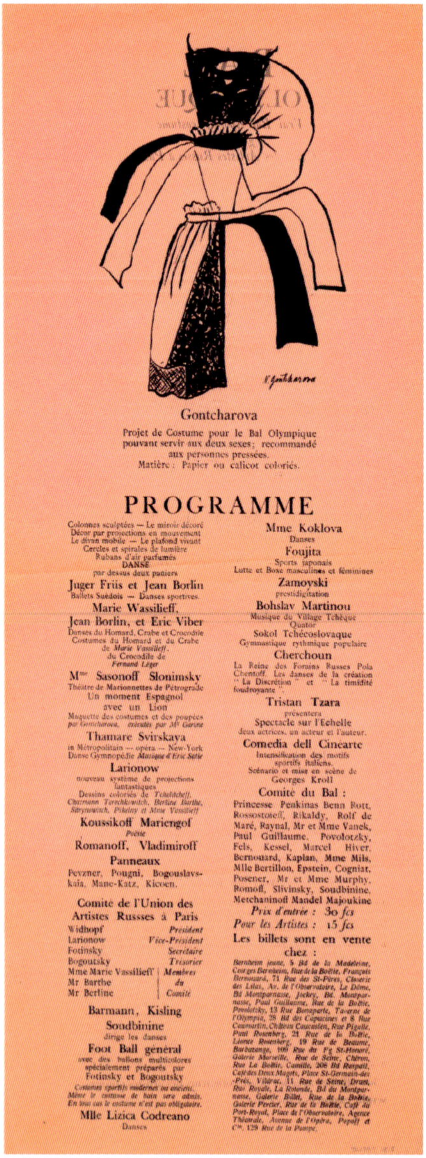

Gontcharova

Projet de Costume pour le Bal Olympique pouvant servir aux deux sexes; recommandé aux personnes pressées.
Matière : Papier ou calicot coloriés.

PROGRAMME

Colonnes sculptées — Le miroir décoré
Décor par projections en mouvement
Le divan mobile — Le plafond vivant
Cercles et spirales de lumière
Rubans d'air parfumés
DANSE
par dessus deux paniers
Juger Friis et Jean Borlin
Ballets Suédois — Danses sportives.
Marie Wassilieff,
Jean Borlin, et Eric Viber
Danses du Homard, Crabe et Crocodile
Costumes du Homard et du Crabe de *Marie Vassilieff*,
du Crocodile de *Fernand Léger*
M^me^ Sasonoff Slonimsky
Théâtre de Marionnettes de Pétrograde
Un moment Espagnol avec un Lion
Maquette des costumes et des poupées *par Gontcharova, exécutés par M^r^ Garine*
Thamare Svirskaya
in Métropolitain — opéra — New-York
Danse Gymnopédie *Musique d'Eric Satie*
Larionow
nouveau système de projections fantastiques
Dessins coloriés de *Tchelitcheff, Chatmann Terechkowitch, Berline Barthe, Sitrynowitch, Pikelny et Mme Vassilieff*
Koussikoff Mariengof
*Poésie*
Romanoff, Vladimiroff
Panneaux
Pevzner, Pougni, Bogouslavskaia, Mane-Katz, Kicoen.

Comite de l'Union des Artistes Russses à Paris

| | |
|---|---|
| Widhopf | *President* |
| Larionow | *Vice-President* |
| Fotinsky | *Secrétaire* |
| Bogoutsky | *Trésorier* |
| Mme Marie Vassilieff | *Membres* |
| Mr Barthe | *du* |
| Mr Berline | *Comité* |

Barmann, Kisling
Soudbinine
dirige les danses
Foot Ball général
avec des ballons multicolores spécialement préparés par Fotinsky et Bogoutsky
*Costumes sportifs modernes ou anciens. Même le costume de bain sera admis. En tous cas le costume n'est pas obligatoire.*
Mlle Lizica Codreano
Danses

Mme Koklova
Danses
Foujita
Sports japonais
Lutte et Boxe masculines et féminines
Zamoyski
prestidigitation
Bohslav Martinou
Musique du Village Tchèque
Quator
Sokol Tchécoslovaque
Gymnastique rythmique populaire
Cherchoun
La Reine des Forains Russes Pola Chentoff. Les danses de la création " La Discrétion " et " La timidité foudroyante ".
Tristan Tzara
présentera
Spectacle sur l'Echelle
deux actrices, un acteur et l'auteur.
Comedia dell Cinearte
Intensification des motifs sportifs italiens.
Scénario et mise en scène de Georges Kroll
Comite du Bal :
Princesse Penkinas Benn Rott, Rossostoieff, Rikaldy, Rolf de Maré, Raynal, Mr et Mme Vanek, Paul Guillaume, Povolotzky, Fels, Kessel, Marcel Hiver, Bernouard, Kaplan, Mme Mils, Mlle Bertillon, Epstein, Cogniat, Posener, Mr et Mme Murphy, Romoff, Slivinsky, Soudbinine, Metchaninoff Mandel Majoukine
*Prix d'entrée : 30 fcs*
*Pour les Artistes : 15 fcs*
Les billets sont en vente chez :
*Bernheim jeune, 5 Bd de la Madeleine, Georges Bernheim, Rue de la Boëtie, François Bernouard, 71 Rue des St-Pères, Closerie des Lilas, Av. de l'Observatoire, Le Dôme, Bd Montparnasse, Jockey, Bd. Montparnasse, Paul Guillaume, Rue de la Boëtie, Povolotzky, 13 Rue Bonaparte, Taverne de l'Olympia, 28 Bd des Capucines et 8 Rue Caumartin, Château Caucasien, Rue Pigalle, Paul Rosenberg, 21 Rue de la Boëtie, Léonce Rosenberg, 19 Rue de Beaune, Barbazange, 109 Rue du Fg St-Honoré, Galerie Marseille, Rue de Seine, Chéron, Rue La Boëtie, Camille, 208 Bd Raspail, Café des Deux Magots, Place St-Germain-des-Prés, Vildrac, 11 Rue de Seine, Druet, Rue Royale, La Rotonde, Bd du Montparnasse, Galerie Billet, Rue de la Boëtie, Galerie Percier, Rue de la Boëtie, Café du Port-Royal, Place de l'Observatoire, Agence Théatrale, Avenue de l'Opéra, Popoff et C^ie^, 129 Rue de la Pompe.*

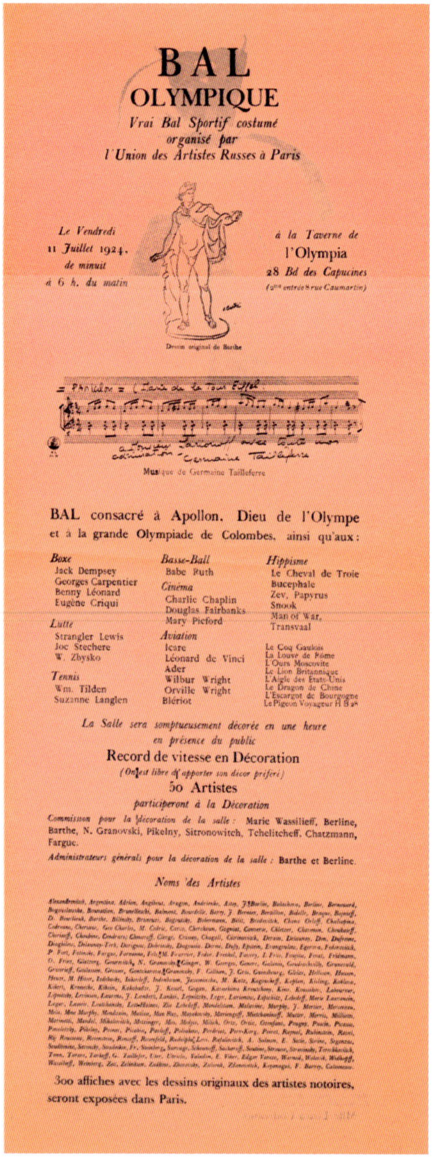

BAL OLYMPIQUE

*Vrai Bal Sportif costumé organisé par l'Union des Artistes Russes à Paris*

*Le Vendredi 11 Juillet 1924, de minuit à 6 h. du matin*

*à la Taverne de* l'Olympia *28 Bd des Capucines* *(2^me^ entrée 8 rue Caumartin)*

Dessin original de Barthe

Musique de Germaine Tailleferre

BAL consacré à Apollon, Dieu de l'Olympe et à la grande Olympiade de Colombes, ainsi qu'aux :

*Boxe*
Jack Dempsey
Georges Carpentier
Benny Léonard
Eugène Criqui

*Lutte*
Strangler Lewis
Joe Stechere
W. Zbysko

*Tennis*
Wm. Tilden
Suzanne Langlen

*Basse-Ball*
Babe Ruth

*Cinéma*
Charlie Chaplin
Douglas Fairbanks
Mary Picford

*Aviation*
Icare
Léonard de Vinci
Ader
Wilbur Wright
Orville Wright
Blériot

*Hippisme*
Le Cheval de Troie
Bucephale
Zev, Papyrus
Snook
Man of War,
Transvaal

Le Coq Gaulois
La Louve de Rome
L'Ours Moscovite
Le Lion Britannique
L'Aigle des Etats-Unis
Le Dragon de Chine
L'Escargot de Bourgogne
Le Pigeon Voyageur H B 28

*La Salle sera somptueusement décorée en une heure en présence du public*

Record de vitesse en Décoration

*(On est libre d'apporter son décor préféré)*

50 Artistes

*participeront à la Décoration*

*Commission pour la décoration de la salle :* Marie Wassilieff, Berline, Barthe, N. Granovski, Pikelny, Sitronowitch, Tchelitcheff, Chatzmann, Fargue.

*Administrateurs généraux pour la décoration de la salle :* Barthe et Berline.

*Noms des Artistes*

300 affiches avec les dessins originaux des artistes notoires, seront exposées dans Paris.

**24.** (cat. 114) After Natalia Gontcharova (1881–1962)
*Costume Project for the Olympic Ball*, on double-sided flyer, 1924
(*Projet de Costume pour le Bal Olympique*)

Printed text on pink-coloured paper with illustration of an original drawing, 65.4 × 25.4 cm
McNay Art Museum, San Antonio, Texas (TL1999.18.5)

This side of the flyer for the varied programme of entertainment at the costumed Ball is headed by an image that could not be more different from the statue of Apollo on the other side and on the programme (fig. 23). Drawn by the organiser, Natalia Gontcharova, it offers a cheap and cheerful dress design for men and women 'in a hurry'.

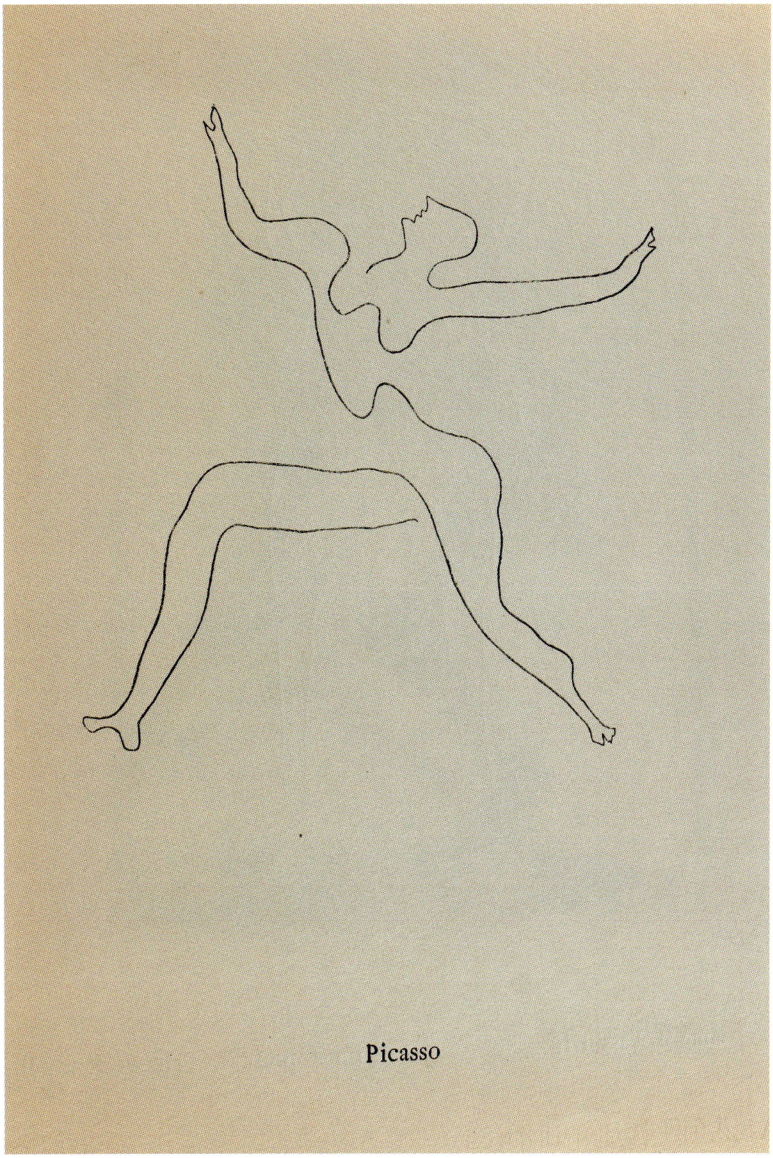


**25.** (cat. 112) After Pablo Picasso (1881–1973); L'Union des Artistes Russes & François Bernouard: Paris, publisher
*Mercury: Study of a Dancer*, in *Olympic Ball, Real Sports Costume Ball*, programme, 1924
(*Mercure: Étude de danseur*, in *Bal Olympique, Vrai Bal Sportif Costumé*)
Printed illustration of an original drawing on heavy paper, 29 × 24.5 cm
Private collection

Pablo Picasso produced the costumes and curtain for the ballet *Mercure*, which premiered the month before this study was reproduced in the Bal Olympique programme. The simplicity that conjures this figure out of a single unbroken line is glossed rather differently by Picasso's collaborator, composer Erik Satie: 'This show is akin to Music-Hall, as it comes without stylisation, and on no account has any connection with art things.'

the most important figures, both for his work with the predominantly Swedish Ballets Suédois, the principal rival to the Ballets Russes as the modernists' company of choice, and his role in bringing African-American entertainer Josephine Baker and the show *La Revue Nègre* to Paris the following year. Another transatlantic figure was the art dealer Paul Guillaume, whose wealth came not only from selling works by Italian artists like Amedeo Modigliani and Giorgio de Chirico but also African statues to the Pennsylvania collector Alfred Barnes.

As this list makes clear, the organisation of the ball was far from confined to those of Russian heritage, and tickets seem to have been available from almost every dealer in modern pictures in Paris. The programme itself was similarly varied, with 'sporting dances' by de Maré's lover, the Ballets Suédois dancer and choreographer Jean Borlin. This was followed by the artist Marie Vassilieff accompanying Borlin and another member of the company in the dances of the Lobster, the Crab and the Crocodile. Vassilieff herself designed the lobster and crab costumes, while the crocodile had been made by Léger the previous year for the Ballets Suédois's *The Creation of the World*.

The early 1920s marked a period of intense collaboration between visual artists, composers and ballet companies, with Gontcharova and Larionov working extensively with the Ballets Russes. Gontcharova's talents as a costume designer are evident in the flyer's suggestion of a costume for the ball, one that rejects the classical style of Victor Barthe's Apollo figure (fig. 23) in favour of a unisex garment of flowing paper or calico ribbons (fig. 24). The snatch of a score below Barthe's work is by Germaine Tailleferre, the only female member of 'Les Six', a young group of followers of composer Erik Satie. As revealed in its dedication to Larionov, it comes from the ballet *Les Mariés de la Tour Eiffel*, commissioned by Maré and choreographed by Borlin. Yet another artistic collaboration is invoked by the programme's reproduction of one of Picasso's designs for the ballet *Mercure* (Mercury), which had premiered a few weeks before (fig. 25). Its title once again reveals the hold that classicism still had on this dynamic, diverse art-scene. Picasso and Satie are listed among the many artists at the foot of the flyer, a veritable 'who's who' of the Parisian art scene of the time, although the extent of their involvement in the evening's proceedings is unclear. Others who definitely did take part were Larionov, with a new system of projections, the Japanese artist Tsuguharu Foujita, who demonstrated Japanese sport and male and female wrestling and boxing, and Romanian Dada poet Tristan Tzara, who offered a display of ladder climbing. The flyer also promised an attempt at the speed record for decoration, to be carried out in front of the guests!

## DELAUNAY'S RUNNERS

Also on the Ball's list of artists were the Delaunays. There is not the evidence to say for certain that they actually attended (though their friendship with Tzara and Sonia's involvement in the previous year's Russian ball make it likely). Even then, Robert's engagement with the Olympics would be more enduring than these overnight shenanigans. Sport was not a new theme for Delaunay: part of his pre-war reputation had been built on his large rugby-themed painting *The Cardiff Team*, which had been hailed by Apollinaire as 'the most modern picture' in the Salon des Indépendants of 1913.[2] But *Runners* marked a departure from his more recent work, and with seven of the series produced between 1924 and 1926 (with only one outlier in 1930), there is agreement that the Olympics acted here as a generalised catalyst.

The version we have in the Fitzwilliam exhibition is from the National Museum of Serbia in Belgrade (fig. 26). Comparing it with the one now held at the Museum of Modern Art in Troyes, France (fig. 27), we find that the latter gives us some clues as to Delaunay's inspiration. The background to the Belgrade work is a patchwork of greys, punctuated, top right, by a red solar disc, a form Delaunay had used many times

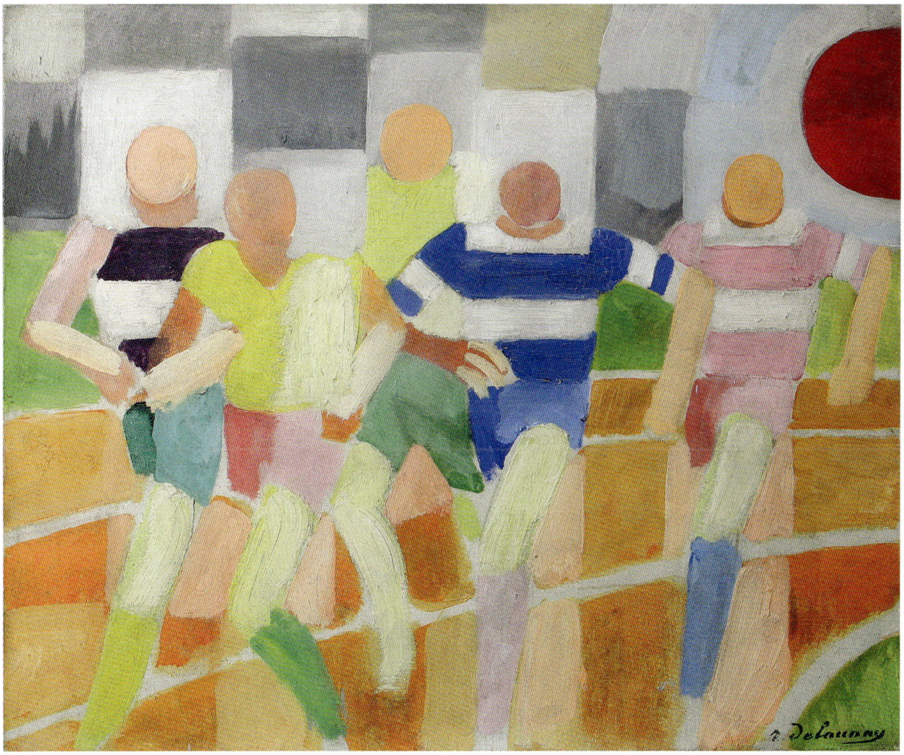


**26.** (cat. 101) Robert Delaunay (1885–1941)
*The Runners*, *c.* 1924
(*Les Coureurs*)
Oil on canvas, 46 × 55 cm
National Museum of Serbia, Belgrade (974)

Robert Delaunay's series *Coureurs* (Runners) was inspired by the 1924 Olympics in his hometown of Paris. Like most of the series, this painting shows five runners taking a bend. Based on new evidence showing the version overleaf as it was exhibited in 1925, it is now possible not just to connect the paintings to the Olympics generally, but to link these works to the 1,500m race won on 10 July by Paavo Nurmi.

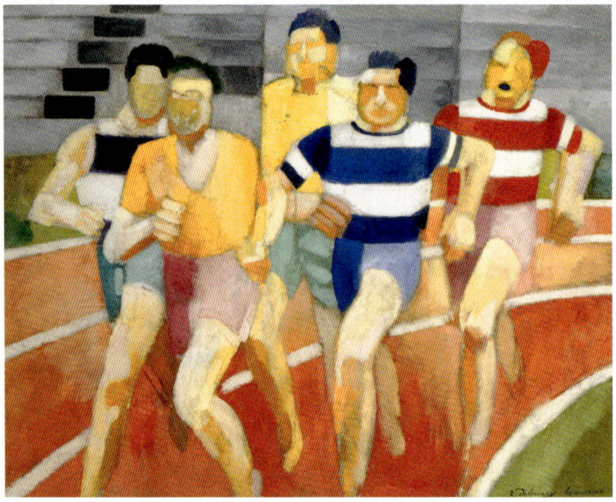

**27.** Robert Delaunay (1885–1941)
*Runners*, 1924
(*Coureurs*)
Oil on canvas, 114 × 146 cm
Troyes, Musée d'Art Moderne de Troyes (MNLP 51)

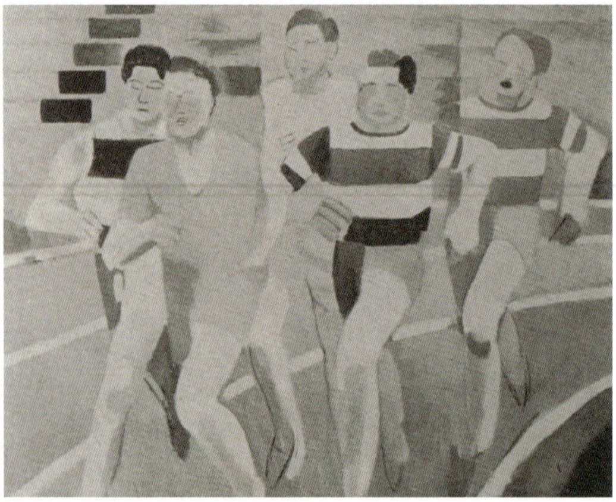

**28.** Robert Delaunay (1885–1941)
*Sketch for 'Record'*, c. 1924
(*Esquisse de 'Record'*)
Reproduced 'Le Salon des Indépendants', *L'Art Vivant*, 1 March 1925, p. 18

previously. Looking at the Troyes picture, we see that this black and grey backdrop is the stadium, with rows of concrete terracing and a blacker set of rectangles that correspond to shadows cast by a fence running up the stand. As the athletes take the bend, the stadium at Colombes, where the 1924 track and field events were held, comes into focus (fig. 16). Also in focus are more individuated runners, with identifiable hairstyles and, in one case, a moustache. In fact, when the Troyes canvas was originally shown in the Salon des Indépendants in 1925, it had both a different title and even greater individuation. The caption to a photograph in the bimonthly art magazine *L'Art Vivant* (fig. 28) titles the work *Esquisse de 'Record'* (Sketch for 'Record'). The photograph also demonstrates that even here, Delaunay had returned to the canvas and obliterated some elements that tie the work more firmly to specific Olympic races.

Before turning to the athletes themselves, a little more about the history of the Troyes painting. In writing later about the piece exhibited in the Salon in 1925, Delaunay dates it to the previous year, and notes how he sold it to fashion designer Jacques Heim in 1928 (a detail that accords with what is known about the painting's provenance).[3] That the Troyes and Salon paintings are one and the same is further attested by the absence of any work titled *Record* or *Sketch for 'Record'* in the posthumous catalogue of Delaunay's works prepared by Guy Habasque.[4] All of this suggests that between the painting's exhibition in 1925 and its sale in 1928, Delaunay made the figures less recognisable, also changing the title to the more generic *Coureurs*, which he added to the lower right of the canvas.

The discernible features in the painting's early life as *Sketch for 'Record'* allow us to speculate on the identities of the runners, who, I suggest, all competed in the 1,500m final on 10 July. The small mouth, high forehead and side parting of the leading runner recall the features of the British athlete Henry Stallard, who would go on to win the bronze medal, while the jet-black hair low on the temples of the runner behind suggests his compatriot and fellow Cambridge student Douglas Lowe, who would finish fourth after taking the 800m title earlier in the week (see Holt's essay). The moustachioed figure on the right, meanwhile, can be connected to the Swiss silver medallist Willy Schärer, and the other hooped figure to victor and phenomenon Paavo Nurmi – a shorter, powerful man with a squarer face whose swept-back hair leaves an expanse of forehead glistening in the strong sun.

It is of course possible that Delaunay was actually in the stadium at Colombes. But even if that were the case, it is extremely unlikely that he would have had access to the centre of the track, which is the supposed vantage point for the painting. Rather, this is an experience as mediated through press photography and the pictures that were appearing in periodicals such as *Le Miroir des sports*. Delaunay's *Cardiff Team* had also been based on a press photograph. These are modern athletes, in a modern stadium, conveyed to Delaunay by the modern mechanical means of the camera and commercial media reproduction. It is a process that he then transforms into the much older medium of oil paint on canvas in its own replica series, which as it develops, becomes less human and more abstract.

As a title, *Sketch for 'Record'* also ties the picture to 10 July. In the space of little over an hour, Nurmi won both the 1500m and 5000m finals, breaking the Olympic record in each (see Young's essay). Perhaps Delaunay changed the title because he wanted to distinguish himself from the Futurists, whose leader, Marinetti, had once praised the 'concept and love of achieving "records"'.[5] But the change also plays its part, together with the abstraction of the background and alterations to the faces, in effacing the initial referents, Nurmi and company at Colombes. In this way, the paintings increasingly distance themselves from the hot summer day that inspired them, turning a single moment of sporting glory into a timeless ideal. In place of distinct physiognomy, we are left with heads as round as the sun – five of them, like Olympic rings.

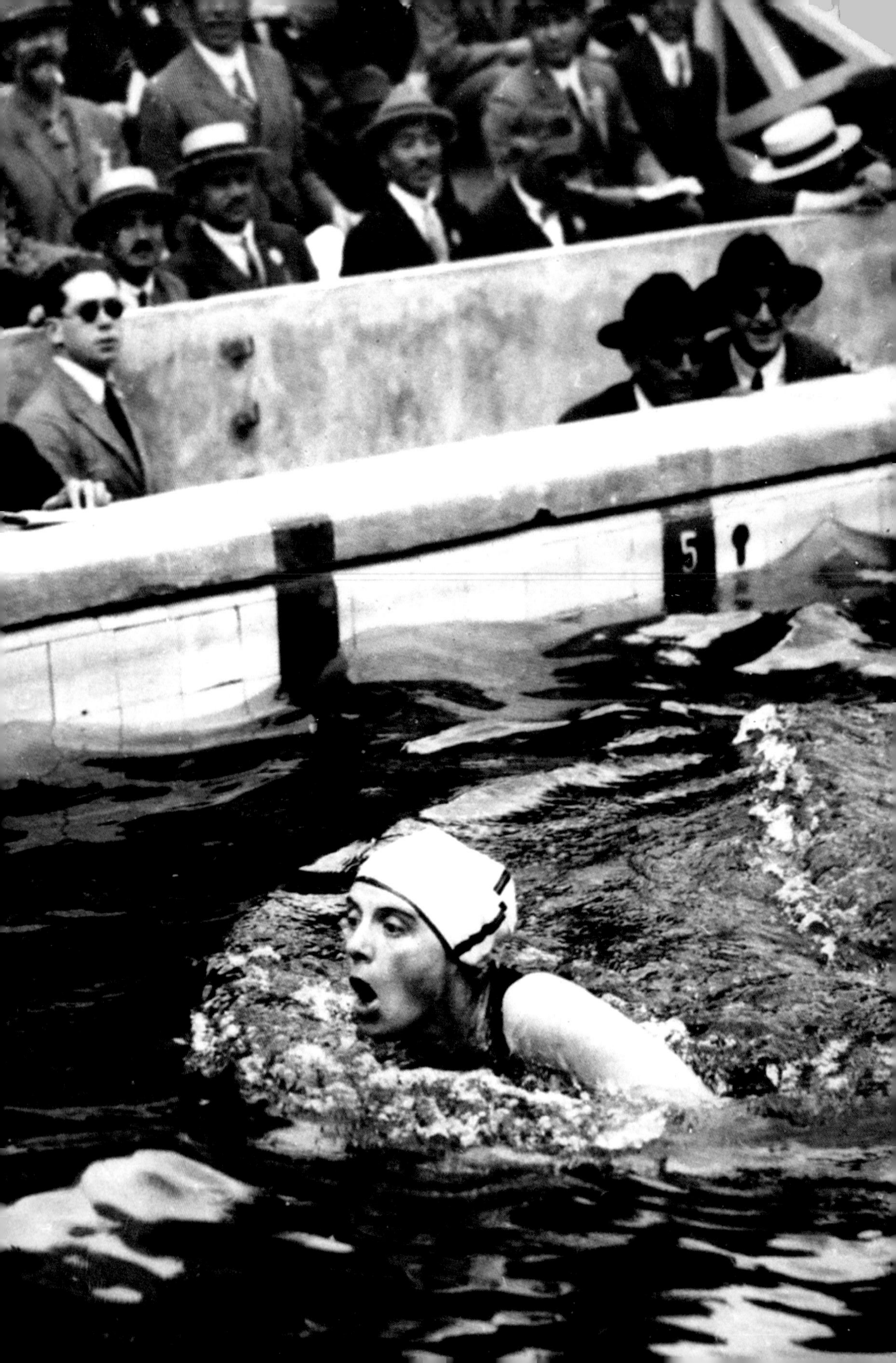
5

# THE GAMES

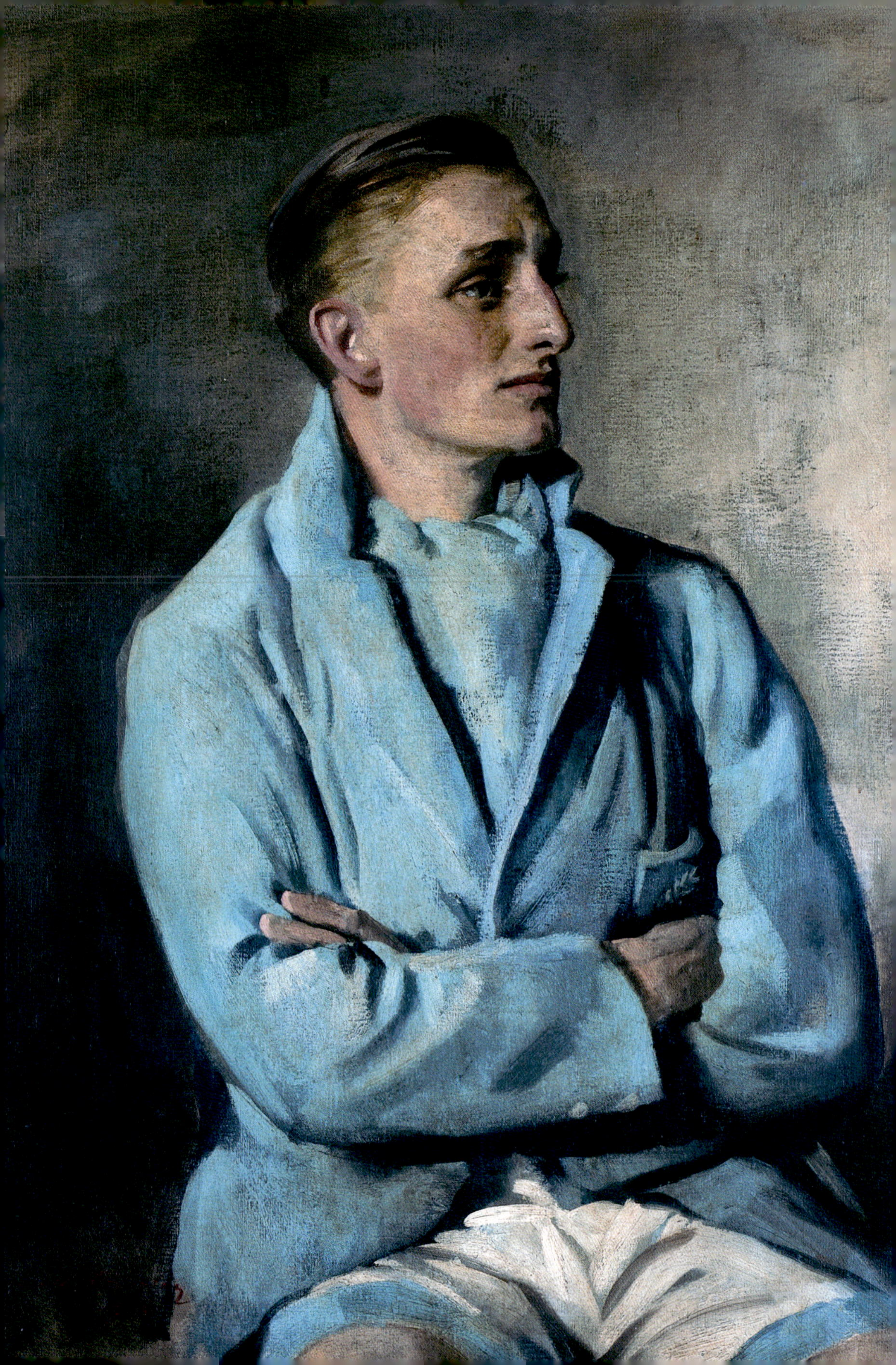

# 3

# CAMBRIDGE, BRITAIN AND THE 1924 OLYMPICS

RICHARD HOLT

'Bliss was it in that dawn to be alive, but to be young was very heaven.' The famous lines of Wordsworth, visiting Paris during the French Revolution, are well suited to a later and happier moment. The Paris Games of 1924 were particularly happy for British Olympism and for Cambridge. Britain came fourth in the unofficial medal table in 1924, their best performance for the rest of the century, with the University's athletes at the forefront. Highlights included gold in the 100m and the 800m, silver and bronze by members of the sprint relay teams and gold on the river for the coxless four (fig. 30). Even Eric Liddell, the Edinburgh University student, who famously refused to run on a Sunday, trained with the Cambridge University Athletic Club (CUAC) and was considered an 'honorary member'. There had been nothing quite like it. Nothing quite like it would happen again.

There is much more to discover about the team of 239 men and 28 women who represented Britain that summer – the neglected working-class boxers, Harry Mallin and Harry Mitchell, both of them gold medallists, and swimmers like Lucy Morton, who was a bigger name in her native Blackpool than Kitty McKane (later Godfree), the reigning Wimbledon champion, whose Olympic medals were the talk of the affluent London suburbs. There were unsung medallists too in unsung events: cycling, race-walking, fencing and wrestling. And there were the self-effacing patricians, Cyril Mackworth-Praed, a Cambridge ornithologist, who won a gold and two silvers for shooting, and Philip Neame, the only Olympic medallist to have also won a Victoria Cross.[1]

**29.** (cat. 26) Sir Oswald Joseph Hornby Birley (1880–1952)
*David, Lord Burghley* (1905–1981), 1926
Oil on canvas, 101 × 74.9 cm
Burghley House, Stamford (PIC 179)

Lord Burghley is painted in his Cambridge Blue's blazer, his head turned to emphasise his aristocratic profile. In between Olympics, he achieved the famous 'dash' round the Great Court of Trinity College, Cambridge, at noon against the striking of the clock, which in the film *Chariots of Fire* is attributed to Harold Abrahams.

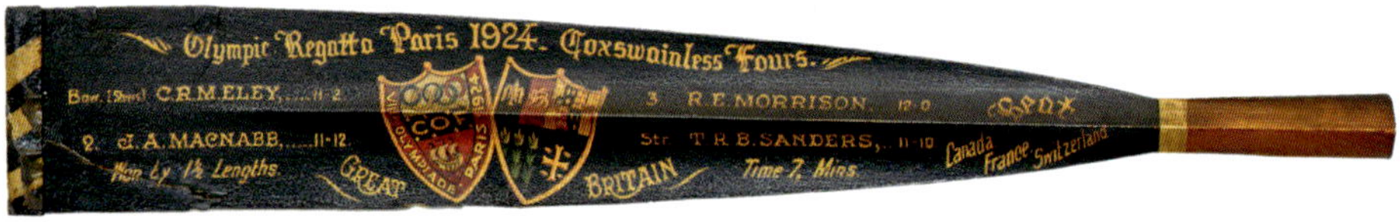


**30.** (cat. 48) Unrecorded maker
Illuminated trophy oar spoon celebrating the men's coxless four Olympic final and painted with the names of the four rowers, Charles Ryves Maxwell Eley (1902–1983), James Alexander Macnabb (1901–1990), Robert Erskine Morrison (1902–1980) and Terence Robert Beaumont Sanders (1901–1985), *c.* 1924

Wood, paint, gold leaf, 96.5 × 15.2 × 5.1 cm
The Macnab Memorial Trust

The gold medal in the 1924 coxless fours was won for Great Britain by a boat from Trinity College, Cambridge. Third Trinity – Macnabb, Eley, Morrison and Sanders – had rowed together since their schooldays at Eton. The oar spoon tells us that they triumphed in 7 minutes and by 1½ lengths. It also records the crews they beat.

## BRITISH SPORT

Prior to Paris, British participation in the early Olympics had been limited. Insularity and imperialism focused attention on the 'Home Nations' and the white 'British world', especially the 'Ashes' cricket series against Australia and rugby against New Zealand. 1908 was the turning point. Britain intervened to host the Olympics in London after Rome pulled out. A purpose-built venue, the White City, was created as part of a vast Franco-British Exhibition, and after a shaky start these London Games were a great success despite several spats between the British Olympic Association (BOA) and the American delegation. The future of the Olympics was secured and, reassuringly, Britain topped the unofficial medal table.[2] They struggled to match this triumph, with a disappointing showing at Stockholm in 1912 and – London railway man Albert Hill's double gold in the 800m and 1500m apart – a mediocre performance at Antwerp in 1920.

Why did Olympic medals matter so much in 1924 and why were the successes of the Cambridge 'Blues' – so called after the traditional colour of the University – so well received? The British emerged from World War I victorious but weakened, facing unprecedented peace-time challenges at home and abroad: vast war debts to the United States; the loss of 'informal Empire' in South America; new League of Nations mandates in the Middle East to add to the burden of imperial defence; the responsibility, shared with France, of policing the Versailles settlement, which the Americans had refused to ratify. In Britain the Anglo-Irish War, the bitter coal strikes, universal suffrage and the rise of Labour challenged the status quo. Success in Paris became a proxy for the revived prowess of the public-school educated elite, and more widely of 'the British race'. For all their deep historic and cultural ties, there was tension between the British 'Weary Titan' and the American 'New Kid on the Bloc'.

These politics form the backdrop to the renewed Olympic rivalry of 1924. Sport was a relatively self-contained sphere, where friends could clash without risking transatlantic solidarity. The American understanding of 'amateur', however, proved a particularly tricky issue for the British, who had been brought up on a diet of Victorian voluntarism, where sport was considered a private matter and subsidy was not 'fair play'. Britain had no college athletic scholarships to support its best sporting talent. Only three universities supplied members of the British team: Oxford, Cambridge and Edinburgh. The BOA rose to the challenge of funding the delegation, raising £24,000 by public subscription. This was more than Britain was used to but still far less than the Americans. Despite the disclaimers of Olympic purists that 'the important thing is not winning but taking part', there was a belief that Britain 'must wake up and get back some of her lost prestige in the world of international sport'.[3] For the British public, on the other hand, only a few Olympic disciplines really mattered. In a climate in which running and boxing captured the popular imagination, 'continental' sports such as fencing and gymnastics were of little interest.

## THE CAMBRIDGE STORY

In 1908, the CUAC had already appointed Alec Nelson as its athletics 'coach', combining the roles of tactician and 'trainer', advising on individual preparation and technique while attending to practicalities as a kind of superior college servant.[4] He was universally liked and formed a close working relationship with Philip Noel-Baker, the only man to win both an Olympic medal (silver in the 1500m at Antwerp) and, in 1959, a Nobel Peace Prize. Noel-Baker was a Quaker, who drove an ambulance in World War I and helped set up the League of Nations after it. A lone socialist voice among the military and imperialist cohorts of the BOA, he was nonetheless respected as a successful athlete and a decorated non-combatant. Nelson's nous and Noel-Baker's moral authority as team captain proved a formidable partnership. *Notes on Athletics by Members of the Cambridge University Athletic Team*, published in 1922, ingeniously combines a belief in natural talent with the need for careful preparation, and the conviction that 'our first class raw material ... can compete on level terms with American and other "specialists"'.[5] On the eve of the 1924 Games, the athletics correspondent for *The Observer* particularly admired 'that electrifying burst of [finishing] speed for which Cambridge men have become justly famous since Alec Nelson took them in hand'.[6]

Could this 'middle way' prevail? Could the best of British – the values of sportsmanship and a sense of fun – be combined with success in an ever more competitive global arena? Eric Liddell (fig. 31), who admired Noel-Baker profoundly, knew his 'windmill'

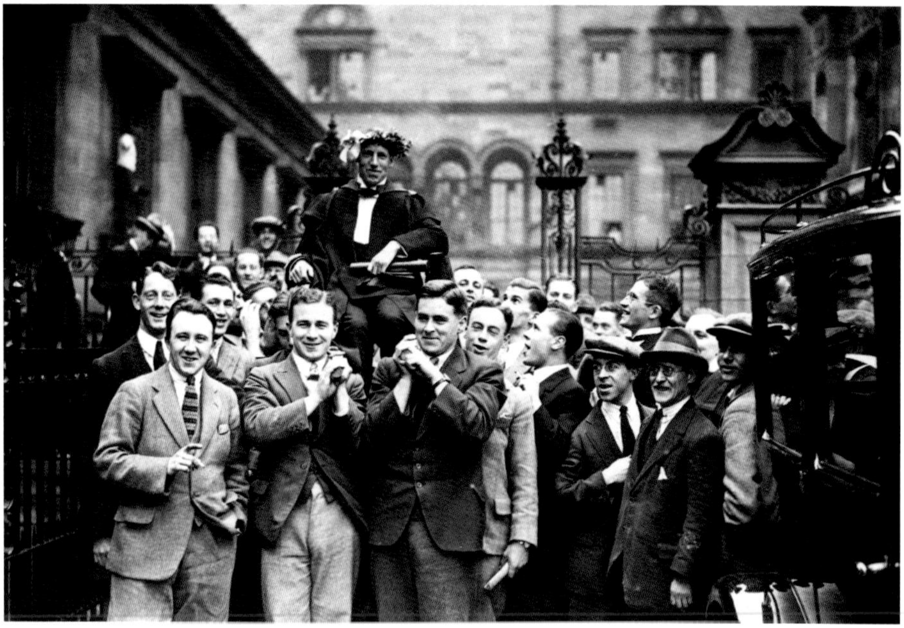

**31.** (cat. 25) Unrecorded photographer
Scottish athlete Eric Liddell (1902–1945) is paraded by fellow students around Edinburgh University after returning victorious from competition at the 1924 Summer Olympics, 18 July 1924
Black and white photograph

As an evangelical Christian, Eric Liddell switched to the 400m in Paris after learning that the 100m would be run on a Sunday. The photograph shows him being carried by his fellow students on his graduation day in Edinburgh, wearing a laurel wreath like an ancient Greek athletic victor.

arms were at odds with the new 'science' of running. He believed 'God made me fast' – technique was secondary. In the final of the 400m, he clutched a scrap of paper with the words 'He that honours me, I will honour' (1 Samuel 2:30) that had been passed to him that morning and 'ran mad' from the start. Some wondered whether he would run out of steam, but his trance-like self-belief saw him home in a world-record time. Moral instinct and British flair had triumphed over American specialisation as Horatio Fitch, the favourite, trailed Liddell by six yards, incredulous that 'a man could set such a pace and finish'.[7] Running with a pulled muscle, Guy Butler, grandson of a famous Harrow headmaster and alumnus of Trinity College, Cambridge, took the bronze behind Liddell. Gonville and Caius College alumnus Henry Stallard, who unselfishly acted as his Cambridge teammate Douglas Lowe's pacemaker in the 800m, despite having beaten him earlier in the year, was another 'moral' man in the Noel-Baker mould. Collectively, they and others fostered the ideal of Britain as a country where competitiveness was contained within a moral culture amid allegations that in the US the reverse was true.

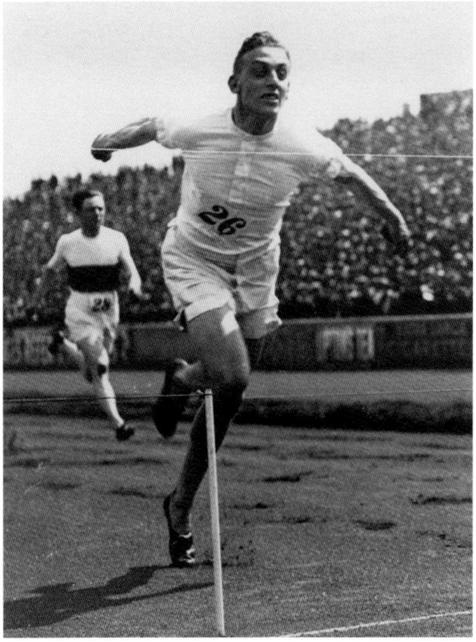

**32.** (cat. 35) Unrecorded photographer
Harold Abrahams (1899–1978) wins the 100-yard dash at the AAA Championships at Stamford Bridge, June 1924

Black and white photograph, 25.4 × 20.2 cm
Gonville and Caius College, Cambridge (PH: 1/50)

A remarkably composed Harold Abrahams dips for the line in the 1924 AAA Championship to win in 9.9 seconds. In Paris, his victory was by a far narrower margin. Abrahams would retire from athletics the following year but remained an important presence in sport as an official, journalist and commentator until his death in 1978.

True or not, the British bought into their own mythology. None more so than David Cecil, Lord Burghley, who was too young to figure in the medals when he competed in Paris but flew the flag for Cambridge in 1928 by winning gold in the 400m hurdles. The portrait of Burghley in his Cambridge Blue's blazer captures the refinement and confidence of the supremely fortunate gentleman amateur, who would be an International Olympics Committee member for 45 years, President of the Amateur Athletic Association for 40, an MP, and a wartime Governor of Bermuda (fig. 29). His daughter recalled: 'What he really loved was the fact everybody was joining in just for the pleasure of racing each other', adding that 'he minded terribly that people shouldn't take part in sport for profit or gain'.[8] Lowe, too, was a staunch amateur, who like Stallard, 'abhorred ostentation', refusing decades later to have his name associated with the film *Chariots of Fire* lest it inflate his achievements.

If Burghley became the most powerful figure in British athletics, his Cambridge contemporary, Harold Abrahams, was almost as influential. They are the two sides of the amateur coin personified – Burghley, old style, an avid fox hunter all his life; Abrahams, the son of an immigrant Jewish financier, who arrived at Cambridge and quickly transformed the 'haphazard' training available to him, winning 58 events in the Cambridge inter-collegiate competitions, the annual Varsity match against Oxford and other meetings, 'an aggregate record which had not been achieved in the history of this university' (fig. 32).[9] He famously employed Sam Mussabini as a personal coach to win the 100m in Paris and spent the next fifty years arguing for a more 'scientific' approach to athletics.

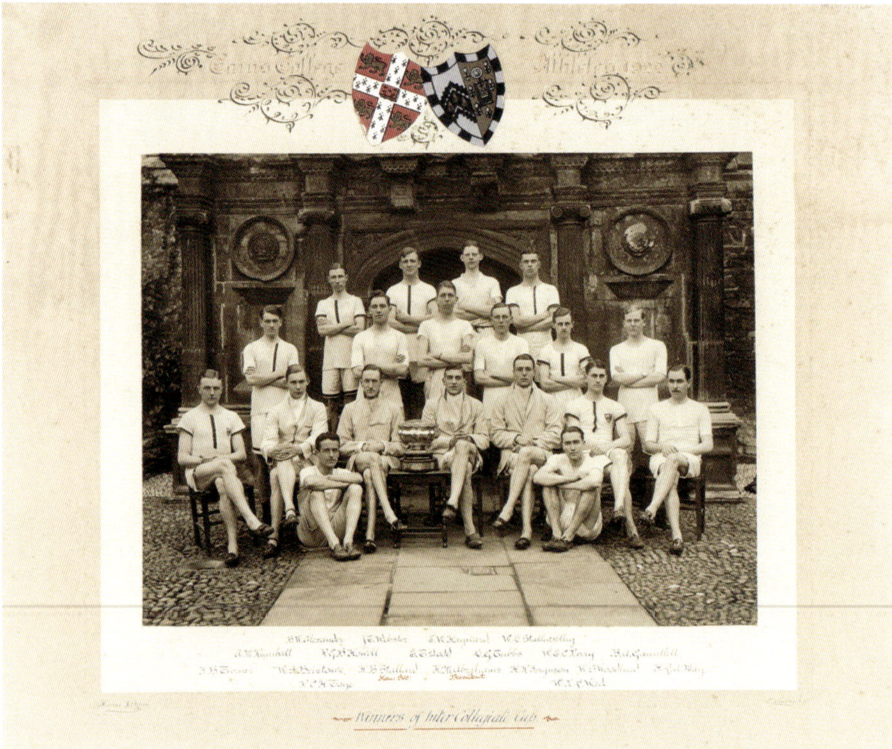

**33.** (cat. 36) Stearn & Sons, Cambridge (founded *c.* 1866)
*Caius College, Athletes 1922, Winners of Inter Collegiate Cup*, 1922
Black and white photograph mounted on board, pen and ink, metallic paint and coloured ink on applied paper, 36.6 × 43.2 cm
Gonville and Caius College, Cambridge (PH.S.7.1922)

This photograph of Gonville and Caius, winners of the colleges' athletics competition at the University of Cambridge in 1922, shows a young Harold Abrahams in his role as President (right of the cup). Left of the cup is the club's Honorary Secretary, Henry Stallard, who would win bronze in the 1500m in Paris, running with a stress fracture.

Abrahams was in a minority, the exception to the multi-sport preference of most of his contemporaries: Liddell played rugby for Scotland, Lowe was a college football captain, Butler a cricketer and a devotee of Eton Fives; Max Woosnam, who competed in the Olympic tennis team, was a Cambridge Blue in five sports. Abrahams was the epitome of the secular anglicised Jew for whom sport, public school and Cambridge were seen as passports to integration, acceptance and status. As a committed Olympian, he refused to support a boycott of the 1936 Olympics in Nazi Germany and later worked as a commentator for the BBC in Berlin (fig. 33).

Jack Beresford, Britain's most successful interwar Olympian with medals in all five Games of the period, had a strikingly similar 'immigrant narrative'. The son of successful

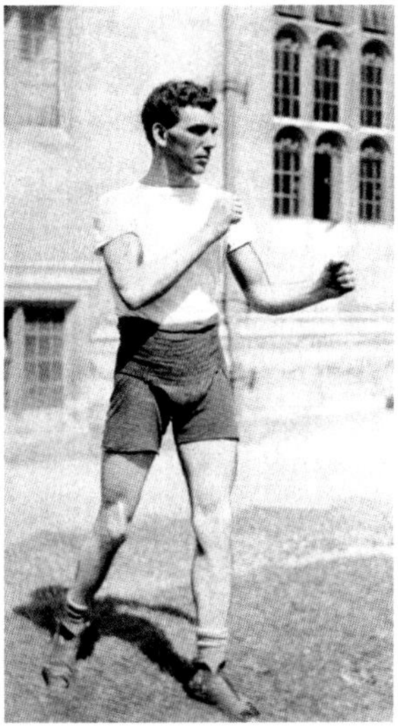

**34.** Unrecorded photographer
Harry Mallin (1892–1969), Great Britain's gold medallist in middleweight boxing, Antwerp 1920 Olympic Games, 12 August 1920
Black and white photograph

This photograph of the working-class amateur boxer Harry Mallin has him pose like a statue in front of a building that could pass for a Cambridge or Oxford college. Paris saw this middleweight successfully defend his title – the first boxer in Olympic history to do so, and the only British boxer until Nicola Adams won flyweight gold in 2012 and 2016.

anglicised Polish immigrants, he went to Bedford (as for a time did Abrahams), a minor public school, and then to work in the family business by the Thames, urged on by his father who had won a rowing medal at Stockholm in 1912. As his coach recalled, 'he was vicious in the boat', dominating at Henley and winning gold in 1924 after a tense struggle with his American rival, William Garrett-Gilmore, avenging a narrow defeat four years earlier at the hands of Hollywood star Grace Kelly's father, Jack. 'We admired him', as one of Beresford's contemporaries recalled, 'but we also regarded him as being a bit unreal'.[10]

## QUESTIONS OF CLASS

Public school athletes and oarsmen got the lion's share of coverage in *The Times* and other broadsheets. But this was only one side of the story. The 1920s were the decade of democracy, of female emancipation and parliamentary socialism. The Paris Games coincided with the first Labour government in Britain (and the first socialist one in France). The mass press – Britain was a nation of newspaper readers – gave column inches to the rest of the British team, especially the boxers. Theirs was a more proletarian masculinity, but one that still held fast to the British ideal of fair play, respect for opponents and sportsmanship.

1924 saw Harry Mallin, a London policeman, defend the middleweight gold medal he had won in 1920 (fig. 34). No boxer had successfully defended a title up to that point. Mallin had won almost 300 fights – he had never lost – when he faced the Frenchman and crowd favourite, Roger Brousse, in the quarter final. The verdict controversially went to Brousse, but Mallin had bite marks on his chest and shoulder. After an appeal from a Swedish official, the result was overturned, and Mallin went on to defeat another British boxer, Jack Elliot, in the final after the ring was besieged by an angry French crowd.[11] This all-British bout, together with two more medals in the light heavyweight and flyweight divisions, went some way to reassure the British of their continued fighting spirit and vitality after the horrors of war.

The boxers fared better than others. Another policeman, Archie Macdonald ('Bonny Archie'), one of the Macdonalds of Skye, was better known as a scourge of Glasgow gangs than as an Olympic wrestling medallist. Cyril Alden, a post-office worker from Bermondsey, won three cycling silver medals, two at Antwerp and another in the 50km in Paris, but never found recognition beyond the cycling fraternity. Gordon Goodwin's silver in the 10,000m walk behind Ugo Frigerio, the charismatic grocer's son and crony of Mussolini, passed almost unnoticed. Sport is a hard school. Most unlucky were those like Ernie Harper, from the Hallamshire Harriers, who ran fourth in the brutally hot cross country event (see Young's essay). Stopping to help a suffering competitor, he sacrificed his chance of a medal. Twelve years later at Berlin, he took silver in the marathon after advising the eventual winner on tactics.

## MEN AND WOMEN

The social divisions within the men's team were reproduced in the smaller female contingent. Women's Olympic sport was still severely restricted – there were no female track events until 1928 – and Britain concentrated on tennis and swimming (the one dominated by wealthy young women, who learned the game on spacious suburban lawns, and the other more socially mixed and based in municipal swimming baths). Both parties held their own against tough American opposition. The 28 women won eight medals comparative to the 239 men's 26 – a strikingly better ratio.

Kitty McKane honed her skills at St Leonards, the exclusive girls' boarding school in St Andrews (fig. 35). She came from a rich and athletic family. Tennis was her game but she could also skate to a high standard and later became a champion badminton player. After taking the first set 6–0 against her French opponent, she lost her singles semifinal in Paris, when the umpire suddenly switched from English to French at the insistence of the crowd. Her sense of British 'fair play' was affronted. She was 'absolutely disgusted' that an official could do such a thing *during* play, lost her composure and the match, but took silver in the doubles with Phyllis Covell, the daughter of another wealthy Home Counties family. 'There wasn't the fuss about the Olympics there is today', she recalled in old age, 'We had a lot of fun. We took it seriously, but not too seriously'. She was unwilling to commit to the relentless routine of her French or US counterparts, Suzanne Lenglen or Helen Wills.[12]

Swimming was more democratic and more like hard work. The Victorian provision of municipal 'baths' meant that swimming as a sport was open to all, including young working-class women. Lucy Morton won gold in the 200m breaststroke despite losing several teeth in a Paris taxi which crashed just before the Games (fig. 36). Her father worked for Blackpool Council and Lucy and her sisters learned to swim in the local

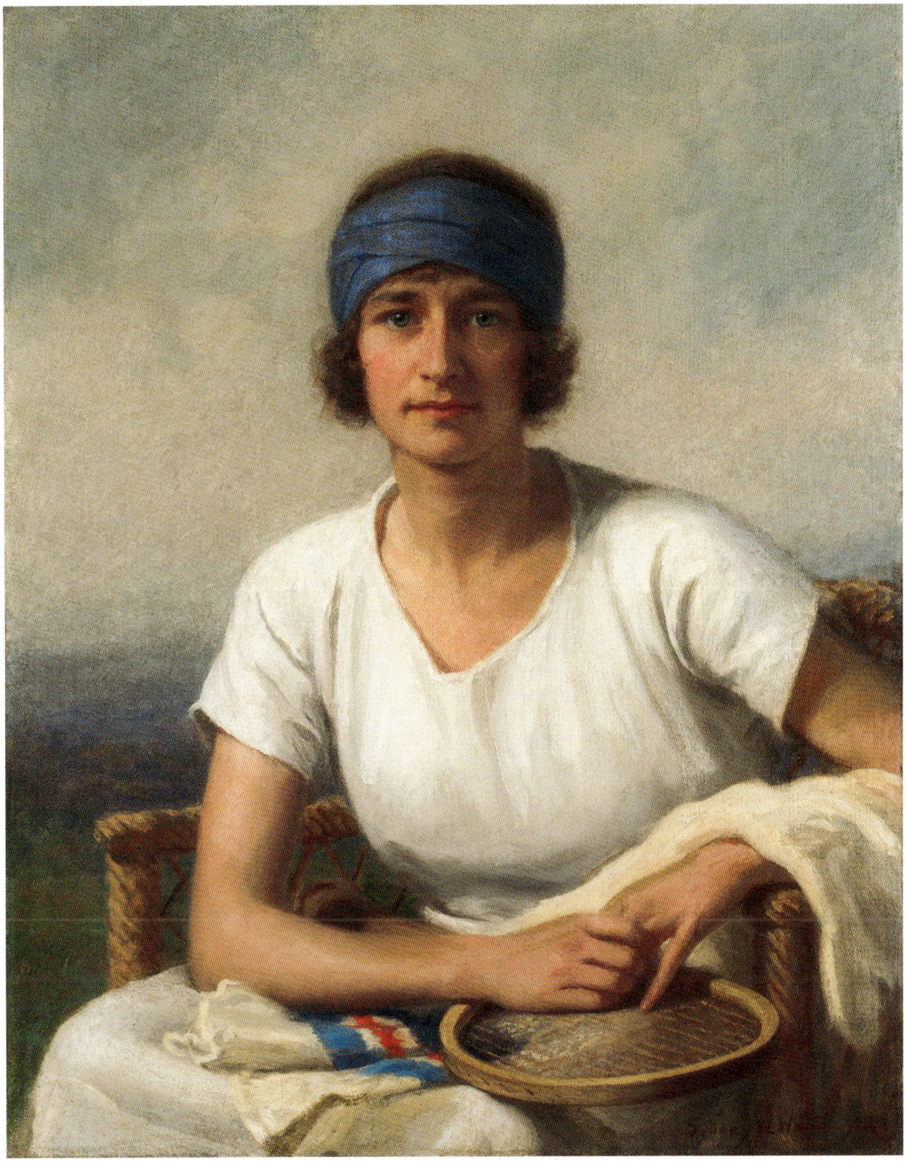

**35.** (cat. 51) Sydney W. White (1870–1945)
*Kitty Godfree* (1896–1992), 1924
Oil on canvas, 86.5 × 69 cm
Wimbledon Lawn Tennis Museum, London (A2073)

Despite playing in the era of the 'greats', Suzanne Lenglen and Helen Wills, Kitty Godfree (née McKane) has an outstanding Olympic record: in 1924, she added a bronze in the singles and a silver in the doubles to the three medals she had won in 1920. The painting captures her as if between games, staring assuredly at the artist.

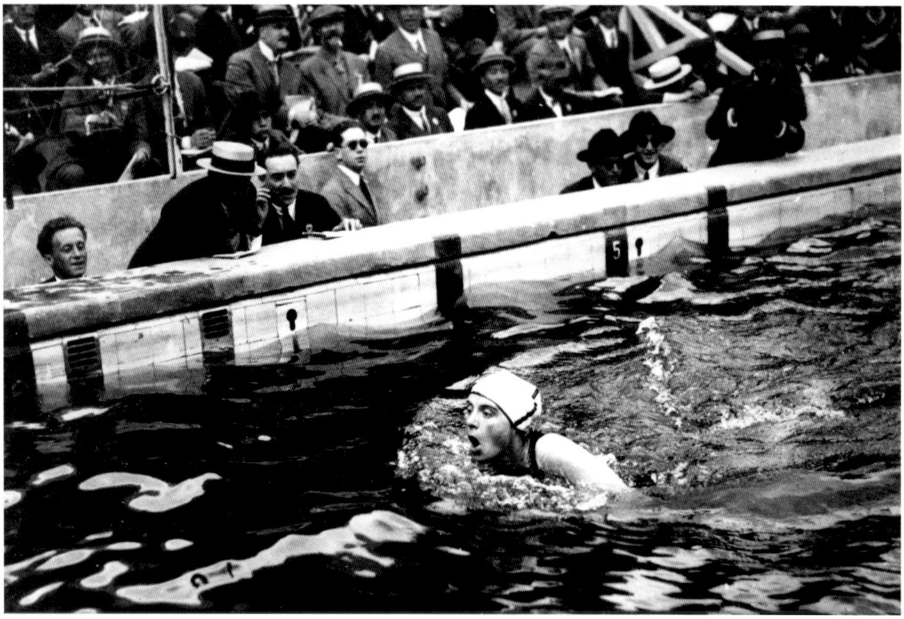

**36.** (cat. 54) Unrecorded photographer
Lucy Morton (1898–1980) competing in the women's 200m breaststroke at the 1924 Olympic Games, 1924
Black and white photograph, 21.4 × 16.7 cm
Showtown, Blackpool (BC.2023.1.22)

Lucy Morton manages a dramatic final spurt to win the 200m breaststroke final – the only gold medal for a British swimmer in the 1924 Olympics. The photograph captures her at that defining moment, watched by men.

baths. She broke two world records in 1913, aged 15, but had to wait until 1924 to compete in the Games (there were no Olympic breast or backstroke events for women in 1920), pulling off a surprising and thrilling victory over the American Agnes Geraghty, who had beaten her in the heats. She retired at her peak, and returned to a hero's welcome in Blackpool, where she was given a civic reception, a bouquet of 'mauve and pink sweet peas' and a piano. Overcome, all she could say was 'thank you'. She repaid her fellow citizens for the next forty years by teaching their children to swim, even giving lessons in the flooded basement of the Blackpool Tower (fig. 37).[13] Gladys Carson, who took the bronze medal behind Morton, was the daughter of a Leicester policeman. She had to train in a canal before going to domestic science classes. Ellen King from Edinburgh, at 15 the youngest of the British team, had to wait another four years for a silver medal, and then like Lucy Morton devoted herself to teaching swimming to schoolchildren. These women never sought or received the national recognition of a Kitty Godfree but were well known locally in a world where familiarity, friendliness and community were prized above national renown.

*

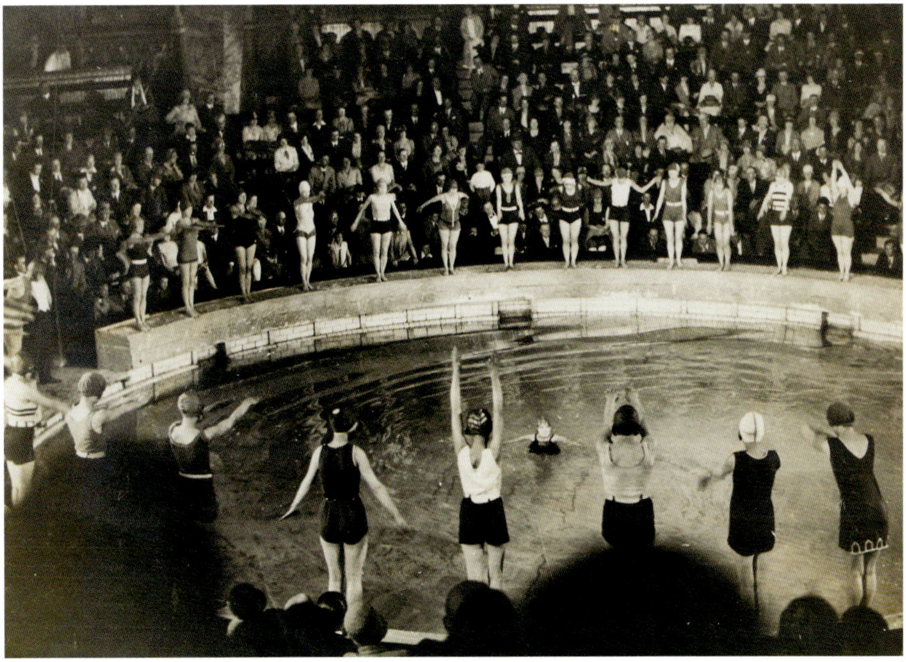

**37.** (cat. 163) Unrecorded photographer
Lucy Morton (1898–1980) performing her swimming classes at the Blackpool Tower Circus, 1928
Black and white photograph, 15.8 × 21.0 cm
Showtown, Blackpool (BC.2023.1.152)

Lucy Morton gives a demonstration at Blackpool Tower Circus in how to teach swimming. Her female pupils line up as if in a beauty parade in front of a packed audience.

Olympism is one lens of many through which to observe the nuances of region, class and gender within British society as well as the shared values so important to British amateurism. In this sense, the Paris Games were little different from the others – with a crucial reservation: no other British Olympians have been the subject of a hugely successful film, which has shaped contemporary understanding. *Chariots of Fire* has obvious and deliberate 'errors': Abrahams never did the 'dash' around Trinity quad; Liddell knew well in advance that the 100m would be held on a Sunday; Burghley (fictionalised as Lord Lindsey) never balanced champagne coupes on his hurdles, and so on. Despite cinematic licence, the film partially succeeded in capturing the Janus-like nature of British Olympism, gentlemanly and Hellenic, democratic and competitive, prejudiced and progressive.[14] Despite some great individual performances – the 'Golden Girls' of the Sixties, Coe and Ovett, Daley Thompson, Linford Christie, Steve Redgrave and many more – the BOA muddled through collectively in Olympic mediocrity. Britain had to wait until the next century – and major investment from a new National Lottery – for the re-branded 'Team GB' to equal Britain's Olympic ranking in the summer of 1924.

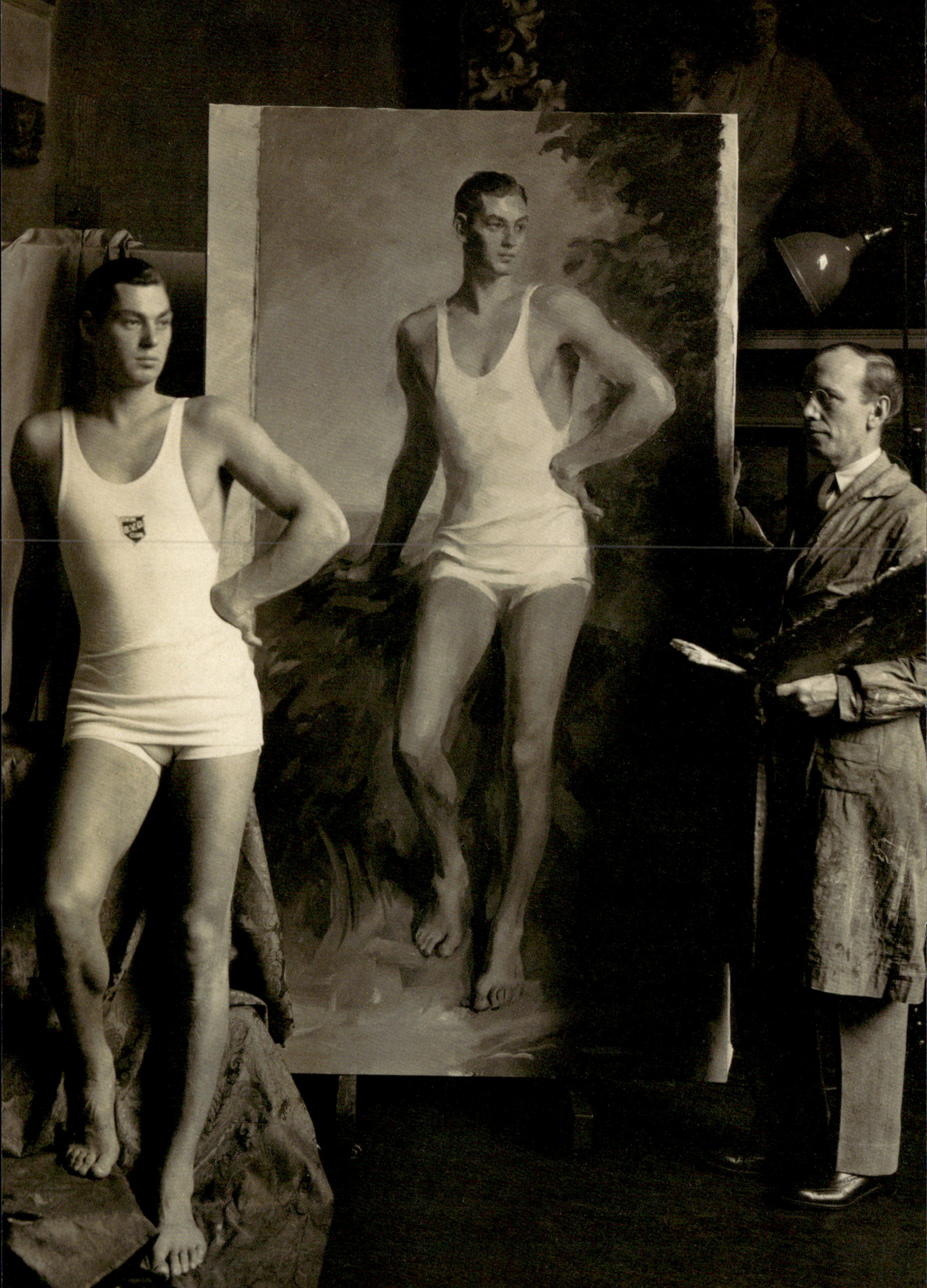

# 4

# THE USA, THE SPORTING SUPERPOWER

MIKE CRONIN

The team from the United States was the second largest at the Paris Olympics after the hosts, and was by far the most successful. Made up of 275 men and 24 women, it won a total of 99 medals, including 45 golds. As *The New York Times* gleefully reported on 22 July 1924: 'the United States ... not only made a clean sweep of all the major branches of Olympic competition but rolled up a points total which clinches the all-round championship of the games'.[1] A few months later, the President of the American Olympic Committee (AOC), Robert Means Thompson, reported to President Coolidge, informing him that the US team had shown the 'cheerfulness in defeat, modesty in victory, fair play, courtesy and courage that characterized the conduct of the American Team'.[2] Thompson's statement, and his embrace of fair play made the US contingent sound like a group of Victorian-minded amateurs simply happy to be taking part. However, the US squad was the best funded and most highly trained. They were in Paris to win, as a way of demonstrating the power and superiority of the American nation.

## THE AMERICAN WAY

In contrast to the European experience of World War I, the US was little touched by the conflict, having not declared war against Germany until April 1917. Compared to the massive losses in Britain and on the Continent the number of Americans to lose their lives fighting in Europe was, though large, still relatively contained. The impact of the war on the home front was also restricted and while there were some price controls,

**38.** (cat. 61) Pach Brothers (active 1867–1993) Johnny Weissmuller (1904–1984) posing for artist John Hubbard Rich (1876–1954), *c.* 1931
Gelatin silver print, 24.1 × 18.6 cm
National Portrait Gallery, Smithsonian Institution, Washington
(S/NPG.93.388.39)

Olympic swimmer Johnny Weissmuller was seen as ideal man and national hero. From 1929 he was contracted for five years to promote New York City swimwear brand BVD and, following his move to Hollywood in 1931, was mythologised by John Hubbard Rich at Rich's studio in the Hollywood Hills, wearing a BVD swimsuit. In 1932 Rich would, like Weissmuller, become an Olympian, when he submitted *The Trojans in Action* to the Los Angeles Games.

there was no rationing. In sporting terms many Europeans witnessed the cancellation of leagues and competitions between 1914 and 1918, whereas in the US sport continued throughout the war. While the National Collegiate Athletic Association (NCAA) season was disrupted in part in 1918 due to the Spanish flu, many sports under its remit, such as track and field, entered the 1920s largely unaffected.

As the governing body for sport across the American university system, the NCAA was instrumental in the success of the US team. Of the 299 athletes who competed in Paris, 63% had recently graduated from, or were attending, university. And, unlike in Britain, where athletes were drawn from the elites of Cambridge, Oxford and Edinburgh (see Holt's chapter), American student athletes were selected from a wide range of institutions across the country, including the University of Minnesota, Syracuse University, Oregon State University and the University of Kansas, as well as the Ivy League colleges of Harvard, Princeton and Yale. The NCAA and individual universities scheduled a regular roster of high-level competition for athletes (the first national NCAA track and field championship was held in 1921) and provided financial support, coaches and facilities for student athletes.

The support for athletes within the university system was mirrored by the approach of Thompson and the AOC. Thompson believed that the US team had to be well funded to achieve the best results. He organised a fund-raising drive and gathered money from corporations, sports bodies, universities and members of the public. In all, the AOC raised $350,000 (the equivalent of $6 million today) to cover the team's expenses in Paris, including accommodation for the majority of the athletes at the Château de Rocquencourt, where alcohol was banned in line with the United States' policy of Prohibition.[3] The single biggest act of philanthropy came from Thompson himself, who had made his fortune in nickel trading. Thompson argued that it was important that as many of the athletes as possible travel together to 'consolidate the men into a real Olympic Team, and [to ensure] America takes part in the solemn opening of the Games or in the ending, both most important functions'.[4] To that end, he rented the luxury ship *America* for the team's Atlantic passage and footed the entire bill himself.[5]

Those athletes travelling on the *America* were better prepared than any other nation competing in Paris. They also embodied a nation that was at the cutting edge of modern life. The US of the 1920s was a fast-growing economy (GDP grew by $1.5 billion between 1920 and 1924), was building its cities anew with skyscrapers and had the highest rates of car and radio ownership in the world. Through the lens of Hollywood, the 'Jazz Age' and a plethora of lifestyle magazines, it was seen as the nation that defined the 'Roaring Twenties'. The US team was also alive to the patriotic and nationalistic opportunities afforded by the Olympics. As scholar Stephen Pope remarked of the American engagement with the Games and the nationalist motivations behind winning rather than simply taking part, 'the Olympics provided an arena in which certain Americans could invent and popularize symbols of their political and sporting culture by linking athletic prowess to national mythology' (fig. 38).[6]

## THE AMERICANS AND THE FRENCH

The sense that the US was sending a team to win was captured by *The New York Times* in a preview of the Games in April 1924. It offered the view that 'athletic observers in other countries, as well as in the US expect the Americans to come off the field with the greatest credit'. 'Thousands of American athletes', it noted, 'are now in training for the Olympics, in colleges, athletics clubs and in the army and navy'.[7] Such intense competition to build the US team resulted in the strong group of athletes that travelled to Paris under the head coach, Lawson Robertson from the University of Pennsylvania, who would be heralded as one of the greatest American athletic coaches in the first half of the twentieth century.[8]

The first competition in Paris, the rugby tournament, took place in May. The US successfully defended the title it had won in 1920, but it was the reaction of the French crowd that grabbed the headlines. *The New York Times* titled: 'U.S. TEAM IS HISSED BY FRENCH WHEN IT WINS OLYMPIC TITLE; Booing Drowns "Star-Spangled Banner" as Police Escort Victors From Field'.[9] It was initially reported that the negative French reaction to the Americans' victory was a result of some rough play during the game. When the main Olympic programme began in July, however, the French crowds continued to heckle many American competitors. The main motivation behind the home nation's disdain for the Americans and what they represented had little to do with sport. In January 1923, the French had occupied the Ruhr Valley after Germany defaulted on the reparations payment forced on them by the Treaty of Versailles. The US criticised the French for their occupation and, through the framework of the Dawes Plan, renegotiated the terms of German indebtedness, agreeing, through the American financier J.P. Morgan, to loan the German government $200 million so it could meet its commitments. The conference that finalised the renegotiated reparations took place during July and August 1924 (thus coinciding with the main Olympic events) and the final settlement, which favoured Germany, was widely derided in France. The presence of American athletes in Paris gave the French audience a target for their frustrations.

## THE STATE OF THE NATION

Alongside the undoubted success of the US team in 1924 were personal narratives that revealed much about the contemporary and future state of the nation. The US athletes were not a homogenous group but reflected differences that existed across American society in terms of class, gender and race. Yale University, to take a prominent example, was in the 1920s a college for the American elite. Within such institutions, rowing was seen as the ideal sport for gentlemen. In the spring of 1924, on the back of beating Princeton, Cornell, Pennsylvania and Columbia, the Yale eight asked the University's rowing committee whether it would support them in travelling to the Olympics. The University committed $10,000 within a few minutes of the request, and the team left for France on 21 June. In Paris, the crew took gold, winning the final by a comfortable margin.

Of the eight, two men illustrate most effectively the cultural transformations that occurred in the US across the twentieth century. The first, James Stillman Rockefeller, captured much of the media's imagination (fig. 39): heir to the Rockefeller fortune, good looking and, after his boat's Olympic victory in July, a national hero who featured on the cover of *Time* magazine, Rockefeller left Yale the following year and joined the National City Bank (later Citibank), where he became Chair. He married Nancy Carnegie, of the famous philanthropic family, and with her became a well-known funder of medical, historic and arts foundations and trusts. He lived the life that may have been expected of him when he was at Yale: he preserved his family wealth, added to it through his own career in business and was a notable and civic-minded philanthropist. He symbolised an older, traditional and conservative America.

Rowing in the same boat was Benjamin Spock, who came from a comfortable Connecticut family. After the Olympics and the completion of his undergraduate degree, Spock studied medicine and became a paediatrician. In 1946 he published *The Common Sense Book of Baby and Child Care*, which became a bestseller. Unlike Rockefeller, Spock was not a conservative: in the 1960s he opposed nuclear proliferation, objected to the Vietnam War from its outbreak and espoused the withholding of tax in protest against it. In 1970 he joined the New Party (a libertarian third voice in American politics) and in 1972 was the party's candidate for President, receiving 0.1% of the vote. Spock was widely condemned for his left-wing political views and there was criticism too that his hugely influential book had ushered in the permissiveness that defined the 1960s. As notorious for their drug-taking and sexual licence as they were for their stance against

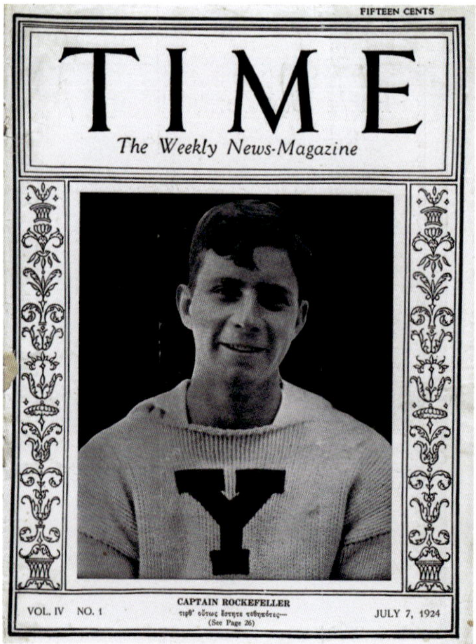


**39.** (cat. 43) Time Inc. (founded 1922)
*Time* magazine, vol. 4, no. 1 (7 July 1924), with cover photograph of 'Captain Rockefeller', James Stillman Rockefeller (1902–2004)
Printing on paper, 20.3 × 27.3 cm
Courtesy of Thomas E. Weil

Rowing captain James Stillman Rockefeller, on the cover of *Time* magazine, 7 July 1924. In the article inside, the author invokes ancient Greece to capture his crew's victory: 'Now he led them forth – the bronze-skinned ones – to conquer the oarsmen of the world, as warlike Menelaus led the bronze-greaved Argives against Troy of old.'

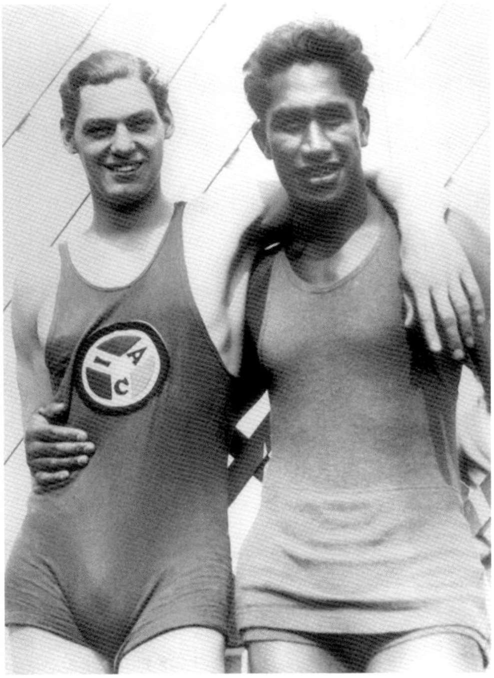


**40.** (cat. 158) Unrecorded photographer
Johnny Weissmuller (1904–1984) and Duke Kahanamoku (1890–1968) at the Paris 1924 Olympic Games, 1924
Black and white photograph

The American press whipped up an intense rivalry between Johnny Weissmuller and Duke Kahanamoku. As one journalist noted: 'Duke was old school: reserved and circumspect. Johnny was jazz age: he liked to play the rogue and was an inveterate skirt chaser ... The anticipation that Duke, the human fish, would face off against Johnny, the human hydroplane, was keen.'

war and in favour of gay and women's rights, the children of the 1960s were deemed 'the Spock generation'.

While Rockefeller and Spock demonstrated how wider divisions over the socially conservative or liberal future of the country were replicated within a small Yale elite, two swimmers who travelled as teammates and opponents reflected other schisms in American society. Neither Duke Kahanamoku nor Johnny Weissmuller had attended university. The former was a native of Hawaii; the latter, born in Szabadfalu (modern-day Freidorf) in what was then the Empire of Austria-Hungary, had entered the US as a one-year-old. Kahanamoku was 14 years older than Weissmuller and had already competed in the Olympics of 1912 and 1920, winning three golds and two silvers. The press positioned the battle for the 100m freestyle as a struggle between experience and precociousness (fig. 40). Weissmuller was described by his coach as having a mass of gleaming black hair and 'a cocky, devil-may-care grin that concealed a Teutonic work ethic'.[10]

Weissmuller prevailed in Paris, Kahanamoku taking silver and his brother Samuel bronze. Overall he won three golds in 1924 and added two more in 1928, by which point he had set 67 swimming world records. He returned to Paris in 1929 to open the Lucien Pollet-designed Piscine Molitor, an Art Deco outdoor lido that became *the* place to be seen during the summer months and where, for the remainder of the summer, he worked as a lifeguard. In 1929 he appeared in his first Hollywood film, and in 1932 starred in the first of 12 *Tarzan* movies (see Michelakis's chapter).

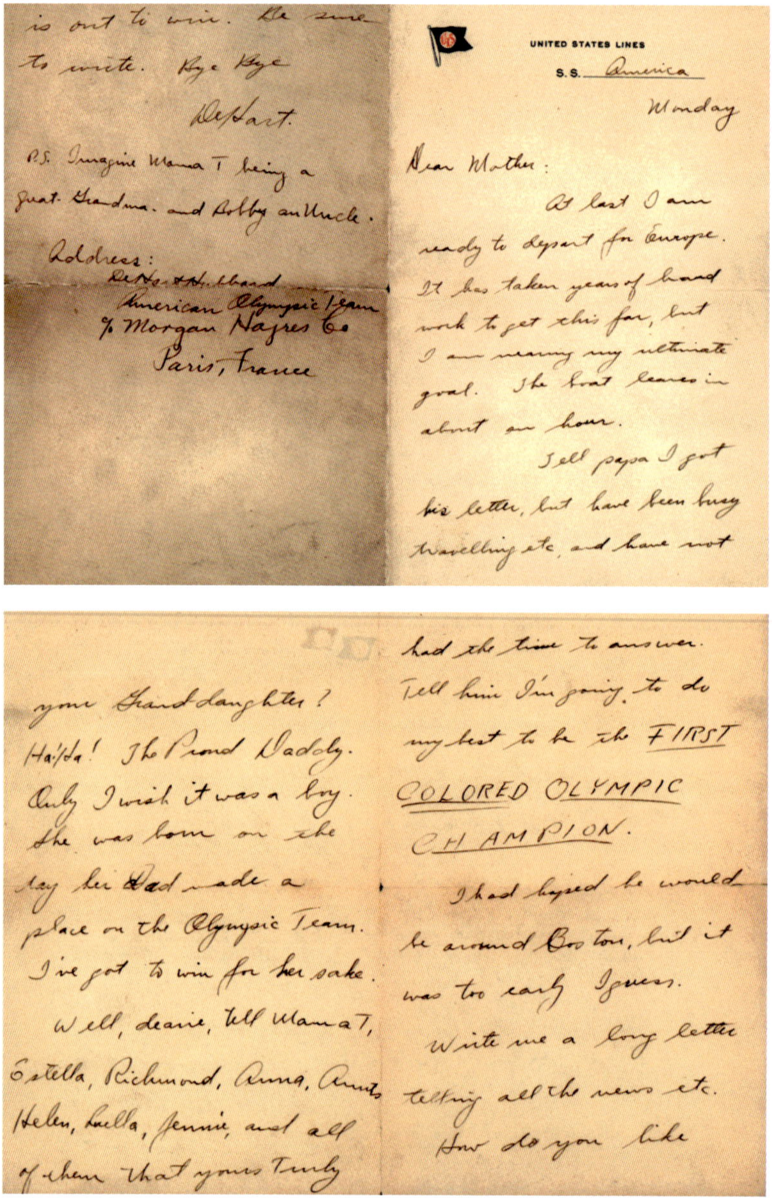

UNITED STATES LINES
S.S. America

Monday

Dear Mother:

At last I am ready to depart for Europe. It has taken years of hard work to get this far, but I am nearing my ultimate goal. The boat leaves in about an hour.

Tell papa I got his letter, but have been busy travelling etc, and have not had the time to answer. Tell him I'm going to do my best to be the FIRST COLORED OLYMPIC CHAMPION.

I had hoped he would be around Boston, but it was too early I guess.

Write me a long letter telling all the news etc.

How do you like your Grand daughter? Ha! Ha! The Proud Daddy. Only I wish it was a boy. She was born on the day her Dad made a place on the Olympic Team. I've got to win for her sake.

Well, dearie, tell Mama T, Estella, Richmond, Anna, Aunts Helen, Luella, Jennie, and all of them that yours Truly is out to win. Be sure to write. Bye Bye

DeHart.

P.S. Imagine Mama T being a great-Grandma. and Bobby an Uncle.

Address:
DeHart Hubbard
American Olympic Team
% Morgan Harjes Co
Paris, France

**41.** (cat. 50) William DeHart Hubbard (1903–1976)
Letter written to his mother on board the SS *America* before sailing to Paris with the US Olympic team, 16 June 1924

Pen and ink on paper with printed letterhead, 19 × 25.5 cm
Cincinnati Museum Center, Cincinnati, Ohio (MSS 1067)

En route to the Paris Games, American long jumper William DeHart Hubbard wrote a letter to his mother instructing her to tell his father that he would 'do [his] best to be the "FIRST COLORED OLYMPIC CHAMPION"'. Hubbard delivered on his promise by taking the gold.

While Weissmuller transitioned from successful Olympian to matinee idol – with the fame and wealth that this entailed – Kahanamoku too attempted to get leading roles in Hollywood only for his Hawaiian background to hold him back. Of the 19 movies in which he appeared, his roles are listed variously as 'Indian Chief', 'Pirate Captain', 'Hawaiian Boy' or 'Native Chief' – minor roles reserved in those days for non-white actors. Where he did gain global fame was as the father of surfing, staging exhibitions across the world to showcase and popularise the sport. He was elected Sheriff of Honolulu from 1932 to 1961, which gave him a base income, but he found himself, by the end of his life, in dire financial straits. The Kahanamoku and Weissmuller life stories demonstrate that while Olympic victory in the 1920s was a route to public acclaim, structural racism and conceptions of the ideal body as white led to quite different outcomes.

Interestingly, in this context, when Michigan student William DeHart Hubbard became the first African American to win an individual medal (fig. 41), there was little mention of his skin colour in the press. Hubbard was a native of Cincinnati and always the fastest runner in his class. He was recruited by the University of Michigan, who secured him on the back of a public fundraising drive for a $3,000 athletics scholarship. During college, Hubbard competed in the NCAA and took the national sprint title in 1925 as well as the long jump title in 1923 and 1925. He qualified for Paris together with the African and Native American athlete Edward Orval 'Ned' Gourdin. Despite carrying an injury, Hubbard pipped him to the gold in the long jump final.

When the major national newspapers reported Hubbard's victory, they attached no significance to its implications for American race politics. In 1925, and in full health, Hubbard broke the world long jump record and equalled the world record for the 100-yard dash. After leaving Michigan, he went to work in the Department of Colored Work in his hometown of Cincinnati. He competed at the 1928 Olympics, again in the long jump, but finished well down the field. Hubbard was elected to the National Track Hall of Fame in 1957 and died in 1976. But his achievements were overshadowed by sprinter and long jumper Jesse Owens, whose four gold medals at the 1936 Games in Berlin were won against the heightened sensitivity of needing to disprove Nazi Germany's racial theories. Now, finally, Hubbard is duly celebrated. In 1924, in contrast, from an American perspective, his victory had not been framed as ideological.

## THE WOMEN'S TEAM

The US took 24 women athletes to Paris, leaving only France and the United Kingdom with a bigger contingent. In line with discriminatory and collegiate attitudes of the period, these women were less likely to have attended university (there was, for example, no financial assistance for women at the time). Of the 24 who made the team, only three, the swimmer Sybil Bauer from Northwestern University, and the tennis players Helen Wills and Hazel Wightman from the University of California at Berkeley had attended, or were attending, college. The remainder, especially the largest group, the swimmers,

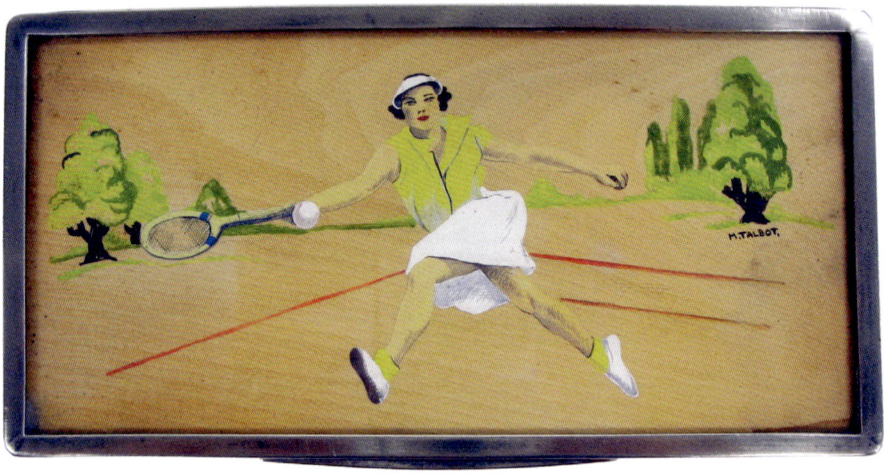


**42.** (cat. 137) James Dixon & Sons (founded 1806); May Talbot (active 1930s), artist
Cigarette box, *c.* 1930
Pewter, wood, glass, oil paint, 5 × 18.9 × 10 cm
Wimbledon Lawn Tennis Museum, London (WTM:2000/29)

Helen Wills stares down opponent and viewer on this cigarette box. In her signature visor and impeccable red lipstick, she is sexy yet sassy, her racket poised to hit a winner.

were from working-class families in the major cities of the North East and the Midwest, many of them, like Weissmuller, the children of immigrants. Martha Norelius, who won gold in the Olympic 400m freestyle, was born in Stockholm but had moved with her family to the US, where her father was coach to her and Weissmuller.

Although a much smaller cohort, these female Olympic champions, like their male counterparts, built on their success to seek financial reward and – in the spirit of the 'Roaring Twenties' – became influential cultural and popular figures. Helen Wills (fig. 42) began playing tennis at the age of eight and joined the Berkeley tennis club at 13, where she proved to be naturally talented and a quick learner. By 1921 she was the Californian singles and doubles champion. The following year, aged 16, she was defeated in the final of the US Championship but, after winning it in 1923, was duly selected to represent the United States in Paris. There, Wills took gold in the singles and, playing with Hazel Wightman, gold in the doubles too. She would eventually retire from tennis in 1943, by which time she had amassed 31 Grand Slam titles, remaining unbeaten in all competitions between 1927 and 1933. She has regularly been heralded as one of the greatest players of the twentieth century. Such was the level of her concentration and steeliness on court that her fellow players felt that she was aloof and distant, referring to her as 'little Miss poker face' or 'the imperial Helen'.

Off the court, Wills was a highly accomplished writer and artist. She was known during her playing career for her grace (fig. 43), elegance and contemporary look, and

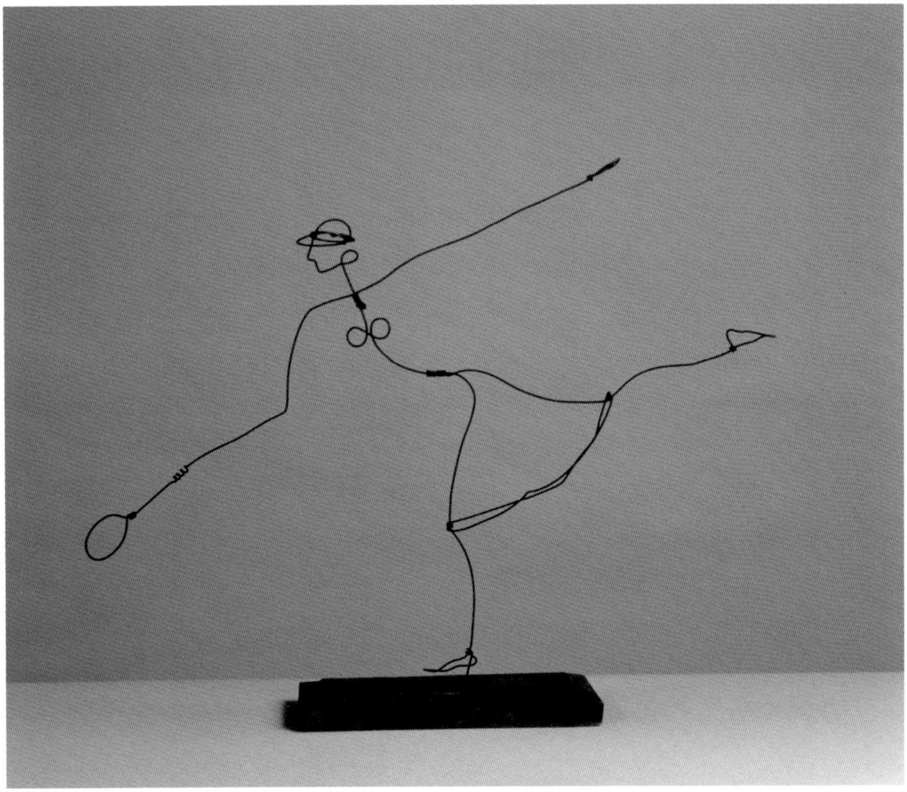

**43.** (cat. 138) Alexander Calder (1898–1976)
*Helen Wills*, 1927
Wire and wood, 33.6 × 43.2 × 20.3 cm
Calder Foundation, New York

Alexander Calder represents Wills through what he sees as essential attributes – racket, visor, skirt and breasts. His technique of wire sculpture, or 'drawing in space', perfectly captures Wills's graceful playing style.

became a regular in women's and fashion magazines. She wrote a playing manual, *Tennis* (1928), a mystery, *Death Serves an Ace* (1939), and collections of poetry. She did all the illustrations for *Tennis* herself, designed fabrics and exhibited her art in galleries in the US and Europe (fig. 44). In 1932 she submitted work to the Olympic Arts Competition in Los Angeles. Wills became an iconic global figure in the interwar years. Her image was everywhere in the media, with one editorialist admitting in 1927 that 'all the males of America from six to sixty, are a little in love with her'.[11] She was, because of her celebrity, sporting fame and connection with the arts and philanthropy, the Californian 'Queen, its "Girl of the Golden West"' (fig. 74).[12]

Gertrude Ederle was born in New York and began swimming and being coached at the age of 12. Within a year, she had broken the world record for the 880-yard freestyle.

**44.** (cat. 119) Helen Wills (1905–1998), designer; Stehli Silks Corporation (founded 1837), manufacturer
*A Game of Tennis*, dressmaking fabric from the *Americana* series, 1926 (detail)

Printed silk crepe, 51.4 × 98.7 cm
Allentown Art Museum, Allentown, Pennsylvania (1978.26.165)

The Stehli Silks Corporation created its *Americana* series of prints between 1925 and 1927 'for modern American women by modern American artists, reflecting the modern American scene'. Wills designed *A Game of Tennis* for Stehli in 1926 and it became a best seller. As she said, she preferred 'to talk of Titian rather than tennis'.

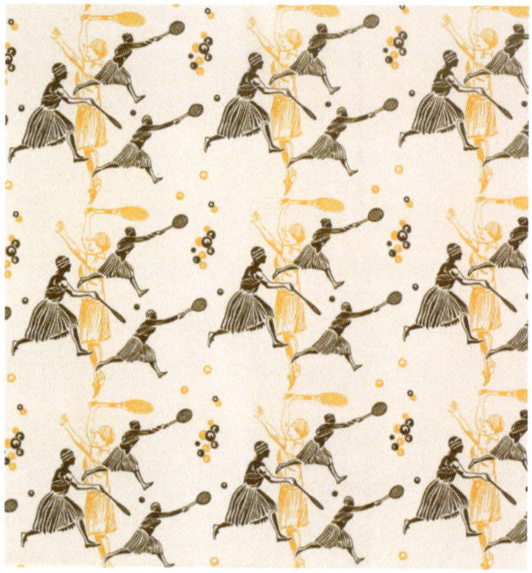

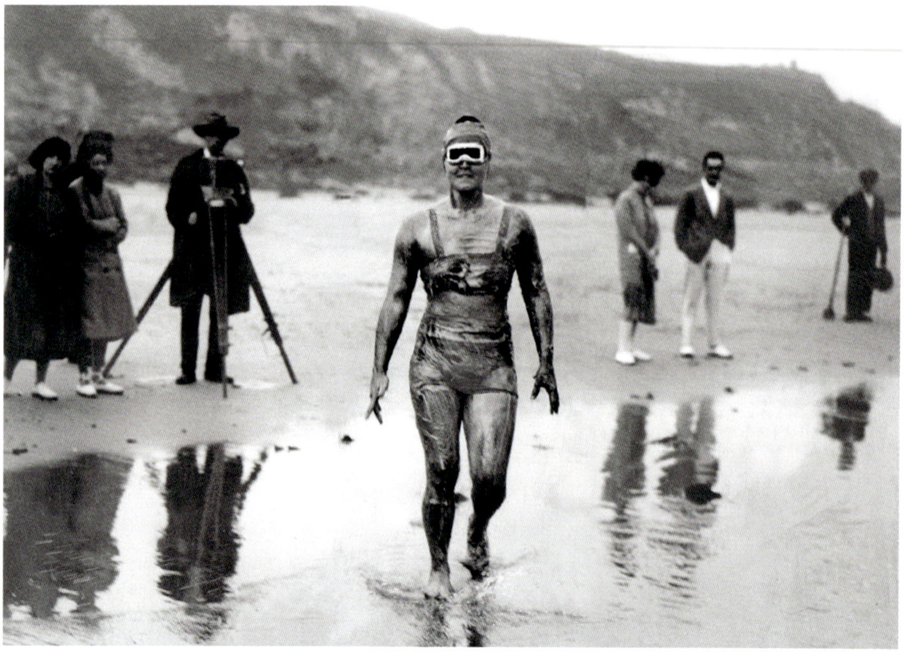

**45.** (cat. 154) Unrecorded photographer
Grease-coated Olympic swimmer Gertrude Ederle (1906–2003) wades into the sea in France on her way to becoming the first woman to swim the English Channel, 6 August 1926

Black and white photograph

In August 1926, covered in grease, wearing a two-piece swimsuit to reduce drag in the water, and donning a pair of motorcycle goggles that she had adapted, Gertrude Ederle, who had won three medals at the 1924 Olympics, became the first woman (and only the sixth person) to swim the English Channel.

Between 1921 and 1925 she went on to set 29 national and world records for various distances. At Paris she took gold with her teammates in the 4 × 100m freestyle relay and a bronze in both the 100m and 400m individual events. Ederle came from a working-class family and, in search of an income, turned professional soon after the 1924 Games. She put on public exhibitions and completed long-distance swimming feats. In 1925 she attempted to swim the English Channel but failed. Sponsored by two US newspapers, she had another go in 1926, completing the crossing in 14 hours and 35 minutes to become the first woman to be successful (fig. 45).

Ederle's fortunes were badly affected by the Wall Street Crash of 1929, but in the years between her Olympic success and the financial collapse, she was one of the US's biggest stars. On her return to New York after her Channel swim, two million people turned out to acclaim her at a ticker-tape parade, and she was welcomed to the White House by President Coolidge. She played herself in the 1927 silent movie *Swim Girl, Swim* (fig. 109), joined the vaudeville circuit and marketed her own brand of swimwear, the 'Trudy swimsuit'.

*

The American team was the dominant force in Paris; it made the 'Roaring Twenties' roar. Unbound by class differentiations and a rigid and restrictive sense of amateurism, as was perhaps the case in Britain, its athletes embraced the allure of belonging to a land of opportunity – an upwardly mobile culture in print and on screen – to trade on their sporting prowess, their speed, strength and beauty. The US athletes embodied their country, and once back home, attempted to capitalise on their medals and fame, seizing the opportunities afforded by their rapidly changing and modernising nation. Weissmuller was the stand-out star. Erdele and Wills cemented their fame by setting records in their respective sports, and Kahanamoku embodied the surfing style of his native Hawaii. Rockefeller and Spock, while both successful, came to represent later divisions in the social fabric of the United States. The 1924 American Olympians reflected the complexities of the nation they represented, and demonstrated that while athletes could be upwardly mobile, significant differences of opportunity still remained in a society stratified by class, gender and race.

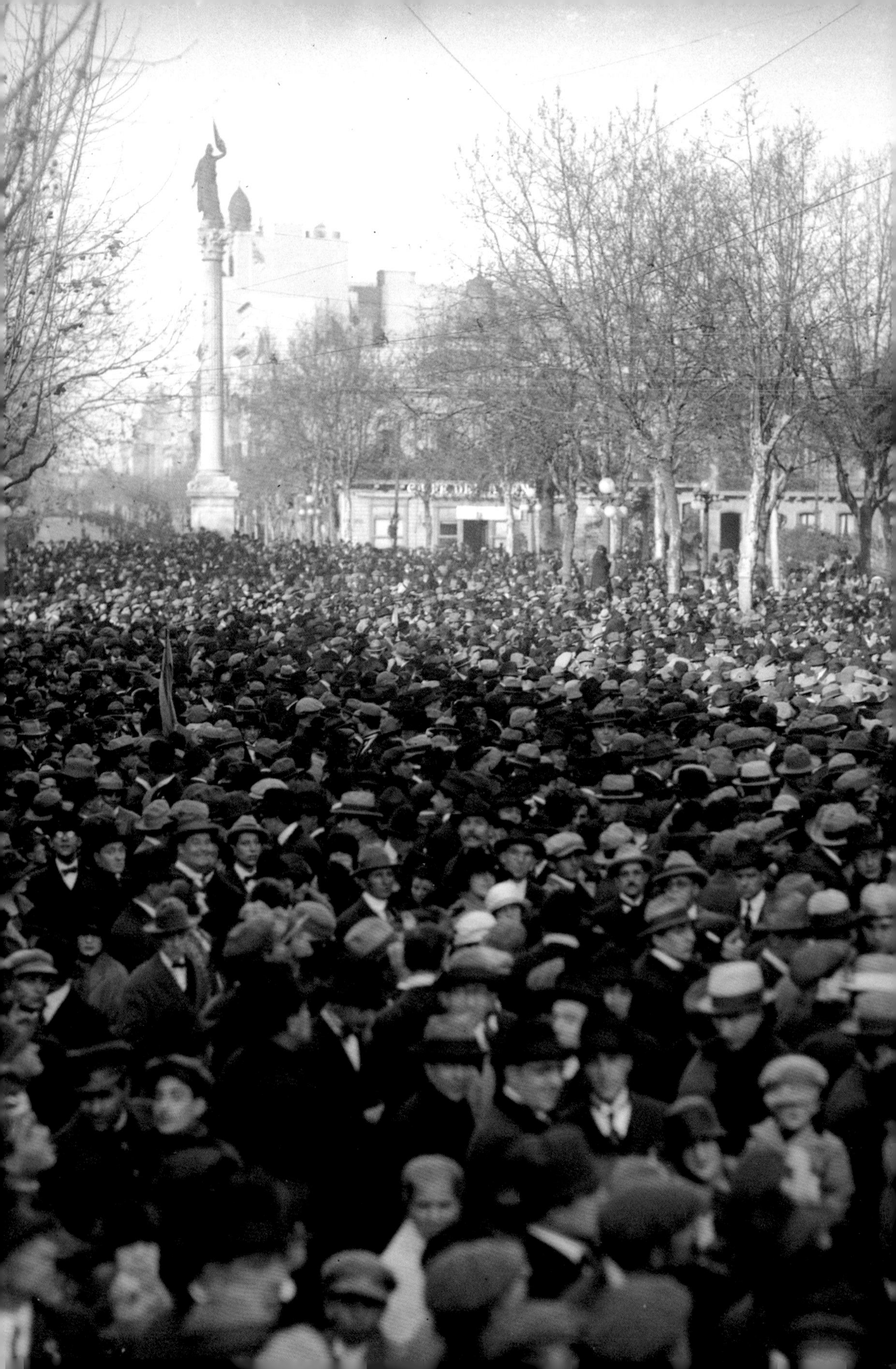

# 5

# URUGUAY, FOOTBALL AND GLOBAL STARDOM

WILL HUDDLESTON

The football tournament at the 1924 Olympics was a critical turning point in the development of the world's most popular game. The best attended and most commercially valuable international competition to date, the Paris Games were also the first to have a truly global character, with worldwide media coverage and representatives from Europe, Africa and the Americas. This was a dramatic departure from previous Olympic football tournaments, which had tended to feature only a handful of European teams, and which could in no sense be considered 'world championships'. In this newly global arena, to almost universal surprise, Uruguay – a tiny nation on South America's Atlantic coast with a population roughly half that of Paris itself – claimed the gold medal by beating Yugoslavia, the USA, France, the Netherlands and Switzerland, scoring 20 goals and conceding only twice. The first Latin American team to play in Europe (fig. 47), Uruguay made an enormous impression on observers in the French capital, producing a style of football that was exhilarating to audiences and unstoppable by opponents. The significance of the victory went far beyond mere results: the 1924 tournament represented a footballing first encounter between the 'Old' and 'New' Worlds, a clash that challenged the assumed hegemony of European football and opened up new horizons for the sport. The triumph was also an essential element in the construction of Uruguayan identity, providing a vivid image of unity as well as a tangible demonstration of the young nation's capacity and cultural distinctiveness both at home and abroad.

**46.** (cat. 69) Unrecorded photographer
Reception of the victorious Uruguayan football team at the Plaza de Cagancha in Montevideo following their return from the Paris Olympics, 18 July 1924 (detail)
Gelatin silver print
Centro de Fotografía de Montevideo

Enormous crowds gather to greet the Uruguayan squad on its return to Montevideo. Images like this one were reprinted for weeks across the country's media, providing a visual example of a nation united. Such pictures suggested that, if only for an afternoon, an overwhelming majority of 'the people' were engaged in the same activity and felt the same patriotic thrill.

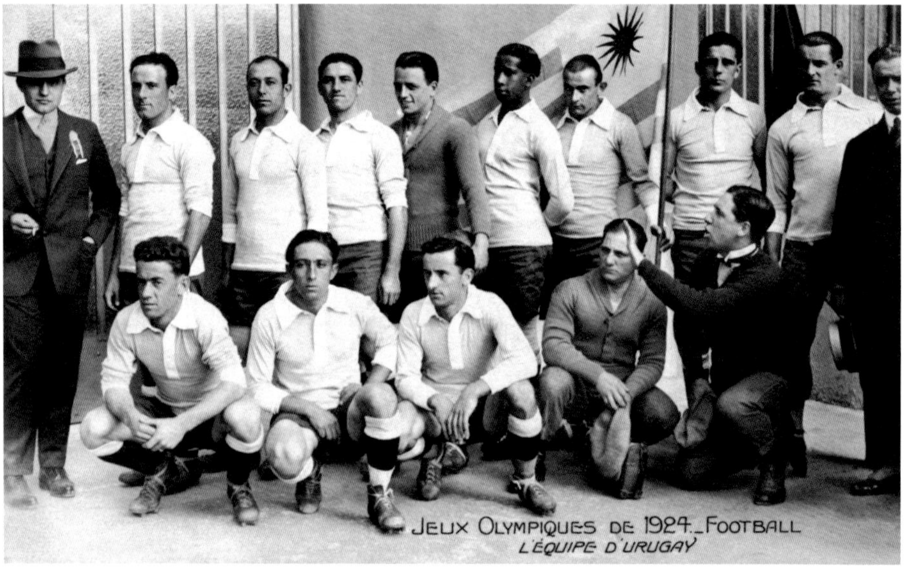


**47.** (cat. 65) Unrecorded photographer
*Olympic Games of 1924 – Football, the Team from Uruguay*, 1924
(*Jeux Olympiques de 1924 – Football, l'équipe d'Uruguay*)
Black and white photograph
Comité International Olympique (CIO)
(PHO10005185)

This image of the Uruguayan squad was produced as a postcard and sold during the tournament. On the far-right, captain and full-back José Nasazzi looms imposingly over his players, while two to his left, the centre-half José Vidal holds the Uruguayan flag aloft. On the bottom right, a member of the official delegation arranges the squad for the photo, trying to perfect an image destined for wide public consumption.

## A SMALL MODEL COUNTRY

The astonishment which Uruguay generated in Paris was enhanced by the fact that, for the vast majority of spectators, the nation was a complete mystery. Constrained by its size, distance from Europe and North America, and relative newness as a stable nation-state, Uruguay was on the disregarded margin of global politics and culture in 1924. Indeed, the media coverage of the tournament was marked by a profound ignorance of the country, with one French journalist going so far as to describe 'my shock at seeing the Uruguayans distinguish themselves in the football tournament, when I had no idea of their existence'.[1] The International Olympic Committee (IOC) itself was almost as ill-informed, having expressed the opinion early in Uruguay's application process for the Games that, 'being a province of Argentina, Uruguay would not be able to participate'.[2] If observers had heard of Uruguay (and knew that it was an independent country), the knowledge they had was typically negative, heavily inflected by pernicious and prejudicial assumptions about the continent as a whole. Frequently, the nation was imagined as primitive, violent and underdeveloped, a rural hinterland that was worlds away from the sophistication of Europe and North America, and therefore unsuited to participate in the Olympic project. As the *Chicago Daily Tribune* caustically remarked, for instance, 'if Uruguay wins a championship, it ought to be in roping steers and jerking beef'.[3]

Such antiquated visions of the country were markedly out of step with the tectonic shifts that had reshaped Uruguayan society, politics and culture since the late nineteenth century. These changes were built on a foundation of unprecedented economic success, as Uruguay enjoyed a commercial boom based on the massive export of wool and cattle products to Western Europe. Britain, in particular, was a key market and stimulated this growth with the enormous investment of capital, technology and human resources necessary to turn Uruguay into a 'supplier of the British dinner-table and textile mill'.[4] Famously, the Fray Bentos tinned meat company fed the United Kingdom's troops during World War I, and by 1923 Uruguay accounted for 12% of the world's total beef exports.[5] On the eve of the Paris Olympics, Uruguay figured among the 15 richest nations on the planet, with the highest purchasing power per capita and life expectancy in South America.[6]

Upon this financial bedrock, a generation of statesmen launched a concerted effort to revolutionise a country that was still considered a 'medieval backwater rather than a nation of the modern world'.[7] In the eyes of many, these 'nations of the modern world' were to be found almost exclusively in Western Europe, and Uruguayan politicians regularly broadcast their aim to convert the nation into a 'Switzerland of the Americas' through a range of progressive socio-political reforms. During the first decades of the twentieth century, Uruguay introduced the eight-hour workday, free and universal public education and the abolition of capital punishment, as well as a range of modernising projects such as the electrification of public transport and the construction of a vast new port in the capital city, Montevideo. These and countless other changes were designed to recast Uruguay as a developed, 'Europeanised' nation: a 'small model country', in the words of two-time president José Batlle y Ordóñez.[8]

## THE BRITISH ROOTS OF URUGUAY'S BEAUTIFUL GAME

Football was both a product and tool of Uruguay's long-term project of national reinvention. The sport first arrived in the late nineteenth century, imported by Britons who had settled in the country to administer the farms, factories and trainlines that made up this latest outpost of the 'Informal Empire'. The British quickly established semi-autonomous communities, chiefly in Montevideo, with their own schools, churches and even hospitals. Crucially, they also formed social and sports clubs, which rapidly adopted football following its codification. The first recorded football match in Uruguay, in 1881, was played between two such institutions: the Montevideo Cricket Club and the Montevideo Rowing Club. The names of the players – Dixon, Walker and Hughes among others – underline that, initially, football was far from a Uruguayan game. From these elite and foreign beginnings, however, the sport gradually found its

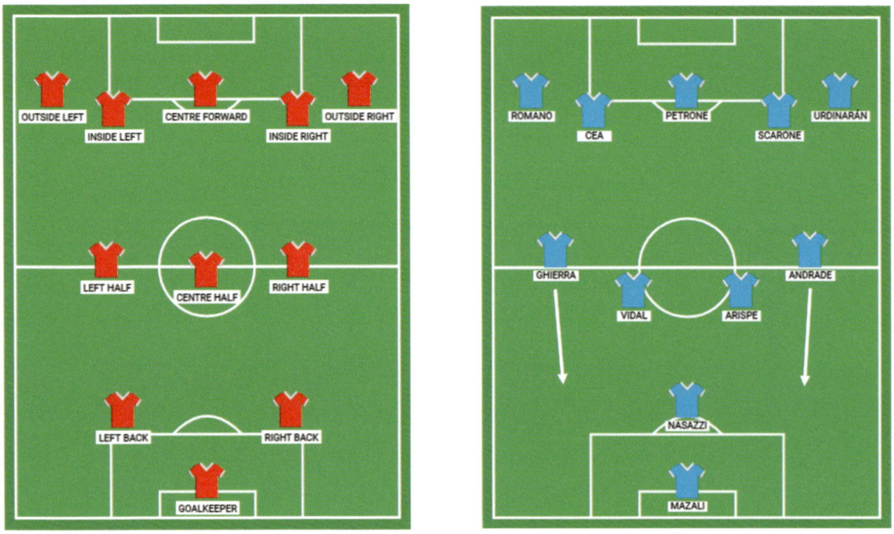


**48.** Graphic diagram created by Will Huddleston using www.homecrowd.io, which compares (*left*) the typical 2–3–5 formation in 1924 and (*right*) the modifications made to it by Uruguay. Diagram based on ideas published in Aldo Mazzucchelli, *Del ferrocarril al tango: el estilo del fútbol uruguayo, 1891–1930*, Taurus 2019.

On the left is the 2–3–5 formation that had dominated football since the 1880s, composed of two defenders, three midfielders and five attackers who worked relatively autonomously. Uruguay lined up in this formation, but were much more fluid, with right-back Arispe pushed into a defensive midfield role alongside centre-half Vidal, while the wing-halves, Ghierra and Andrade, pushed wide and dropped back to mark opposition wingers. This left Nasazzi alone to play as a sweeper and organise the defence.

way to a wider social base, largely through the work of men like William Leslie Poole, the 'Father of Uruguayan Football'. Following his studies at the University of Cambridge, Poole moved to Montevideo in 1885 to teach at the English High School, where he introduced the game to his charges. They subsequently formed their own football clubs and leagues. As the sport spread, Uruguayan statesmen and educators quickly adopted it as a way of emulating the British and improving the nation's youth. In the 1890s, for example, the Rector of the Universidad de la República, Alfredo Vásquez Acevedo, implemented an extensive programme of physical education which included football, arguing that the sport 'will bring great benefits, and ensure that the Latin race will one day be the equal of the Saxon'.[9]

Thirty years later, these hopes of societal improvement appeared to be confirmed, as Uruguay effortlessly imposed itself on the Olympic tournament, demonstrating to the world the nation's self-confidence and progress. Most notably, Uruguay's tactical approach was light years ahead of its opponents, based on rapid, coordinated movement

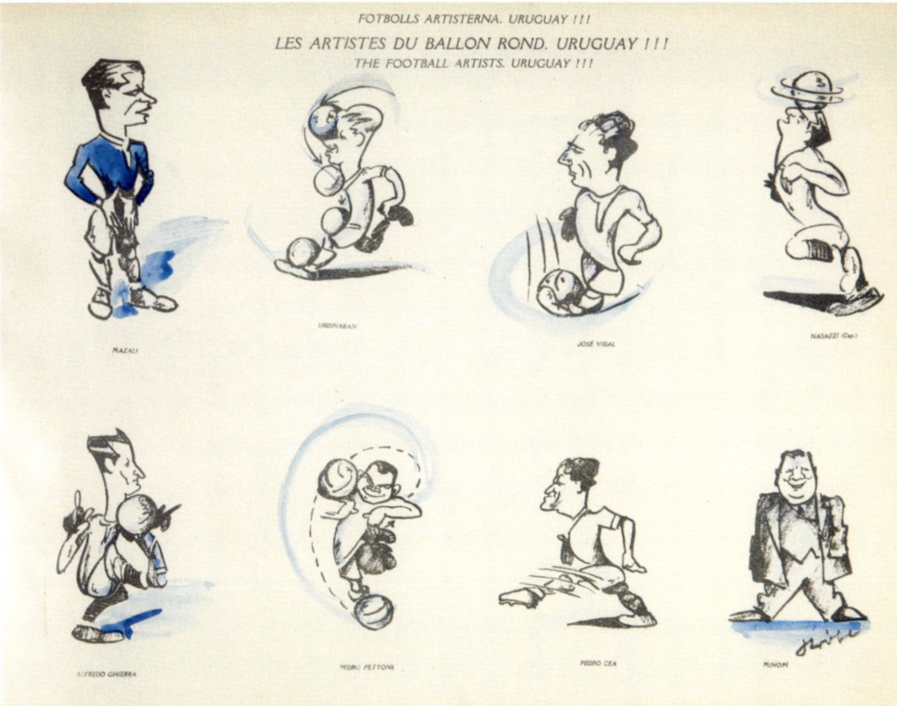


**49.** (cat. 66) Stefan Strobl (active 1920s)
*Fotbolls Artisterna. Uruguay !!!; Les Artistes du Ballon Rond. Uruguay !!!; The Football Artists. Uruguay !!!*, in *1001 Champions, VIII Olympiade, Caricatures par Derso, Kelen, Strobl*, c. 1924
Lithograph with hand-colouring, in bound volume, 28.4 × 36 cm
Olympic Museum Collections, Lausanne (C-J01-1924/001)

The title of these caricatures of the Uruguayan squad is given in Swedish, French and English, underscoring their wide potential audience. Framed by the goalkeeper, Mazali, and coach, Fígoli, six members of the Uruguayan squad perform seemingly impossible feats of juggling, shooting and dribbling. These drawings match the typical depiction of the Uruguayans as otherworldly talents, more akin to magicians and artists than footballers.

between attacking and midfield lines, and an innovative defensive shape that relied on players fluidly swapping positions (fig. 48). Observers regularly stressed the precision, intelligence and 'science' of the Uruguayan squad, which was juxtaposed with the apparent backwardness of their rivals from Europe and North America. The language of 'science' which was used to describe Uruguay's play dovetailed perfectly with the nation's Positivist creed in the early twentieth century, according to which the human body – and society at large – could be trained and perfected by medical, technological and scientific innovation.

Paris provided ample vindication of this belief, with observers struck by the South Americans' 'new conception of special training. A doctor and a physical training expert were as important elements of the staff as the coach himself. They saw to it that their charges reached perfect physical condition.'[10] The squad's training regime was rigorously maintained despite the difficulties of 1920s travel. During the three-week journey to Europe, goalkeeper Andrés Mazali took charge of the physical preparation, leading calisthenics sessions and running laps on the deck of the *Desirade*. On arrival in France, these efforts bore fruit, with observers struck in particular by the titanic strength of full-back José Nasazzi, the boundless endurance of midfielder José Vidal and the lightning pace of the 19-year-old centre-forward Pedro Petrone, who finished as the tournament's top scorer with seven goals. Although these individuals stood out, the squad as a whole was fitter, stronger and quicker than any other in Paris, and reporters constantly praised these 'excellently formed athletes, stunningly agile and fast as the wind'.[11]

Alongside this advanced approach to physical preparation, the technical skill, verve and flair of the Uruguayan squad was a revelation, delighting spectators and journalists hungry for a new expression of the game. As opposed to the long passes and physical belligerence favoured in Europe, the Uruguayans preferred to play with short passes, quick, intelligent movement and excellent close control, best exemplified by the mercurial inside-forwards Pedro Cea and Héctor 'El Mago' Scarone. This distinction was immediately noticed by the European media, which lyrically described 'the beauty, the lines, the suppleness and the symmetry of the Uruguayan game'.[12] The aesthetic quality of their play was emphasised by the players themselves, who expressed in interviews a fresh attitude to football, based on a devotion to beauty over functionality, and artistry over force (fig. 49). In one revealing discussion with a Spanish newspaper, members of the squad noted that 'for us, sport and art are one and the same', adding that 'in our country, football isn't played with force, but with beauty. We want to win, but win well, which is to say, beautifully.'[13] Such stress on playing (and winning) 'beautifully' was a valuable means of demonstrating cultural distinction in a highly visible arena of global culture. On the pitches of Paris, Uruguay's exquisite dribbling and dizzying passing patterns marked the nation's divergence from the sporting and cultural models of the 'Old World' and enchanted audiences with an extraordinary new style of football. So fresh was this approach that European newspapers even adopted Uruguayan terminology to explain it, referring regularly to the *gambeteos*, or rapid, evasive dribbling between opponents, with which the South Americans carved through defences.

## SPORTING DIPLOMACY AND THE 'BLACK MARVEL'

The Uruguayan team's fabulous skill and willingness to entertain made them arguably the biggest single attraction at the Paris Olympics (fig. 50). The football tournament alone accounted for more than a third of the spectators to the Games – 201,324 from a total of around 600,000 – with the final alone bringing in 516,575 francs.[14] Probably for the first time in its history as an independent nation, Uruguay had captured the focus of Europe, and took full advantage to make a positive introduction to a previously

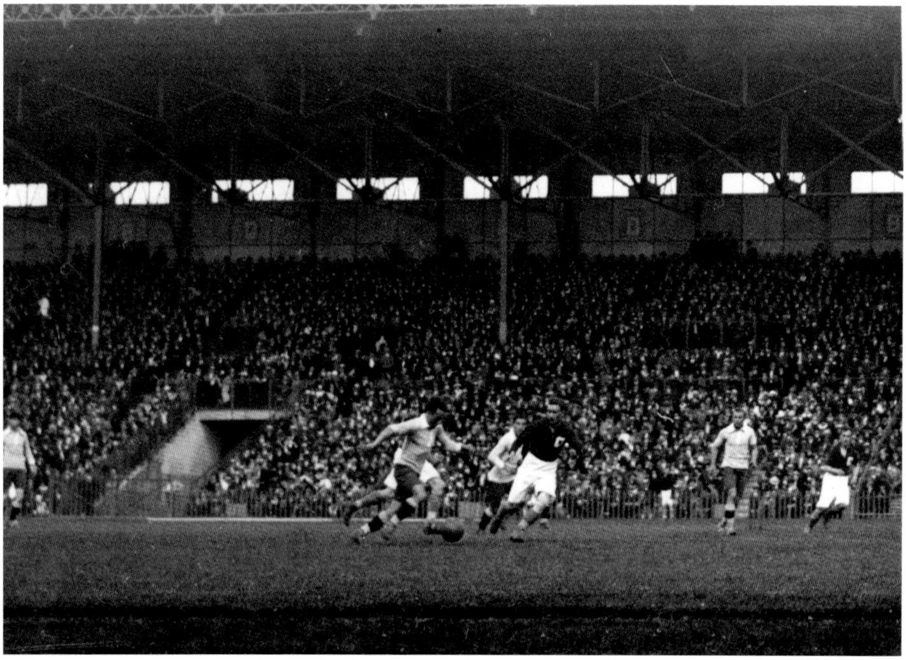

**50.** (cat. 68) Unrecorded photographer
Action in the quarter-final match between France and Uruguay, with Uruguay on the attack, at the 1924 summer Olympics in the Stade Olympique in Colombes near Paris, France, 1 June 1924
Black and white photograph

In this scene from Uruguay's knock-out game against France, which the South American side won 5–1, a Uruguayan player (possibly the outside-right, José Naya) holds off pressure from two French opponents. Behind him, a Uruguayan forward prepares to dart behind the defence. Surrounding the pitch, the stands are packed, highlighting the immense interest the squad generated. The 30,868 spectators smashed the previous attendance record in the Olympic Stadium.

ignorant Western world. The Uruguayan delegation deliberately cultivated and directed this popular interest, conscripting the squad – often referred to as 'our footballing embassy' – into a well-marshalled campaign of sporting diplomacy. Throughout their time in Paris, Uruguay's players visited embassies, attended ceremonial dinners and conducted public relations stunts on and off the pitch (fig. 51), most obviously running out for matches carrying both the Uruguayan flag and an enormous French Tricolour. Uruguay's calculated approach to public relations was clearest in their dealings with the media, as the delegation visited press offices across Paris and invited journalists to their camp in Argenteuil, in the northwestern suburbs of the city. There, in the grounds of a château owned by an elderly Frenchwoman named Madame Pain, the squad acquainted reporters with some of the key elements of Uruguayan life, including *tango*, *mate* (a traditional infused herbal drink) and *asados* (large barbecues on an open flame)

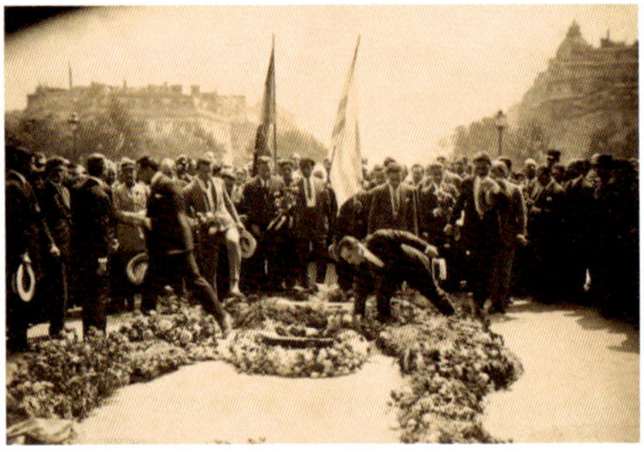

**51.** Unrecorded photographer
Members of the Uruguay football team lay flowers on the Tomb of the Unknown Soldier at the Arc de Triomphe, Paris, 1924
Black and white photograph

Shortly before the final, the Uruguayan squad visited the Arc de Triomphe and the Tomb of the Unknown Soldier, just one of the public relations engagements they carried out in Paris. In the foreground, captain José Nasazzi bends to lay a wreath, while behind him, José Leandro Andrade holds the Uruguayan flag aloft, to leave no doubt as to who was honouring the hosts.

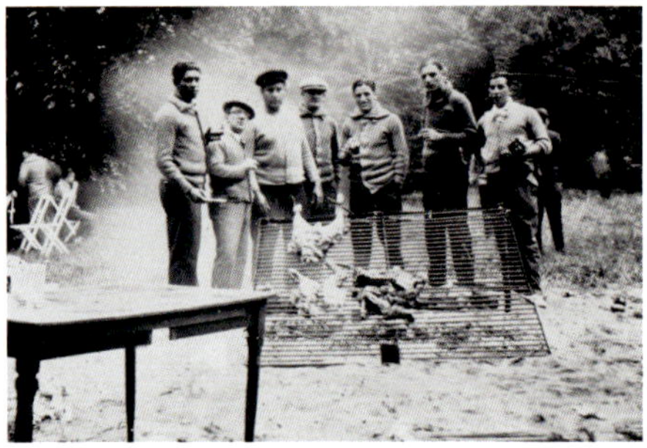

**52.** (cat. 67) Unrecorded photographer
Footballers from the Uruguay football team pose as they prepare a barbeque at the team's Argenteuil base during competition in the football tournament at the 1924 summer Olympics in Paris, France, probably May 1924
Black and white photograph

The Uruguayan team enjoy a traditional *asado criollo* on an open fire or *parrilla* at their camp in Argenteuil. José Leandro Andrade is far left and Pedro Cea is in the centre, holding a glass of beer. The presence of a number of unnamed foreign journalists in the midst of this typically Uruguayan scene underscores the delegation's efforts to spread and share their culture with a receptive global audience.

(fig. 52). The enthusiastic reports which resulted from these encounters were greeted with delight by Uruguayan media and officials, who praised the team for having 'spread the nation's name with positivity to all corners of the globe, as those who previously had the least idea of its existence ... duly informed themselves, and were even moved to learn about other aspects of national life and culture'.[15]

By far the most famous member of the Uruguayan squad in Paris was the right-half, José Leandro Andrade. One of the finest footballers of the age, Andrade was 'a player with the most refined technique and exemplary tactical qualities, a player who could do everything ... with the grace of a tap-dancer and the fairness of a true sportsman' (fig. 53).[16] A fearsome alloy of power, intelligence and technical ability, he was also the first Black footballer to compete in the Olympic Games, and his immense achievements and undeniable quality challenged widespread assumptions about race that emphasised the physical and mental superiority of Whites. The 'Black Marvel', as he was nicknamed in the press, was treated with a curious mixture of fascination, admiration and exoticisation by the European media, in line with the racist tropes prevalent in 1920s Europe (fig. 54).

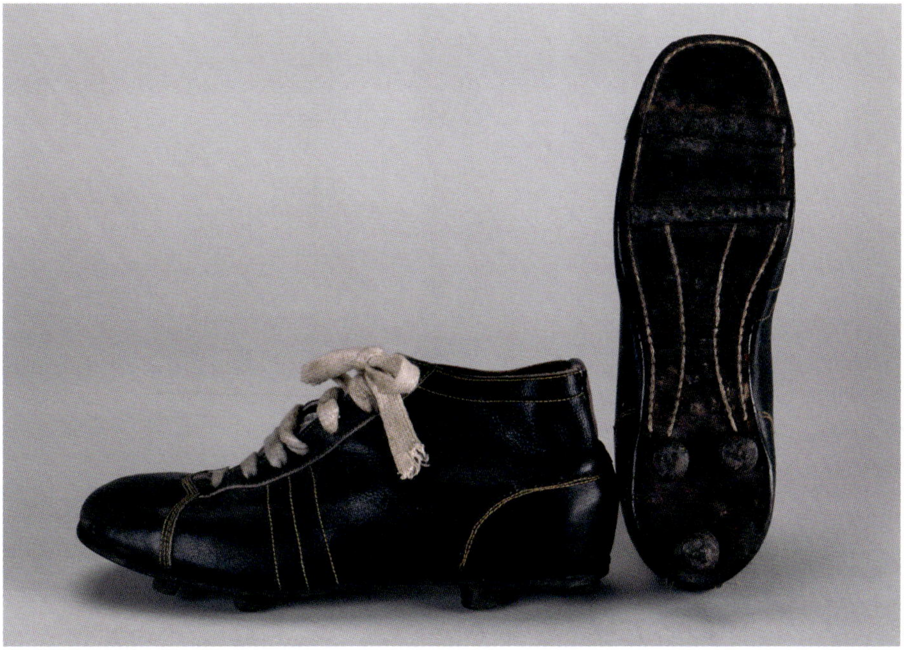

**53.** (cat. 70) Unrecorded maker
Pair of football boots worn by José Leandro Andrade (1901–1957) in the match between Uruguay and Argentina in the final of the first FIFA (Fédération Internationale de Football Association) World Cup competition in 1930, *c.* 1930

Leather, textile, iron, 11.5 x 25.5 x 16 cm (shoe size 9)
Musée National du Sport, Nice (MNS 2007.7.53)

Similar to the pair that shot him to fame in Paris, these boots bore Andrade to immortality in 1930. Defeating their greatest rivals, Argentina, on home soil, Uruguay added to the Olympics victories of 1924 and 1928 to claim their third global title in a row. Not even Pelé and Brazil matched this feat.

**54.** (cat. 72) Unidentified artist, signed with initials *Ad.v.B*
*The Black Marvel*, caricature of José Leandro Andrade (1901–1957), 1924
(*La merveille noire*)

Photograph of an original drawing

France's caricaturists were drawn to the competitors of the 1924 Olympics. Here José Leandro Andrade juggles four balls at once to the clear dismay of his opponent in the background. His five legs emphasise this coordination and dexterity while also making him seem insect-like. This sense of Andrade as a strange, inhuman creature feeds into a stereotypical representation, the racist undertones of which are today fully acknowledged.

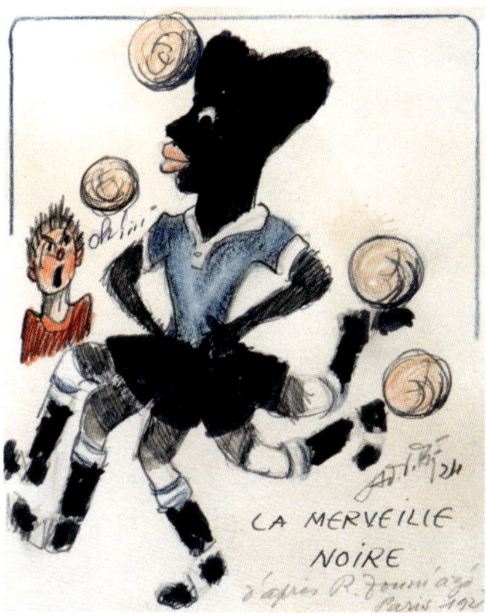

A few years after the tournament, Andrade would reflect on the attitudes of Parisians towards him: 'they confused me with the Prince of Abyssinia, who had been in Paris not long before ... in the cabarets they called me "your highness", and a French woman offered me a great many things so I would take her into my Harem'.[17] As this anecdote indicates, Andrade's on-pitch feats received as much attention as his off-field adventures. Six-foot tall, strikingly handsome and an accomplished musician, Andrade's activities in the cabarets and bars of the city made him a celebrity on the level of Paavo Nurmi and Johnny Weissmuller, one who inspired constant media interest and who featured in advertising campaigns for whiskey, chocolate and a range of other products during his time in Europe. In the words of the great Uruguayan writer Eduardo Galeano, Andrade 'was black, South American and poor, the first international idol of football'.[18]

## CHAMPIONS OF THE NEW WORLD

If Andrade as an individual challenged racial prejudices, Uruguay's performance as a whole posed a powerful retort to assumptions about Latin America's subaltern position relative to Europe. The squad's starring role in Paris was interpreted by Europeans and South Americans alike as the latest blow in an intercontinental combat, with the squad presented as 'champions of the New World coming to conquer the Old one'.[19] The prejudices that had dogged South America for centuries – that it was unsophisticated, underdeveloped and incapable of catching up with Europe – were shattered by the precision and refinement of Uruguay's play and the modernity and rationality of its sporting organisation, advances that were strikingly contrasted with the archaic methods of their European and North American opponents. The results spoke for themselves, with Uruguay scoring seven goals against Yugoslavia and putting five past the hosts, playing with their helpless opponents 'like a cat plays with a mouse'.[20] Uruguay's 3–0 victory in the final against Switzerland served as a neat parable in itself, with the nation effortlessly overcoming the model it had previously tried to emulate. This shift must be viewed in the context of a broader belief, following World War I, that a 'young South America was on the rise while a decrepit Europe was losing its central place in the world'.[21] Football was just one arm of a much wider cultural reinvention in the 1920s, as South American writers, musicians and artists sought to prove the potential of their continent, especially its capacity to equal and surpass the achievements of the 'Old World'.

While the triumph in Paris undoubtedly had continental ramifications, the achievement was ultimately a Uruguayan one. As the prominent diplomat Enrique Buero noted, 'the victory of our team has been a victory for Uruguay as a nation',[22] a feat that demonstrated the country's capabilities and provided an enormous boost to a national identity that was still coming into formation in the 1920s. This was especially important for Uruguay, which had endured an almost constant cycle of conflict since gaining independence in 1828. The country's most recent civil war had ended in 1904, just 20 years before the Uruguayan squad crossed the Atlantic. Their victory, as the representatives of a united country, provided a tangible reference point for a common identity untainted by political violence. The ultimate demonstration of the harmony inspired by footballing success came over a month after the tournament, when the squad returned home after another three-week journey, this time aboard the *Valdivia*. On 31 July, which had been declared a national holiday by the Uruguayan senate, the ship docked in the port of Montevideo, and the squad were met with enormous crowds for a celebration which had 'the character of a true apotheosis', as Uruguayans 'from all over the country' flocked to 'the extraordinary reception of their brave compatriots'.[23] The extraordinary scenes of these festivities (fig. 46) provided an unmistakable image of national unity and suggested a sense of shared mission, which had previously been sorely lacking in Uruguay.

*

Uruguay's startling display in Paris was not just a landmark in the nation's history, it also marked a new era in the history of football. The 1924 Games demonstrated to both the world football body FIFA and enchanted spectators the potentially boundless horizons of a game that was rapidly growing beyond the confines of the Olympics. Six years later, after Uruguay had claimed a second consecutive football gold medal at Amsterdam in 1928, FIFA launched its own competition: the World Cup. It is no surprise that the organisation chose Montevideo to host the inaugural tournament, which also marked the Centenary of Uruguay's first Constitution and birth as a modern nation-state. Today the FIFA Men's World Cup is the most widely viewed single sporting event in the world and FIFA the wealthiest single sports body. Uruguay's contribution to the growth of football is often overlooked, but few nations have been more crucial to the global spread of the game. Uruguay was undoubtedly the best international team in probably the most important decade in the expansion of world football. Uruguay was essential to the development of football, and football, in turn, was essential to the development of Uruguay, allowing the nation to project itself abroad and highlight its extraordinary advances to a global audience that had previously paid little attention. In Paris, the Uruguayan representatives demonstrated a unique national style and approach to the game, one that shattered pre-conceptions of the country and the continent, and engendered a vibrant and confident Uruguayan identity.

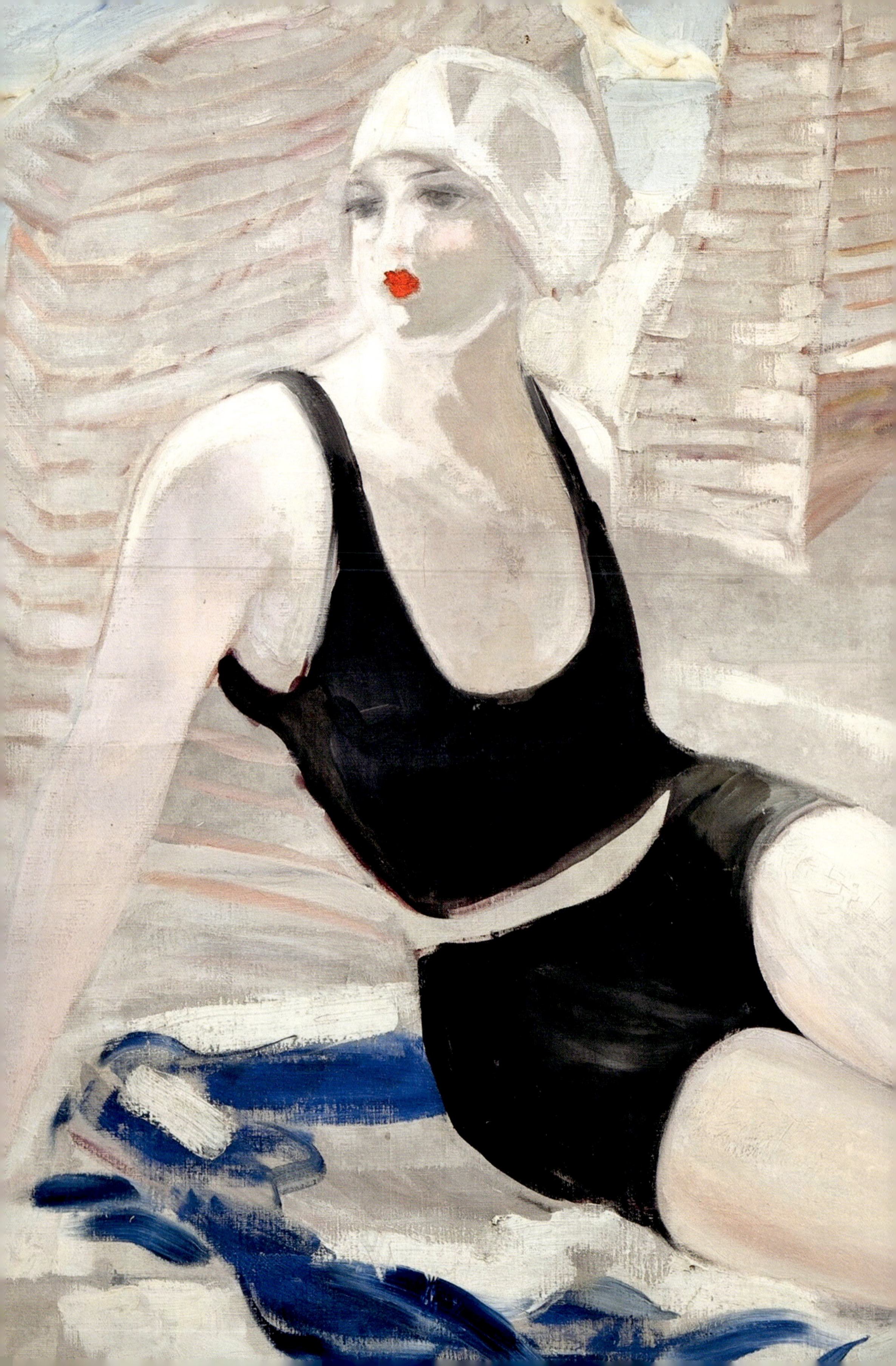

# SOCIETY

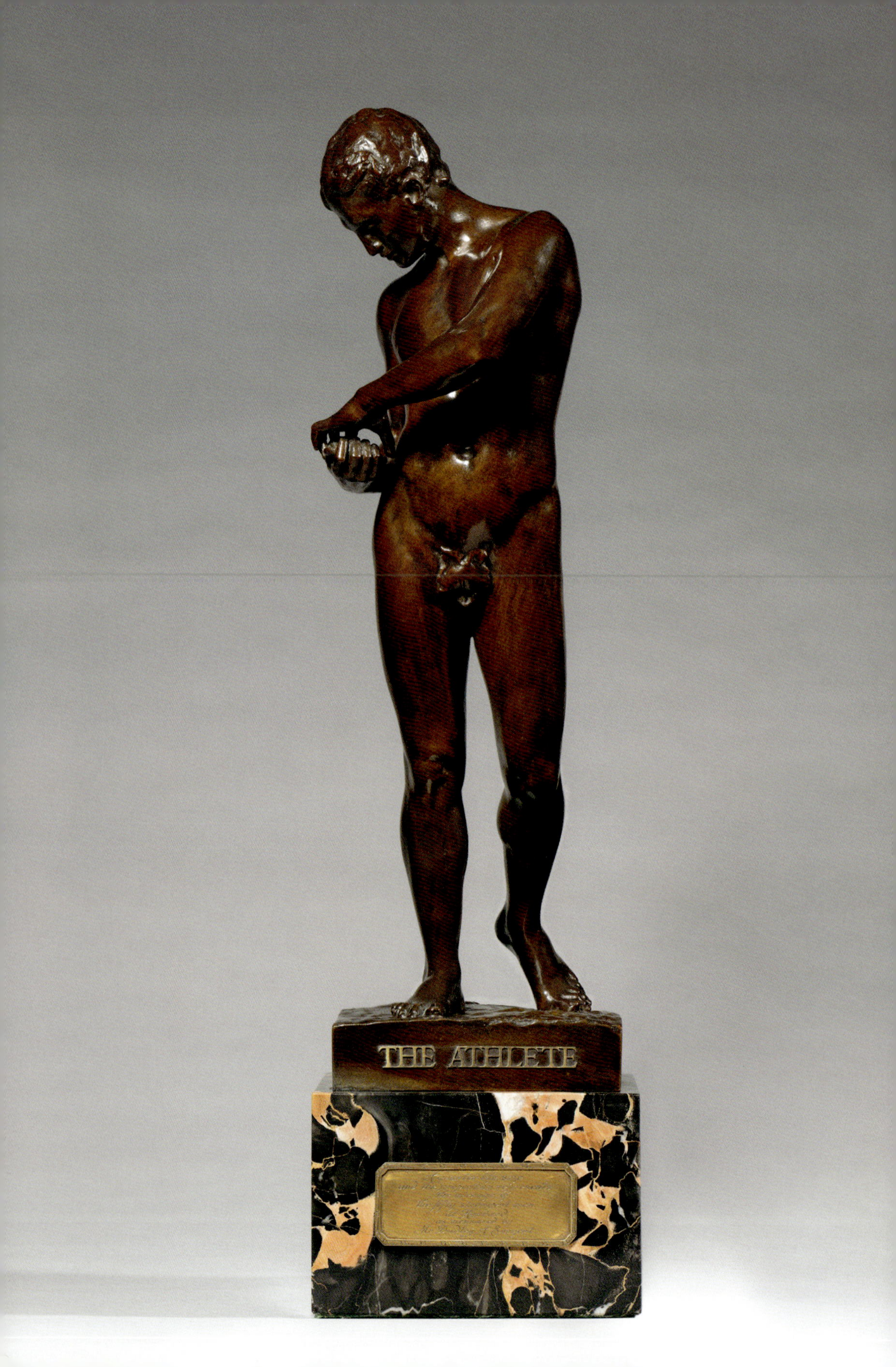
THE ATHLETE

# 6

# SPORT, SCIENCE, PUBLIC HEALTH

VANESSA HEGGIE

The Paris Olympiad stands at a pivotal point in the relationship between sport, science and health. For much of the previous century, individual European nations had developed and disseminated distinctive cultures of physical exercise, from the 'Turnen' Gymnastics of Germany to Sweden's Ling method, after Pehr Henrik Ling, and the team sports of Britain and the US. By the end of that century, interested researchers from both medical and scientific backgrounds were improving human performance with modern technologies – particularly the camera, but also electrical apparatus, thermodynamic theories and new methods of nutritional analysis.[1] Increasingly doctors and others with medical training claimed expertise in sporting activities, intervening in 1920, for example, to demand changes to the timing of the Olympic marathon to prevent heat exhaustion. By 1924 it was commonplace, at least for the wealthier teams, to bring a variety of medical personnel including doctors and masseurs with them, and to embrace 'scientific' methods of training and nutrition. From this point onwards, medical and scientific intervention increased and diversified. Not only did the 1928 Amsterdam Olympics witness a major at-event physiological study and anthropometric survey and the 1932 Los Angeles Games the first Olympic Village with a medical clinic, but – very differently – there were already accusations of gender fraud at Berlin 1936.

## SHIFTING IDEALS

Two events in 1924 show how far elite sport and professional sports medicine were distinguishing themselves from more general exercise and healthy living. The first is the formation, just before the Paris Games, of the first sports medicine organisation

**55.** (cat. 80) Robert Tait McKenzie (1867–1938), sculptor; cast at Roman Bronze Works, New York City (founded 1897)
*The Athlete*, 1903
Bronze and marble, 43.3 × 13.2 × 13.5 cm
National Trust Collections, Anglesey Abbey, Cambridgeshire (NT 515046)

In the late nineteenth and early twentieth century, many doctors and physical educators collected measurements of athletic bodies to try to understand the physical (and possibly evolutionary) basis of performance. Tait McKenzie used such measurements to inform his artistic representations of athletes in motion. He considered the face as well as the body, trying to model the typical features of exhaustion or concentration (as seen in the *Sprinter*, fig. 58) and to represent national 'types'.

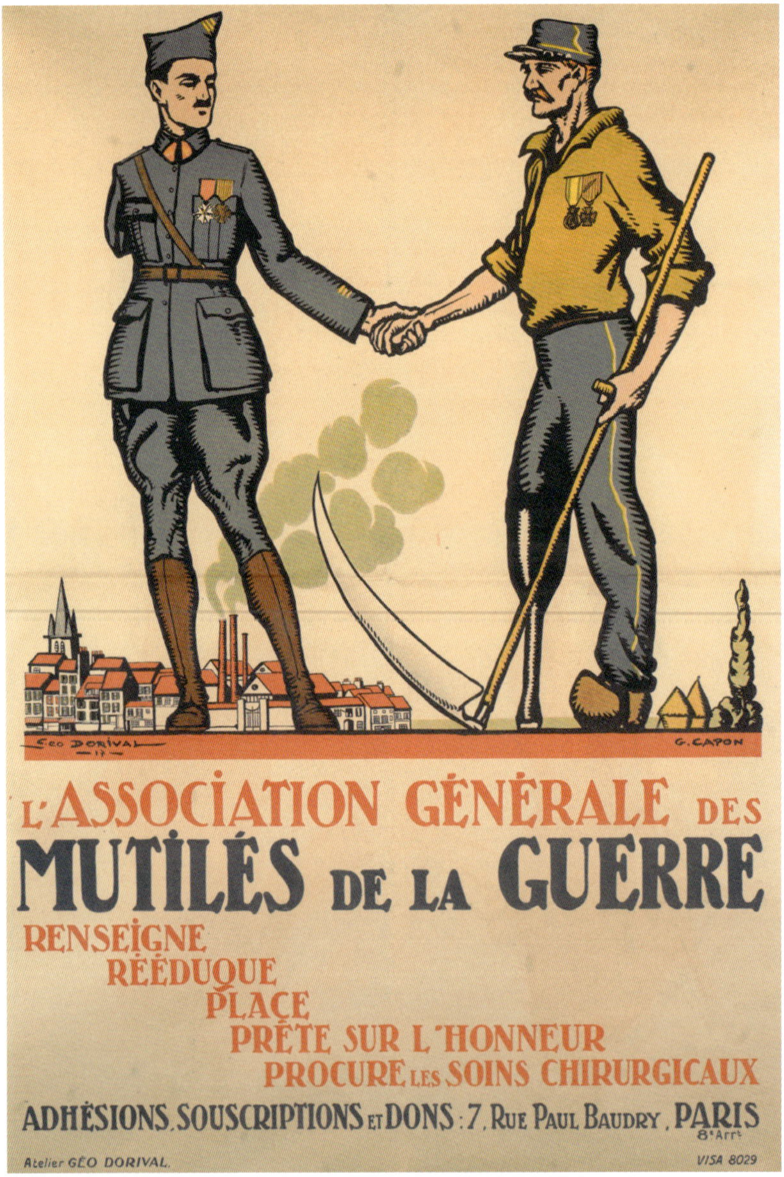


**56.** (cat. 77) Justin Marie Georges Dorival (1879–1968), artist; Georges Capon (1890–1980), artist; Atelier Dorival, Paris (active *c.* 1910–28), printer
*General Association for the War Disabled*, poster, 1917 (*L'Association Générale des Mutilés de la Guerre*)
Colour lithography on paper, 118.3 × 79.8 cm
IWM (Imperial War Museums), (Art.IWM PST 11165)

The Association Générale des Mutilés de la Guerre was founded in 1915 to support injured French servicemen, and in this poster promised medical and financial support, as well as assistance finding employment. Representing the city and the countryside, the imagery understandably focuses on visible physical injuries as opposed to the invisible sensory and psychological disorders that also affected ex-service personnel after the war.

for doctors, the German Medical Association for the Promotion of Physical Exercise (Ärztebund zur Förderung der Leibesübungen). This was followed just four years later by the International Federation of Sports Medicine – the Association International Médico-Sportive, later renamed the Fédération Internationale de Médecine du Sport.[2] These organisations were global expressions of professional identity among a small group of doctors and other health professionals who began to recognise their expertise as unique.[3] The other significant event took place immediately after the Games – the first ever Silent Games, later to become the World Games for the Deaf. These Games attracted nearly 150 participants to compete in 31 sports and gymnastics demonstrations. Founded largely by Deaf activist Eugène Rubens-Alcais, in part as a form of disability activism, the Silent Games were an expression of Deaf identity and Deaf ability. While the Paralympics tends to trace its history to the late 1940s and to the work done with soldiers who had spinal injuries, the use of sport and exercise in the treatment and liberation of people with a wide variety of disabilities had been long established before the first Stoke Mandeville Games for the Paralyzed in 1948.[4]

World War I had been a mass disabling event across much of Europe, and in France, as elsewhere, the absence of sufficient state support prompted private and charitable organisations to help discharged soldiers with both physical and mental injuries (fig. 56). The General Association for the War Disabled (Association Générale des Mutilés de la Guerre, or AGMG) was succeeded by more specialist organisations that focused on particular injuries, including those to the eyes or lungs.[5] The lived reality and visibility of such injuries, not just on posters but also on the streets, where veterans were forced to beg for support, led to reconsiderations of what the male body was and could do. Despite their obvious injuries, the men on the AGMG poster are represented as war heroes and physical labourers; sport was another field in which the masculinity of the disabled body could be proven.[6] Invisible injuries – whether the aural disabilities of the 'mass deafening event' that was the Great War or trauma and shellshock – were obviously harder to see, but sporting moments like the Silent Games made them visible as they were overcome.[7]

New models of masculinity and femininity are discussed elsewhere in this volume (see Vout's chapter). With these models came a revision of what counted as a 'normal', healthy body, with emphasis, even beyond the Games, on sport as a means of keeping disabled bodies strong. Physician, athlete and artist Robert Tait McKenzie authored books on physical training in which he included separate chapters on the 'Blind and the Deaf-Mute', and on the application of sports and exercise in a range of other conditions, from scoliosis to flat feet and diseases of the nervous system (fig. 57). Tait McKenzie had a deep and lifelong interest in finding the winning formula for a healthy body; in this he was significantly influenced by the director of Physical Education at Harvard University, Dudley Allen Sargent, who in the late nineteenth century instigated a programme of 'anthropometry', measuring the bodies of young athletes there in the hope of turning physical education into a science that could be mathematically understood

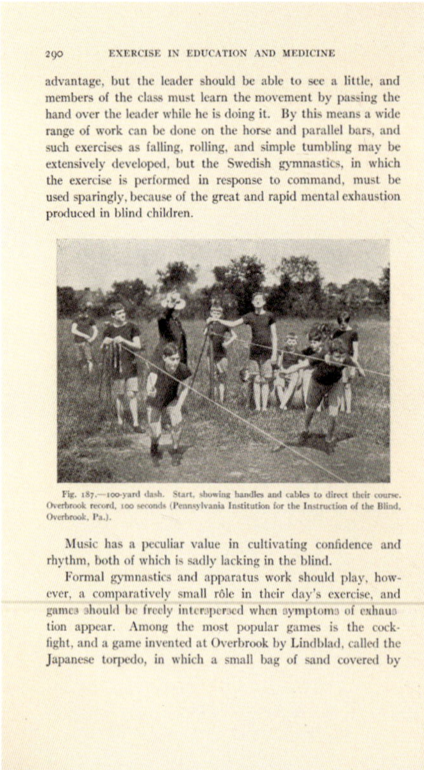

290 EXERCISE IN EDUCATION AND MEDICINE

advantage, but the leader should be able to see a little, and members of the class must learn the movement by passing the hand over the leader while he is doing it. By this means a wide range of work can be done on the horse and parallel bars, and such exercises as falling, rolling, and simple tumbling may be extensively developed, but the Swedish gymnastics, in which the exercise is performed in response to command, must be used sparingly, because of the great and rapid mental exhaustion produced in blind children.

Fig. 187.—100-yard dash. Start, showing handles and cables to direct their course. Overbrook record, 100 seconds (Pennsylvania Institution for the Instruction of the Blind, Overbrook, Pa.).

Music has a peculiar value in cultivating confidence and rhythm, both of which is sadly lacking in the blind.

Formal gymnastics and apparatus work should play, however, a comparatively small rôle in their day's exercise, and games should be freely interspersed when symptoms of exhaustion appear. Among the most popular games is the cockfight, and a game invented at Overbrook by Lindblad, called the Japanese torpedo, in which a small bag of sand covered by

**57.** Robert Tait McKenzie (1867–1938), *Exercise in Education and Medicine*, 1915 (2nd edition, W.B. Saunders Co. Philadelphia; London), p. 290, fig. 187

Black and white photograph

Tait McKenzie's training textbook included chapters on the use of physical exercises to improve the bodies and minds of people with physical, sensory and mental disabilities. In this illustration from the book, rope guides enable children with visual impairments to take part in running races.

and underpinned. Tait McKenzie used these measurements in his sculpture to create 'ideal' images of athletes engaged in a range of sports, all of these athletes nude in debt to ancient Greece (figs 55 and 58).[8]

This 'anthropometry', or 'man-measurement' – height, chest size, length of arm to leg, maximal oxygen consumption – aimed at discovering the invisible laws of nature that govern performance. But it was also a mode of classification that divided men. And in the context of the emerging field of eugenics, it was used to argue for the superiority of some ethnic groups over others. In a world in which Greek statues, long stripped of their original pigment, dictated Western art, it was white European bodies that were deemed perfect (cat. 156).[9] Small wonder that these are the bodies that Tait McKenzie depicts in three dimensions, despite using images of athletic Black bodies in his training books, and despite working in bronze. Small wonder too that throughout the twentieth century the idea that specific ethnicities or races had 'unfair' physical advantages continued to be discussed, and the messy reality of biology undermined sports organisations' obsession with dividing competitions into male or female categories.[10]

Beyond sports, Tait McKenzie's work also suggests that there are perfect 'national' types, as illustrated by his series of war memorials, which usually featured 'typical'

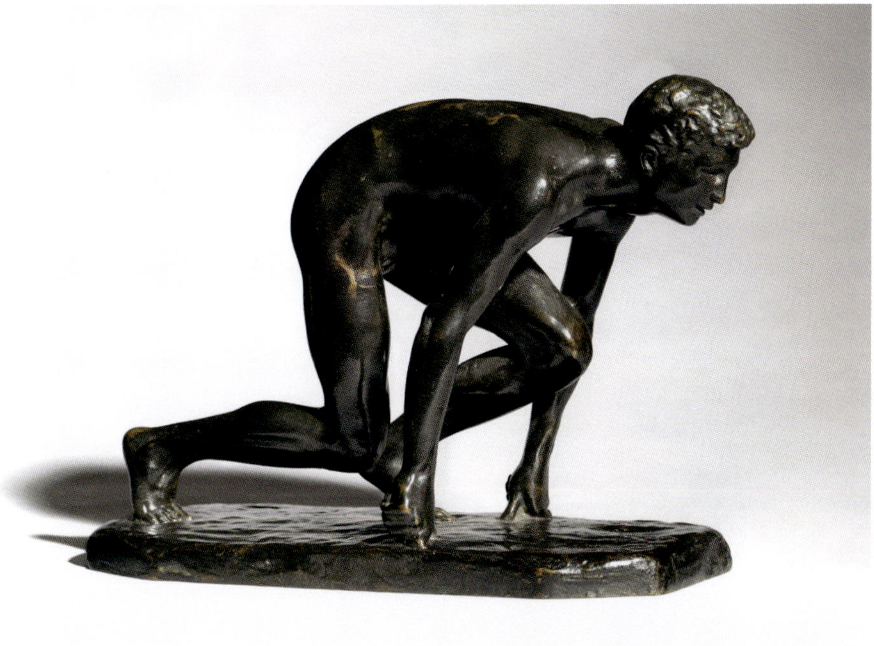

**58.** (cat. 78) Robert Tait McKenzie (1867–1938), sculptor; cast at Roman Bronze Works, New York City (founded 1897)
*Sprinter*, 1902
Bronze, 22.3 × 29.1 × 15 cm
National Trust Collections, Anglesey Abbey, Cambridgeshire (NT 515040)

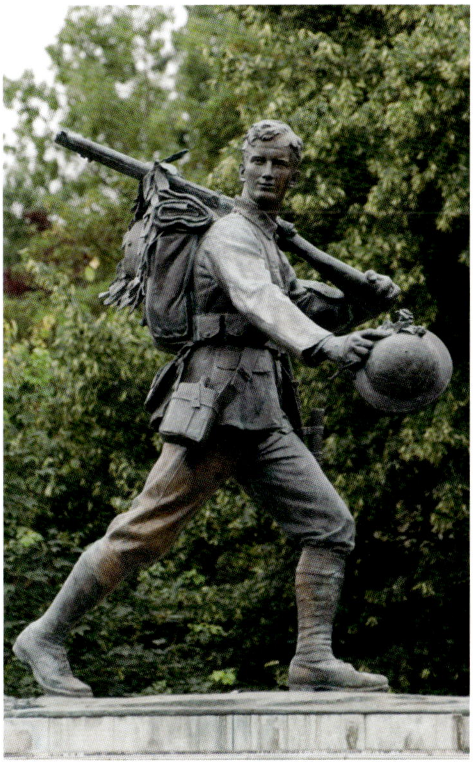

**59.** Robert Tait McKenzie (1867–1938)
*The Homecoming*, Cambridge War Memorial, 1922
Bronze, height 210 cm
Cambridge City Council, Cambridge (CB2_JB_S005)

All but one of McKenzie's war memorials feature male figures, often in motion or, like his sports sculpture *Sprinter*, ready to spring into action. In these artworks the facial features were particularly important. McKenzie wanted to represent the ideal national type – young, male, able-bodied, active and virile.

young and able-bodied men (fig. 59).[11] There is a tension here in sports medicine and science between the idea that performance and ability are inherent, inherited and fixed, and the assertion that scientific training and sports medicine could build, develop and improve not only performance, but health and mental wellbeing. Tait McKenzie himself straddles this divide: his art points one way and his written work the other, endorsing sports and exercise as a space for the personal improvement of every body.

## SPORTS 'SCIENCE'

The increased scrutiny of athletes and their performances allowed doctors, physiologists and a range of other interested parties to design systems of training and exercise that claimed to be scientific. Even nations that clung, at least rhetorically, to the notion of amateurism, had by 1924 embraced medical and scientific assistance for their elite athletes. Dr Adolphe Abrahams, older brother of the sprinter Harold Abrahams (fig. 60), had attended several previous Games as an unofficial medical advisor for the track and field team before being appointed, in 1924, as the British Olympic Team's Honorary Medical Officer. Adolphe Abrahams had a longstanding interest in sports medicine, and eventually positioned himself as the UK's leading expert, founding the British Association of Sports Medicine in the 1950s. Despite bemoaning the 'preposterous standard' of Olympic sports, which increasingly demanded significant time and effort put into training, and extremely distinctive and unusual physical development, he also strongly advocated 'rational' and 'scientific' training methods – encompassing diet, sleep hygiene and psychology as well as strength and endurance routines.[12] Adolphe Abrahams also commercialised his expertise (see Introduction) – after Harold's career was cut short due to an injury, the two co-wrote a training manual, *Training for Athletes*, published in the Olympic year of 1928 (fig. 61).[13]

By 1924 it was generally expected that Olympic organising committees would listen and respond to medical advice when considering the planning and logistics of the Games. At first this focused on the most physically demanding race, the marathon. After a rather chaotic event in St. Louis in 1904, the London Olympic Organising Committee introduced a pre-entry requirement for letters of support from doctors (focusing on cardiological fitness) and regular refreshment stations along the route. The death of a participant at Stockholm in 1912 led to further medical requirements about the timing and first aid staffing of this event; in 1924, Adolphe Abrahams suggested that this level of medical consideration should also be extended to the 10,000m cross country race. Fully trained doctors were not the only ones to critique the infrastructure of the Games when it came to biomedical issues: the US rowing coach, Ed Leader, was apparently so horrified at the breakfasts provided in the Olympic Village – 'an orange that was no bigger around than, say a 50c piece ... just dry pith inside. There was no juice to spoon out. And there was one croissant roll and a curl of butter' – that he moved the whole team into a privately hired apartment and had them eat out in a local restaurant. Even there,

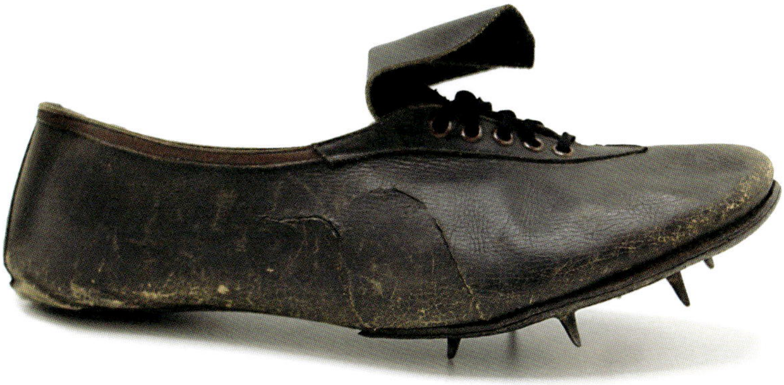

**60.** (cat. 99) J.W. Foster & Sons (Athletic Shoes) Limited (founded 1895)
Running shoe, 1920–29
Leather, metal, textile, 9.5 × 25 × 9 cm
Reebok Brand Archive, Boston, Massachusetts (RF-5233)

Harold Abrahams won his 1924 gold medal in spiked running shoes made by Bolton-based Joseph William Foster and Sons. They had the advantage of securing a better grip. The company would later boast of being worn by 'successful athletes at the Olympic Games since 1908' and name its building 'Olympic Works'. Foster's grandsons founded Reebok, named after the fast running, jumping antelope.

he had to work to secure his preferred system of safe meats and vegetables, turning down a celebratory 24-lobster platter brought out for 4 July![14]

Nutrition was but the tip of the iceberg: Harold Abrahams famously used the professional trainer Sam Mussabini (fig. 62) to prepare for the 1924 Games, and one of Mussabini's new 'scientific' approaches was photographic. The ability to analyse images of the moving as well as static body was a valuable resource for the new scientific trainer, and while sport films initially produced for entertainment had many purposes, they were also pored over by participants and their trainers for insights into technique and performance. Even more useful was chronophotography – the use of rapid shutter speeds and often multiple camera angles to 'capture' motion in minute detail. Pioneered by Eadweard Muybridge in the late 1870s and early 1880s (see Michelakis's chapter) to demonstrate animal movement, it was developed by Etienne-Jules Marey into a biomedical technology that could, like anthropometry, reveal hidden secrets about the body and performance (fig. 108).[15] Indeed, Marey had used it at the first Paris Olympic Games in 1900; his footage of the rowing event reassured the French team that American success in this sport was to do with efficiency of movement, rather than being an indication of American physical superiority over a 'degenerate' French race.[16]

Such work frequently figured the human body as a machine, governed by static and predictable laws of physics – input and output that could be calculated and tweaked to

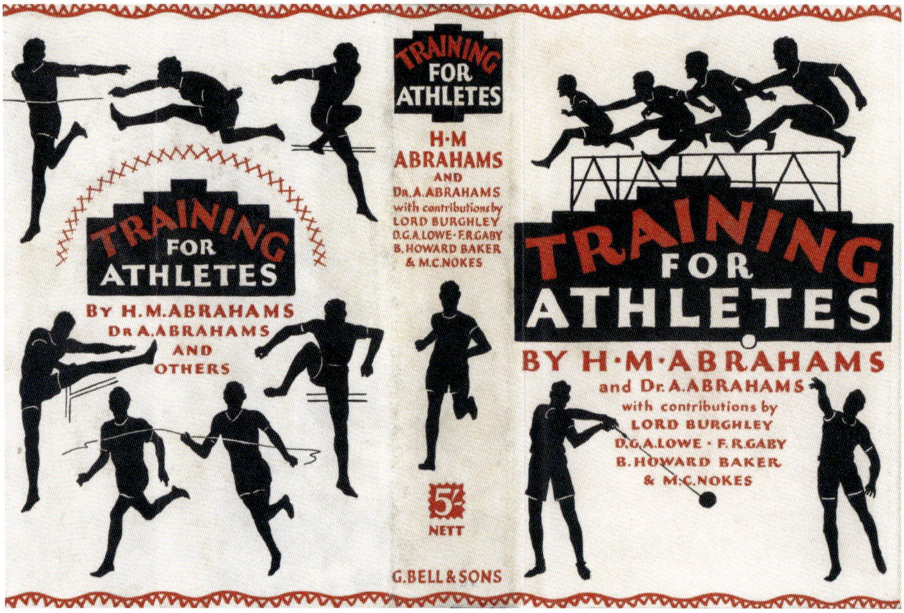


**61.** (cat. 100) Unrecorded artist
Original book jacket design for Harold M. Abrahams (1899–1978); Dr Adolphe Abrahams (1883–1967)
*Training for Athletes*, George Bell and Sons Ltd: London, 1928

Colour printing on paper, 19.3 × 29.3 cm
Cambridge University Library, Cambridge (9514.d.15)

Harold Abrahams takes lead billing in the authorship of this training manual, co-published in 1928 with his medically qualified brother, Adolphe. Harold's sporting career came to an end in 1925 when he broke his leg long jumping, but he continued to use his expertise, captaining the British Olympic Team in 1928, working in sports journalism and revealing his training secrets to the public in *Training for Athletes*.

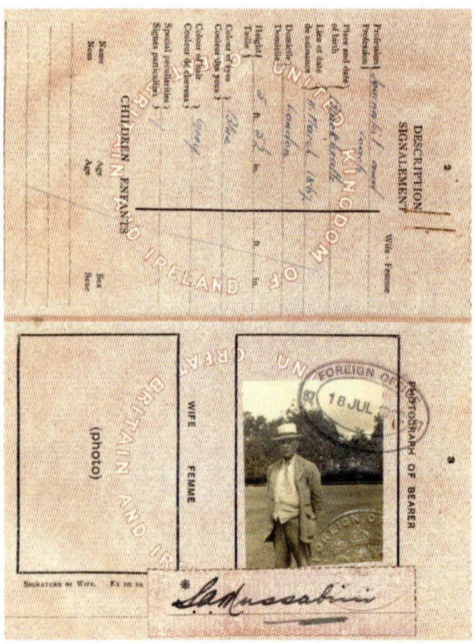


**62.** (cat. 18) UK Passport of Scipio Africanus ('Sam') Mussabini (1867–1927), 1922–31
Printed paper, covered boards, pen and ink, ink stamps, paper stamps, black and white photograph, 15.1 × 10.9 × 8 cm

Cadbury Research Library, University of Birmingham (MS935/2)

'Sam' Mussabini (1867–1927) was a professional athlete in the 1890s, before turning to coaching to make a living. He worked not only with Olympic medal-winning athletes such as Harold Abrahams, but also with at least one professional cyclist. Mussabini advocated scientific techniques, including the use of chronophotography, to analyse and improve movement. This study of movement also informed his personal success at, and publications about, billiards.

provide the most work for the least energy. And it led to the development of 'scientific management' by the likes of American engineer Frederick Winslow Taylor, whose system of 'Taylorism' sought to make industry more efficient by minutely managing the movements of workers as well as machines. The promise, and the peril, of this man-as-machine metaphor is visible in the work of art movements of the early twentieth century (fig. 9) – with Muybridge's chronophotography most famously and directly referenced in Marcel Duchamp's *Nude Descending a Staircase, No. 2* (1912).

## MAN AS MACHINE

The apogee of efficient movement at the 1924 Games was reached with the Finnish middle-distance runner Paavo Nurmi, who took gold in the 1500m, the 5000m, the cross country, and helped his national team to win the 3000m and cross country team events (see Young's chapter). Although not allowed by the Finnish authorities to enter the 10,000m, on his return to Finland he set a world record for that distance, so that he simultaneously held the world record for the 1500m, the 3000m, the 5000m, the 10,000m and the mile. A crucial part of Nurmi's method was to run with a stopwatch, allowing him to pace himself and spread his energy in an efficient and – as the records showed – extraordinarily effective way. The stopwatch was a visible marker of a regime about which Nurmi was generally reticent – cross training with periods of running and walking and forms of calisthenics (fig. 63). Unusual for the time, this training was the source of speculation and scrutiny, especially after his publicity tour of the US in 1925. If his success was not due to his genetics, or the Scandinavian diet of black bread and raw dried fish (see Introduction), perhaps it was due to his unique preparation.

Nurmi's unwillingness to talk to the press facilitated his image as a man-machine, a production-line runner whose movements were systematic and standardised, or, as one widely quoted US sports journalist, George Trevor, put it, an 'inscrutable Robot', a 'mechanical Frankenstein created to annihilate time'.[17] This narrative of Nurmi's unusual or even abnormal ability was encouraged by the medical observations of the Finnish team organisers, who confirmed Nurmi's extremely low resting pulse rate. As one of the 'hidden secrets' of the body, pulse-rates were widely scrutinised. In the 1920s, the prevailing cardiological assumption was that a low resting heart rate – usually anything below 50 beats per minute – was indicative of real or potential heart disease; this would have been a key indicator of problems for the doctors asked to provide health certificates for the Olympic Marathon. But the mass screening of otherwise healthy young men, not only in the context of enormous international sporting events, but, most significantly, through recruiting for two world wars, would reveal a very different picture of cardiological health, encompassing a much broader range of healthy anatomy and function, and eventually recognising the hypertrophied, slow-beating athletic heart as a positive adaptation, not a pathological deviation from the norm.[18] Indeed, in the 1940s Adolphe Abrahams was one of the key figures who admitted a change of heart (pun intended) in

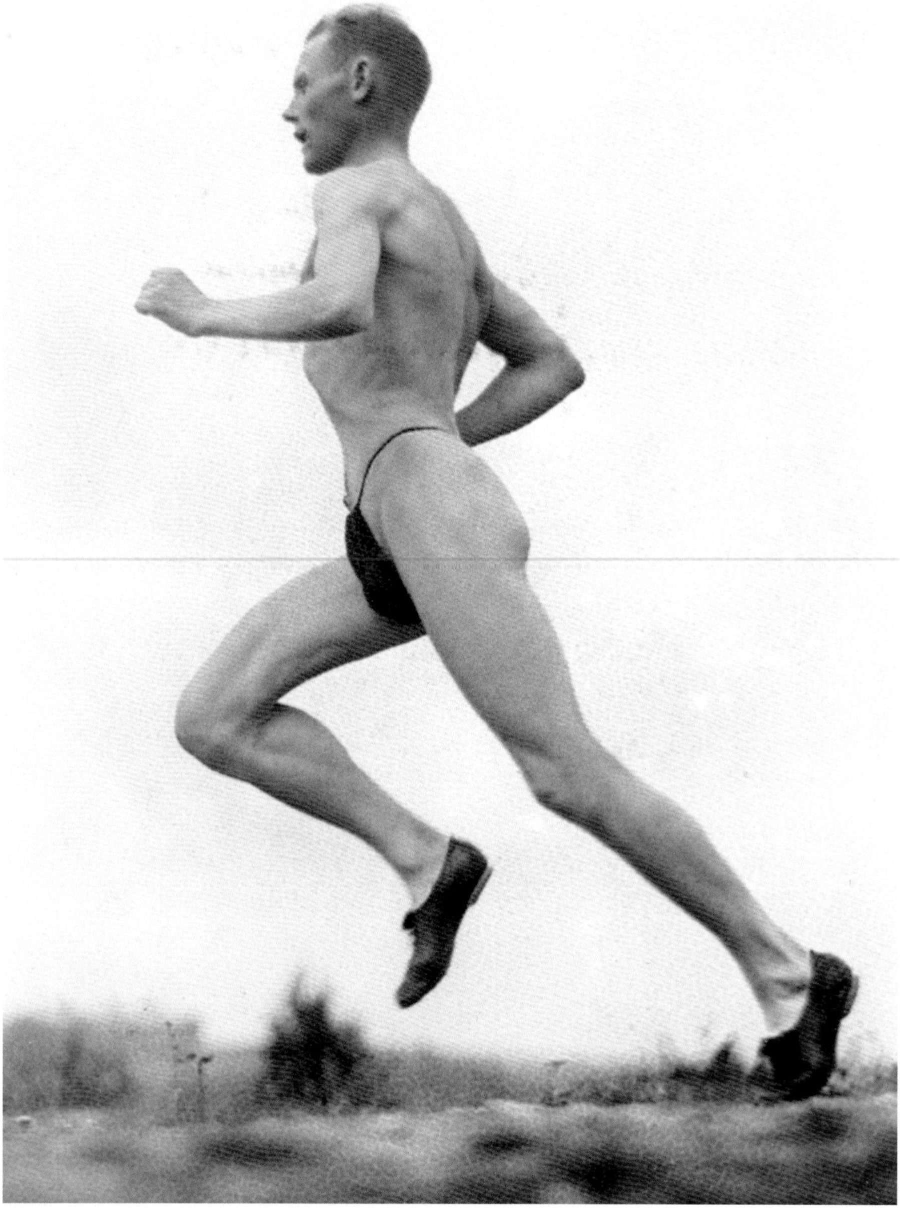

**63.** (cat. 74) Unrecorded photographer
Paavo Nurmi (1897–1973) pictured during his training regime, 1925
Black and white photograph
Sports Museum of Finland, Helsinki

Nurmi systematised his training regimes, not only using a stopwatch to measure his pace and progress, but also engaging in a form of cross training which involved walking, calisthenics and running in a single 'system'. A fairly reticent performer, he is perhaps pictured here in publicity shots for his tour of the USA in 1925.

understanding athletic physiology, a process which by the mid century recognised the elite athlete as a form of physiological *super*human.[19]

The idea that athletes could be *ab*normal and *super*human, covered mental fitness too, an area in which Nurmi is also important. Nurmi had a taciturn nature, and he self-diagnosed as neurasthenic, a generalised term encompassing a range of mental ill health that could include depression, 'nervous exhaustion' and chronic fatigue.[20] His assertion that the rigour and routine of sport and exercise could effectively treat his psychological problems was a positive point of hope in a decade struggling with a male mental health crisis; a health and exercise connection that had long been explored in the host nation, France.[21] While post-war trauma was obviously not limited to men, mental illness – like physical disability – posed particular questions about healthy masculinity in those recently released from active service.[22]

*

A century later, the organisers of the 2024 Olympic Games in Paris have announced that they will provide the first ever mental health hotline for competitors and access to other mental health support, such as subscriptions to a wellness app. While this may seem slow progress, it does reveal the 1924 Games as a moment when the relationship between sport and all forms of health began to change. New scientific understandings of bodies and their potential variety were being developed; new scientific training was on display and increasingly valued; and simultaneously, the medical appreciation of the role, and limits, of sport in maintaining physical and mental health was being actively reshaped.

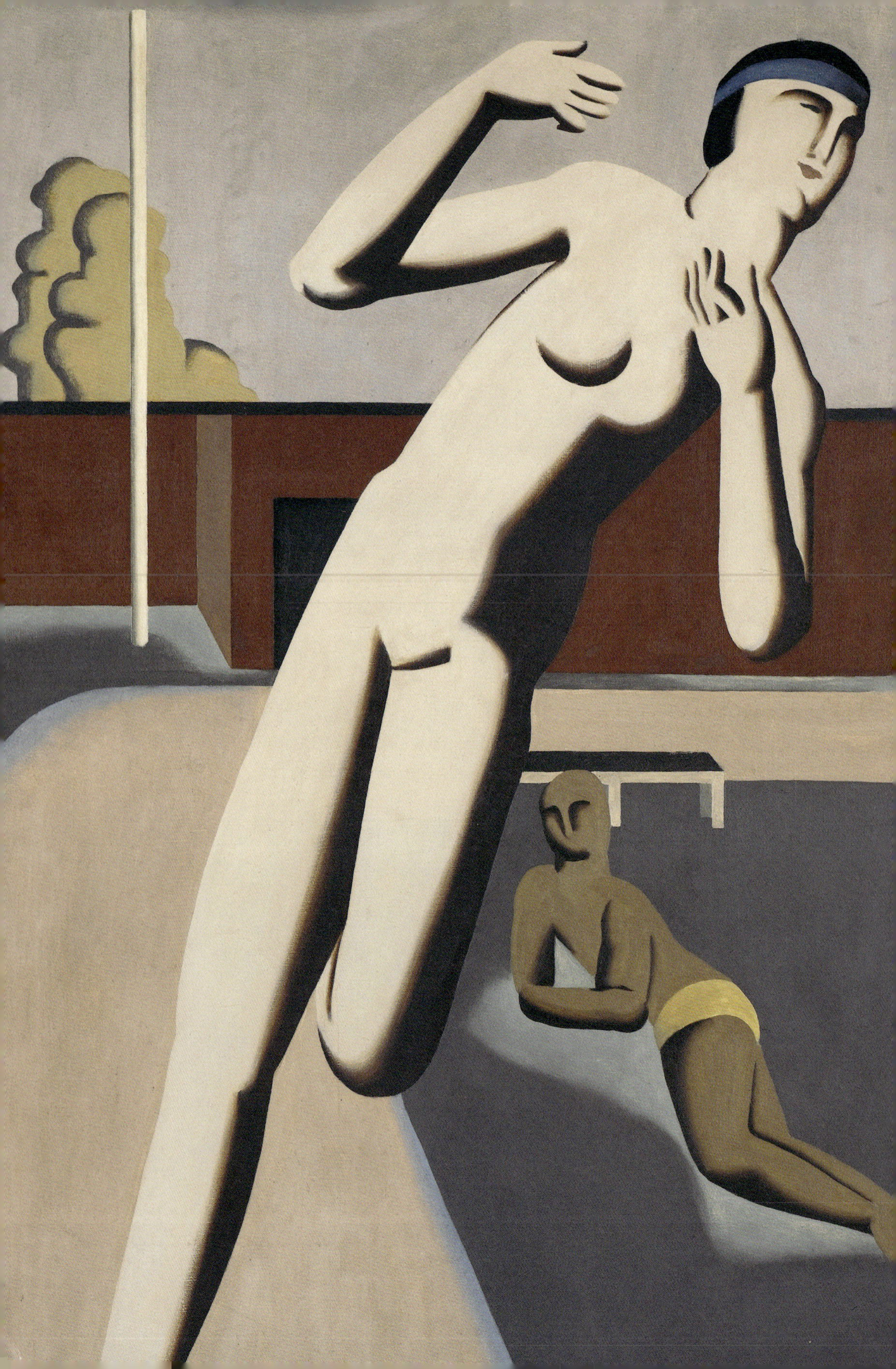

# 7

# SEX, GENDER, BODY IMAGE

CAROLINE VOUT

For the ancient Greeks, whom Pierre de Coubertin so admired, good looks and moral goodness went hand in hand. Working out in the gym and competing in the stadium turned men into admirable citizens. Exercise also demanded that they train or compete naked. Not even they could agree on the origins of this nakedness, but it distinguished them from non-Greeks, and inevitably made their best athletes objects of desire as well as paragons of virtue. Poets of the period draw attention to their straight limbs, strong hands, necks glistening in the sun; sculptors airbrush them into impossibly beautiful nudes that pander to the adult spectator (fig. 2).

The importance of these male nude statues, and of centuries of responding to them, cannot be overestimated, and not just for any Olympic revival, but for European ideals of masculinity more broadly. From at least the Renaissance, their shapely bodies have dictated what physical and ethical fitness looks like, and inspired desire and empathy. Although ancient Greek women normally neither took part in sport nor appeared unclothed in the sculptural record, images of Greek goddesses have done similar work for femininity, casting women as fabulously fertile Aphrodites/Venuses or as celibate and sporty Artemises/Dianas. Women in ancient Greece were prohibited from watching the Olympic Games, but that did not stop them oohing and aahing over male athletes in other contexts.[1] Pentathletes were especially admired: their varied training made them the complete package. But the dialogue between real bodies and bronze/marble bodies was most compelling. Writing under the Roman empire, one Greek author observes: 'when he stopped exercising and the crowd began to draw away, we studied him more closely. He was just like one of the most carefully wrought statues.'[2]

**64.** (cat. 133) Willi Baumeister (1889–1955)
*Female Runner II*, 1925 (detail)
(*Läuferin II*)
Oil on canvas, 119.5 × 80 cm
Staatsgalerie, Stuttgart (3042)

This runner is part of a series painted by Baumeister between 1922 and 1934, and could not be further from the rounded Venuses of classical antiquity, emphasising dynamism over desirability. Baumeister represented Germany in the Olympic Arts Competitions in 1928 and 1932, but did not win a medal.

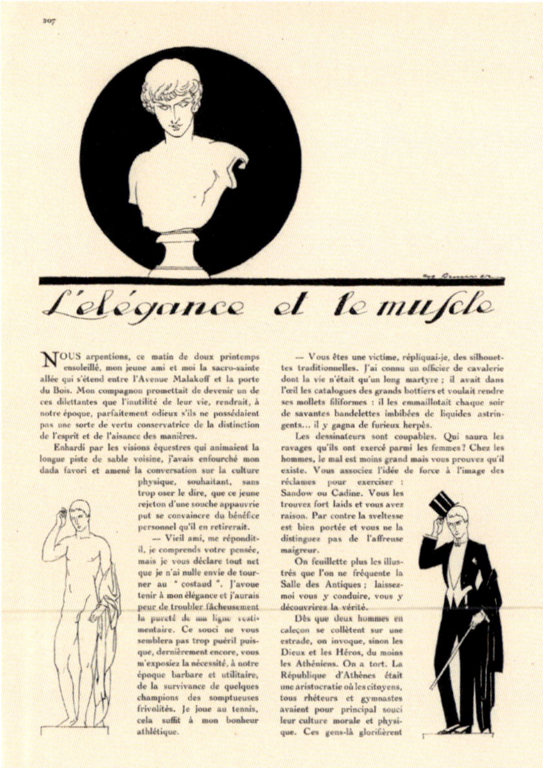
207

L'élégance et le muscle

Nous arpentions, ce matin de doux printemps ensoleillé, mon jeune ami et moi la sacro-sainte allée qui s'étend entre l'Avenue Malakoff et la porte du Bois. Mon compagnon promettait de devenir un de ces dilettantes que l'inutilité de leur vie, rendrait, à notre époque, parfaitement odieux s'ils ne possédaient pas une sorte de vertu conservatrice de la distinction de l'esprit et de l'aisance des manières.

Enhardi par les visions équestres qui animaient la longue piste de sable voisine, j'avais enfourché mon dada favori et amené la conversation sur la culture physique, souhaitant, sans trop oser le dire, que ce jeune rejeton d'une souche appauvrie put se convaincre du bénéfice personnel qu'il en retirerait.

— Vieil ami, me répondit-il, je comprends votre pensée, mais je vous déclare tout net que je n'ai nulle envie de tourner au " costaud ". J'avoue tenir à mon élégance et j'aurais peur de troubler fâcheusement la pureté de ma ligne vestimentaire. Ce souci ne vous semblera pas trop puéril puisque, dernièrement encore, vous m'exposiez la nécessité, à notre époque barbare et utilitaire, de la survivance de quelques champions des somptueuses frivolités. Je joue au tennis, cela suffit à mon bonheur athlétique.

— Vous êtes une victime, répliquai-je, des silhouettes traditionnelles. J'ai connu un officier de cavalerie dont la vie n'était qu'un long martyre ; il avait dans l'œil les catalogues des grands bottiers et voulait rendre ses mollets filiformes : il les emmaillotait chaque soir de savantes bandelettes imbibées de liquides astringents... il y gagna de furieux herpès.

Les dessinateurs sont coupables. Qui saura les ravages qu'ils ont exercé parmi les femmes? Chez les hommes, le mal est moins grand mais vous prouvez qu'il existe. Vous associez l'idée de force à l'image des réclames pour exerciser : Sandow ou Cadine. Vous les trouvez fort laids et vous avez raison. Par contre la sveltesse est bien portée et vous ne la distinguez pas de l'affreuse maigreur.

On feuillette plus les illustrés que l'on ne fréquente la Salle des Antiques ; laissez-moi vous y conduire, vous y découvrirez la vérité.

Dès que deux hommes en caleçon se collètent sur une estrade, on invoque, sinon les Dieux et les Héros, du moins les Athéniens. On a tort. La République d'Athènes était une aristocratie où les citoyens, tous rhéteurs et gymnastes avaient pour principal souci leur culture morale et physique. Ces gens-là glorifièrent

**65.** D. Strohl (active 1920s); Zyg Brunner (1878–1961), artist
'L'Élégance et le muscle',
*Monsieur* (September 1921), p. 207

An ancient bust of Antinous, young lover of the Roman emperor Hadrian, casts its sartorial gaze over a two-page article that advocates for the new athletic body by imagining the Louvre's *Marcellus* and other classical statues looking dapper in contemporary clothing.

Cut to 1921 (fig. 65), and an article on 'elegance and muscle' in French men's magazine *Monsieur* is still citing Aristotle on the beauty of the pentathlete, promoting the sleek yet strapping silhouettes of ancient Greek statue-types like Myron's *Diskobolos* (*Discus Thrower*) (fig. 76), and scoffing at girls who are keen to exercise, but worry what it will do to their arms and legs. 'Can you see Diana the huntress in a dance hall or the Venus de Milo in a Lanvin dress?' The male author replies in the affirmative – as he must, if he is to reconcile the latest art and fashion with the lifestyle changes that came of economic prosperity, transforming the bodies of both men and women through sport and leisure, and distinguishing them from their pre-war parents. With the mass dissemination of print media, especially photography, and the advent of commercial cinema, the relationship between art and life became more intense, and an audience more likely to fall for these bodies or want to follow in their footsteps. The growth of advertising further closed the gap between spectacle and spectator. One such advertisement joked, '*A Spalding suit won't teach you to swim* ... But it will make you feel like an Olympian champion!'[3]

Daydreaming was imperative. The deaths and disability directly caused by World War I, as well as the demands it had made on the women left behind, had inevitably thrown the vulnerabilities and capacities of male and female bodies into stark relief and highlighted the need for greater resilience, as well as for new realities. These hopes coalesced with the fight for female suffrage and the potential freedoms that came with that, even as the loss of young life and declining birthrate consolidated women's role at the heart of the nuclear family. It would take France until 1944 to give its women the vote, which seems late for a country that had, exceptionally, since 1791 not criminalised same sex relations between consenting adults in private. Not that homosexuality was not as stigmatised there as it was everywhere. But Paris's salons and nightclubs were home to a thriving gay and lesbian subculture, which meshed with the city's status as a centre of art, fashion, ballet and jazz to make it what we might call a queer capital. 1924 saw the publication of André Gide's dialogues on homosexuality and of the first homosexual review, *Inversions*, which lasted just over a year before obscenity laws did for it. Testing the limits was what much of this was about. Masculinity and femininity were being redrawn with optimism and anxiety and, especially in France, where in 1923 Greek and Latin were made compulsory in secondary schools, analogies with classical culture deployed to support a range of options.

## MODERN WOMAN

Seeing sporting bodies in the stadium, or up-close and personal in the cinema or in the sports sections of newspapers and in magazines played a major part in this culture and is inseparable from it. Women did not just watch sports and often violent sports (fig. 66), where they also, of course, eyed up one other, they competed in sports in ways that rivalled men, and even broke men's records. Which sports were suitable for women without compromising their femininity was a live question, asked particularly by those keen to maintain gender norms. But, as the 1924 Olympic gold medal winner in the tennis singles and doubles, Helen Wills, later put it: 'The ideas and, along with them, the inhibitions imposed upon us by the previous generation are being dispelled.'[4] Women like her were rewriting the script, and not just by their appearance on court, but by their influence beyond it. The control over their bodies that their training regimes and ground strokes demanded spoke to women taking control over their bodies in other ways. It is indicativative that the cover of the August 1924 issue of the American magazine *Physical Culture* carries a graphic of an athletic young woman, playing tennis on a beach in a close-fitting swimsuit, and the line 'Some Plain Facts About Birth Control' (fig. 67).

These new swimwear designs (cat. 123), like the men's in their worsted yarn and tank-top shape, along with shorter, lighter tennis dresses were as emancipatory as any ground or breast stroke. The August issue of the fashion magazine *Art-goût-beauté* carried an advertisement for the 'New Olympic Corset', 'without laces at the back, 'giving every freedom [*liberté*] of movement for all sports' as modelled in a drawing of a female tennis player, with modish bobbed hair and head band (fig. 68). On her tiptoes, her back arched, she resembles a dancing maenad (frenzied female follower of Greek god Dionysus), or Isadora Duncan dancing as a maenad, unencumbered by the constraints of society and

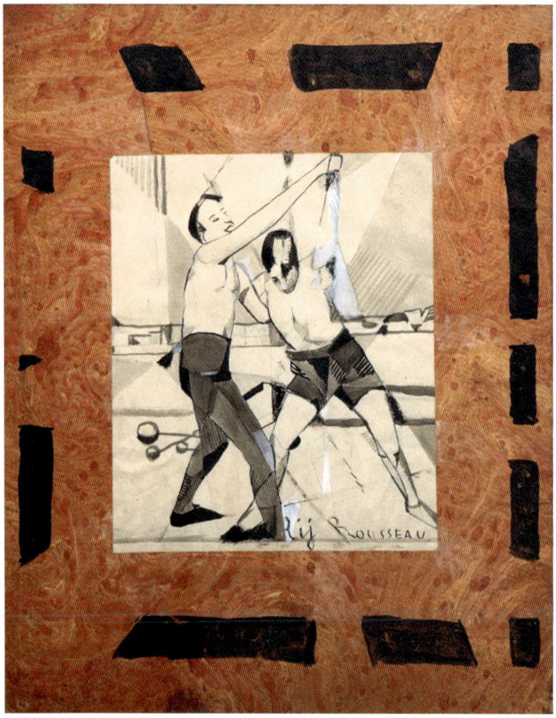

**66.** (cat. 126)
Jeanne Rij-Rousseau (1870–1956)
*The Wrestlers*, 1924
*(Les Lutteurs)*
Ink and gouache on paper,
60 × 48 cm
Private collection

French-born Rij-Rousseau lived and worked in Paris, where in the 1920s she produced a series of works inspired by sport. This work on paper is one of several to take wrestling as its theme, subjecting one of the most masculine of sports to a female gaze. She also produced a tapestry on the subject, a medium often associated with women.

principles of female decorum. At the height of the Games, *The New York Times* warned that the corset was doomed as the 'style sportive' of Coco Chanel and Jean Patou and the 'thousands of women athletes attracted to the games as participants or enthusiastic onlookers' rejected stays in favour of a more flexible future.[5]

Willi Baumeister's *Female Runner II* of 1925 captures something of this exhilaration and iconoclasm (fig. 64). The nude athlete is now an aerodynamic female who leaves the male spectator beached in the background. One of the many artists that Wills inspired, sculptor Charles Sargeant Jagger would describe her too as having 'a supple figure, long legs and small head' as in Baumeister's painting, together with 'the classic features of the ancient Venuses'.[6] Wills was widely regarded by her fans as a goddess, though more usually a Juno or Diana (see Cronin's essay). French girls were Venuses, claimed Patou; American ones Dianas, with 'muscles well-developed' and 'short bust'.[7] This is why, for his 1925 Paris fashion shows, he brought women from across the Atlantic to model his designs. Bodies were changing apace with ways of dressing and depicting the body: if there is a Venus in Baumeister's image, it reclines in yellow Speedos.

Baumeister's *Runner* is more androgynous than Wills: a better parallel might be the 'long limbed, lightly poised and slimly built' women that an athletic director from Yale University had already, in an article on 'What Sport Can Do *For* Girls' in the November

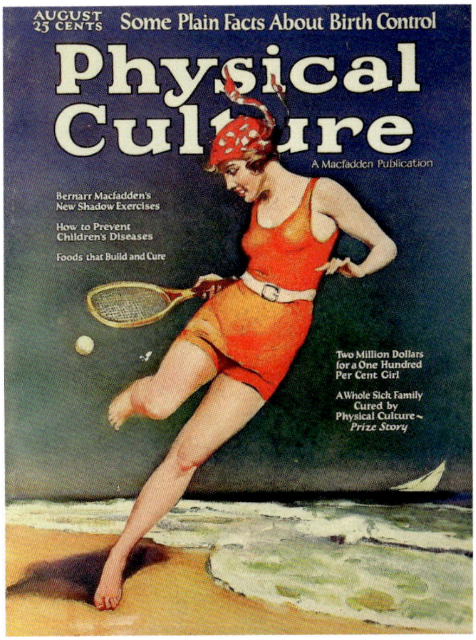


**67.** Macfadden Publications Inc. (1899–1944)
*Physical Culture*, vol. 52, no. 2 (August 1924), cover

*Physical Culture* was an American magazine on bodybuilding, health and fitness. Founded in 1899 by fitness guru Bernarr MacFadden, by the 1920s it had a circulation of 500,000. MacFadden met his third wife, swimmer Mary Williamson, when she won his competition to find the 'most perfect specimen of English womanhood'. She would, during divorce proceedings, describe his methods as 'crackpot'.

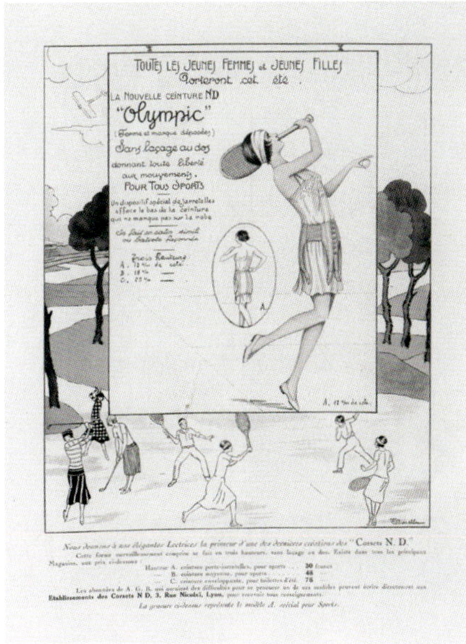


**68.** Unidentified artist, signed; Éditions d'art: Paris, publisher
Advertisement for the new 'Olympic' corset, *Art-Taste-Beauty: Pages of Feminine Elegance (Art-goût-beauté: feuillets d'élégance féminine)*, no. 48 (15 August 1924), np

The advertisement first appeared just after the Paris Olympics, in the August edition of the monthly French fashion magazine, *Art-Gout-Beauté*. The corset, available from a company in Lyon, might be said to facilitate participation in all sports, but the landscape surrounding the central image shows only the 'feminine' sports of golf and tennis.

1922 issue of the American monthly *Woman's Home Companion*, termed 'the third sex'.[8] Within a few years of Baumeister painting this picture, French surrealist Claude Cahun was producing her *I am in Training; Don't Kiss Me* photographs – self-portraits of the artist in a nude bodystocking and boxing shorts, complete with barbell.[9] Her experiments with boxing here and elsewhere remind us of contemporary French sportswoman Violette Morris, who regularly sparred with men and won gold in the discus and shot put in London's 1924 Women's Olympiad (fig. 69 and cat. 130). Smoking heavily at Montmartre's Lesbian nightclub, Le Monocle, she took the 'garçonne look' made famous by Coco Chanel to extremes. She played into the hands of those who still had a problem

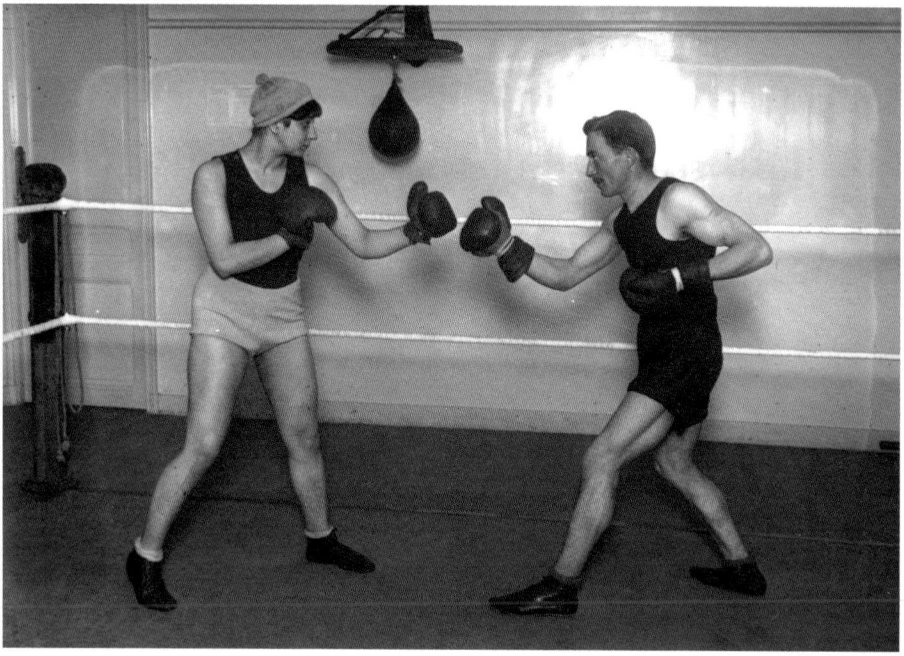

**69.** (cat. 129) Agence Rol photographic agency (founded 1904)
Violette Morris (1893–1944) boxing with a sparring partner, 1913
Glass-plate negative
Bibliothèque nationale de France, Paris (Rol, 33393)

'I am a woman and do not have to answer to anyone for what I do', appealed Morris in 1930 as she fought her exclusion from the French Federation of Women's Sport (Fédération Française du Sport Féminin). Her doing it 'her way' was already international news – on 18 March 1929, New York's *Time* magazine reported: 'Because Nature had not shaped her conveniently for the accomplishment of her athletic ambitions, she last week horrified Paris by having a surgeon remove both her breasts.'

with women participating in competitive sports and had her license to participate in the 1928 Olympics revoked (one of the arguments against her being that she wore trousers in public without applying for the requisite permit from the Paris Préfecture de Police that allowed a woman to dress as a man). Undeterred, in 1929, she elected to have a double mastectomy.[10]

Less controversial, but just as pioneering, was Switzerland's Ella Maillart (cat. 131), the only female competitor in the 1924 Olympic monotype sailing and an international skier and hockey player. Maillart became a photographer and travel writer, driving to Kabul with her boyish, bisexual friend, Annemarie Schwarzenbach. Her account of the trip is as much about being a woman in a modern world as it is about the unfamiliarity of Afghanistan. There, she muses, 'no more high-heeled sluts in short frocks: you've come to the country where women are not seen'.[11]

## WOMAN AS SEX-SYMBOL

'A woman was never more under observation that when on a court', claimed Wills's fiercest opponent and rival, French player Suzanne Lenglen.[12] Lenglen milked the attention for all it was worth, arriving at matches in make-up, silk, ermine and jewellery, and sipping alcohol at changeovers. Her extraordinary style and agility were visually appealing: the bandeaux in our images are a nod to her signature look (fig. 70). Even the American press responded enthusiastically: Lenglen was 'the best-beloved young nymph that ever volleyed the white ball out of her opponent's reach', with 'the figure of those Spartan girl athletes we still see in marble across the ages'. She might serve with the 'male athlete's power of "throw" (a movement supposed to be denied to woman's anatomy)' but she was neither overly masculine nor menacing because of it. In contrast, she made people fall in love. She is similar to the god of love, Eros/Cupid: 'Her volley is not a timid push, but an arrow from the bow. And an arrow from the bow is Suzanne herself.'[13]

Truth was that spectatorship and consumerism combined to turn even the most trailblazing player into a sex object, not advancing the feminist cause but threatening to set it back 50 years. In his entry to the 1924 Olympic Arts Competition, essayist, poet and novelist Henry de Montherlant conjures a female athlete readying herself for her run: 'I particularly recall the moment when she sat down on the grass and the masseur

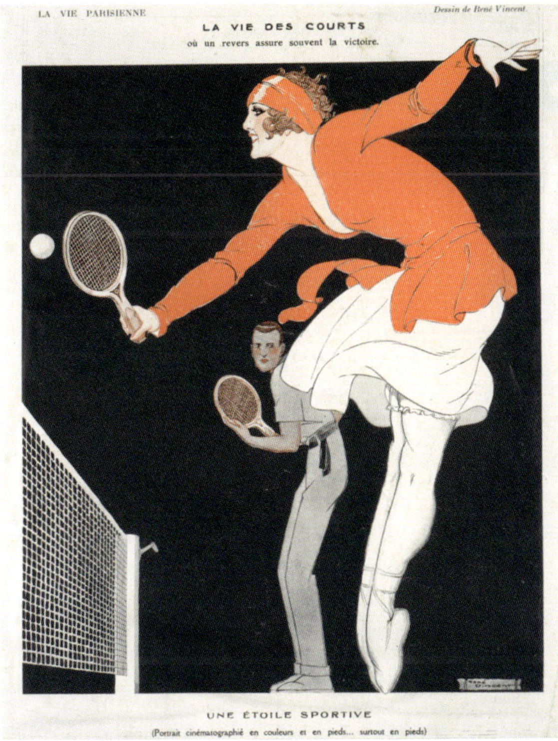


**70.** (cat. 139) René Vincent (1879–1936)
*'Life on the Courts ... A Sports Star'*, *La Vie Parisienne*, vol. 59, no. 23 (4 June 1921), loose sheet
(*'La Vie des Courts ... Une Étoile Sportive'*)
Colour lithography on paper, 33 × 24 cm
Private collection

Vincent's portrait of a 'sports star' captures the frisson of seeing female tennis players like Suzanne Lenglen dance around the court. A glimpse of underwear leaves her male partner distracted and blushing.

… massaged her legs … And while the artist's hands climbed high, quivering like flames, very high, until they went under the wide openings of her shorts, I watched the young girl's face with sneaky and intense attention … but … her gaze remained fixed in the distance'.[14] In art too, a player like Wills was reduced to her skirt, visor, and breasts or red lips. The exploitation of women's bodies is of a piece with this essentialism.

Sport made men men, but what it made women was still up for grabs: there was no sudden gender or beauty revolution. Wills may have been a goddess, but, after a screen-test in 1927, she was still considered too heavy for Hollywood. Conversely, the women's rackets that she and her fellow players endorsed boasted of smaller handles 'to fit a woman's hand'.[15] It was a similar story in swimming: a feature in *Current Opinion* 1922 shows a 17-year-old Johnny Weissmuller about to dive, eyes on the prize, and, next to him, three-times gold medal winning swimmer at the 1920 Olympics, Ethelda Bleibtrey, posing, hand on hip, in her swimsuit in the sunshine, staring back at the (we assume, male) photographer like a beauty pageant queen. His caption is, 'The Fastest Swimmer in the World'; hers, 'A Modern Mermaid with No Rival'.[16]

## DIVERGENT MASCULINITIES

By 1929, after winning five gold medals of his own, Weissmuller would be the face and body of the BVD brand of swimwear (fig. 38), and the *Los Angeles Times* would refer to male surfers as 'mermen'.[17] Spectatorship and consumerism conspired to make objects of the gaze out of male athletes too. Young male athletes had been the subject of some of the earliest photography: in 1843, Edinbugh-based duo David Octavius Hill and Robert Adamson capitalised on the outdoor setting demanded by the calotype technique to capture a handsome Real Tennis or racket player in slim fitting shirt and trousers poised as if mid-action. In the years that followed, the same magazine that informed its readers about birth control offered images of muscular men, lit like classical statues. Another magazine carried photos of the winners of the 'Most Beautiful Athlete in Europe' competition, third place going to French weightlifter André Rolet, who had competed in the 1924 Olympics and now entertained as a 'vaudeville tableau-poser'.[18]

Both male and female audiences swooned. But the Greek heritage that the Olympic and physical-culture movements channelled was renowned for the premium it put on male-male desire in particular. Ancient Athens viewed older men's courtship of adolescent males as a normal and educative element in the latter's transition to manhood and encouraged it in its celebration of athletic male bodies in poetry, philosophical dialogue, sculpture and pot painting. In the eighteenth century, the influential writings of Johann Joachim Winckelmann turned this desire into art historical appreciation, locating these bodies in a cloud-free utopia in which men could love men without stigma. By the end of the nineteenth century, 'Greek love' had become code for the love that dared not speak its name. And the word 'homosexuality' had entered the vocabulary, configuring this love as an identity and encouraging a certain kind of self-imaging.

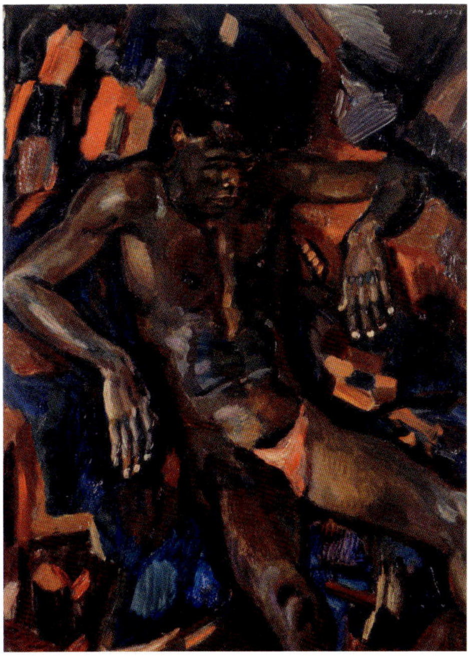

**71.** (cat. 128) Jan Sluijters (1881–1957)
*The Boxer Rolf*, c. 1918
(*Der bokser Rolf*)
Oil on canvas, 143 × 104.5 cm
Het Noordbrabants Museum,
's-Hertogenbosch (7762)

Sluijter's boxer sits in the corner of the ring, giving the artist opportunity to zoom in on his body. As the protagonist slumps, exhausted, it is the viewers of the painting who are encouraged to be active as their gaze ranges over his body.

All of this ensured that images of male athletes had homoerotic appeal long before the 1950s American magazine, *Physique Pictorial*, aimed its classically posed bodybuilders at a gay readership. One just has to look at Robert Tait McKenzie's *Athlete*, flexing his muscles and courting admiring glances by avoiding the audience's gaze and looking down to the ground (fig. 55), or the similarly contemplative photographs of Weissmuller, taken by George Hurrell after the swimmer's signing as Tarzan in 1932, his chest again bare and his skin shining like bronze (fig. 75). Both deploy features familiar from classical statuary to activate a tradition of male viewing of male bodies that are as passive as they are active – compatible, as the *Monsieur*'s article on 'elegance and muscle' shows – with the masculinity of dandified bohemianism. Small wonder that French activist Daniel Guérin (1904–88) should confess in his autobiography of delighting in, and sometimes masturbating over, the sports pages of the daily papers, and their pictures of 'beautiful Scandinavian athletes with fair hair and long muscles'.[19]

For all that participation in sport was generally seen as a safe outlet for men's energy and fortifying preparation for fatherhood, some sports (rugby, football and boxing) were considered manlier than others, and excessive training was considered to be as disfiguring as spectatorship might be sordid. Like ancient Rome's gladiators, boxers were a 'bit of rough', often from society's working classes (see Holt's chapter), whose violence in the ring fuelled the sense of illicit eroticism. Several of the professional boxers of the period were also Black (fig. 71),[20] and in a colonial context that rendered them 'the

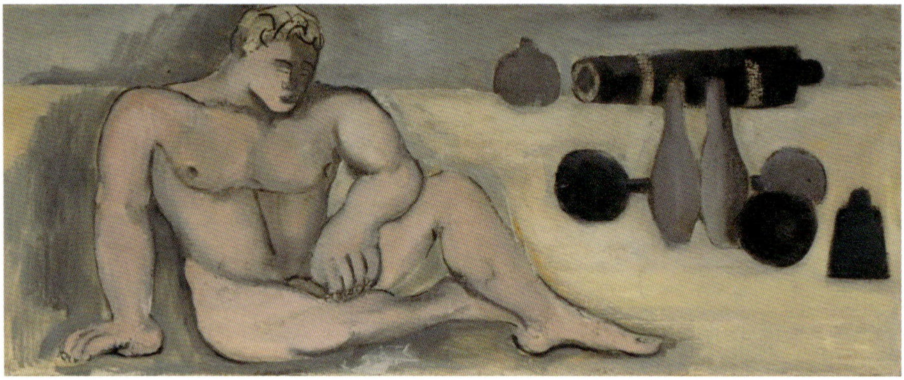

**72.** (cat. 132) Marsden Hartley (1877–1943)
*The Strong Man*, c. 1923
Oil on canvas, 33 × 81.9 cm
The Vilcek Foundation, New York
(2006.03.05)

Hartley was drawn not to the French art scene but to Germany, and hid his homosexuality from almost everyone. *The Strong Man* is one of several muscular male figures that he painted in the 1920s and references both the gymnasium and the circus. It raises the question of what a picture must look like in a period of repression to be read as alluding to homosexuality.

subjected other', their bodies all too readily fetishised as hypersexual. In Paris in 1924, Black athletes did win medals in other events, challenging normative masculinities that had for centuries – supported by classical marble statues, stripped of their original pigment – bound the moral goodness associated with male fitness to whiteness.

What a healthy man was was up for grabs also. The radical redefinition of women's role in society saw to that and reimagined the male sporting body accordingly. At one end of the spectrum, 1923 saw female impersonator 'Barbette' perform high-wire and trapeze acts in drag to packed cabaret halls in Paris, only to reveal an exaggerated masculinity in the finale. Jean Cocteau was not alone in being enchanted. At the other end of the spectrum is Marsden Hartley's painting of the same year, *The Strong Man* (fig. 72). Is he a push-over like the skittles next to him or as pugnacious as the cannon behind? Hartley was insistent that his art owed little to classical tradition, yet his weightlifter poses like *The Dying Gaul* (fig. 73), an ancient statue identified in the Renaissance as a gladiator but later recognised as a Galatian Celtic chieftan and Greek and Roman enemy. Whatever his and Barbette's bodies were, they too were 'other'.

*

Today, sport is still a vehicle for debating and shaping sex and gender. From the outset, the Paris 2024 Olympics promised an equal number of men and women athletes and the same number of events for each. They boasted of being a more diverse and inclusive

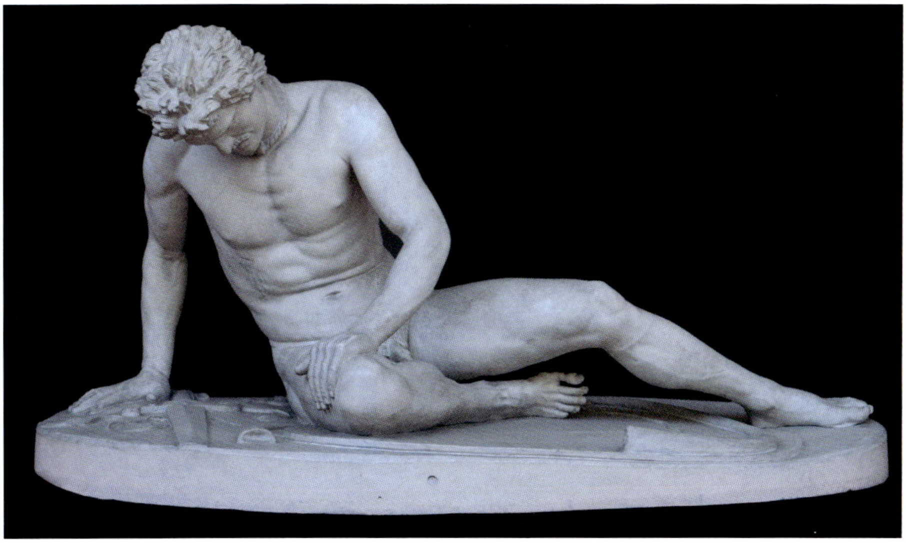

**73.** Domenico Brucciani and Co., London (1841–1900s); after unrecorded Roman maker (Capitoline Museum, Stanza del Gladiatore 1, Rome, *c*. 60–40 BCE or later, marble); after unknown maker (probably bronze, now lost, *c*. 230–220 BCE) *The Dying Gaul*, *c*. 1884

Plaster, 73 × 93 cm
Museum of Classical Archaeology, Cambridge (377)

Famous since the Renaissance, *The Dying Gaul* is a study in an athletic body spent. Already *The Penny Magazine* of 12 January 1833 had described its subject as a 'man of toil', casting him as a working-class hero. Ancient author Diodorus Siculus describes the Galatian enemy as 'tall of body, with rippling white flesh' and blond hair.

Games, advertising an official slogan, *Ouvrons grand les jeux* (Games wide open), a riff on *ouvrons grand les yeux* (eyes wide open), and a partnership with LGBTIQ+ hub Pride House. And then there were the headlines – on French sprinter, Halba Diouf, who was training to compete in the 200m, only for World Athletics to ban transgender women athletes from taking part; on whether tennis player and ambassador for French fashion house, Dior, Emma Raducanu, would or would not make the British team; on her 'incredible 12-month body transformation' from 'slim' and 'slender' to 'leaner' and 'muscular'.[21] Classical culture too continued to be relevant: the twin mascots for the 2024 Summer and Paralympic Games are shaped like conical Phrygian caps that signalled liberation in antiquity and again in the French Revolution. Yet even these have been received in sexual terms, each of them likened to a 'clitoris in trainers', a welcome departure from the phallic Eiffel Tower.[22] Not that its shadow can be escaped. As Olympic sporting events in venues across Paris and beyond interact with Parisian culture, its art and its life, what we think about our bodies is again likely transformed.

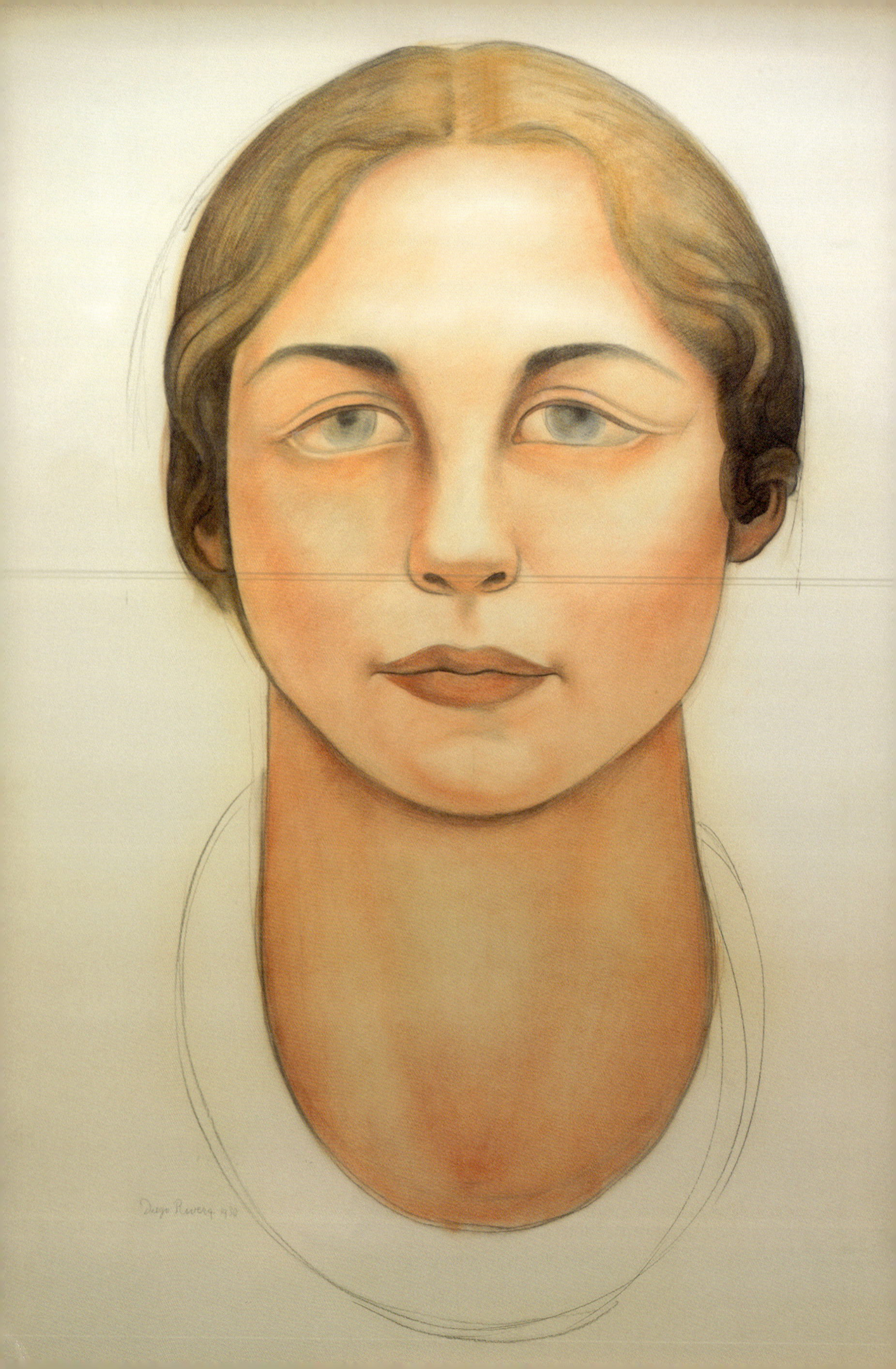
Diego Rivera

# 8

# THE OLYMPICS, NATIONHOOD AND THE RISE OF FASCISM

DAPHNÉ BOLZ

Pierre de Coubertin's Olympic vision was typical of the late nineteenth century: it was of a piece with the national identities then emerging in Europe and characterised by a marked universalism. In one sense, it was a patriotic vision. Coubertin's initial project had been to integrate sport into French schools, drawing on the culture of the British Empire he so admired to reinvigorate the nation's youth. In another sense, it was shaped by his status as a member of a privileged European elite, who were used to travelling abroad, had world-wide connections and affiliations and spoke several languages. Combining the celebration of men's physical education with praise of nationhood in a harmonious international setting, therefore, came naturally to Coubertin and presented him with no contradiction. As the Olympics developed, however, and sport became a showcase of diplomatic tensions, the essential balance between the national and the international became increasingly hard to manage. Slowly but surely, Coubertin's understanding of nationalism as a force for good turned into divisive nationalist sentiment.[1] Paris 1924 is important in this regard, on the cusp of a period in the late 1920s and 1930s when the politicisation of sport at the Olympics was magnified by Fascist regimes.

## NATIONAL IDENTITY

Even in their earliest incarnations (see Introduction), the modern Olympics were no stranger to nationalist fervour. Both the use of basic symbolism such as anthems and flags and the exercise of sporting judgment – at a time when international federations were only just forming to agree the rules of competition – stoked underlying tensions. In

**74.** (cat. 164) Diego Rivera (1886–1957)
*Mrs Helen Wills Moody*, 1930
Pastel on paper, 227.7 × 160.2 cm
Tate, London (T00200)

When Mexican artist Diego Rivera painted his *Allegory of California* on the wall of the San Francisco Stock Exchange, local girl Helen Wills inspired the central figure. She was at the same time the 'nearest living perfection of the old Greek ideal' and 'an ideal American beauty'. This pastel gives some sense of the mural's style and scale. It turns the 'girl next door' into a goddess.

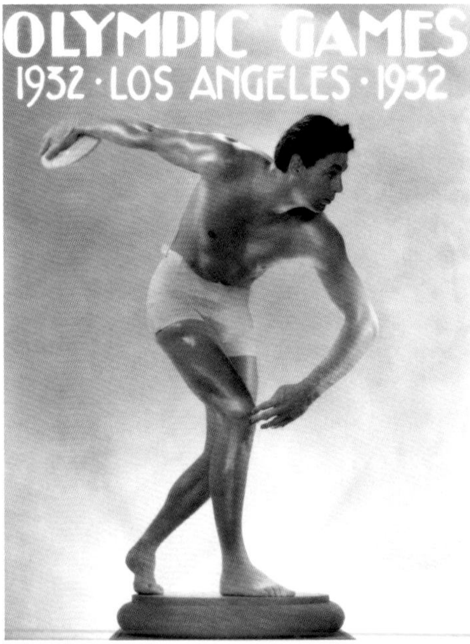


**75.** (cat. 166) George Hurrell (1904–1992) Actor and Olympian Johnny Weissmuller poses as the *Discus Thrower* (*Diskobolos*) for the 1932 Los Angeles Olympic Games, 1932

Black and white photograph

In 1932, glistening in baby oil to resemble the bronze original, Weissmuller posed as the ancient Greek *Diskobolos*. The photo is part of a shoot for American media company Metro-Goldwyn-Mayer Studios, Inc., who had just signed the Olympic swimmer to play Tarzan. By stepping into ancient Greek shoes, Weissmuller becomes the ideal man.

London in 1908, the Finns were reluctant to walk behind the flag of the Russian Empire and the Americans caused upset by refusing to dip theirs before the British monarch; the Americans continued to rile the hosts over the question of Irish Home Rule and took badly the decisions of the sporting jury. It was at a closing banquet that Coubertin cited the now famous dictum that the important thing was not the winning but the taking part.

Four years later, at the widely acclaimed Games in Stockholm, a Finnish anthem was 'mistakenly' played during the Opening Ceremony, and the decisions of the sporting jury were deemed so controversial throughout that the International Olympic Committee (IOC) launched an inquiry afterwards. After World War I, the return of peace did little to prevent the Games becoming a place to affirm nationalist feelings. Not long after the hostilities, it was clear that the Olympic ranking of nations was problematic and something that Olympic leaders had to mitigate. At the Olympic Congress in Lausanne in 1921,

**76.** (cat. 165) Domenico Brucciani and Co., London (1841–1900s); after unrecorded Roman maker (British Museum, London, Townley Collection, 117–38 CE, marble); after Myron (bronze, now lost, *c*. 460–450 BCE)
Plaster cast of *Discus Thrower* (*Diskobolos*), *c*. 1880

Plaster, metal, paint, 176 × 58 × 115 cm
Museum of Classical Archaeology, Cambridge (118)

The *Diskobolos* was made in bronze in ancient Greece, where it stood in a sanctuary as evidence of man's god-given beauty. That bronze was melted down, but not before the Romans copied it for gyms, gardens and bathhouses. The British Museum version that this plaster cast reproduces was wrongly restored in the eighteenth century, but quickly became iconic.

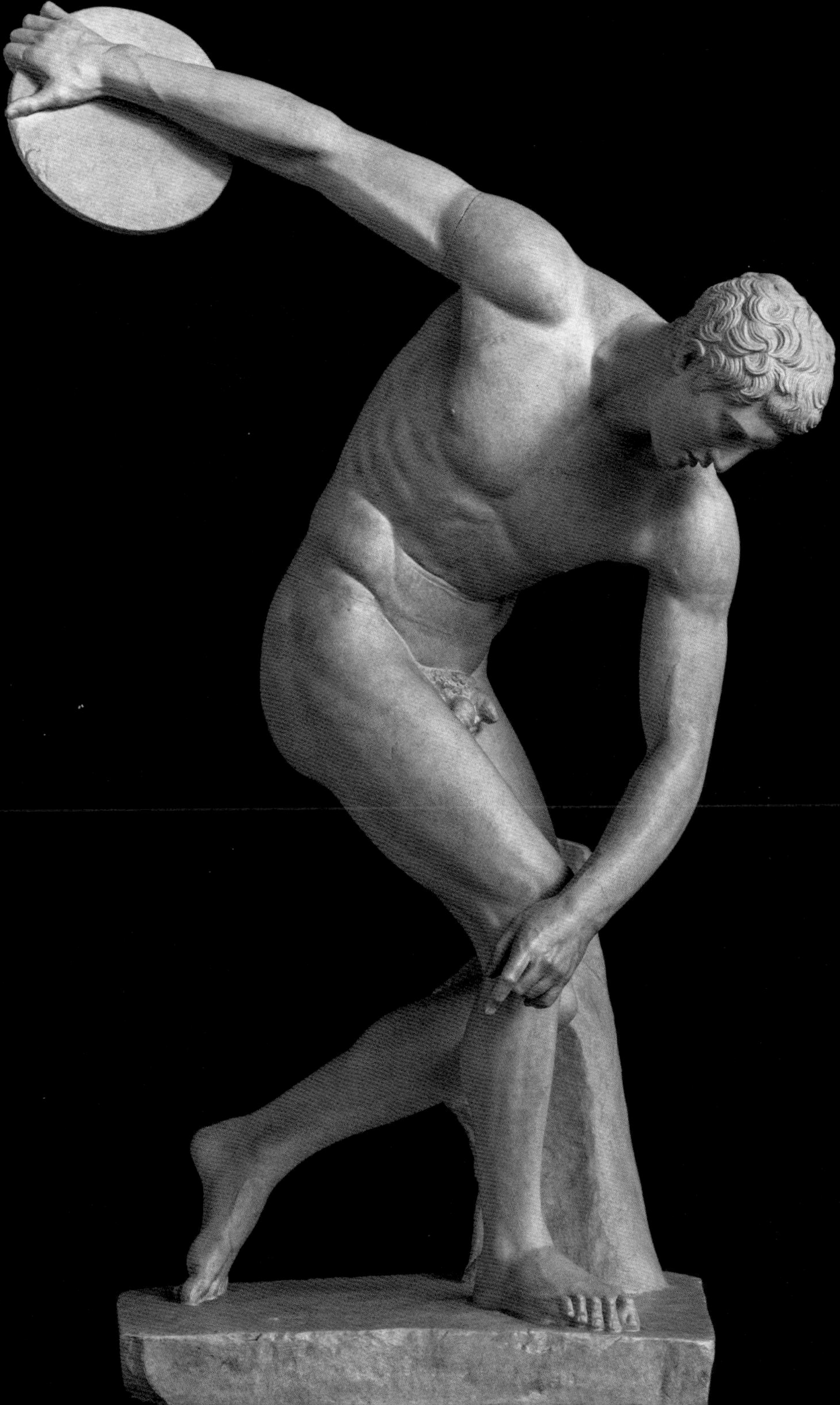

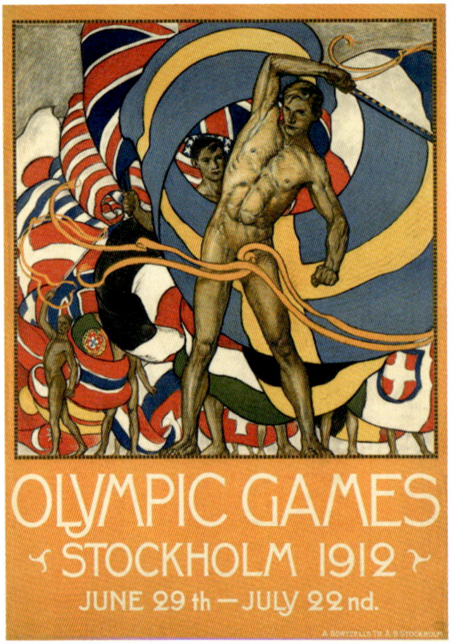


**77.** Olle (Gustaf Olof) Hjortzberg (1872–1959), artist; A. Börtzells Tr. A.B., Stockholm, printer
Official poster for the 1912 Stockholm Olympic Games, 1912
Colour lithography on paper, 75.5 × 107 cm

Before the creation of the five Olympic rings motif in 1914, Olympic posters had to find other ways of advertising the international dimension of the event. This one, for Stockholm 1912, uses a variety of flags from countries in various continents. The athletes' swirling of these flags introduces dynamism and drama.

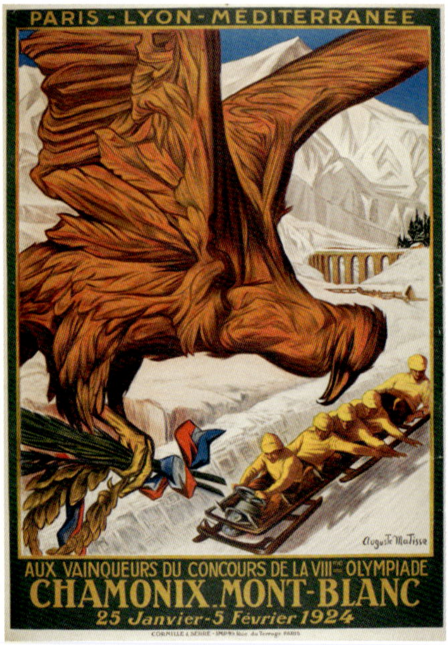


**78.** (cat. 12) Auguste Matisse (1866–1931), artist; Cornille & Serre, Paris (active 1910–26), printer
*To the Winners of the Eighth Olympiad*, poster, *c.* 1924
(*Aux Vainqueurs du Concours de la* VIIIme *Olympiade*)
Colour lithography on paper, 105.5 × 75 cm
Victoria and Albert Museum, London (E.23-1926)

France hosted the 1924 Summer and Winter Olympics. This advertising poster for the Paris-Lyon-Méditerranée rail company commemorates the 'victors of the eighth Olympic competition' and the setting of the Winter Games in Chamonix-Mont-Blanc. The eagle conjures not ancient Greece but Rome and the ideas of imperial power which that brings with it. The laurel in its talons is tied with the French flag.

the IOC outlawed the tables. But as Allan Guttmann stressed, despite this 'stand against the publication of point tables, which they rightly saw as an invitation to chauvinism ... it was impossible to prevent the outbreaks of nationalism at the Games'.[2] The tables, popular with the press and public, continued informally and were as widely read as ever.

Sports of all kinds were becoming increasingly popular in the 1920s. The period saw the emergence of an ideal trained body, promoted by, and disseminated in, photography and film. The model for this new aesthetics were mostly sportsmen – and sometimes sportswomen, some of whom participated in the Olympics. US swimmer Johnny

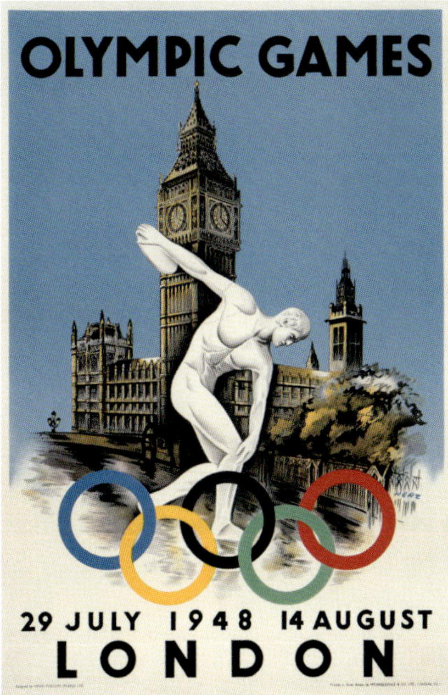


**79.** (cat. 168) Walter Herz (1909–1965), artist; McCorquodale & Co. Ltd (1846–1937), printer
Official poster for the 1948 London Olympic Games, 1948
Colour lithography on paper, 100.5 × 62.5 cm
Olympic Museum Collections, Lausanne (81722)

Like most Olympic posters of the late nineteenth to the early twentieth century, the 1948 poster for the London Games integrates sports elements such as the Greek *Diskobolos* statue with national emblems like the Houses of Parliament in London. They are bound by the symbol of universality that is the Olympic rings.

Weissmuller, who won four medals in Paris, exemplifies this look (figs 75 and 76). His muscular body proved perfect for playing the rope-swinging lord of the jungle, Tarzan, in no fewer than eight films (see Michelakis's chapter). The modern woman, meanwhile, with an unprecedented mix of elegance and strength, is perhaps best represented by his teammate, tennis player Helen Wills (fig. 74), or by her French rival, Suzanne Lenglen, who, having won the women's singles at the 1920 Olympics and at Wimbledon five years running, was set to add to her trophy cabinet until injury forced her to withdraw from Paris (fig. 70).

Sport stars like these were representatives of national systems that clashed at an Olympics that was now – thanks to mass media – a global arena. Organising the Games and thus attempting to own this global arena became an attractive means of promoting a country's image and authority. This is exemplified by Olympic posters of the period (figs 7, 77, 78 and 79; cat. 13), which emphasise national landmarks or flags as much as they do sporting activity. Numerous cities began bidding to host: for the 1924 Games, interest was expressed by no less than 13 cities – Amsterdam, Havana, Rome, Atlantic City, Barcelona, Boston, Budapest, Halifax, Lyon, Los Angeles, Paris, Prague and Reims. As a new showcase of 'soft power', the Olympics seemed just the place to affirm one's potential or even one's existence on the international scene. Among the 44 nations represented in Paris, one could note, for instance, the first autonomous participation of Ireland and the presence of Hungary, which had been excluded from the 1920 Games and attended for the first time as an independent nation. Alongside Austria, Bulgaria and Turkey were Lithuania, Latvia and Poland, as well as the more distant countries of Ecuador, the Philippines and Uruguay (see Huddleston's chapter). All five continents were represented, demonstrating the strength and scope of the Olympic movement. The Olympic Arts Competition, carefully staged in France, the cultural capital of the world, had similarly vast horizons, featuring 24 countries (see Osgood's chapter). The question now was how to keep these countries united in the Olympic spirit, despite their competing star athletes, traditions and political agendas.

## A NEW WORLD ORDER

A series of sporting scandals shows how difficult that task proved to be for the organisers of the 1924 Games. Crucially for the present argument, each of these included some nationalist element. Even before the splendour of the Opening Ceremony (see Introduction), there were major ructions at the rugby tournament, which had kicked off the Games two months earlier. Having come bottom in that season's Five Nations Championship, the French were favourites to win gold in their national team sport after England, Scotland, Ireland and Wales declined to enter. The tournament was contested by only two other countries, the inexperienced Romania and the US, but this did not incline the hosts to be hospitable.[3] The US team was hassled at their port of entry, denied suitable training facilities and, on one occasion, robbed of their clothes. When they comprehensively defeated France in the final, the violent encounter on the pitch spilled over into the stands, with the winners requiring a police escort to reach the safety of the changing rooms. The hosts had been denied the first gold at their own Olympics, but their disgruntlement can be read as something more profound: the Allied victory had revealed the important contribution of the Americans, who were beginning what would turn out to be a long and influential presence on the global stage (see Cronin's chapter). In the aftermath of the war, France and the US had already clashed over the terms of the peace treaty. The Americans' victory in a sport that was not really their own signalled something bigger than sport itself – and it went down very badly with the home crowd.

The rugby tournament was a taster of what was to come once the Games proper got underway. Anticipating problems, the IOC had created a Jury of Honour in 1923 with the responsibility for settling the most serious disputes concerning Olympic regulations, the ultimate aim being to 'ensure an atmosphere of fair-play throughout the event'.[4] It is no surprise that the Jury had to deal with cases concerning sportsmen or officials from powerful countries like the United Kingdom, Argentina, Austria, Belgium, France, Hungary, Italy and the US.[5] The regulations, which were not always detailed, often led to grey areas and protests. The tensions over sports issues were not minor, as they implied strong nationalist feelings and ultimately jeopardised the future of the Games. A key case in point came with boxing (fig. 80), the three-round form of which relied on transparent and reliable judging. This was felt to be lacking; controversy followed controversy, leading to ringside shenanigans bordering on rioting.[6] The British were

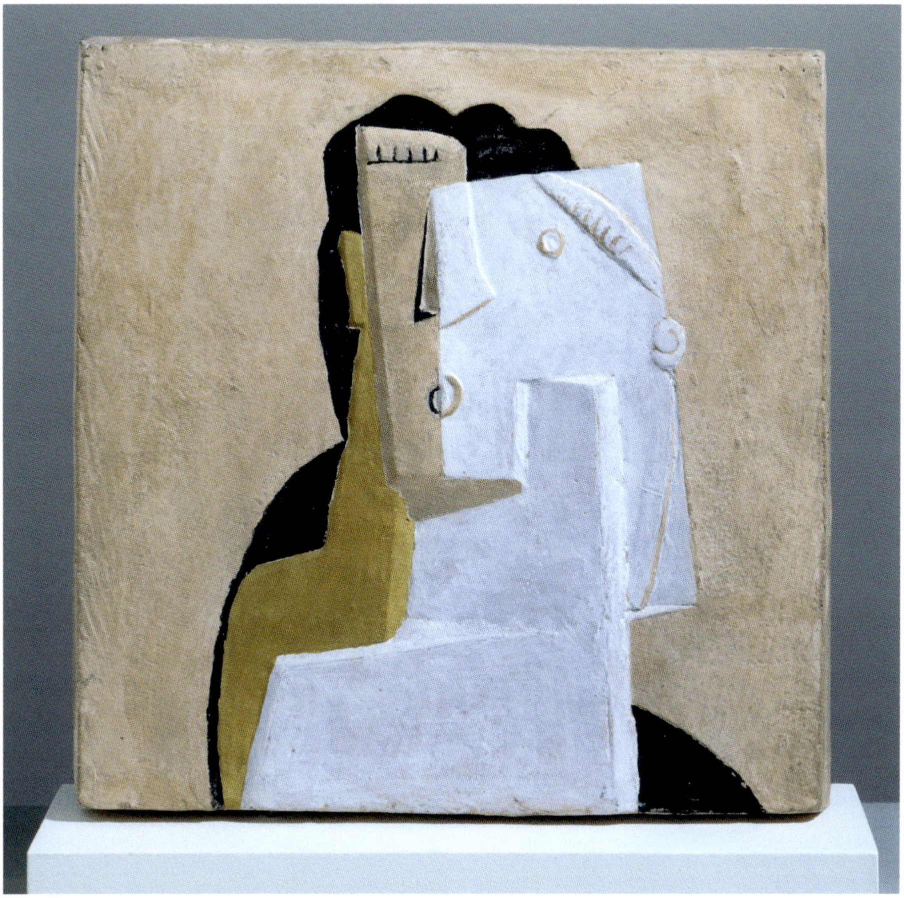

**80.** (cat. 117) Henri Laurens (1885–1954)
*Head of a Boxer*, sculpted 1920, cast 1921
(*Tête de boxeur*)
Painted terracotta, 24.2 × 23.8 × 2.5 cm
Tate, London (T06833)

Paris-born Laurens's painting of a boxer is inspired by his regular attendance at fights. The breaking down of the boxer's head into various planes is typical of French Cubism and works with the disjointed nose to conjure the breaks and cuts often inflicted in the ring.

particularly critical of the refereeing and claimed it was unlikely their boxers would ever participate in the Games again.

In the British press, the 1924 scandals led to fierce criticism of the Olympic movement generally. Despite some famous victories on the track, the British clearly sensed they were losing ground to the highly trained Americans and new emerging 'sports countries' like Italy (see Holt's chapter). Such sports-related tensions expressed the jockeying for position of these countries, and explain why the British and American media were the first to emphasise how much the Paris Games 'exacerbate international bitternesses instead of soothing them'.[7] This sentiment, first expressed in the London *Times*, was quickly taken up by *The New York Times*, which claimed: 'LONDON SEES END OF OLYMPIC GAMES: *The Times* Says World Peace is too Precious to be Upset by Athletic Outbreaks.'[8] While these headlines were clearly exaggerated, they reveal the underlying national component in the disputes among sportsmen and spectators alike. They also speak to the reshaping of the world order in light of the US alliance as a new power to a United Kingdom exposed to fresh diplomatic challenges.

The exclusion of German athletes from the 1920 and 1924 Games also jeopardised the development of the Olympic movement. Coubertin himself was aware of this risk but could not oppose the stance of the French government, which refused to invite its former enemy. This attitude led to significant criticism from the German press, which did not hesitate to highlight the problems that arose in Paris.[9] Moreover, German sports functionaries scrutinised individual performances, comparing them to current German standards and inviting world-class athletes visiting Europe to come and compete against their own in front of German crowds. Much to the delight of spectators, the home athletes often fared well against the opponents they might have beaten had they been allowed to compete in Paris.

## SURVIVAL AND EXPANSION

Despite 1924 being the largest Games with the broadest media following to that point, the Olympics were still not fully established as the world's premier sporting event. As sport developed apace in the 1920s, its forms and forums splintered, with individual sports finding unique routes to mass spectatorship and profit. From the mid 1920s, neither tennis nor football could square themselves with the IOC's increasingly stringent amateur regulations and had lucrative ambitions of their own to pursue. 1924 would be the last Olympic tennis tournament until 1988, the Grand Slams picking up momentum; and in 1930, the international football federation (FIFA) created the World Cup, which rapidly established itself as the world's premier football tournament (see Huddleston's chapter). In tandem, large groups with rival ideologies were entering the field. In 1925, on the back of a small-scale, locally organised counter-Olympiad in Paris, the Socialist Workers' Sport International organised the first official Workers' Games in Frankfurt. The aim was to offer an alternative to the 'bourgeois' system proposed by Coubertin's Olympic movement, which was chaired exclusively by, and representative of, the elite. The event was very well organised and allowed for high-quality sport: some 3,000 athletes competed, 450,000 attended, and there was even an official film. A further, long-term threat to the Olympics was the Soviet Union, which never expressed an interest in competing until conditions changed in the Cold War, and they participated, with outstanding results, from the Helsinki 1952 Games onwards. The USSR teams had their own sports system, which was both keen to expand internationally and based on the idea of international friendship, but free of the nationalism that characterised 'bourgeois' Olympism.

For the IOC, retaining leadership in international sport meant having to exploit national feelings to promote 'Olympic values' worldwide. This meant finding ways to legitimise its profile as the principal sporting body by collaborating with, as well as controlling, most international federations. From the Antwerp Games in 1920, the IOC's intention was to bring together as many countries as possible, with a view to expansion, and with little regard for individual political situations. The first step in Antwerp was to avoid offending the Allies, and the second, in Paris, to reintegrate former enemies, with just Germany having to wait until 1928. Already in 1924, however, the election to the IOC of two new German members, Theodor Lewald and Oskar Ruperti, demonstrated this unifying ambition. Including as many countries as possible in the movement was a way to avoid them opposing its aims. The same principle applied to the inclusion of women athletes, which grew, albeit gradually, from one Olympiad to the next. The IOC's policy thus adapted to diplomatic realities while remaining constant in its goal: to bring people together around the sporting values proclaimed since its foundation.

Competition between countries was one of the reasons for the expansion of sport in the interwar period. This signalled significant social and cultural change, as in many countries sport went from being a private activity to a state-driven tool to develop fitness in and out of school. Nationalism was considered a minor problem in comparison to the other dangers and threats faced by the movement, namely professionalism, workers' sport and women's participation. On the contrary, nationhood and nationalism helped the Olympic movement expand on a global scale.[10] Coubertin was very pleased with the global reach of the movement during these years,[11] which was reflected in increasing participation from Asian and African countries, turning the Olympics into a real 'world Games'. This expansion was largely due to the activism of Henri de Baillet-Latour, who was elected IOC President in 1925. Baillet-Latour had the tact of a diplomat and travelled the world to spread the Olympic idea and strengthen his and the institution's leading position.[12] He made a deal with the youth movement, the Young Men's Christian Association (YMCA), which had similar worldwide ambitions. The IOC would take over the YMCA's involvement in the Indian Empire Games of 1909 and in the Far Eastern Games, held between 1913 and 1934, and would give its patronage to the Latin American Games of 1922.[13] In return, the same countries were allowed to enter the IOC.[14] This was a win-win deal: new countries were acknowledged and the Olympic movement grew. The development of sport in Africa culminated in the Alexandria Pan-Arab Games of 1953, as emphasis shifted from celebrating European values to nations and states on an international stage.

## OLYMPISM AND FASCISM

From a European perspective, however, the 1924 Paris Games also foreshadowed dramatic events to come. Exploiting national feelings and ambitions was a dangerous game and before too long, the Olympic movement was becoming caught in a trap of its own making. In Paris, the main dispute brought to the Jury of Honour concerned the Italian

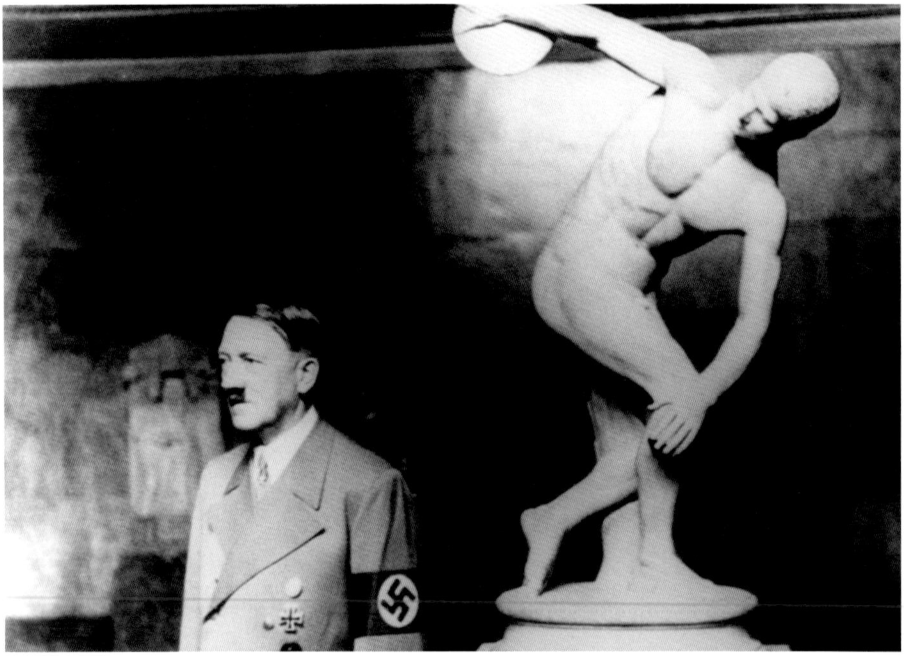

**81.** Unrecorded photographer
Adolf Hitler at the exhibition of the Palombara *Diskobolos* at the Glyptothek in Munich, Germany, 7 October 1938
Black and white photograph

Hitler was obsessed with history and fascinated by Greek antiquity. Ancient statues like the *Diskobolos* have, over time, lost their original pigment and been admired in the modern period for a beauty bound to a mistaken idea of whiteness. Hitler saw the whiteness of this statue as a fitting representation of his racist ideology and, as such, had it displayed in Munich.

fencer Oreste Puliti, whose attitude exemplified the aggressive and uncompromising stance of Fascist Italy, not just in sport but in home and foreign policy. Dissatisfied with the referee's decision, Politi left the room with his teammates, all of them singing a Fascist song. His behaviour anticipated the ideological exploitation of sport by totalitarian regimes, a reality that the IOC was ill-equipped to handle. In 1924, Benito Mussolini's government had yet to outline a consistent sports policy; but it already had a clear idea of what constituted a 'Fascist attitude': a mixture of aggressiveness, honour, pride, action and the defence of the fatherland at all costs. The tagline was to 'live dangerously'. The Puliti affair was not just a sports quarrel, but an occasion for the Fascists to stage and perform the nature and character of the Fascist 'New Man'. From the 1920s onwards, the regime identified sport as a powerful ideological tool. In 1932, the Italian government sent a large contingent of athletes to the Los Angeles Games. 'Mussolini's Boys' performed well and came second in the medal table to the USA. By then, physical training and sport were overtly considered by the Fascists as a means for the New Italians to polish and refine a combative and modern image of their country. In 1934, the country held the Students' Games in Turin, and then the second football World Cup, a perfect sports and political event, which culminated in the Italian team winning the final just a few months before the Fascist Empire was proclaimed.

Germany experienced mixed fortunes at the Olympics during the Weimar Republic. Drawing on massive grassroots participation, an excellent network of sports education and commercial sponsorship that permitted targeted preparation for selected athletes, it came second overall on its return to the Games in Amsterdam in 1928. The effects of the Depression and, in comparison with Italy, lack of state backing, led to a steep decline at Los Angeles 1932. But when, a year earlier, the IOC had awarded the 1936 Games to Berlin, they could not have foreseen how the event would be exploited for ideological purposes under Hitler's regime. Having pushed back initially over the question of Jewish participation, the IOC accepted the overtly nationalist feelings of the Nazis and caved in. One shared reference between the IOC leaders and Nazi ideologues was the primacy of Greek antiquity (fig. 81): ancient Greece was considered the cradle of European culture by sports leaders, and the symbol of racial purity by the Nazis. This ancient heritage gave the IOC and the German government common ground to work hand in hand. At the Berlin Games, the Nazis set temporarily aside their disdain for the pacifism and racial neutrality central to Olympism in order to organise a grandiose event showcasing the superiority of the Nazi regime and the German people.

*

While nationhood had been valued as a cultural component since the founding of the Olympic movement, from the 1920s the IOC faced the challenge of the ideological use of sport by governments. This was against the original Olympic ethos, which saw sport as an educational activity for the betterment of the individual, not a political one. The Paris 1924 Games were held at a time when political ideologies were beginning to percolate more than ever before through international sport. This led to conflicts that were not good publicity for the Olympics. However, the exacerbation of nationalism in the inter-war period was also exploited by the IOC. By integrating new countries into the Olympic movement, the IOC leaders, directed from 1925 by Baillet-Latour, worked towards the globalisation of the movement and towards reinforcing the institution's position in an international sporting arena. The accommodation of the Fascist states and organisation of the 1936 Berlin Games were just one aspect of this trend. In the end, the way the Olympic leaders handled the issue of nationalism in the 1920s and 1930s – deploring it in principle but largely ignoring it in practice – best demonstrates their capacity, diplomatically and expediently, to adapt to the political circumstances. While claiming to keep politics out of sport, they exploited ideological ambitions and developments in sport to assert the IOC's continued domination.

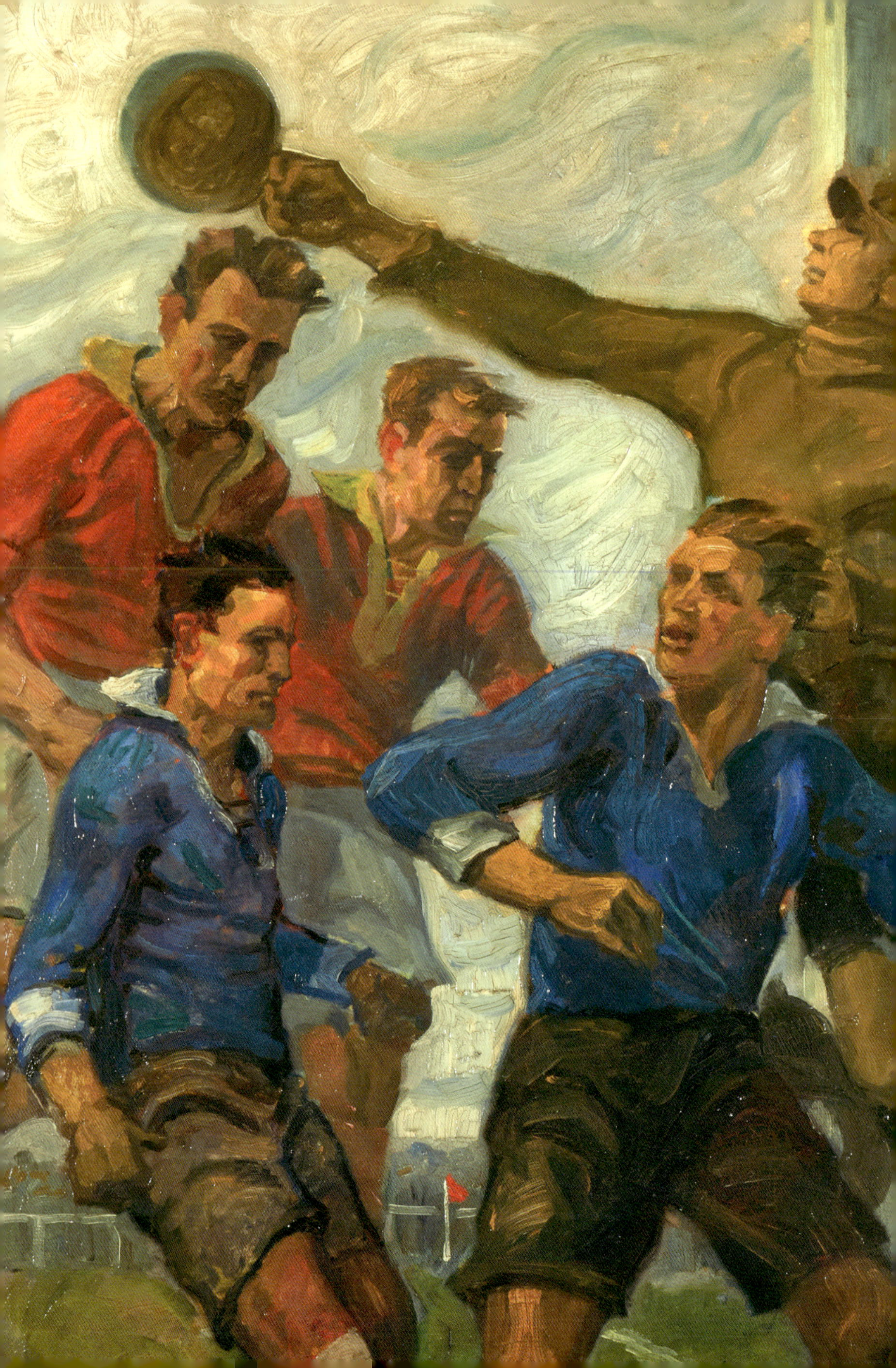

# THE ARTS

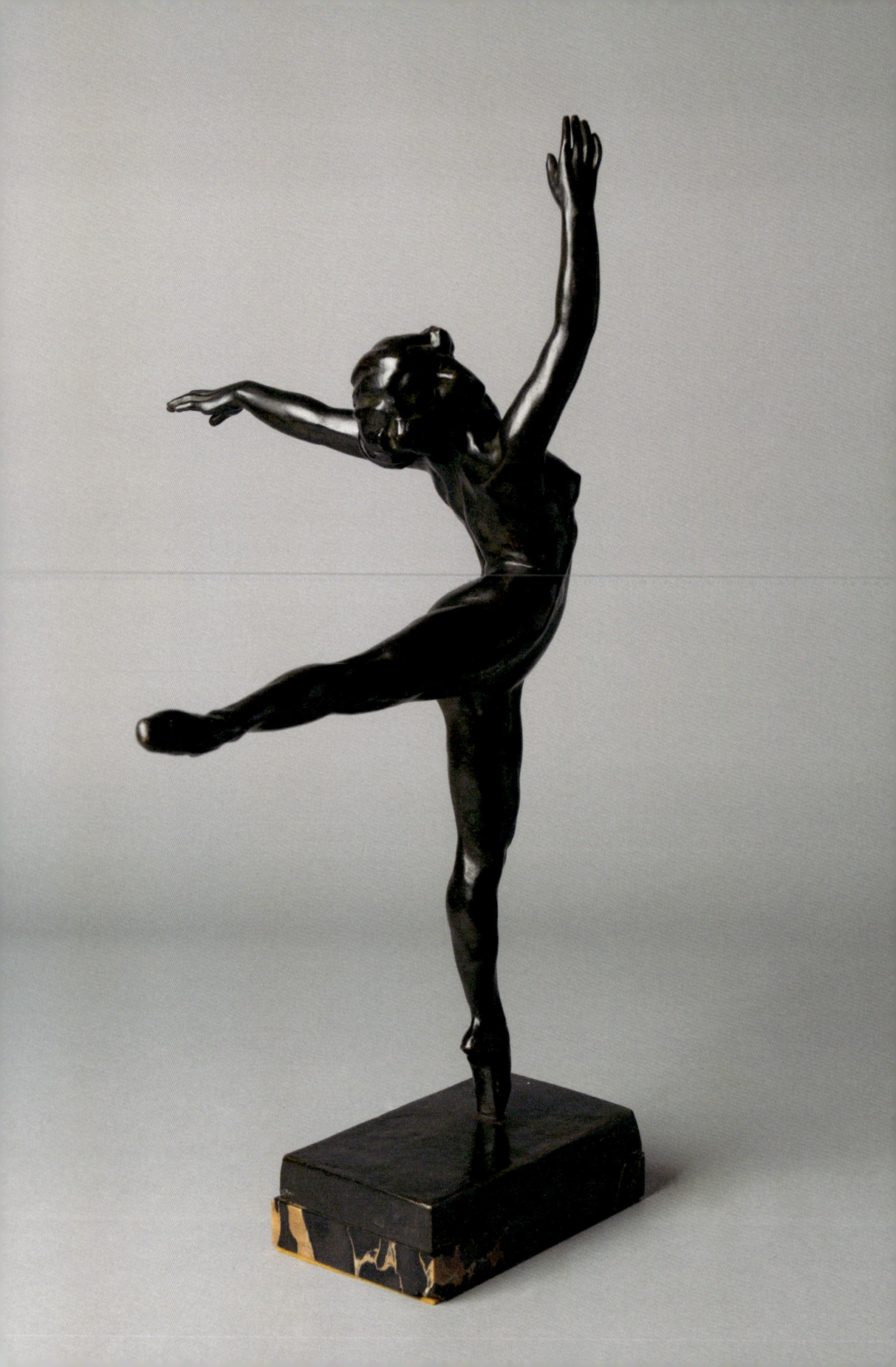

# 9

# PARIS AND THE OLYMPIC ARTS COMPETITION

MILES OSGOOD

What does it take for an artist to win an Olympic medal? According to what standard does an Olympic jury distribute gold, silver and bronze to three different painters, sculptors, or writers (fig. 83)? Over the four decades that the modern Olympics held official Arts Competitions, there was never a fixed answer to this question. From 1912 to 1948, thousands of artists submitted their work to official competitions in architecture, literature, music, painting and sculpture, and 156 of them won genuine Olympic medals, but the results were impossible to predict. Some of the major modern artists in the Fitzwilliam Museum's exhibition – including George Grosz, Willi Baumeister and Wäinö Aaltonen – competed in different editions of the Olympic Arts Competitions and failed to make the rostrum. Meanwhile, otherwise unheralded artists from unexpected corners reached the height of their careers at the Games. Not one of those snubs or selections was ever explained. It would be up to gallery visitors, after the prizes had been announced, walking through the Grand Palais in 1924 or the Fitzwilliam Museum in 2024, to play out the contest in their minds and make their own inferences.

## THE HOUSE OF TASTE

It was in Paris in 1906 that Pierre de Coubertin first made a formal call to Olympic officials to establish art contests. Standing in the foyer of the Comédie Française, Coubertin had two proposals for the competitions' future judges: first, to find among a new generation of artists 'labourers of intellect who are at the same time also athletes'; and second, to

**82.** (cat. 111) Serge Youriévitch (1876–1969)
*The Dancer Nattova*, 1930
(*La danseuse Nattova*)
Bronze, marble, 41 × 25 × 20 cm
Northampton Museum and Art Gallery, Northampton (2002.78.35)

For the Arts Competition of 1924, Youriévitch exhibited a version of this graceful dancer next to his own gargantuan *Wrestler*. In keeping with Nattova's famously difficult poses, the figure seems to find and follow all of the axes of three-dimensional space with almost perpendicular precision. In 1927, a critic described the piece, with its 'brutal, geometric, and exquisite movement', as 'equal, in the psychological domain of dance, to Rodin's *Thinker*'.

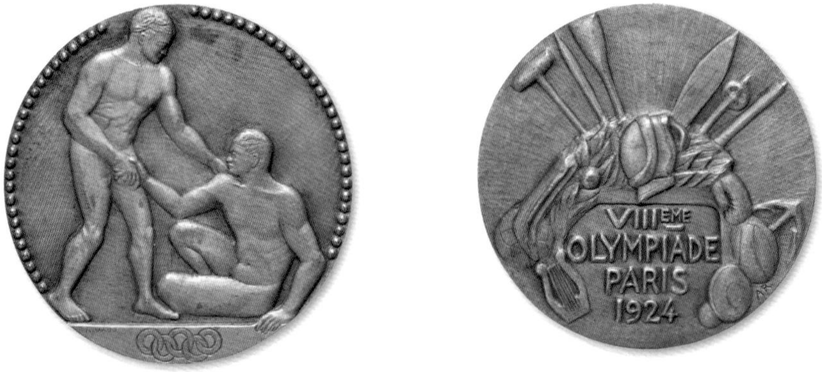


**83.** (cat. 107) André Adolphe Rivaud (1892–1951), designer; Monnaie de Paris (founded 864), manufacturer
Olympic silver winner's medal awarded to Jack Butler Yeats (1871–1957) in the Arts Competition, 1924
Silver, 5.5 cm
Yeats Archive, National Gallery of Ireland, Dublin (IE NGI/YA/Y1/JY/10/2/2)

Irish painter Jack Yeats won this silver medal at the Paris 1924 Olympic Arts Competition for his painting *The Liffey Swim*. The 1924 Olympic medals, designed by André Rivaud and awarded to both athletes and artists, feature an athlete helping his rival on the obverse, and on the reverse, a collection of sporting equipment – along with a lyre to represent the art contests. All contributors to the Olympic Arts Competition also received a bronze participation medal (cat. 32).

find works that would contribute to what Coubertin called 'eurythmy', or a concentric harmony bringing together spectacle and setting, athletes and audience. Public festivals and sporting events had always failed the test of good taste, according to Coubertin, as he gestured around for a point of contrast. 'This, here, *par excellence*, is the house of taste. It is recognized as such by the whole world.' His gesture indicated, most immediately, the baroque adornments of the theatre hall around him, but also – by the concentric logic of eurythmy – the rest of the French capital. 'The first stone of the edifice we hope to place could not have been fashioned elsewhere with the same guarantee of success.'[1]

Perhaps it was a mistake, then, to entrust the inaugural contests to other hosts. The first set of rules, put together by London's Royal Academy for 1908, were comically constraining: painters in the 'Cartoons' category, for instance, were asked to depict 'The battle of the Greeks and Amazons' in a frieze 10 feet long by 4 feet high, sketched at one-fourth the size.[2] In Stockholm in 1912, the judges confused matters further by rewarding Coubertin himself with literary gold and then rebuking him for submitting a bilingual text under two pseudonyms: 'It's preferable for presented works to carry the mark of a national genius and not to try to cross borders.'[3] After World War I, the judges for the Arts Competition in Antwerp 1920 overcorrected in this patriotic direction, awarding half of the medals (and all three for sculpture) to local Belgian artists.[4]

So, when the organisers for Paris 1924 set their ambitions to legitimise the 'Pentathlon of the Muses', they started with the rulebook. The Marquis Melchior de Polignac – an

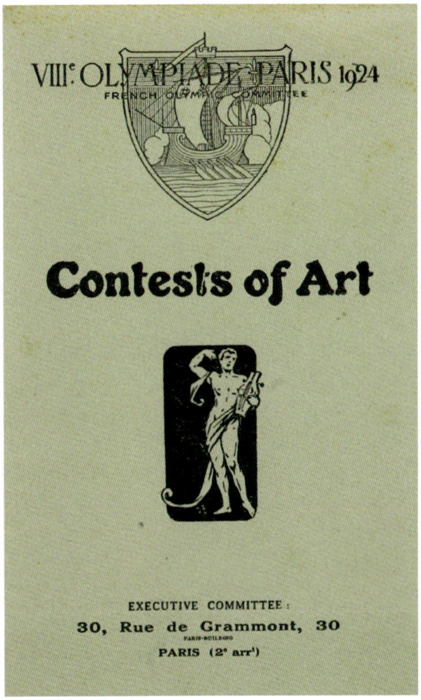


**84.** Executive Committee, French Olympic Committee (founded 1894)
*Eighth Olympiad Paris 1924: Contests of Art*, *c.* 1923–24, cover of the rulebook for the 1924 Olympic Arts Competition

The executive committee of the Paris Olympiad published this booklet in 1923 to promote the third iteration of the Olympic Arts Competition. Printed in French, Spanish and English and sent to the foreign press, the 30 pages open with lists of Olympic committee members and the five art juries – a striking catalogue of around 125 international artistic celebrities – before turning to the rules.

impresario behind France's first aviation tournament and a 'Collège d'athlètes' in Reims – envisioned an ambitious 'Grand Season of Arts' running alongside the sporting events in the heart of the city.[5] First and foremost, he would use the experience and the networks of 'the most illustrious French artists' to bring together an international 'assembly of the world's elite'.[6] The Official Report of the Paris Olympics records that each of these councils, deliberating over rules and expectations for the events, made 'magnificent suggestions': the sculpture council saluted the return of ancient humanism; the composers imagined powerful open-air performances; and the architects wanted reservoirs cleared for swimming competitions.[7] Ultimately, the most important contribution of this 'Grand Season' was that, as opposed to the sporting events in the suburbs of Colombes, it brought the Olympics into the centre of Paris: three months of musical and theatrical performances were planned for the Théâtre des Champs-Elysées – including Jean Cocteau's ballet *Le Train Bleu* (The Blue Train, cat. 121) – while the Arts Competition would take over four rooms at the Grand Palais. To make sure these rooms would be filled, Polignac circulated booklets on the 'Concours d'Art' to the city's foreign embassies, translated into three languages and adorned with an ancient Greek statue-type known as *Apollo Lykaios* (fig. 84).[8] Paris, famous for both its artistic freedom and its arbiters of taste, would be crowning champions of Olympic art in 1924 not on the basis of stringent regulations but on the prestige of its peerless juries.

## THE JUDGMENTS OF PARIS

The most alluring feature of the rule books, and the most bewildering, was the prefatory catalogue of juries, with its impossibly impressive list of approximately 125 international judges. For the first and only time, the composition of the Olympic art juries would be advertised ahead of the events, as the principal attraction of the contests. Far-flung artists would have gawked at the opening pages, which promised that Maurice Denis, Tsuguharu Foujita and John Singer Sargent would be just three of the 30 judges evaluating the painting submissions; that Béla Bartók, Maurice Ravel and Igor Stravinsky were all on the jury for music; and that the jury for literature included Gabriele D'Annunzio, Maurice Maeterlinck, Paul Valéry and Edith Wharton.[9]

For a prospective competitor, the appeal of so distinguished an audience would have been hard to pass up – but how would this crowd of luminaries work in practice? Here, side by side, were standard-bearers of symbolist drama and naturalist fiction, of De Stijl and Art Nouveau, of Les Nabis or Les Six. It was hopeless to find a winning strategy for this outsized, overstuffed set of referees. Amid the loosely defined rules for each of the five Olympic art events, a repeated directive insists on maintaining the mystery: 'The deliberations of the Jury will be secret'.[10]

There are two judges, however, who give us a glimpse. The first is the writer Jean Giraudoux, who served on each of the five juries and who, in an essay titled 'L'Olympiade de 1924', wanted to reform existing Olympic orthodoxy. Whereas organising committees, Giraudoux noted, were always on the lookout for the 'complete man', he took the contrary view that the most thrilling athletes and artists were eccentric experts. It was far less compelling to watch the same body-types work through the events of the decathlon, he argued, than to cheer for cyclists, jumpers, or wrestlers, whose physiques had undergone or overcome incredible 'deformations' in pursuit of victory. And similarly, as a literary principle, 'The French language has been improved not at all by those complete writers ... but by those who had quirks, like Montaigne, or tics, like Rabelais, whose style struck through its deformations'.[11] Giraudoux later characterised these deformation experts as true 'champions', indispensable to literature and to sport.[12]

As a spectator and a judge, Giraudoux would be looking for unique stylists, not consummate performers – but he acknowledged that his was a minority position. This might explain how two of the more individualist and modernist writers in the literature competition ended up short of the rostrum: Robert Graves, who used the occasion of a new 1924 Paris tribunal to take shots at the Versailles Treaty in his boxing poem 'At the Games', and Henry de Montherlant, who played upon the homoeroticism of male athletic camaraderie in *Paradise in the Shadow of Swords*. By contrast, Dorothy Margaret Stuart won the silver by presenting herself as something of a 'complete' writer, with her cycle of poems titled *Sword Songs*, which takes the reader through four imaginative episodes in the history of sword combat in as many different verse forms (fig. 85).

The second judge to speak out was the journalist and critic Jean de Pierrefeu, who promoted remarkably more conservative tastes in an assessment of the Paris contests.

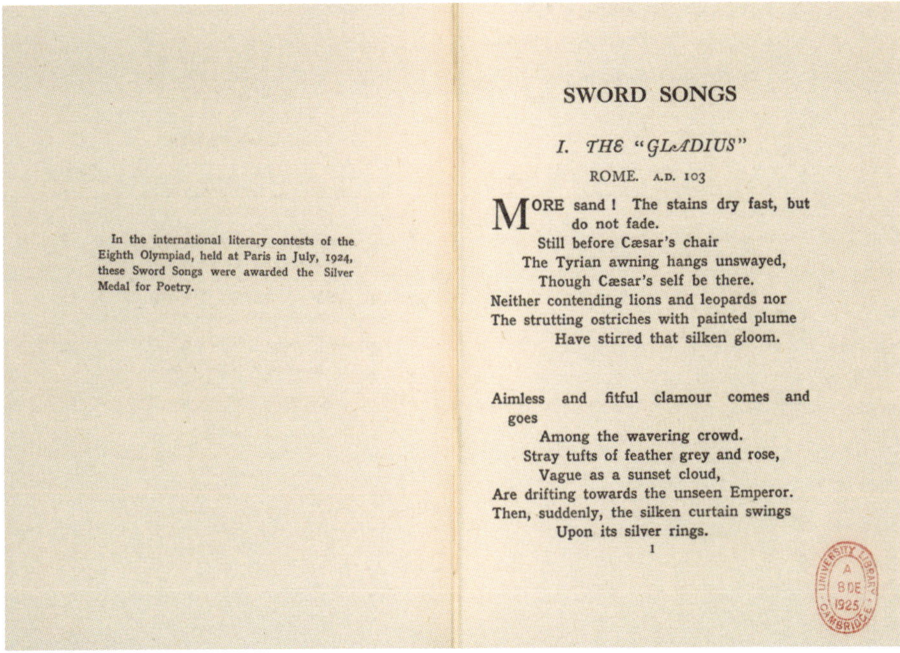

In the international literary contests of the Eighth Olympiad, held at Paris in July, 1924, these Sword Songs were awarded the Silver Medal for Poetry.

SWORD SONGS

I. THE "GLADIUS"

ROME. A.D. 103

MORE sand! The stains dry fast, but
do not fade.
Still before Cæsar's chair
The Tyrian awning hangs unswayed,
Though Cæsar's self be there.
Neither contending lions and leopards nor
The strutting ostriches with painted plume
Have stirred that silken gloom.

Aimless and fitful clamour comes and
goes
Among the wavering crowd.
Stray tufts of feather grey and rose,
Vague as a sunset cloud,
Are drifting towards the unseen Emperor.
Then, suddenly, the silken curtain swings
Upon its silver rings.

1



**85.** (cat. 109) Dorothy Margaret Stuart (1889–1963) *Sword Songs*, with illustrations by Gerald Spencer Pryse, Methuen and Co.: London, 1925

Printing on paper, covered boards, 19 × 12.2 cm Cambridge University Library, Cambridge (1925.7.4776)

English writer Dorothy Margaret Stuart won a silver medal at the Paris 1924 Olympics for this book of poems. Starting with a dramatic account of Roman gladiatorial combat ('The Gladius') and moving forward in time through Renaissance fencing to couplets about a bout of honour in Dunkirk c. 1785 ('The Small Sword'), Stuart sums up the whole of her project in her epilogue: 'I sing of the spirit that dwells in the bright grey blade.'

As an opening, Pierrefeu recalled Coubertin's hopes for athletic art from 1906 and repeated the patriotic sentiment that the contest of 1924 gave this entire endeavour 'exceptionally favourable conditions, since it took place in Paris, at the very centre of all intellectual activity'.[13] He was disappointed, then, to find that, among the contestants, the ancient precedent of the Olympics had not sufficiently revived Pindaric lyricism in poetry (*lyrisme*), living and liberated nudes in the plastic arts (*nudité*), or majestic seriousness in music and theatre (*gravité*). Looking for an alternative model, Pierrefeu points to the bright, airy stadium-scenes of painter Georges Leroux, 'who knows how to translate new sights into a classical style', but who did not enter the Olympic contest (fig. 86). Pierrefeu resigns himself to the possibility that modern sport, with its tennis or football players, instead favours only 'minor genres', such as a humourist's caricature, a wood engraving, or the metal-work of Claude-Léon Mascaux, whose designs for a series of

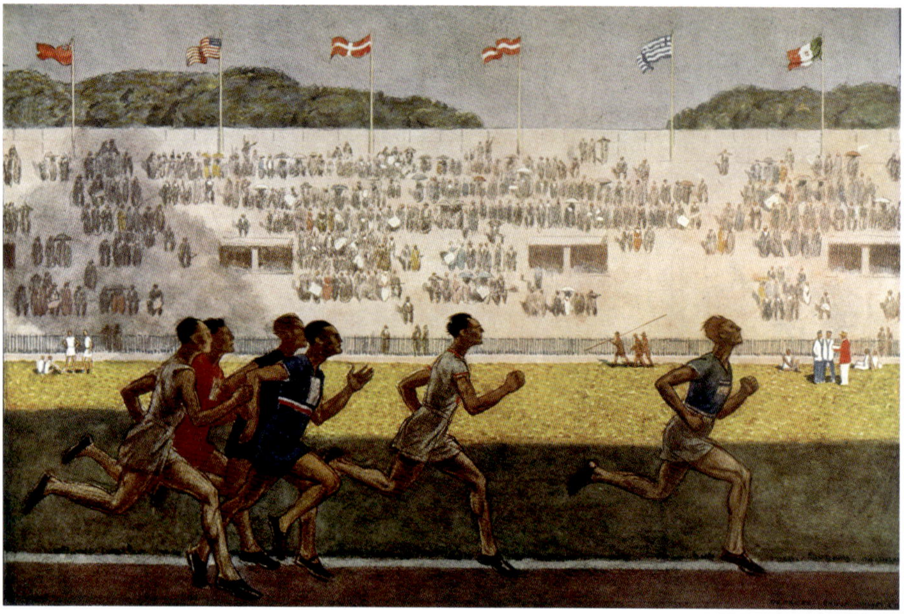

**86.** Georges Paul Leroux (1877–1957)
*At the Stadium of Colombes during the 1924 Olympic Games*, c. 1924
Watercolour
Private collection

Georges Leroux did not enter the Olympic Arts Competition, but judge Jean de Pierrefeu singled out this watercolour as an example of what he hoped the contests would inspire. At a glance, the painting seems to exhibit some of the flaws of modern sport that Pierrefeu maligns (awkwardly fitting uniforms, flat featureless bleachers, a scattered and listless crowd), but the clustered sprinters, with their muscular legs and upturned chins, are also reminiscent of runners on ancient Greek vases. A Finn is in the lead, as was often true on the track in 1924.

Olympic medals won bronze in the 1924 competition.[14] In the aftermath of 1924, Olympic officials agreed with Pierrefeu and legitimised these genres, developing sub-categories for 'Applied Arts & Crafts', 'Engravings & Etchings', 'Reliefs & Medallions' and even 'Town Planning'.[15] As the contests continued in Amsterdam, Los Angeles and beyond, individual Futurists, Dadaists and other modern stylists answered Giraudoux's call for avant-garde challengers, but the Olympics as an institution sided with Pierrefeu's taste for conservative content and narrow form.

## ARTISTIC TYPES AND ATHLETIC TACTICS

It is too simple, however, to confine Olympic artists to these camps. Looking carefully at the essays by Giraudoux and Pierrefeu – not just for the basic aesthetic categories they preferred, but for the conventions they criticised and the aspirations they targeted – we

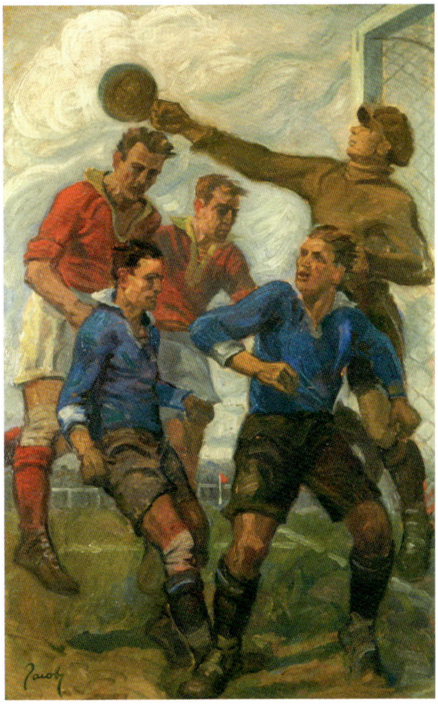

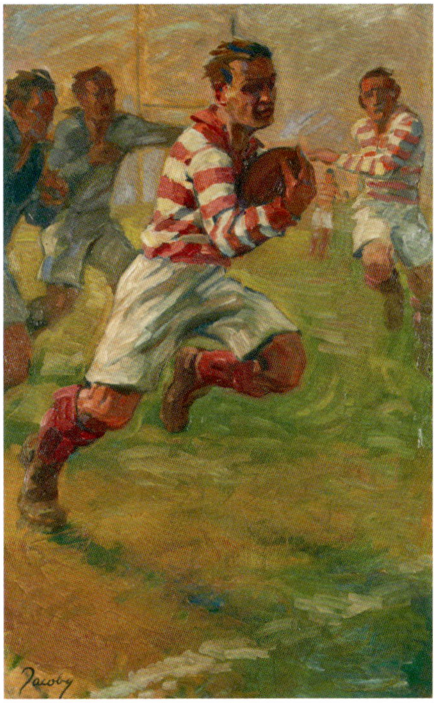

**87.** (cat. 102) Jean Jacoby (1891–1936)
*Corner*, from the *Sport Studies* triptych, 1924
(*Études de Sport*)

Oil on canvas, 104 × 67 cm
Olympic Museum Collections, Lausanne (81598)

**88.** (cat. 103) Jean Jacoby (1891–1936)
*Rugby*, from the *Sport Studies* triptych, 1924
(*Études de Sport*)

Oil on canvas, 99 × 59.5 cm
Olympic Museum Collections, Lausanne (81599)

Jean Jacoby, the most decorated contestant in the history of the Olympic Arts Competition, won his 1924 gold medal with a sports triptych, two parts of which are featured here. A professional sports illustrator in Luxembourg, Jacoby makes his athletes serious in demeanour but exuberant in light and colour. The newspaper *L'Auto* commended 'the powerful style and beautiful charm' of his rugby scene.

can identify at least four types of artists at the Games, each with his own resemblance to a type of athlete. We have already touched on the first two. While dismissed by Giraudoux, the 'complete artist' was evidently still appealing to other judges. Capable of rendering numerous sporting subjects with undeniable skill (albeit at the expense of personal flair), Jean Jacoby belonged to this category.[16] Having trained at the École des Beaux-Arts in Strasbourg and become a commercial sports illustrator, Jacoby submitted a *Sport Studies* triptych (featuring *Corner* and *Rugby*) for Luxembourg, showing off the appeal of sport for the eye attuned to colour, light, shadow and motion, with similar pleasure and simplicity as we find among Georges Leroux's runners (figs 87 and 88).[17]

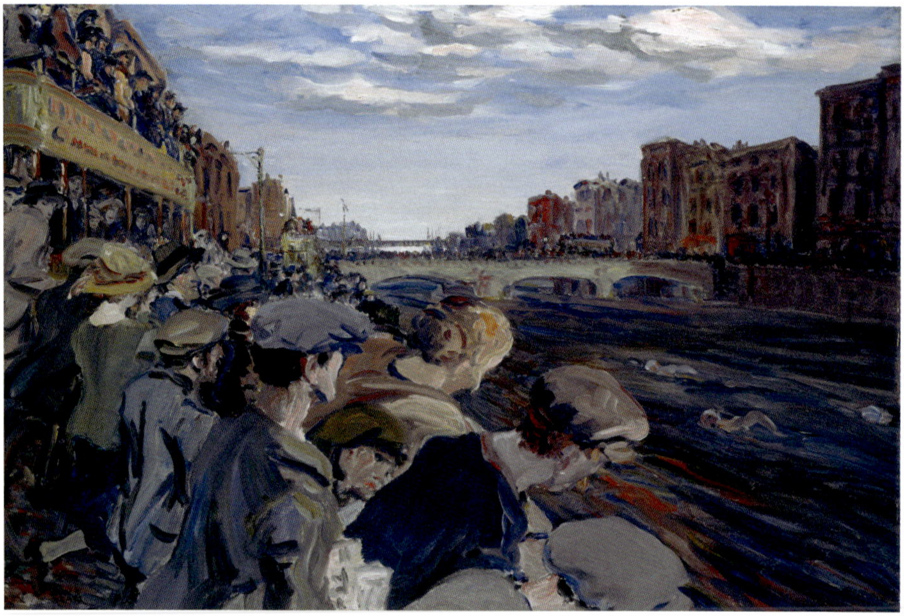

**89.** (cat. 106) Jack Butler Yeats (1871–1957)
*The Liffey Swim*, 1923
Oil on canvas, 61 × 91 cm
National Gallery of Ireland, Dublin
(NGI.941)

Jack Yeats's *The Liffey Swim* won a silver medal at the 1924 Olympics, where it was known simply as *Swimming*. In 1925, *The Sunday Independent* praised it for its 'tremendous vigour', remarking of his paintings: 'If you had one in your room you would never wish you were dead; you'd look at it and give life another chance.' The male face turned outwards may be Yeats's own.

Jacoby's broad interest in sport made him the ideal 'complete' artistic Olympian: he would end up submitting 32 works over four Olympiads, earning more accolades than any other Olympic artist by winning two gold medals and two honourable mentions. Among other Olympic artists, only the Canadian sculptor Robert Tait McKenzie was more devoted to the contests (with 58 submissions over five Olympiads), and he never reached the same heights – a single bronze medal in 1932, for *Shield of the Athletes* (see Heggie's chapter).

Second is the 'deformation specialist'. Artists in this category, praised by Giraudoux as the manic stylists of the past, ought to have been especially abundant in 1924. As we see in the exhibition, numerous artists of the interwar avant-garde brought their unique visual signatures to the subject of sport: Robert Delaunay (figs 26–8), Pablo Picasso (cat. 122), Henri Laurens (fig. 80; cat. 121) and Jeanne Rij-Rousseau (fig. 66) all found inspiration in Olympic sports, even if they never entered the official contests. Within the Competition, the one painter who found success for his distinctive modern style was Irish artist Jack Butler Yeats with *The Liffey Swim* (fig. 89). Yeats made an important turn toward Expressionism in the early 1920s, in the same years that Ireland was fighting its revolutionary and civil wars. In this context, his canvas transcends athletic art to become an aesthetic and political manifesto. The titular swimmers are barely perceptible as translucent, wriggling brushstrokes, whereas a unified citizenry stands together in the light of the foreground, and the face of the artist himself (perhaps) looks outwards at the city. Memorialising a real annual swimming race between Guinness's Brewery and Butt Bridge, Yeats ingeniously converts Dublin itself into a stadium, putting spectators not only on both banks of the river, but also on O'Connell Bridge and in a passing tram: a democratic reimagining of spectating sections.[18] Yeats distinguishes himself even from other Expressionists, finding in the mass of the crowd not dread but excitement. Compare *The Liffey Swim*, for example, to Edvard Munch's painting *Workers Returning Home* (1913–15), which uses the same colour palette and vanishing lines but confronts us with the hollow-eyed spectres of tired labourers advancing upon us. By contrast, Yeats places himself and his viewer inside the crowd, looking over their shoulders. Entering the Paris contest in 1924, Yeats deformed the tropes of both Olympic art and modernist painting – and *The Liffey Swim* secured Ireland one of its two medals (the other a bronze for poetry, won by Oliver St. John Gogarty).

The third and most popular type of Olympic artist is the 'naked classicist'. For all of Pierrefeu's protestations that modern sport had not sufficiently inspired a taste for *nudité* among Olympic artists, there were many such attempts in the 1924 sculpture competition, visible together in their corner of the Grand Palais – from a neoclassical saluting youth by Frantz Heldenstein to a modern Black heavyweight rendered by Jean-René Gauguin, winning silver and bronze respectively. Triumphing over them was Kostas Dimitriadis, a graduate and future director of the Athens School of Fine Arts, and a foreign fixture of Paris's academies and salons since moving to France in 1903. Dimitriadis worked for seven months on a new *Diskobolos* (fig. 76), studying the strenuous, stretched poses of Finnish discus thrower Armas Rudolf Taipale, who had won Olympic medals in 1912 and 1920 (figs 90 and 91). While Taipale offered Dimitriadis several of the positions of a modern discus thrower, the sculptor opted instead for a unique alternative, inspired by ancient statues, vase paintings and coins: a stance distinct from the ubiquitous versions of Myron's *Diskobolos*, but also never taken by competitors today.[19] The sculptor's anachronistic throwing tactic seems to have worked: whereas Taipale placed twelfth at the Paris Games, Dimitriadis placed first. Greeks immediately took pride in their artistic victory, with the writer Zakarias Papandoniou praising Dimitriadis for having 'definitively attained, in this most recent work, the highest realm of classical art', 'fascinating by the richness of its pose, marvellous in the harmony of its lines, the only work that aligns athletic training with the balance of physical beauty'.[20] Celebrated as the 'new Myron', Dimitriadis received a Gold Cross from the President of the Greek Republic one month after his win and a Legion of Honour award in Paris.[21] A copy of his sculpture has stood outside the Panathenaic Stadium since 1927.

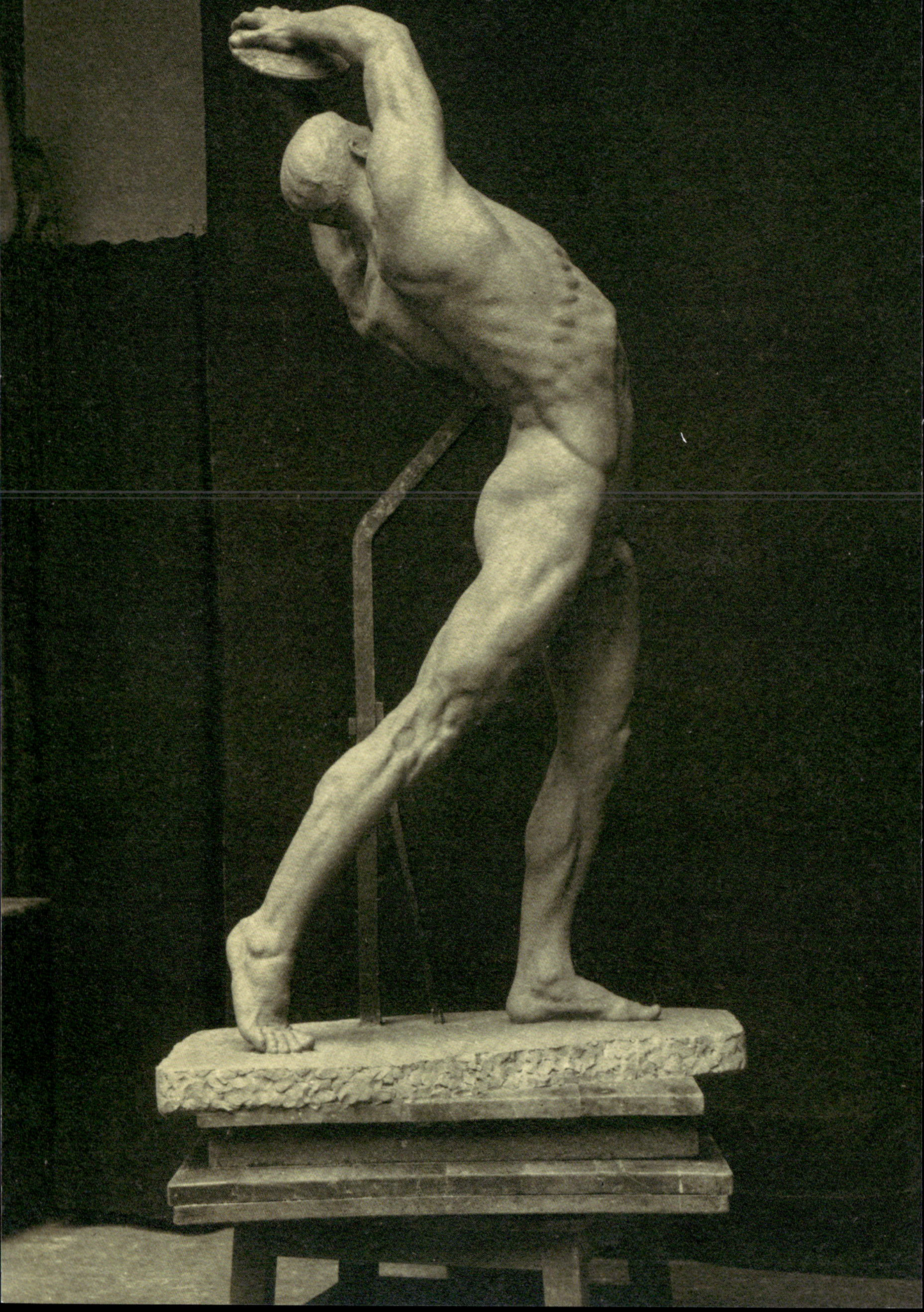

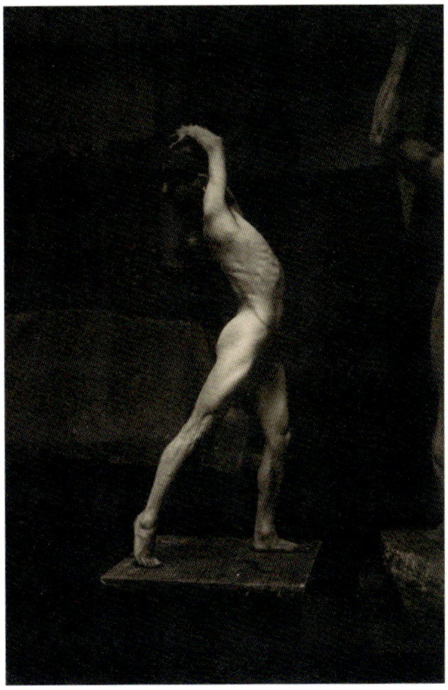

**90.** (cat. 104) Unrecorded photographer
*Finnish Discus Thrower* by Kostas Dimitriadis (1879 or 1881–1943) seen in his Paris studio, *c.* 1924

Black and white photograph

**91.** (cat. 105) Unrecorded photographer
Finnish Olympic discus thrower Armas Rudolf Taipale (1890–1976) poses in the Paris studio of Kostas Dimitriadis for the sculpture *Finnish Discus Thrower*, *c.* 1924

Black and white photograph
Both Dimitriadis archive, Hellenic Literary and Historical Archive / National Bank of Greece Cultural Foundation

The artist and his athletic model tried several modern stances before settling on this more unusual, ancient position, with the discus over the athlete's head. According to Zakarias Papandoniou, who visited the Olympic sculpture gallery in the Grand Palais, 'this pure and imposing work' was the clear victor: 'the other statues in the hall paled by comparison'. After his *Finnish Discus Thrower* won the gold medal, Dimitriadis's name was engraved at the Panathenaic Stadium in Greece, and a copy of the statue erected there in 1927.

Fourth and finally, there is the 'minor-event upstart', whose goal, according to Pierrefeu, is to 'fix the expressive character, the anecdotal turn, the spiritual trait, the specific accent of living reality'.[22] In her repeat billing in the 1924 exhibition and our exhibition, the figure who springs to mind is *La danseuse Nattova* (fig. 82). The sculptor, Serge Youriévitch, was hardly a 'specialist' craftsman: born in Paris but educated in St Petersburg, he had served in the court of Tsar Nicholas II and as a diplomat in France, working as a published psychologist before a health crisis pushed him into sculpture, when (in 1903) he began to train with Rodin and then (in 1920) started exhibiting sculptures at major Paris salons.[23] It is his subject, rather, who embodies a consistent and unique artistic calling: Natacha Nattova (born Natalia Schmit) was a celebrity of the Paris stage for her 'adagio' dances, in which she performed a series of precarious and elegant acrobatic poses.[24] Youriévitch and Nattova, both living far from Bolshevik Russia after the October Revolution, shared new success in the expatriate haven of Paris. Youriévitch's tribute replicates the deceptive difficulty of Nattova's dances, requiring the sculpture to perform its own delicate balancing act: her limbs and features radiate, but the star stands on a single point. When the first version of the statue appeared, in plaster, at the Salon d'Automne in 1923, the American critic Florence Heywood noted the flurry

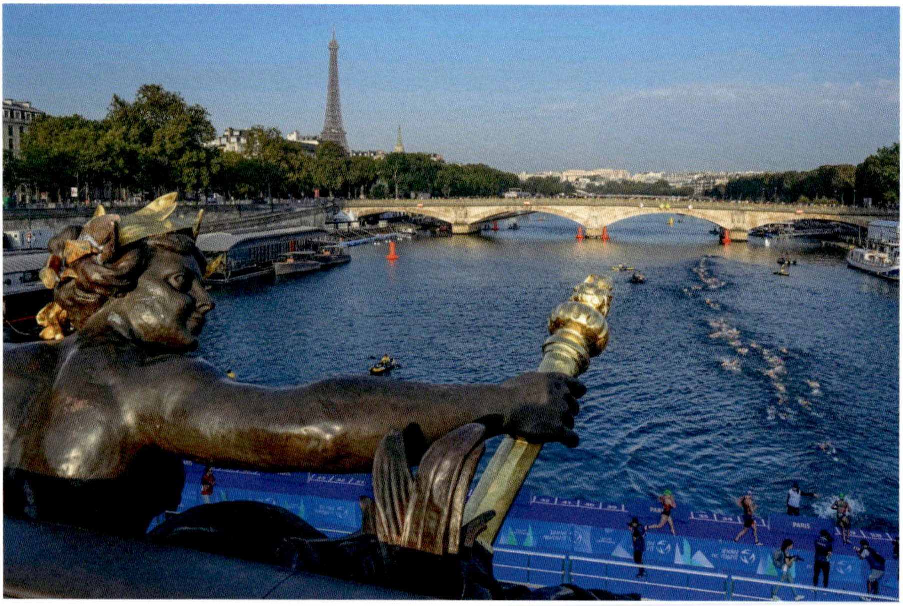

**92.** Athletes in the River Seine during the Women's Triathlon Test event for the Paris 2024 Olympic Games, August 2023

Colour photograph

This photograph, taken from Paris's Pont Alexandre III, depicts a women's triathlon event in the Seine in summer 2023. This event was used as a test for the marathon swimming and triathlon and paratriathlon swimming events in the 2024 Olympics.

of attention it received and marvelled at how this 'life size' figure was also, somehow, 'on tip of toe, light of movement as a bird'.[25] At the Paris Olympics the following summer, a bronze copy of the sculpture, specially requested by the City of Paris, received no awards (perhaps in part because Russia was not officially competing in the Games), but it went on to become Youriévitch's biggest triumph.[26] Even working in the universalising genre of the nude, Youriévitch captures the hair, the upturned eyes, the slight smile and the ballet slippers that bring Nattova's expressive, anecdotal, spiritual and accented features into Pierrefeu's 'living reality'.

Thanks to Giraudoux and Pierrefeu (as outspoken representatives of the otherwise secret juries) and thanks to the four competitors in our exhibition (as distinct strategists in an otherwise chaotic field of play), some of the standards of the Olympic Arts Competition are accounted for. But what of the standards of Coubertin, the original founder behind the contests? There are two artist types I have neglected: the 'athlete-artist', who competes in two contests, and the 'eurythmic harmonist', who can bring the entire Olympic festival together aesthetically. Among the 'athlete-artists', the quintessential crossover champion is the breakout tennis star of Paris 1924, the

American Helen Wills (fig. 44), with her 31 Grand Slams and her twelve drawing submissions to the Olympic Arts Competition of 1932. Among the 'eurythmic harmonists', it is worth pointing to Géo-Charles, whose play *Jeux Olympiques* took the 1924 gold for literature with its imaginative 'open-air theatre' around a boxing ring, complete with a modernised Greek chorus (a sports crowd) and *deus ex machina* (an aeroplane).[27] After winning over the prestigious literary jury at the Olympics, Géo-Charles took a victory lap at the avant-garde Bal Olympique (see Vere's chapter), where he was a guest of honour.

Ultimately, each of the Fitzwilliam Museum's *Paris 1924* exhibition's competing Olympic artworks contributes, in its own way, to Coubertin's vision of 'eurythmy'. Jacoby represents multiple colourful games as a unified triptych, celebrating the diversity of Olympic sport. Dimitriadis ends up planting his *Diskobolos* sculpture outside his home stadium in Athens, completing the neoclassical ambitions of the modern Olympic revival. And Yourievitch brings together the Olympics and modern dance around a Russian star, just as Jean Cocteau would do in *Le Train Bleu* for the Ballets Russes (ballerina and choreographer, Bronislava Nijinska).

It is Jack Yeats, though, who best predicts where this Olympic eurythmy is headed, one hundred years later. With the early plans to put Paris's marathon swimmers in the Seine under the Pont Alexandre III, where fans can crowd the banks and the bridge, *The Liffey Swim* comes to life in a new city (fig. 92). If the Olympic Arts Competitions – with their rulebooks, juries and medals – once convinced art to imitate sport, it is now time for sport to imitate art.

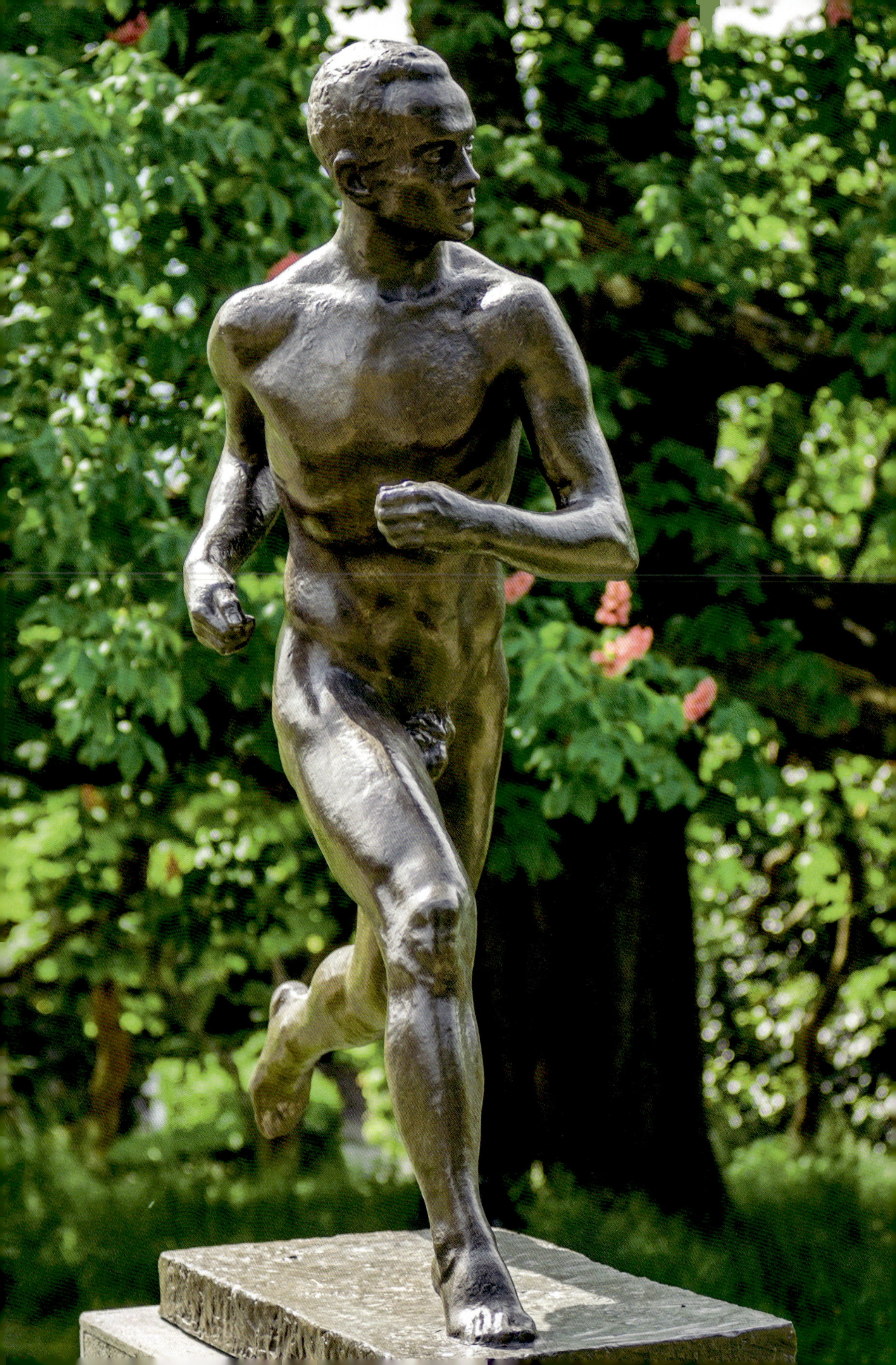

# 10

# PAAVO NURMI IN PROSE, POETRY AND SCULPTURE

CHRISTOPHER YOUNG

It is hardly surprising that visitors to the Olympic Museum in Lausanne today are greeted by a bronze statue of Paavo Nurmi (fig. 93). 'The Flying Finn', as he was widely known, is arguably the greatest long- and middle-distance runner of all time. In a career spanning 14 years, he set 22 outdoor world records over distances between 1500m and 20k, and is the only athlete in history to hold these in the mile, the 5000m and the 10,000m simultaneously. Between 1920 and 1928, he won nine gold and three silver medals at the Olympics – a feat not matched in track and field until 1996 by Carl Lewis. This haul might have been larger still had Finnish coaches not excluded him, much to his annoyance, from the 10,000m in 1924 (an event at which he was never beaten) and had the International Amateur Athletic Federation (IAAF) not controversially banned him for infringing amateur regulations just days before Los Angeles 1932, where he had hoped to bow out with a victory in the marathon. Paris was Nurmi's pinnacle. There he won five gold medals (three individual, two team), drawing the largest crowd since the Opening Ceremony to witness him clinch the 1500m and 5000m titles in little over an hour. In 1925, America beckoned. Over five months he sold out venues from coast to coast, won 51 of his 55 races and was received at the White House by President Coolidge.

Nurmi's statue in Lausanne is one of four large-scale versions of an original made by Wäinö Aaltonen in 1924 and is the only one to stand outside Finland. The 1920s were a period in which the Finns were forging their collective identity with a renewed sense of purpose after recent independence from Russia, and Cubist-inspired Aaltonen was

**93.** Statue of Paavo Nurmi outside the Olympic Museum in Lausanne
Colour photograph

Wäinö Aaltonen's large-scale sculpture of Paavo Nurmi was commissioned by the Finnish government in 1924. Despite being based on photographs from a book on Nurmi's training techniques, it takes the creative liberty of placing the athlete on his toes, when in fact he planted the whole of his foot. The image here is of the 1994 copy imposing itself on the park that rolls from the Olympic Museum in Lausanne to the lake shore.

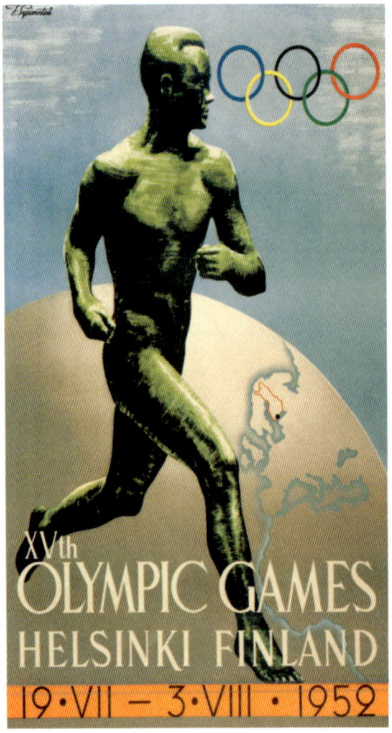


**94.** Ilmari Sysimetsä (1912–1955), artist; Oy Tilgmann Ab (founded Helsinki, 1869), printer
Official poster of the 1952 Helsinki Olympic Games, 1951

Colour lithography on paper, 100 × 62 cm
Olympic Museum Collections, Lausanne

In 1952, Nurmi was still bestriding the world. Originally created for the 1940 Olympics, which were cancelled due to World War II, Sysimetsä's poster was lightly updated and reproduced in over 100,000 copies, in 20 languages, when the Games finally came to Finland. Aaltonen's bronze is rendered here in copper with, appropriately, a golden hue.

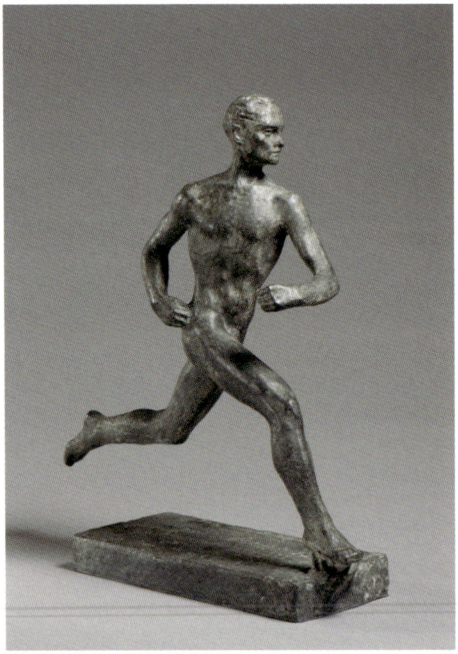

**95.** (cat. 142) Wäinö Aaltonen (1884–1966)
*Paavo Nurmi*, 1950–53

Metal (probably zinc), 44 × 41 × 13 cm
Finnish National Gallery, Helsinki
(SKOP-3740)

Size matters. In the early 1950s, small-scale replicas of the 1925 statue, based on a reworking by Aaltonen himself, were mass-produced in bronze and other metals to raise money for student facilities and the Olympic Village. Although popular, they could hardly capture the dominance of the original in front of the stadium or, more dramatically still, dwarfing the globe on the official poster.

becoming a crafter of the national image. Having first worked on war memorials, he went on to produce monumental sculptures of famous Finnish figures, including a bust of the composer Jean Sibelius (1928) – the only person to rival Nurmi in the national imagination[1] – and was tasked with producing sculptures for the new parliament building in 1932. After the Paris Games, he was engaged by the state to make the first sculpture of their superstar athlete. It was a commission that could have been given at the ancient

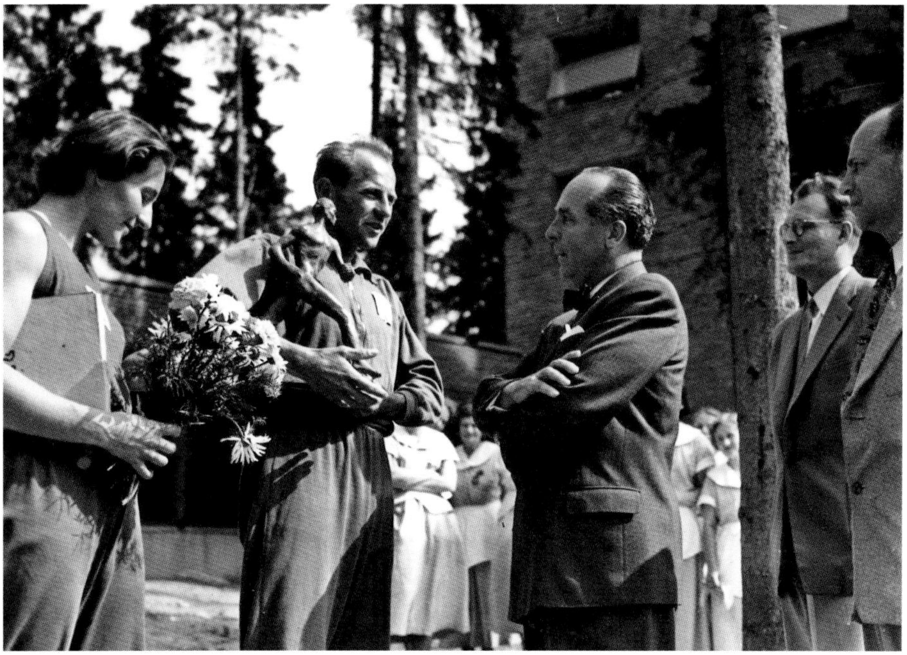

**96.** (cat. 141) Unrecorded photographer / Hede Foto (Osvald 'Hede' Hedenström) (*c.* 1938–60s)
Czech long-distance runner Emil Zátopek (1922–2000) receiving a Paavo Nurmi statue from Ilmari Harki in Otaniemi, Espoo, during the 1952 Olympic Games in Helsinki, *c.* 1952
Black and white photograph

One happy recipient of a *Nurmi* was Czech middle-distance star Emile Zátopek, pictured here during the 1952 Games. At Helsinki, he became the only athlete to win the 5000m, 10,000m and marathon at a single Olympics. Unlike Nurmi, however, Zátopek was known for his open and friendly personality; in 1966, he passed on one of his golds from Helsinki to Australian runner Ron Clarke, who despite breaking 17 world records never managed to win one.

Games, when winners whose families or cities could afford it were cast in bronze and positioned for immortality at Olympia or back home. Aaltonen's *Nurmi* is both classical and non-classical: on the one hand, it is a muscular male nude, but on the other – as is unusual in classical sculpture – it captures the athlete in full flow.[2] The sculpture became iconic in its own right. As late as the 1952 Olympics in Helsinki, it featured on the poster (fig. 94), was erected outside the stadium, where Nurmi lit the flame, and appeared on stamps and banknotes. Just prior to this, miniatures were sold to raise funds for student sports facilities and the Olympic Village (figs 95 and 96).

But Nurmi did not just belong to the Finns. At the height of his fame, he was a source of fascination across the worlds of sport and wider culture. In 1924, he set Austrian Willy Meisl (1895–1965) on the path to become Europe's leading sports writer. In 1926 and 1927, he fired Renée Sintenis (1888–1965), one of Germany's most significant sculptors

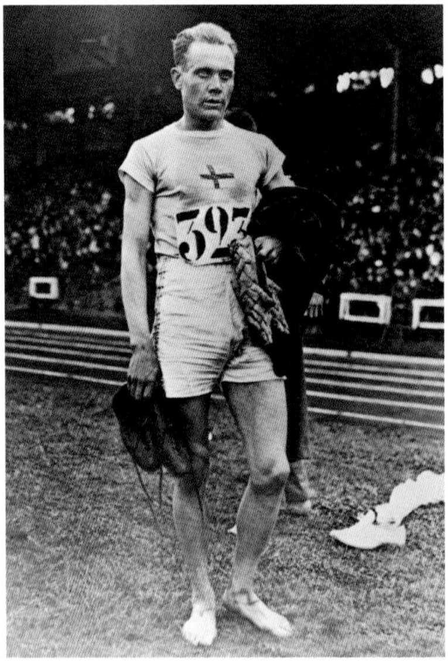

**97.** (cat. 75) Unrecorded photographer
Paris 1924 Olympic Games, Athletics, Paavo Nurmi (Fin) 1st in 1500m Men, 5000m Men, Team 3000m, Individual and Team Cross Country, 1924
Black and white photograph
Comité International Olympique (CIO) (PHO10004733)

If ever a picture captured the 'Phantom' rather than the 'Flying' Finn, this is it. Taken after he had won the 1500m and 5000m finals in just over an hour on 10 July 1924, it shows him taciturn, intense, and apparently oblivious to the record crowd that had turned out to witness the miraculous feat. The following year, French writer Jean Prévost likened Nurmi's achievement to 'a moment when the heavens are empty'.

of the interwar period, and Kazimierz Wierzyński (1894–1969), one of Poland's greatest poets of the twentieth century, to some of their finest work. All three of these highly significant figures would enter the 1928 Olympic Arts Competition in Amsterdam. That they handled the greatest athlete of their day tells us much about the sport's cultural capital in the 1920s. How they handled him tells us not only about them, and about the different ways that sport could be conceived in the period, but also about Nurmi himself. For the 'Flying Finn' was also the 'Phantom Finn', an enigma to everyone, even his closest teammates (see Heggie's chapter). He paid more attention to the stopwatch in his hand than his fellow competitors, gave virtually no interviews and left the stadium immediately after his victories (fig. 97). As Gabriel Hanot – later the creator of football's European Cup (Champions League) – wrote in the illustrated weekly *Le Miroir des sports*:

> Paavo Nurmi lies beyond humanity ... There is such coldness in him and his self-control is so great that never for a moment does he show his feelings ... We have now found the Finnish champion thinner, ruder, even more silent and withdrawn than before, more ethereal ... This extraordinary runner ... will soon have to give us an answer to the living mystery that he constitutes.[3]

As Meisl, Wierzyński and Sintenis turned to that living mystery, they were confronted with a paradox: the world's best-known athlete – arguably the world's most famous man – was a blank canvas.

## THE JOURNALIST: WILLY MEISL

Meisl had little time to capture Nurmi. Like all journalists, he was in as much of a hurry as the athletes he described. But special circumstances compounded the habitual rush. Still barred from the Olympics since World War I, Germany imposed a reporting ban on Paris, which was broken by only two newspapers,[4] and the vacuum gave Meisl a chance to shine. A talented sportsman in a number of disciplines (in football, to name but one, he played in Vienna under the legendary English trainer Jimmy Hogan, and coached in Sweden), he was also a formidable intellect (on his return from the War he completed a doctorate in Law).[5] From the start, in the early 1920s, his work combined a practical and scholarly knowledge of sport with a literary style more commonly found in the culture sections. Ten days after the close of the Paris Games, he finished a book that would bring the Games alive for a German audience and secure him the job of transforming the sports coverage of one of Berlin's foremost broadsheets, the *Vossische Zeitung*. The appointment was wholly justified. *Die Olympischen Spiele 1924 in Wort, Bild, Statistik* (The Olympic Games 1924: Word, Image, Statistics) is one of the finest books written about any Olympics.[6] Covering ancient Greece, the modern Games, the ceremonies, rugby, football, athletics and swimming, the work was conceived, as Meisl put it, as an experiment in mixing facts and figures, epic and lyric that would 'captivate readers and allow them to experience it as if they were there, even to feel some emotions' (p. 5). It brims with sporting insight, literary techniques and classical references, often heaped on top of one another in an infectious jumble: a sprinter's style (pp. 35–6) is expertly deconstructed into its component parts and at the same time related to Tutankhamen on an Egyptian relief or runners on an ancient Greek vase.

Meisl admired the British for their fighting spirit – Harold Abrahams 'throws himself into the race like a rugby player' (p. 36); Eric Liddell's 'style is not a style, he races rather than runs' (p. 52). But he adored the Finns – 'little Finland' took ten golds in track and field against 'great America's' twelve (p. 64) – and marvelled at Nurmi and his rival Ville Ritola, who, between them, accounted for eight of those victories. Of Nurmi, though, he was in awe: 'Nurmi is inscrutable, incomprehensible, a staggering puzzle, a mystery of the track' (p. 40). Yet, unlike his French counterpart Hanot, he felt no urgency to penetrate the mystery. For Meisl, there was no way of understanding Nurmi, and somehow that was the point. Meisl revelled in different images and modes of explanation for his speeding round the track. There is the powerful, 'Nurmi runs a mighty stride, his legs devour space in front of you' (p. 47); the whimsical, 'Nurmi's legs have taken on a life of their own. They live their own life of record breaking and one day they might well say: why do we need Nurmi at all, we'll declare ourselves independent and break the world record on our own!' (p. 42); and the abstract, 'he runs against the unfathomable, the invisible, against the scheduled time he holds in this right hand' (p. 43). But perhaps most devastatingly, there is the effect Nurmi appears to have on others, for instance on the Cambridge athlete Henry Stallard (whom Meisl neglects to say was carrying a foot injury and viral infection) in the first of his back-to-back finals:

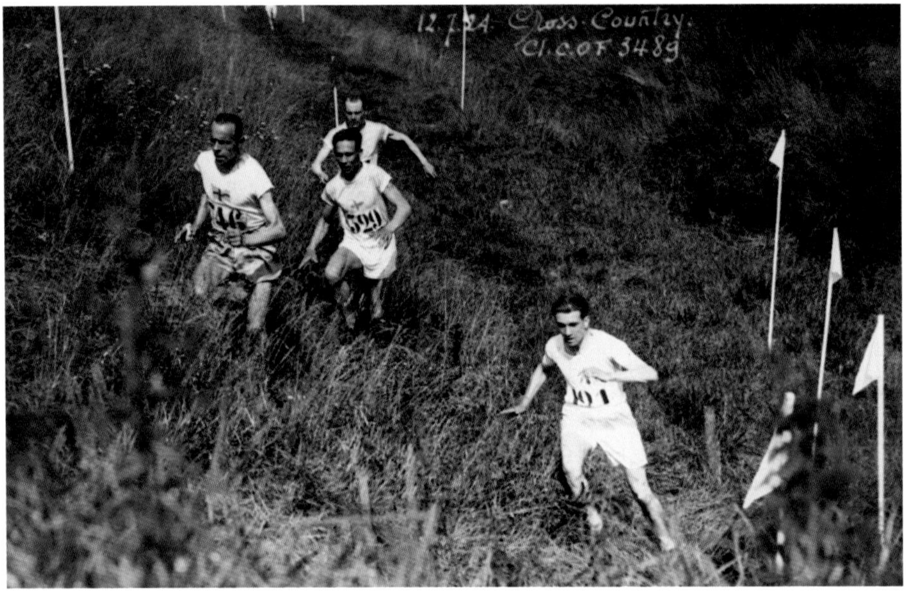


**98.** Unrecorded photographer
Paris 1924 Olympic Games, Athletics, Individual Cross Country, Men – Edvin Wide (Swe) no.746, before Ville Ritola (Fin) 2nd no. 329 and Paavo Nurmi (Fin) 1st, 1924
Black and white photograph
Comité International Olympique (CIO) (PHO10004978)

An image that deceives: during the cross country event, four contenders appear like a herd of deer in a sunlit clearing. Nurmi, the eventual winner, is tucked in at the back. In fact, the sun was scorching, and in his book, which reprints the picture, Willy Meisl describes it as the most brutal race in the history of the Olympics. It was never run again.

> All down the back straight, Stallard gave it his all and had to be carried away on a stretcher, like a hero on his shield. Storms of applause engulfed him on his desolate passage back to the changing room. It would be half an hour before he regained consciousness. Not long after, Nurmi, the superior being, stepped up to run the 5000m, a race, again, he went on to win, in an Olympic record, just as he had planned it. That's Nurmi. (p. 45)

Of course, Meisl's skill as a writer went beyond the turning of a well-wrought phrase. He could trace the arc of a race from start to finish and had a penchant for recounting not just *what* he saw but also *how* he saw it. Harold Abrahams's victory in the 100m, for instance, is told in three phases: the athletes' languid warm-ups; the blur of the runners after the gun; and, only after the cheering abates, a dissection of what actually happened, stride by stride, in an action replay (some thirty years before this was 'invented' on American television). Nearly sixty years later, the sequence would be depicted almost identically in *Chariots of Fire* (1981, see Michelakis's chapter). There is no better example of Meisl's visual mode than his account of the cross country event, a race so brutal that it was immediately struck from the Olympic programme. Forty runners started, but in temperatures approaching 45 degrees, only 11 made it to the finish (fig. 98). Amidst rumours of deaths, ambulances scoured the course late into the evening searching for missing athletes. Nurmi is not the focus, but while Meisl narrates what he can and cannot see, every word consecrates the Finn as a phenomenon (pp. 57–9). Long after the stadium tannoy falls silent, leaving spectators to imagine what is happening outside, Nurmi arrives to claim a perfunctory victory, with the scale of his achievement only subsequently revealed in the sickening disarray of those who trail behind. After a graphic description of their wretched condition, Meisl concludes (p. 59): 'a shameful chapter in the history of sport; a heroic chapter for Nurmi ... Nurmi whom not even the most ferocious sun can fluster, whom a race does not appear to tire but rather to refresh. Nurmi the hero of distance-runners.'

## THE POET: KAZIMIERZ WIERZYŃSKI

The Polish poet Kazimierz Wierzyński might well have read Meisl (he studied German at university and his poem 'The Spartan' repeats the image of a middle-distance runner being born away on his shield) – but the Nurmi he produced is quite different. Despite the lag in Poland's sporting development – the result of nearly a century of tripartite rulership under Prussia, Austria and Russia[7] – Wierzyński, like Meisl, admired sports. Like Meisl too, he was starting his career after World War I, in which he fought (as Meisl had) for the Austrian army, escaped from Russian captivity and engaged in an underground network in Kiev. But unlike Meisl, he was finding his way within a pronounced new national framework. What Aaltonen was to Finnish sculpture, Wierzyński was to Polish poetry. Poland's full independence, sealed with a final victory over Russia in 1921, heralded an era of political, social and cultural nation-building. Warsaw, its booming centre, was every bit as dynamic as Paris and Berlin. Wierzyński – and a handful of other poets, named 'Skamander' after the river on the Trojan plain of Homer's epic poem, *The Iliad* – were a vital part of the scene. The Polish 'Skamanders' each had distinct emphases, but they were united in their rejection of Symbolism's opaqueness and the conventional gloom of Polish lyric and animated by a desire to make their poetry speak to audiences – and to forge a world of future possibilities. It is in this context that *Laur olimpijski* (Olympic Laurel), Wierzyński's fourth collection, was composed from 1925 and published in 1927, with the poem 'Nurmi' at its heart.

The fifteen poems of *Laur olimpijski* treat a range of sports – athletics, football, boxing, even polar exploration – in a neoclassical style. As Donald Davie observed over 60 years ago, in the first (and to date only) English translation of Wierzyński's work, this marked both a return to the classical tradition, of which the Poles had always viewed themselves custodians, and, in the new atmosphere of the 1920s, a search 'for an alternative view of art and life'.[8] Greek in conception – 'manly, direct, energetic and disciplined' – the collection drew its inspiration from Pindar's *Olympian Odes*. The resonances are manifest:

the focus on individuals, the abundance of metaphor and hyperbole, the prevalence of hexameter form, the allusions to Greek myth. But, as Barry Keane astutely notes, Wierzyński was seeking to move beyond Pindar 'in favour of a new mythology that the modern Games provided'.[9] Examined for their 'strength and optimism' and a 'seemingly limitless ability to pass the boundaries set by their predecessors', Wierzyński's Olympians exemplify the potential of all humankind. They stand for a broader, moral good but exist also in a philosophical realm that allows 'the metaphysical concepts of time and space' to 'become momentarily imaginable'. Wierzyński's poetry is controlled and ambitious, and it is accomplished 'without emotional involvement'. His Nurmi is as different from Pindar as it is from Meisl.

Wierzyński's 'Nurmi' poem is worth reading in full. It is given here, for the first time, in a literal English translation.[10]

My step is a dance march,
My step, like a heart, beats,
I am a clock of breath,
I am floating in the air like a tower.

My rhythm merges with the earth,
Beats on it with a resounding foot,
I am running around the world,
Through America and Europe.

My movement after movement comes,
It turns into a moving wheel,
I am a clock of effort,
I am a record of inspiration.

I jump over the stands,
I pass screaming stadiums,
The wind of my wings carries me,
The wind great and inexhaustible.

I chant the pace and increase it,
I am just moving to the finish line,
Tell these crowds of people –
Let them be silent, let them be quiet.

I don't want any victory,
I don't want their applause or screaming,
I want to break the tape and rest
On an old Greek monument.

With its repetitions and, in the original, ABCB rhyme scheme (the ballad quatrain beloved of English folk music), 'Nurmi' appears simple, even simplistic. But it is far from it. It unfolds within a poetic universe that is spun throughout the rest of the collection. It is a universe that is both bounded by the endless metaphysical ideas of time and space and moored at a distant anchor point in the classical world (America and Europe are traversed, but ancient Greece is reached). It remains dispassionate, the first-person perspective only enhances its coolness of tone. And it sets aside stardom in search of a greater good. Like the other pieces in *Laur olimpijski*, the poem seeks to align the uniqueness of the subject with the universal too. Given Nurmi's exceptionalism, this demands considerable artistry. While rhythm and rhyme (more obvious in the original) establish the steady lapping of the track, Nurmi both merges with it and floats above it. While Wierzyński's other protagonists struggle for breath, Nurmi not only becomes breath, but does so with a continuous conversion of poetic oxygen: metaphors become similes, similes metaphors; images clash, resolve, and clash again; abstraction becomes literal, the literal in turn figurative. Like Nurmi, the poem is constantly on the move. And as it moves, Nurmi's and Wierzyński's virtuosity elide: displaying Nurmi's prowess is also about the poet displaying his own. The judges in the 1928 Olympic Arts Competition were impressed and awarded Wierzyński the gold in the 'Lyric' section.

## THE SCULPTOR: RENÉE SINTENIS

Another medallist in the 1928 Competition, Renée Sintenis, who took bronze in the 'Sculpture' section, was equally captivated by Nurmi. Born in Lower Silesia and brought up in rural Brandenburg and Berlin, she began sculpting and exhibiting before World War I, but her career took off rapidly in the 1920s. Signed up by Alfred Flechtheim, a respected Jewish dealer who represented leading artists across Germany, she became part of the capital's cultural circles. Flechtheim protected and projected his protégés in equal measure, through his fabulous soirées, his magazine *Querschnitt* (Cross-section), which became *the* culture periodical of the Weimar Republic, and careful placement of his talent in the public realm.[11] Sintenis's look and persona fitted Flechtheim's model of artist as star. Tall, slender and striking, she sported an Eton bob and drove around town in a Studebaker. The very personification of the Weimar 'New Woman', she advertised for cigarettes and luxury Swiss watches. She was also known for her athleticism. She enjoyed playing table tennis and rode every morning through the city's central Tiergarten park, retiring afterwards, still in full gear, to a café on the stylish Ku'damm to breakfast conspicuously with the English papers. She was a frequent spectator at boxing and cycling events at the Sports Palace, where she watched the fighters she knew from Flechtheim's gatherings, some of whom (notably future World Heavyweight Champion Max Schmeling) she also sculpted.

It is easy to assume that Germany was awash with sports-themed art in the 1920s. The works in our exhibition by Willi Baumeister (fig. 64) and George Grosz (fig. 9) are ubiquitously referenced in cultural histories of Weimar, and Germany had one of the largest submissions to the Arts Competition in 1928. But such impressions are misleading. A show put on in 1927 by the Berlin Secession (a famous group of progressive artists) and the German Museum for Physical Culture in fact bemoaned the dearth of good art on sport,[12] and the German entries the following year in Amsterdam were the result of a concerted push by Edwin Redslob, the Reich Art Commissar in the Interior Ministry tasked with representing democratic Weimar at home and abroad. When the Museum of Modern Art in New York showcased the latest trends in German art in 1931, only a handful related to sport. Preeminent among them was *Nurmi* by Sintenis (fig. 99), whose work by this stage had been displayed in Paris and was held in nearly 30 museums and galleries around the world. The 1931 MoMa catalogue called her 'the most distinguished German sculptor'.[13] Rivals might have questioned that claim, but certainly not when it came to sport. As in Sintenis's other sporting figures, *Nurmi* lives off a combination of oppositions. There is flow and arrested moment: the athlete's foot is like the stick of the

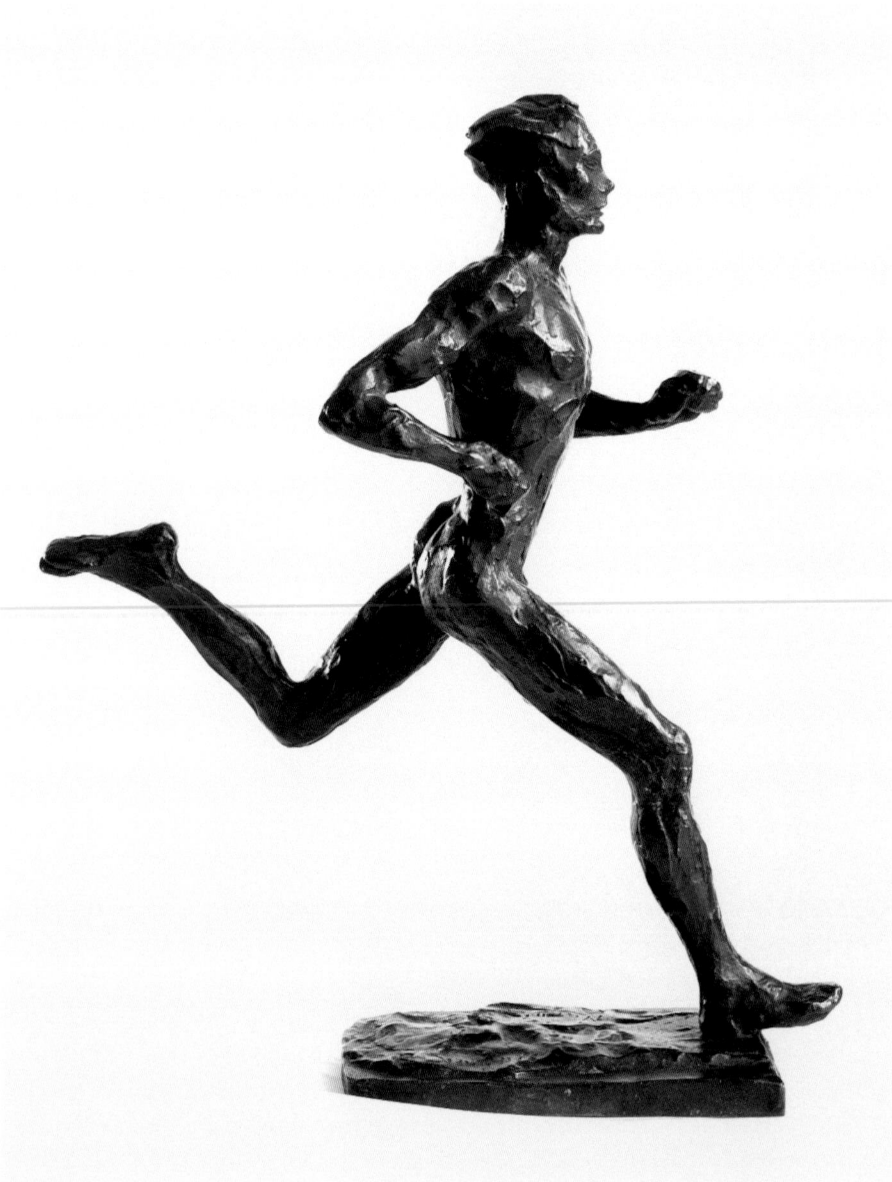

**99.** (cat.73) Renée Sintenis (1888–1965)
*The Athlete* (*Nurmi*), 1926

Bronze, 41 × 34.5 × 16.5 cm
Leicester Museums and Galleries, Leicester (Y.F1.2014.0.0)

Overlooked by the judges in the Olympic Arts Competition in 1928 in favour of her *Footballer*, Renée Sintenis's *Nurmi* went on to become her most celebrated sports piece. It captures the athlete's three distinctive features: massive stride and fully planted feet; arms pumping at mid-chest level; upright torso and motionless head. A 'statuesque' runner (as Peter Lovesey put it), Sintenis's *Nurmi* is also, unusually, human.

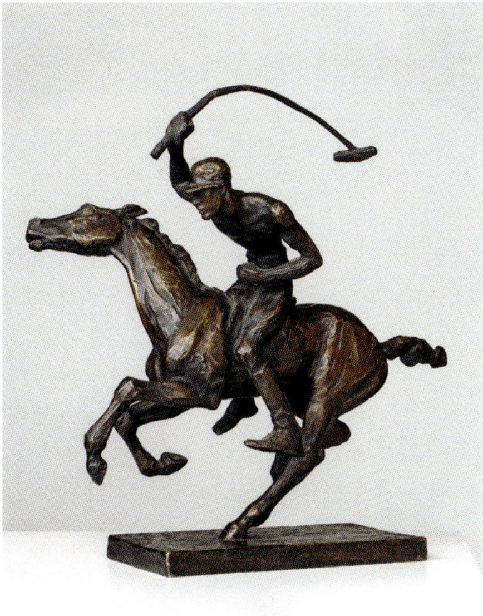

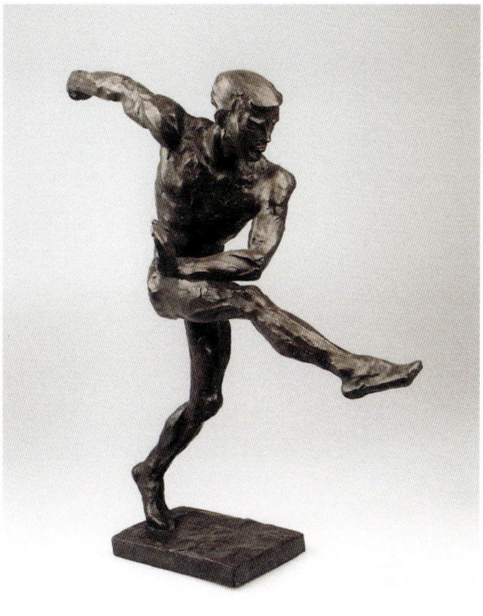

**100.** Renée Sintenis (1888–1965)
*Polo Player*, 1929
(*Polospieler*)
Bronze, 41 × 41.8 × 17.5 cm
Neue Nationalgalerie, Berlin (NG 66/81)

Sintenis's *Polo Player* was entered in the 1932 Olympic Arts Competition – a year after her *Nurmi* was selected for the MoMa show on German art – but came away without a medal. It shows Sintenis's two favourite subjects – animal and athlete – in contradictory but harmonious movement.

**101.** Renée Sintenis (1888–1965)
*The Footballer*, 1927
(*Der Fußballspieler*)
Bronze, 40 × 15.2 × 37.5 cm
Kröller-Müller Museum, Otterlo
(KM 113.238)

Invited to the Games for the first time since 1912, Germany came roaring back in Amsterdam 1928, placing second in the medal table to the United States. They were no less prolific in the Arts Competition, claiming the most medals overall (eight). Sintenis's bronze-winning entry, *The Footballer*, typifies her skill with sporting subjects: balance, power and exertion are arrested in a single moment that suggests speed and fluidity.

*Polo Player* (which she submitted to the 1932 Competition in Los Angeles), coiled and caught in the infinitesimal pause before it snaps forward again (fig. 100).[14] There is ease and strenuousness. There is explosion and calm. Each of these oppositions is held in balance, and – like *The Footballer* (fig. 101), which was awarded the medal in 1928 – the work is about balance itself. Completed largely from memory (probably after Nurmi's 3000m world record in Berlin in spring 1926), it is a remarkable piece.[15]

But to really understand *Nurmi* we need to look elsewhere in Sintenis's oeuvre. For what distinguishes it from Meisl's and Wierzyński's renderings is its sense of intimacy. Sintenis is termed an Expressionist, but her work bears none of the movement's chief hallmarks (such as anger, mourning, despair),[16] and she uses Impressionist techniques (such as the roughing of surfaces) as well. Her work nestles in a niche of its own. From the beginning, she devoted her attention to small-scale sculptures of animals – a product of her childhood in the countryside and a motif she continued after starting on sport. Foals, deer, horses and dogs abound, static at first, increasingly mobile. They are marked by a desire to capture the animal as its own living being, without projection of human thought or concern.[17] In fact, when asked about her choice of favourite subject, she responded that animals, unlike humans, expected nothing of her.[18] Sintenis's creatures radiate closeness, affinity and warmth, from artist to animal and vice versa. The pieces were popular and sold very well; later, her *Berlin Bear* (1956) became the symbol of the city and is still awarded as a trophy at the Berlinale Film Festival. Attempting to describe her work in 1927, author Hans Siemsen noted that when you picked a Sintenis up, you never wanted to put it down again. 'Should I concoct something clever to say about the meaning of Renée Sintenis?', Siemsen asked, adding, 'I would rather look at [her work] for the thousandth time!'[19] And this is what *Nurmi* is all about: the invitation to look, touch, hold in both hands, just as the artist had – to take Nurmi as he is, in his own terms. One lucky owner who had this opportunity was Ernest Hemingway.[20]

*

Arguably unlike any athlete before or since, Paavo Nurmi pushed the bounds of understanding. His achievements were exceptional, his manner eccentric. Giving so much but giving away so little, he permitted people to make of him what they wanted. We have looked at four such people here – leading exponents of their respective crafts, from Finland and Central Europe. At critical moments in their careers, these writers and artists rose to the athlete's challenge, producing their own distinct visions of him: Nurmi the national hero; Nurmi the superhuman phenomenon; Nurmi the epitome of human achievement, surging through time and space; Nurmi open and understandable. Each to their own. As Ron Clarke, one of the best distance runners of the 1960s, wrote: 'Even to [those who knew him best], he was enigmatic, sphinx-like, a god in a cloud. It was as if he was all the time playing a role in a drama. Yet, often the man seemed true to the legends that were woven around him.'[21]

# 11

# CINEMA AND THE SPORTING BODY

PANTELIS MICHELAKIS

Sport and film have been 'intimately connected from the very inception of moving pictures'.[1] Among the earliest sports films were those covering football, baseball, boat races, cricket, motor racing and, above all, boxing. The appeal of such films was twofold: athletic prowess and dramatic tension. Although the modern Olympics and moving pictures emerged in the same year, 1896, the first Games were not filmed. Chronophotographic studies of athletes were produced at the Paris Games of 1900, but it was not until the one-off, so-called Intercalated Games of 1906, which took place in Athens halfway between the 1904 Games in St. Louis and the 1908 Games in London, that the film industry took an interest in the Olympics. The surviving film footage from Antwerp 1920 limits itself to a handful of newsreels, a reflection of the limited conditions so soon after World War I, but the coverage of the earlier Games of 1908 in London and of 1912 in Stockholm is certainly more ambitious: moving decisively in the direction of sports films, rather than just sport news on film, it includes not only 'ritual and ceremony' but also 'individual sports and athletes'.[2]

## THE 1924 OLYMPICS

For the 1924 Olympics, three films were produced by Jean de Rovéra and his company Rapid Film: a three-hour film of the Summer Olympics in Paris, a thirty-five-minute film of the Winter Olympics at Chamonix and an eight-minute tribute to the ancient origins of the Games entitled *The Olympic Games As They Were Originally Practised in Ancient Greece Shown in Living Pictures*. All three of them are now digitally restored by the International Olympic Committee (IOC) as part of a larger project of restoring Olympic films, and are available for viewing on DVD and online.[3] The Official Report of the 1924 Games suggests that the French Olympic Committee team identified three reasons why filming them was important: accessibility of the Games by the wider public, sports documentation and information dissemination. As for the decision to assign the filming to a single company, this was the direct result of the size of the event. As the Official Report puts it: '45 nations are involved; 43 are participating in athletic sports alone. Assuming that each nation delegates a camera operator, which is a minimum, there will always be at least 43 operators around the track of the Athletic Stadium, in addition to the official judges ... There was no serious organization to be hoped for with such an overcrowding.'[4]

In addition to the three official films, footage survives from other events related to the 1924 Olympics: this includes glimpses of athletes practising in their own countries, a festive reconstruction of the ancient Olympics at Montmartre, performances in the Théâtre des Champs-Élysées and at least one sports documentary on running produced in the immediate aftermath. Footage also survives from other athletic events of the same year, such as tennis in Wimbledon and elsewhere, and sports from Ireland's Tailteann Games, which were inspired by early Irish history and held for the first time in September 1924.[5]

The impact of the 1924 Olympics on the screen extends beyond such film footage to include more recent fiction films (*Chariots of Fire*, dir. Hugh Hudson, UK, 1981) and TV documentaries (*Paris Jeux t'aime*, dir. Julien Faraut, France, 2005; *The Real Chariots of Fire*, aired on ITV1, UK, on 2 July 2012). Whether directly or indirectly, the impact of the Olympics was also felt very quickly across a number of cinematic genres, including not only sports documentaries but also animation (*Barnyard Olympics*, dir. Paul Terry, USA, 1924; *Animal Athletes*, dir. Grantland Rice, USA, 1924); physical culture (*Wege zu Kraft und Schönheit / Paths to Strength and Beauty*, dir. Wilhelm Prager, Germany, 1925); romantic comedy (*The American Venus*, dir. Frank Tuttle, USA, 1926; *Swim Girl, Swim*, dir. Clarence Badger, USA, 1927; *College*, dir. James W. Horne and Buster Keaton, USA, 1927); science fiction (*Metropolis*, dir. Fritz Lang, Germany, 1927); and action and adventure films (twelve *Tarzan* films featuring the American Olympic swimmer Johnny Weissmuller between 1932 and 1948). Looking sideways, we may also want to consider the role of the 1924 Olympics in the history of another twentieth-century mass medium, radio: the French journalist Edmond Dehorter would experiment with live broadcasting of key events of the Games on Radio Paris (see Dine's chapter); and one of the greatest British athletes of the Paris Olympics, Harold Abrahams (see Holt's chapter), would go on to become another pioneer of the art of sports commentary for the BBC.

## GAMES ANCIENT AND MODERN

If we put Jean de Rovéra's films for the 1924 Olympics alongside other contemporary and later films related to the Games, three main issues come to the fore: modes of cinematic storytelling, slow motion as a film technique and self-actualisation in and through the cinematic screen.

'The 1924 Games were the first which were marked by the production of a full-length feature-type film.'[6] The film of the Summer Games begins with the arrival of dignitaries and the Opening Ceremony (fig. 102) and it concludes with the most cinematic of early twentieth-century sports, boxing. 'All the principal events are recorded in the film, each followed by a portrait of the winner, still puffing, face-on to the camera. The film is also

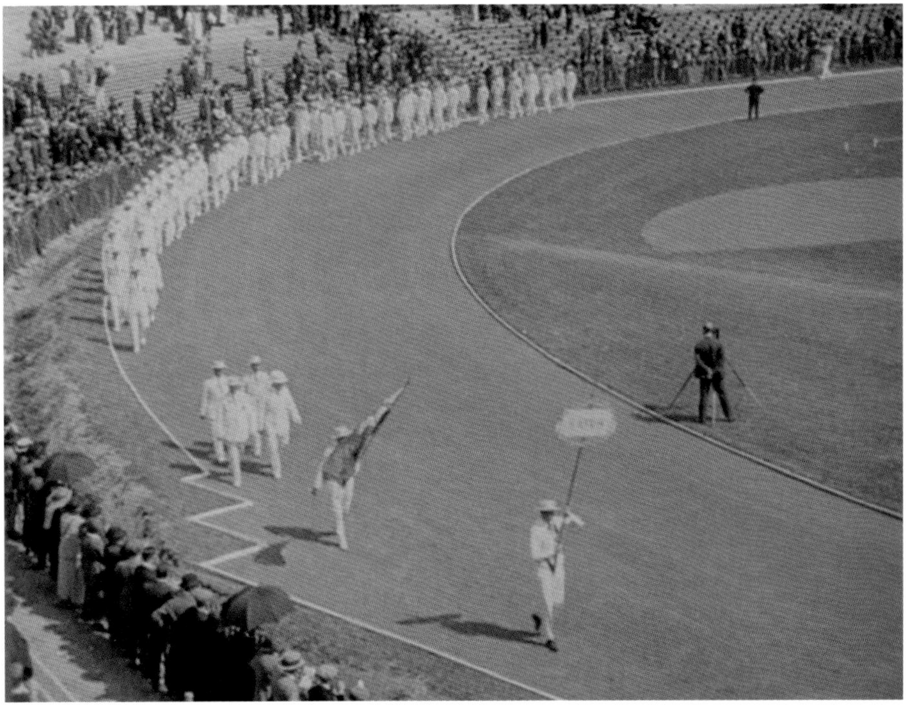

**102.** (cat. 1) Still from Jean de Rovéra (1898–1939), director; Rapid Film, production company *The Olympic Games in Paris 1924*, official film, 1924
Comité International Olympique (CIO)

The two films produced by Jean de Rovéra of the Winter and Summer Olympics of 1924 are based on the premise of unmediated access to ritual and athletic bodies, the lavish spectacle of ceremony and the dramatic spectacle of athletic endeavour. Occasionally, however, they also provide glimpses of a more complex historical reality that involves not only spectacular bodies but also contemporary crowds as well as film cameras and their operators.

of interest in that it attempts to illustrate the range of Olympic events, including the swimming, gymnastics and equestrian sports, in addition to track and field events in the main stadium.'[7] Despite the scale of its coverage of the Games, however, the film suffers from an episodic structure. Extensive coverage allowed for length to accumulate, for all the different disciplines to be represented, for leading athletes to make an appearance and for factual information about timings and scorings to be communicated through title cards after each victory, but it lacked coherence and an overarching story or style to hold it all together.

The film of the Winter Games at Chamonix was shorter, but it was produced in the same manner and had the same drawbacks. The visual interest of its subject matter had to do with the intensity of specific moments and the achievements of specific

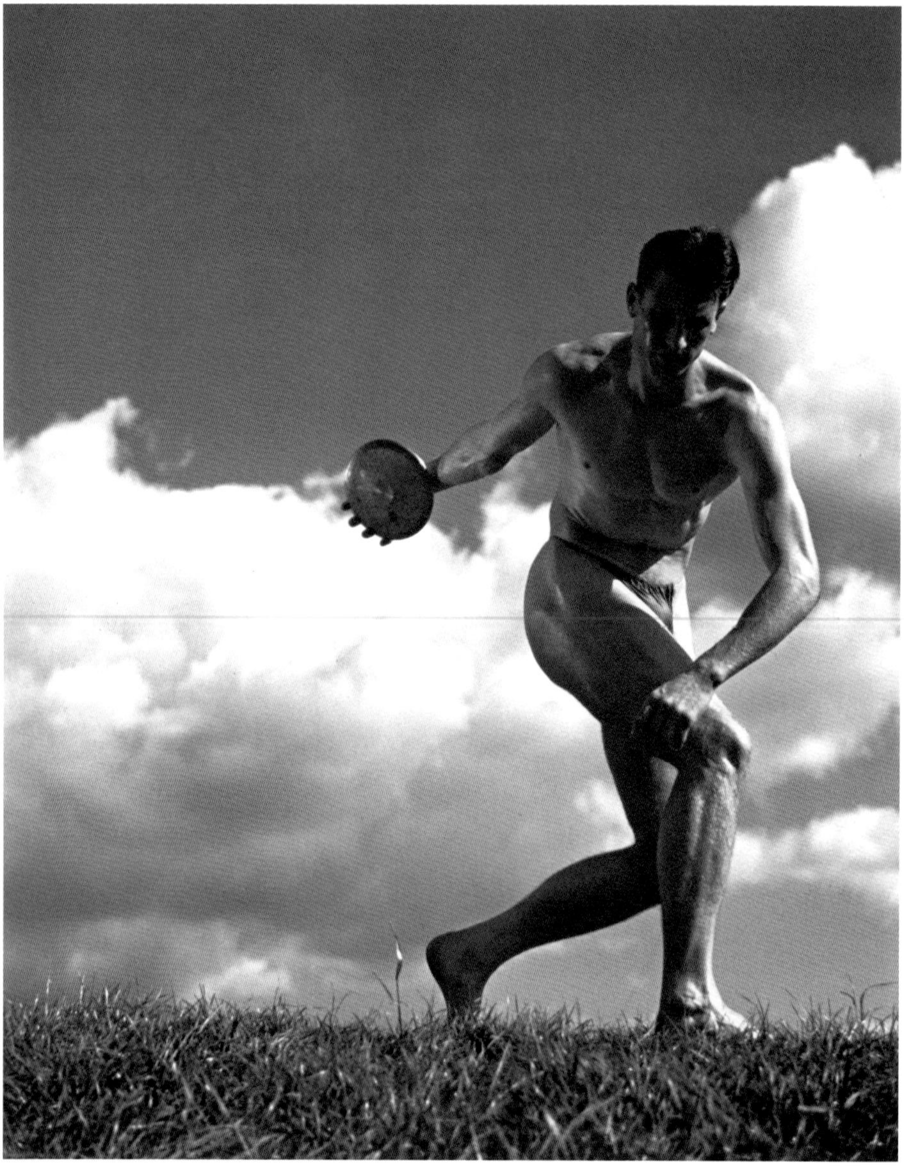

**103.** (cat. 167) Willy Zielke (1902–1989)
Production still from the prologue to Leni Riefenstahl's (1902–2003) film *Olympia*, Germany, 1938
Black and white photograph

The statue of Myron's *Diskobolos* (Discus Thrower) (fig. 76) comes to life as German Olympic athlete Erwin Huber in the prologue to Leni Riefenstahl's film documentary of the Berlin Olympics of 1936. This powerful transition from antiquity to modernity, from stone to flesh, and from stillness to life is heavily indebted to the recognisability and status of Myron's statue, which derive from its countless reproductions, imitations and uses in the arts, in popular culture and in politics.

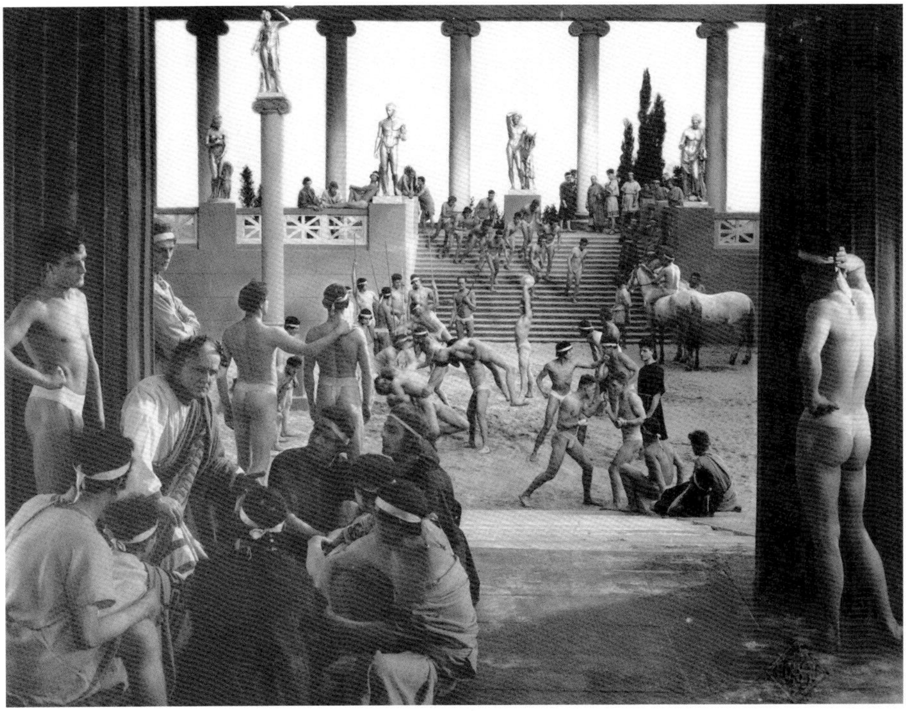

**104.** Publicity still for the film *Ways to Strength and Beauty* (*Wege zu Kraft und Schönheit*), directed by Wilhelm Prager (1876–1955) and produced by Nicholas Kaufmann (1892–1970), Germany, 1925

In the German physical culture film *Ways to Strength and Beauty*, the almost naked, healthy, active bodies of Greco-Roman antiquity provide a foil for the unhealthy bodies of modernity, but also a vision for what the future of modernity could look like if a culture of physical exercise was promoted.

individuals that played no role in the rest of the narrative. This probably helps explain why the distribution and exhibition of the two films was so limited (there is no evidence they were ever shown outside France and Britain), and why they have left almost no visible trace in the film trade magazines of 1924.[8] Even today, the official website of the International Olympic Committee breaks down the films to shorter 'highlights' that can be viewed selectively and out of sequence, effectively reverting to the presentation mode and narrative conventions of the newsreel: brief sequences, focused on spectacle or display rather than on narrative, with fluid boundaries, available for repeat viewings and replication through recombination.

Taken together, it is clear that Rovéra's films attempt to bring the worlds of modernity and antiquity closer together, while also policing the boundaries that keep them apart, in separate narratives. Two of them capture the modern world of international sports. The third focuses on an ancient world of athletics reconstructed for educational

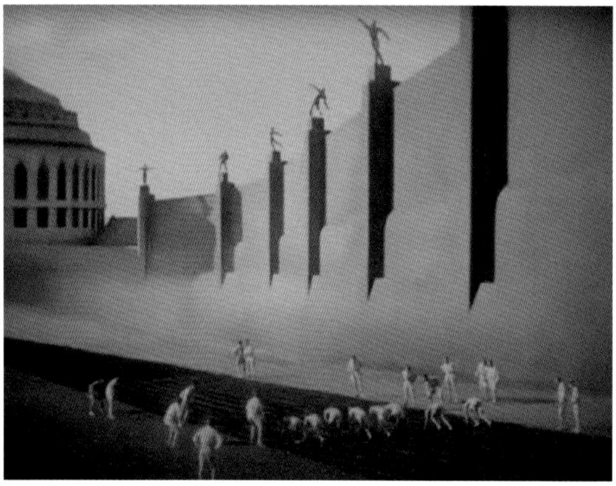

**105.** Still from the film *Metropolis*, directed by Fritz Lang (1890–1976), Germany, 1927

In the futuristic year of 2026, in the city of Metropolis, sports are reserved for the city's blonde, slim and radiant elite. The classicising track-race sequence in an open-air stadium is elaborated from the novel by the German writer Thea von Harbou, which was first published in 1925, in the aftermath of the Paris Olympics.

purposes. The dynamics of the relation between the two worlds is left to the viewer to configure. And yet, long before Leni Riefenstahl's film for the 1936 Olympics in Berlin, whose prologue offers the fantasy of a seamless transition from antiquity to modernity (fig. 103),[9] other films, contemporary with our period, also provided examples of how antiquity and modernity can be interwoven within the same narrative. In the German physical culture film *Paths to Strength and Beauty*, ancient sport and beauty appear as the opposite of an unhealthy modern lifestyle, but also as a model to which a modern culture of physical exercise can aspire (fig. 104). In this film, antiquity and modernity are juxtaposed through a history of decline, but they are also seen in terms of an analogy, with Greek ideals being reclaimed as 'empowering for the citizen and crucial for the nation-state'.[10] Similarly, in Fritz Lang's *Metropolis*, under an open sky, the glow of white stone and the gaze of statues, the 'gilded youth' of this futuristic city enjoys track races 'as carefree but controlled diversions' (fig. 105).[11] As Siegfried Kracauer has suggested in his discussion of this ornamental style in *Metropolis*, its cultural and political implications are not to reaffirm but, in Thomas Elsaesser's words, 'to blur the opposition between myth and reason in modern, industrialized societies'.[12] Another film of the same period that blends the worlds of ancient and modern sport is the American animation picture *Barnyard Olympics*, released in the immediate aftermath of the 1924 Games. At the end of the film, the hare and the tortoise, Aesop's 'ancient rivals', return to the screen for one more race (fig. 106). This race has a double twist. The tortoise wins because it is faster than the hare. It is faster than the hare because, as it turns out, it is a fake tortoise (a dog and a cat emerge from inside its shell). The lessons to be learned from the racetracks of modernity may not be the same as from those of antiquity, but the celebration of speed and victory remains a constant, providing a bridge between the two worlds.

Rovéra's short film *The Olympic Games As They Were Originally Practised in Ancient Greece Shown in Living Pictures* deserves a closer look. As the opening title card of the film suggests, it consists of a series of 'living pictures'. Athletes pose against a dark

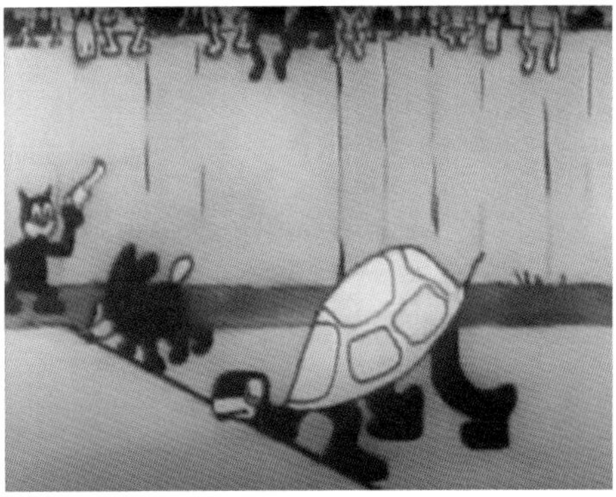

**106.** Still from the animation film *Barnyard Olympics*, from the series *Aesop's Fables*, directed by Paul Terry (1887–1971), 7 September 1924

One of the earliest cinematic responses to the Olympic Games of 1924 is the short animation film *Barnyard Olympics*, released in early September 1924 as part of Paul Terry's long-running animation series *Aesop's Fables*. The film features animals training for the Olympic Games, and it concludes with a playful nod to Aesop's fable 'The Tortoise and the Hare'. The topic was revisited by Walt Disney in a Mickey Mouse cartoon that bears the same title in the year of the Los Angeles Olympics (1932).

stage background and perform traditional sports with the help of costumes and props: jumping, javelin throwing, discus throwing, running, fighting with spears and swords, and wrestling. Thematically, the poses offer compositions reminiscent of ancient marble sculpture and vase paintings (fig. 107). Occasionally, they are modelled on specific artworks, inviting the viewer to try and identify how many and which ones are being 'illustrated'. The reconstruction of Greek athletics, however, is achieved with the help not only of classical art but also of contemporary performance. More specifically, it relies on stylised acrobatics and stillness within the frame, drawing on the specialised acts in vaudeville theatre. Living tableaux and statues were an important part of early twentieth-century popular entertainment: cinema would embrace them from the very beginning for their power not only to educate but also to surprise and excite by blurring the distinction between art and life. The world of the ancient Olympics, however, is *also* reconstructed with the help of cinematographic tools: the camera explores the arrangement and movement of different characters with the help of tracking shots and slow motion. For instance, the throwing of the javelin and the discus is demonstrated with the help of multiple athletes holding poses next to each other to represent sequential movement.

In scientific films and in motion-picture photography, the camera is an aid for the human eye, allowing it to catch what it would otherwise miss: 'the concrete visual details of ... dexterity, speed, and elegance' (fig. 108).[13] Often joined by replays from varying angles, slow motion is used to give access to what really happened and how. In athletic films, slow motion has two primary aims: it helps demonstrate skill and style. It stresses a moment in time, captures it and makes it available for storage and retrieval. And indeed this is how it is employed in Rovéra's two films for the Winter and Summer Olympics. In *The Olympic Games As They Were Originally Practised in Ancient Greece*, on the other hand, slow motion, and more generally the lack of stability between stillness and movement, does not only help demonstrate skill and style. It is a device for forging

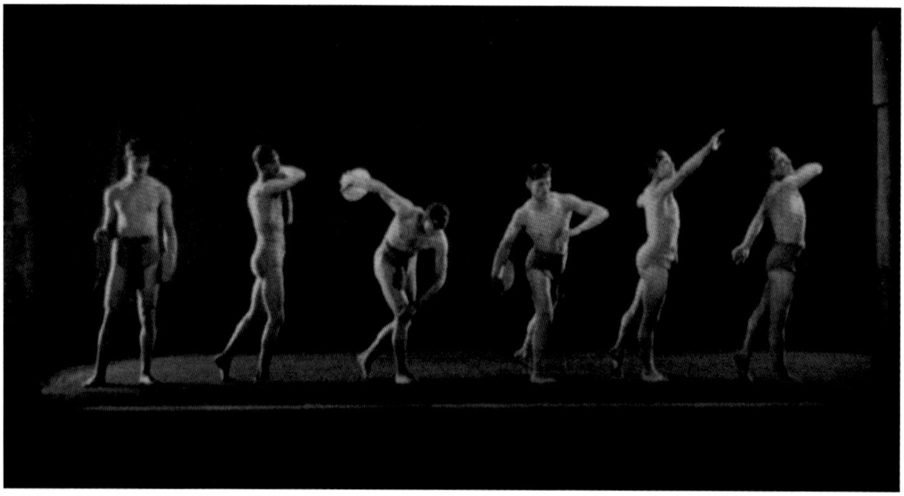

**107.** (cat. 9) Jean de Rovéra (1898–1939), director; Les Films Sportifs, production company
*The Olympic Games as They Were Originally Practised in Ancient Greece Shown in Living Pictures*, 1924
Comité International Olympique (CIO)

Athletes hold poses next to each other to demonstrate sequential movement in the throwing of the discus as practised in ancient Greece. The subject matter and costume aim to educate the viewer in ancient athletics, while the composition is indebted to the aesthetic qualities and narrative conventions of classical sculpture and vase painting. It is also indebted to motion-picture photography and to the playful stylisation of 'living statues' (actors in costume imitating statues or paintings) in vaudeville theatre.

an ideal: bodies 'stripped bare of cultural and historical marking, achieving a new level of perfection and empowerment in [their] performance, cinematographically captured in a way that enables [them] to float outside time'.[14] In the early 1920s, slow motion emerges as a technique in flux and in flex. It opens up the documentary to other film genres, and cinema itself to the other arts. It blurs the boundaries between fact and fiction, action and re-enactment, but also the boundaries between cinema, photography, painting and theatre. For instance, it is exploited in sports and educational films to create a dream-like atmosphere, as is the case with the 1924 sports film *Running – A Sport That Creates Both Bodily and Mental Health*.[15] As it says in the title card for a race in slow motion, 'This is the kind of thing runners *dream about* the night before the race'. For these reasons, the technique of slow motion is also a feature of later films that capture Olympic athletes: for instance, in Riefenstahl's *Olympia* and in Hudson's *Chariots of Fire*, slow motion joins replays and varying camera angles to convey not objectivity but quite the opposite, a sense of 'personal time as dramatically slowed or arrested and the emotions surrounding it',[16] or the coupling of harmony and rhythm, the beauty of form and the beauty of movement.

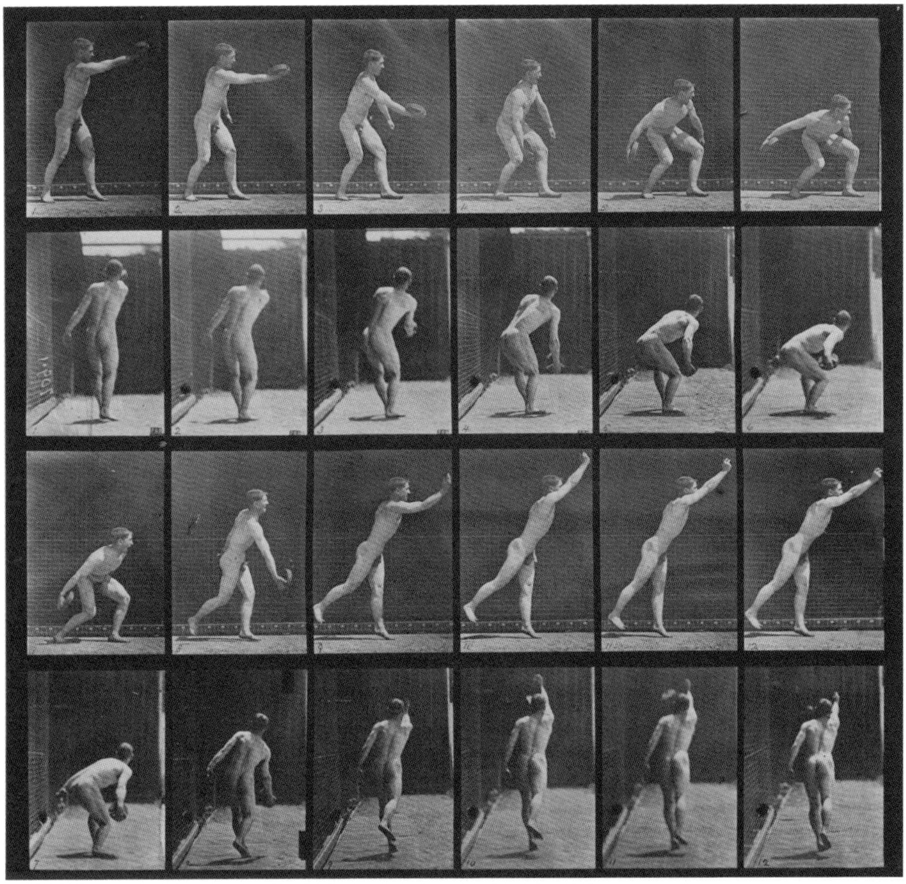

**108.** After Eadweard Muybridge (1830–1904)
Man throwing the discus, plate 307 from Muybridge's chronophotographic series *Animal Locomotion: An Electro-Photographic Investigation of Consecutive Phases of Animal Movements*, 1887
Collotype, 26.5 × 27.5 cm
Wellcome Collection, London (27779i)

Motion-picture photography draws on the cultural value and recognisability of Greco-Roman athletics and sculpture, and on the modern desire to embody them anew. Through the rapid taking of multiple sequential photographs of a nude athlete in motion, it does not simply emulate the ancient Greek statue of Myron's *Diskobolos* – it brings to life the world of antiquity.

## THE ART OF SELF-ACTUALISATION

The audio-visual material on and around the Paris Games offers opportunities to reflect not only on competing attitudes towards antiquity and towards the body in time but also on shifting attitudes to the concept of 'self-actualisation' as it circulates among individuals and collective entities. At one end of the spectrum there is the celebration of individual autonomy and empowerment, the sense of realising one's full potential. The celebration of this paradigm can be found in the cheerfulness and radiance of the gilded

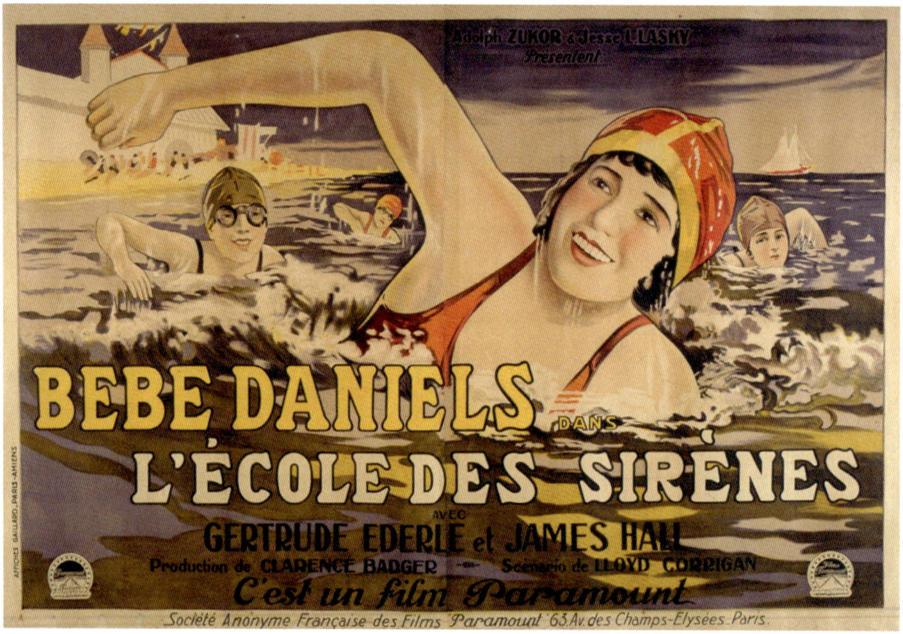


**109.** (cat. 153) Affiches Gaillard, Paris, Amiens (active 1920s)
*School of Mermaids*, film poster, c. 1927
(*L'École des Sirènes*)
Colour lithography on paper, 162.5 × 236 cm
Musée National du Sport, Nice
(MNS 1993.38.8)

The now-lost American silent romantic comedy *Swim Girl, Swim* (or, as it was called in its French release, *School of Mermaids*) starred Alice Smith as Bebe Daniels and had a guest appearance by the 'Queen of the Waves', English Channel swimmer Gertrude Ederle (fig. 45). Like numerous other films of the 1920s spanning a range of genres, it focused on swimming as a physical activity that valorises female agency and autonomy.

youth in the track-race sequence of Lang's *Metropolis*. It can also be traced in many of the recreation culture films that emerge in the 1920s, for instance those featuring open-air swimming, which 'redefine the very image of femininity in the popular imagination' (fig. 109).[17] It is also present in popular accounts of Johnny Weissmuller's transformation from Olympic swimmer to cinematic Tarzan, 'the ultimate self-taught, self-made man', 'a climber both of trees and of the evolutionary and social ladder' (fig. 110).[18]

At the other end of the self-actualisation spectrum, we have not so much mastery in modernity over the human body's frailties but rather release from or transcendence of them. This is arguably the case with many of the victorious athletes that pose for Rovéra's camera while still gasping for air after their intense physical and emotional strain: it is their endeavour that comes through rather than their victory. This attitude to self-actualisation can also be linked to the modern characters in the *Paths to Strength and Beauty*, who display their determination to pursue body aestheticism by escaping

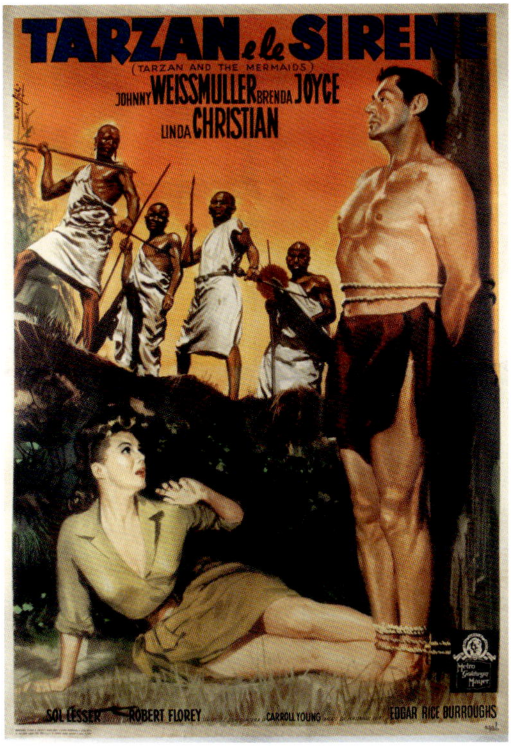


**110.** (cat. 157) Enzo Nistri (1923–2008), artist; A.G.A.F, Florence (active 1940s–60s)
*Tarzan and the Mermaids*, film poster (Italian release), *c.* 1948 (*Tarzan e le Sirene*)
Colour lithography on paper, 192.2 × 134.6 cm
Musée National du Sport, Nice (MNS 84.6.7)

Weissmuller's Tarzan encounters figures that, from antiquity onwards, have been seen as beyond civilisation (barbarians, Amazons, huntresses and mermaids) in Africa, the 'savage' continent of the British Empire. More than any other cinematic hero of the period, his Tarzan celebrates a vision of white male self-actualisation that transcends the divide between body and mind, civilisation and the wilds of nature.

modernity and training like the Greeks. It informs, very differently, the show of athleticism that, despite all odds, is displayed by the totally inept character of Buster Keaton at the end of *College* (1927). It can be found in the metamorphosis of Harold Abrahams in *Chariots of Fire* from a religious and social outcast to a gold medallist. And it can even, perhaps, be linked to the reinvention of the historical Harold Abrahams, following the abrupt end of his athletic career due to injury in 1925, to a radio commentator who would go on to shape the listening habits of millions of people. Curiously, national self-actualisation would need to wait until Riefenstahl's film of the Berlin Games of 1936 to make an impact on cinematic depictions of the Olympics – and this despite the fact that national character was important in discourses around the modern (and ancient) Olympics from their very inception.[19]

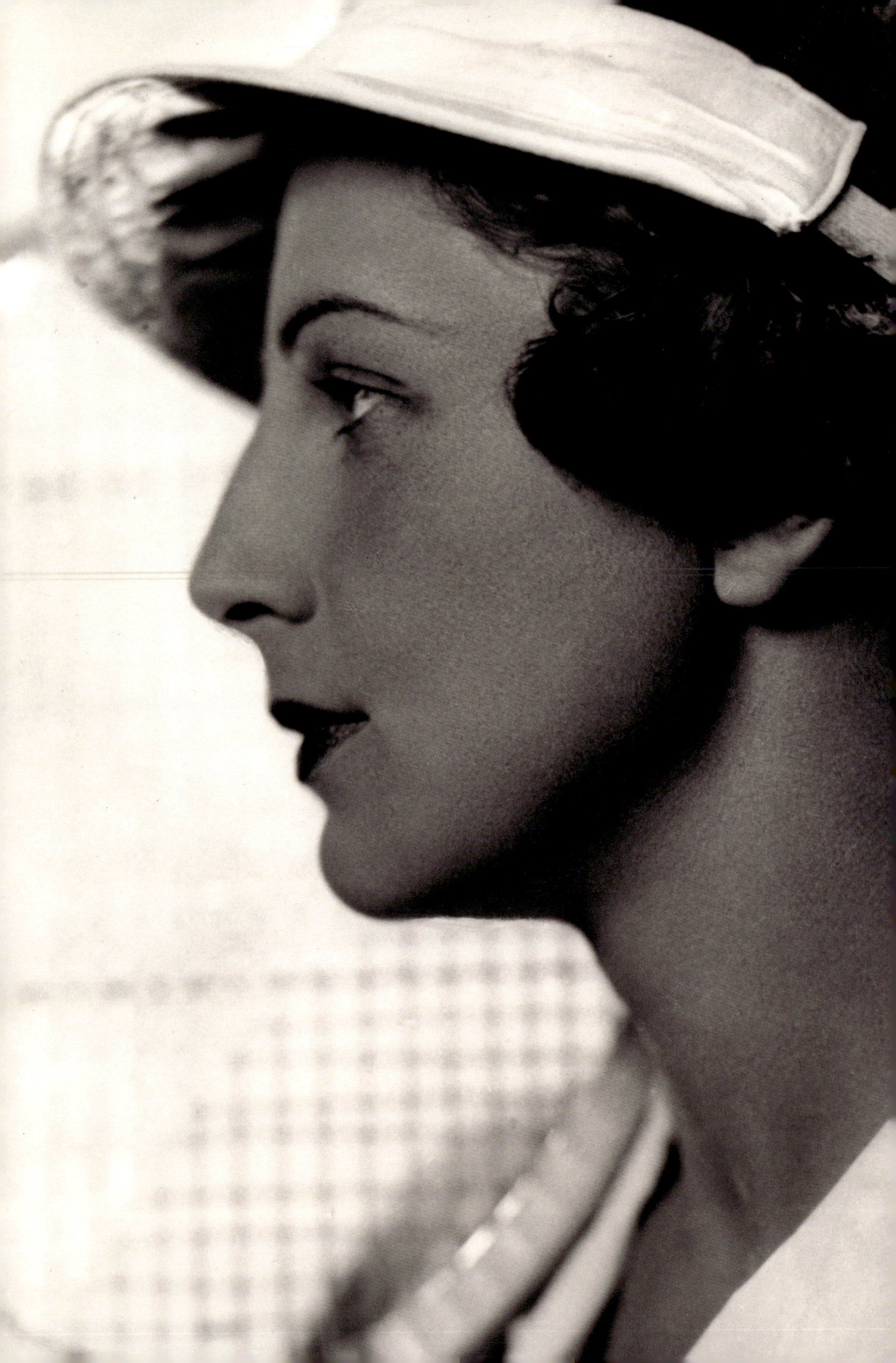

# CATALOGUE

## INTRODUCTION

This year, the Olympics return to Paris for the first time in a century. The 1924 Olympics were the earliest truly international Games and took place at a crucial moment in the histories of sport and art. Paris was establishing itself as *the* modern city, crucible for art, jazz and fashion.

The founder of the modern Olympics, Pierre de Coubertin (1863–1937), was born in Paris. He was inspired by ancient Greece, where the Games began, and by sporting practices emerging in Britain and the United States. His admiration of ancient Greek ideals competed with radically new ways of representing the body, with the realities of World War I casualties and with innovations in science and technology. Newspapers and magazines, photography, radio and cinema broadcast the Paris Games to unprecedented audiences, blurring the boundaries between documentary and artistic styles, and making sport more commercial.

This commercialisation had a profound effect on how sport was – and still is – seen. The bodies it celebrated challenged ideas of beauty, gender and race, and impacted on painting and sculpture. This exhibition highlights how sport *is* culture.

**1.** (fig. 102) Jean de Rovéra (1898–1939), director;
Rapid Film, production company
*The Olympic Games in Paris 1924*,
official film, 1924
© 2010, Comité International Olympique (CIO)

**2.** (fig. 2) Domenico Brucciani and Co., London (1841–1900s); after unrecorded Roman maker (British Museum, London, 117–38 CE, marble); after Polykleitos (bronze, now lost, *c.* 440 BCE)
Plaster cast of *Ribbon Binder*, *c.* 1880
Plaster, metal, paint, 197.7 × 98.4 × 61.8 cm
Museum of Classical Archaeology, Cambridge (185)

**3.** Cast by unrecorded maker;
after unrecorded Roman maker
(The Uffizi, Florence, 100–1 BCE or later, marble);
after unrecorded Greek maker (bronze, now lost, 300–200 BCE)
Plaster cast of *The Wrestlers*, *c.* 1800
Plaster, metal, paint, possibly wood, 97 × 114.5 × 73.5 cm
Museum of Classical Archaeology, Cambridge (390)

**3 ▼**

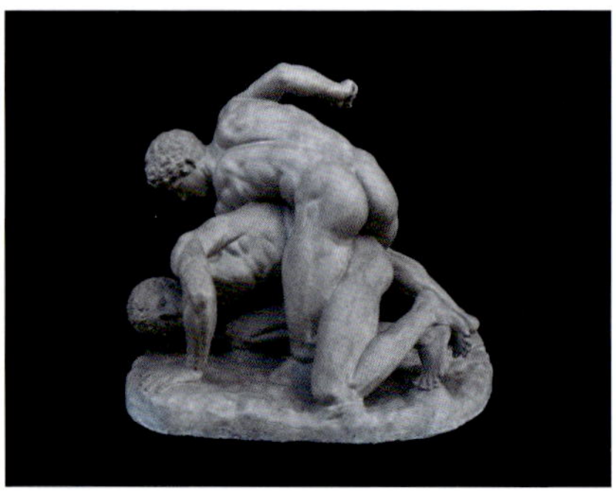

**4.** Unrecorded Roman maker
Herakles wrestling with Antaios, 1–200 CE
Copper alloy, 14.5 × 7.5 × 3.75 cm
The Fitzwilliam Museum, Cambridge, bequeathed by Sir Robert Hyde Greg, 1954
(GR.4.1954)

**5.** (fig. 8) Pheidippos (active 525–510 BCE), painter
Kylix (cup), *c.* 510 BCE
Red-figure pottery, 13.9 × 42 × 33.6 cm
British Museum, London, purchased from Campanari, 1846 (1846,0512.2)

**8 ▼**

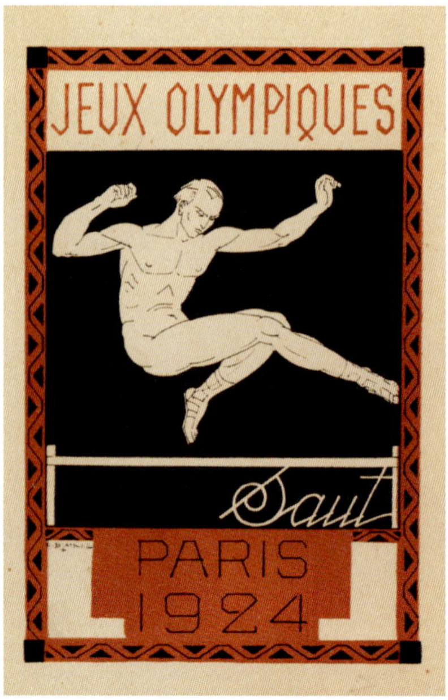

**6.** Unrecorded maker
Panathenaic prize amphora, 336 BCE or earlier
Black-figure pottery, height 83.8 cm
British Museum, London, purchased from Alessandro Castellani, 1873 (1873,0820.371)

This vessel contained olive oil for an athlete victorious in Athens's Panathenaic Games. These games were held every four years in a religious festival in honour of the goddess Athena, who gave the city its name. The other side shows her between columns next to the inscription 'τῶν Ἀθήνηθεν ἄθλων' ([one] of the prizes from Athens).

This side of the amphora shows boxing. Two heavy-set nude figures fight, their hands bound with leather thongs. A third (the winner's next opponent?) eyes them from the sidelines. On the right, the winged goddess Nike (Victory) is ready to award the winner's palm branch.

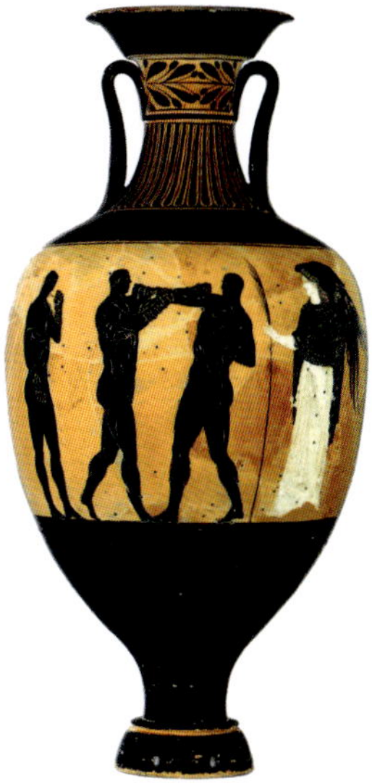

**7.** Émile Louis Bracquemond (1889–1970), maker;
Octave Denis Victor Guillonnet (1872–1967), designer;
Sèvres Porcelain (founded 1740), manufacturer
Paris 1924 Olympic Games, gold-medal winner's vase, 1924
*Pâte-sur-pâte* porcelain, paint, gold leaf, 33 × 13.9 × 6.3 cm
Markus Osterwalder, Switzerland, Olympic historian and collector

This vase is one of four types made for the 1924 Olympics by the Sèvres porcelain factory and given by the city of Paris to gold medallists in individual events. Though smaller than its Greek counterpart and without handles, its narrow neck and nudity are familiar. The roundel shapes echo ancient engraved gemstones. Greek inspiration continues with the gold-laurel detailing.

This classicism is balanced by the modernity of the sports depicted (football, rowing, rugby and diving) and by the aeroplane shapes around the lip. This example went to Swiss horse rider Alphonse Gemuseus, winner of the individual jumping.

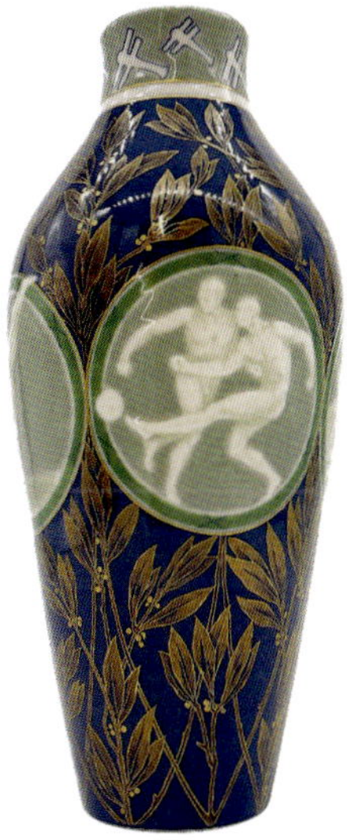

**8.** E. Blanche (active 1914–20s), artist;
Henri François, Paris (active 1920s), printer
*Jump, Olympic Games Paris 1924*, from a set of eight souvenir postcards, 1924
Printing in red and black ink on tan-coloured paper, 14 × 9 cm
Musée National du Sport, Nice, France
(MNS 2006.6.24)

**9.** (fig. 107) Jean de Rovéra (1898–1939), director;
Rapid Film, production company
*The Olympic Games as They Were Originally Practised in Ancient Greece Shown in Living Pictures*, 1924
© 2010, Comité International Olympique (CIO)

## 1. STAGING THE OLYMPICS

The eighth modern Olympics officially opened in Paris on Saturday 5 July 1924. The main stadium was an expensive train ride from the centre in a smoky industrial suburb. Surviving black and white footage is deceptive. The parade of over 3000 uniformed athletes, with their national flags, was as colourful as it was choreographed, making an artwork of the ceremony.

Unlike in the ancient Olympics, women paraded with the men. This was their only appearance in the stadium: they competed at other venues in a limited number of sports – tennis, fencing, swimming and diving.

As the Prince of Wales underlined two days later, each athlete was 'a *sportsman* in the truest sense of the word'. Official stamps and posters juggled modernism and tradition to reinforce this manly message. But being man enough had its limits: the Americans requested hot showers in every room of what was the first Olympic village in history.

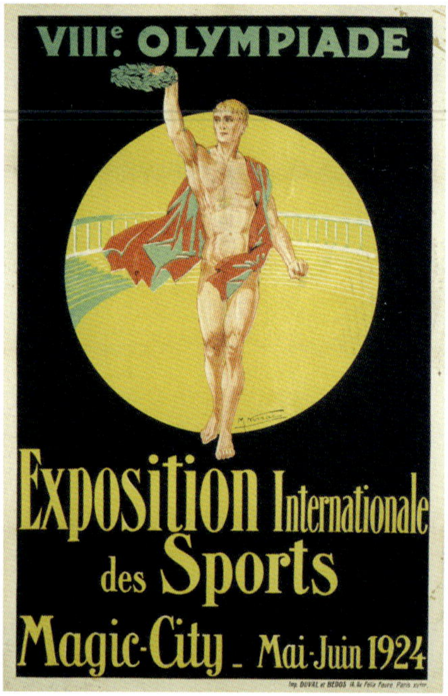


**10.** Marcel Norsac (active 1920s–40s), artist;
Duval and Bedos, Paris (active 1920s–30s), printer
*Eighth Olympiad, International Exhibition of Sport, Magic-City, May–June 1924*, poster, 1924
Colour lithography on paper, 79.5 × 119 cm
Musée National du Sport, Nice, France
(MNS 1989.134.1)

The Olympics spread well beyond Paris's stadiums. This poster advertises the international exhibition of sport held at Paris's Magic-City from 1 May to 31 July 1924. It brought sports organisations and industry together to showcase everything connected with sport and physical education – from gliders and bicycles to equipment, clothes, demonstrations, films and dances.

The Magic-City venue, on the left bank, was known for its masked balls, popular with Paris's gay community. The poster's spotlighting of a flamboyant figure, drapery flying, plays to new and existing audiences: he is like an old-school Apollo, god of sun and light, but also deliciously camp.

**11.** (fig. 7) Jean Droit (1884–1961), artist;
Hachard & Co., Paris (active 1920s), printer
Official poster for the Paris 1924 Olympic Games, 1924
Colour lithography on paper, 116 × 79.6 cm
Victoria and Albert Museum, London, purchased with the support of the American Friends of the V&A in honour of Diana Quasha (E.329-2006)

**12.** (fig. 78) Auguste Matisse (1866–1931), artist;
Cornille & Serre, Paris (active 1910–26), printer
*To the Winners of the Eighth Olympiad*, poster, *c.* 1924
Colour lithography on paper, 105.5 × 75 cm
Victoria and Albert Museum, London, given by Auguste Matisse (E.23-1926)

**13.** Italo Orsi (1889–1947), artist; Comité Olympique Français (founded 1894), publisher
Programme for the Olympic Games Paris 1924, with cover illustration by Italo Orsi, 1924
Colour printing on paper, 26.6 × 21.5 cm
On loan from Wimbledon Lawn Tennis Museum (WTM:2006/62)

The cover of this programme for the tennis competition at the 1924 Olympics is decorated with one of two official poster designs for the Games (for the other, see fig. 7). Orsi's javelin thrower resembles a bronze statue, though he is not nude like ancient Greek athletes, but a modern man in shorts and t-shirt.

The globe signifies the universalism of a Games set against Paris's distinctive skyline, the Basilica of the Sacré Coeur in the foreground. 10,000 copies of each poster were printed, and over half shipped overseas in a celebration of an event shaped by its locale and aimed at world audiences.

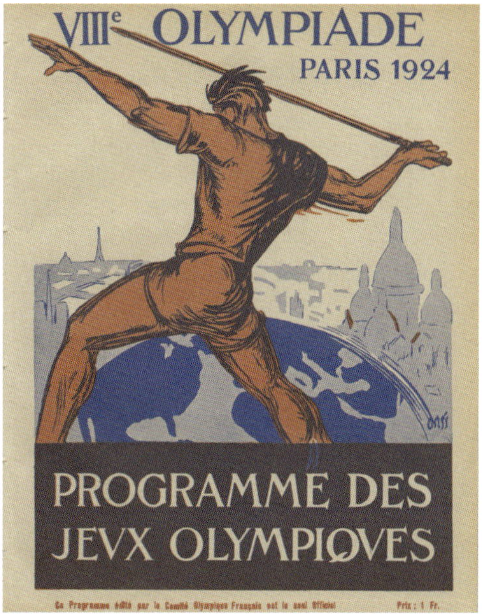


**14.** H.L. Roowy (active *c.* 1900–30), artist; La Lithographie Parisienne, Paris (founded 1866), printer
*Olympic Games, Paris 1924, Tennis; Discus* (illustrated); *Hurdles; Rugby; Swimming*, five souvenir postcards from a set of ten, 1924
Colour lithography on paper, 13.9 × 8.8 cm; 8.8 × 13.9 cm
On loan from Wimbledon Lawn Tennis Museum (WTM:2012/6.1-5)

**15.** (fig. 3) Unrecorded maker
Used admission ticket to the Olympic stadium at Colombes, Paris, 1924
Colour printing on orange-coloured paper, 17.6 × 7.9 cm
Markus Osterwalder, Switzerland, Olympic historian and collector

**16.** Unrecorded maker
Admission ticket to the Winter Olympics in Chamonix, 1924
Printing in black ink on green-coloured paper, 17.5 × 6.6 cm
Markus Osterwalder, Switzerland, Olympic historian and collector

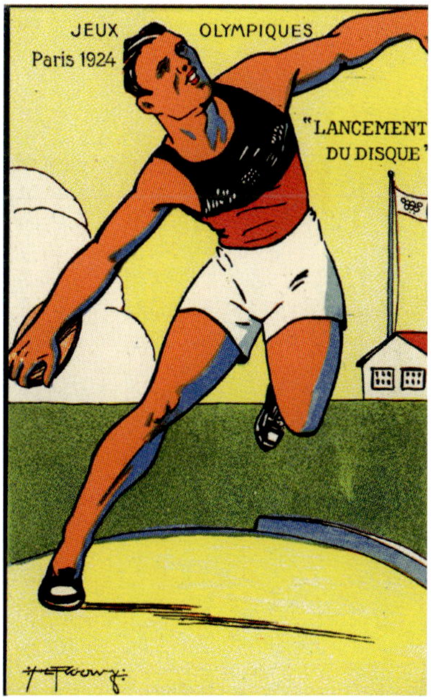


**14 ▲**

**17.** (fig. 6) The British Olympic Association (founded 1905)
'A Sportsman' from *The Eighth Olympiad Paris 1924*, booklet, 1924
Printing on paper, 14 × 22.4 cm
Churchill Archives Centre, Papers of Sir Arthur Marshall (MSHL Acc 2082)

**18.** (fig. 62) UK Passport of Scipio Africanus ('Sam') Mussabini (1867–1927), 1922–31
Printed paper, covered boards, pen and ink, ink stamps, paper stamps, black and white photograph, 15.1 × 10.9 × 8 cm
Lent by the Cadbury Research Library, University of Birmingham (MS935/2)

**19.** Georges Daussy (1862–1951), engraver; Gaston Parison (1889–1959), engraver; after Edmond Henri Becker (1871–1971), designer
Paris 1924 Olympic Games commemorative postage stamps, 1924
Letterpress, glued to a paper envelope with Paris postmarks dated 10 August 1924, 14.5 × 11.2 cm
Markus Osterwalder, Switzerland, Olympic historian and collector

**20.** (fig. 11) Unrecorded photographer
Paris 1924 Olympic Games, Olympic Village, the entrance
(A.N. Paris postcard series, no. 1), 1924
Black and white photograph
© 1924, Comité International Olympique (CIO) (PHO11106719)

**21.** (fig. 16) Unrecorded photographer
Paris 1924 Olympic Games, Opening Ceremony, parade of athletes, Great Britain (GBR), 5 July 1924
Black and white photograph
© 1924, Comité International Olympique (CIO) (PHO11072465)

**22.** (fig. 5) Unrecorded photographer
Paris 1924 Olympic Games, Opening Ceremony, parade of athletes, the delegation in the middle of the Olympic stadium, 5 July 1924
Black and white photograph
© 1924, Comité International Olympique (CIO) (PHO11072460)

**23.** (fig. 19) Unrecorded photographer
Paris 1924 Olympic Games, men's water polo, general view at the Tourelles Olympic swimming pool, 4 May 1924
Black and white photograph
© 1924, Comité International Olympique (CIO), United Archives (PHO10483875)

**19 ▼**

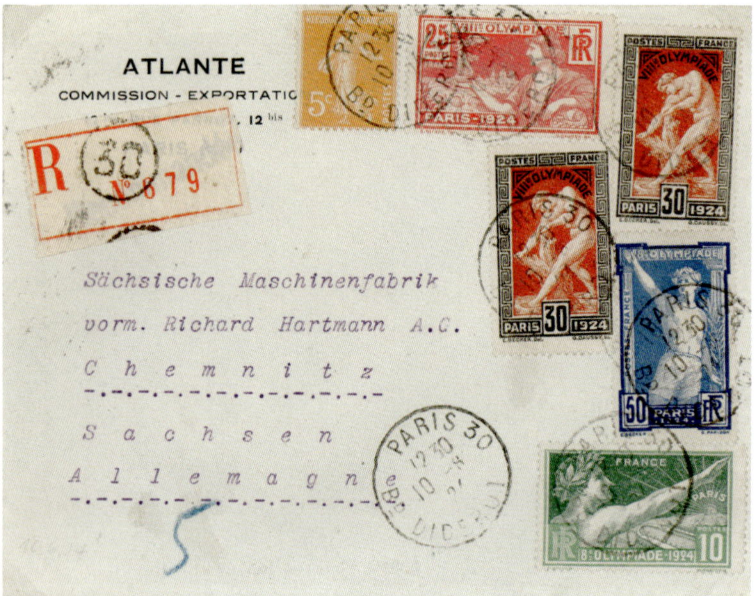

## 2. WHOSE SPORT?

The Paris Olympics attracted the brightest stars and made new ones. Formal portraits, popular images, action-shots, medals and memorabilia relived experiences and created heroes.

Only amateurs could participate in the Olympics. At one end of the spectrum were college athletes: those from the University of Cambridge won more medals than most countries. At the other end of the spectrum, sports such as swimming encouraged wider participation. Lucy Morton, from a Blackpool working-class family, won gold in the 200m breaststroke.

William DeHart Hubbard became the first African American to win an individual gold, and newcomers, Uruguay, triumphed in football with a Black player, José Andrade, in the spotlight.

Paris was an unequal city as intrigued by its visitors as they were by its multiculturalism. Its caricaturists had a field day. But they devoted their greatest energies to competitors, like Hubbard and Andrade, whose bodies challenged the whiteness of Coubertin's Greek statues.

**24.** Unrecorded photographer
Studio portrait of Eric Liddell (1902–1945), wearing the 1924 Olympic team kit of Great Britain, July 1924
Black and white photograph, 10.5 × 17.5 cm
Lent by the Liddell Family

**25.** (fig. 31) Unrecorded photographer
Scottish athlete Eric Liddell (1902–1945) is paraded by fellow students around Edinburgh University after returning victorious from competition at the 1924 Summer Olympics, 18 July 1924
Black and white photograph
Hulton-Deutsch Collection/Corbis via Getty Images

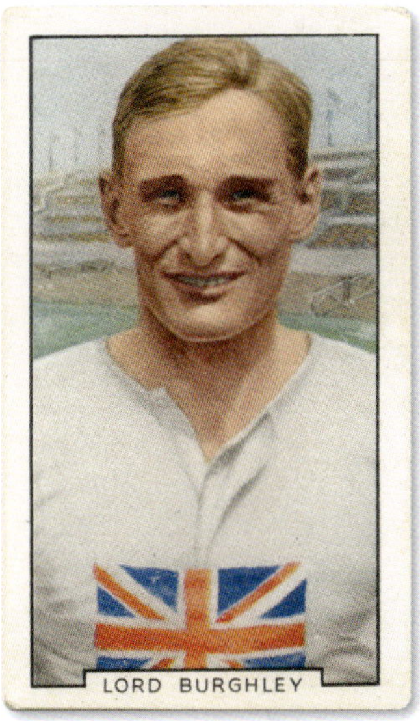


**29** ▲

**26.** (fig. 29) Sir Oswald Joseph Hornby Birley (1880–1952)
*David, Lord Burghley* (1905–1981), 1926
Oil on canvas, 101 × 74.9 cm
The Burghley House Collection (PIC 179)

**27.** Bassano Ltd (active 1901–62)
*David George Brownlow Cecil, 6th Marquess of Exeter* (Lord Burghley) (1905–1981)
Modern print, 2002; from a whole-plate glass negative, 24 September 1924
Black and white photograph, 20.5 × 15 cm
Lent by the National Portrait Gallery, London (x122918MP)

**28.** Unrecorded photographer
David, Lord Burghley (1905–1981) at the University of Pennsylvania's Penn Relays Carnival, *c.* 1926
Black and white photograph, 25.4 × 20.3 cm
The Burghley House Collection

**29.** Gallaher Ltd (founded 1857)
*Lord Burghley* (1905–1981), cigarette card from the 'Champions' set, 1936
Colour relief halftone print on paper, 6.3 × 3.7 cm
Lent by the National Portrait Gallery, London (D48955)

**30.** Unrecorded maker
British team blazer pocket, Paris 1924 Olympic Games, worn by Sir Arthur Marshall (1903–2007), 1924
Embroidered textile, coloured silk, 16.2 × 13.5 × 0.3 cm
Marshall of Cambridge

**31.** Raoul Bénard (1881–1961), designer; Monnaie de Paris (founded 864), manufacturer
Participation medal, Paris 1924 Olympic Games, 1924
Bronze, 5.5 cm
The Fitzwilliam Museum, Cambridge, bought from the Baldwin sale, 21 November 2016 (CM.639-2016)

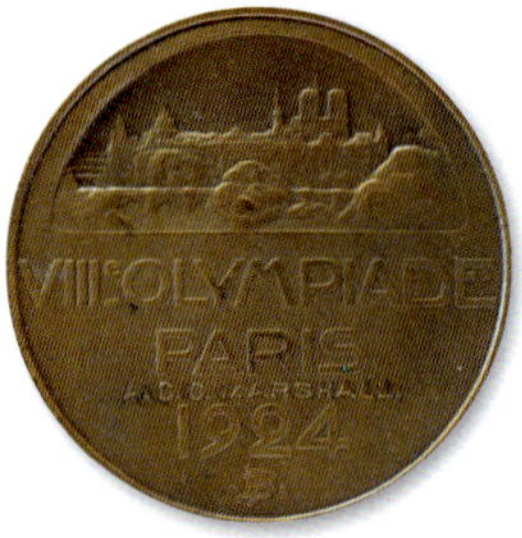

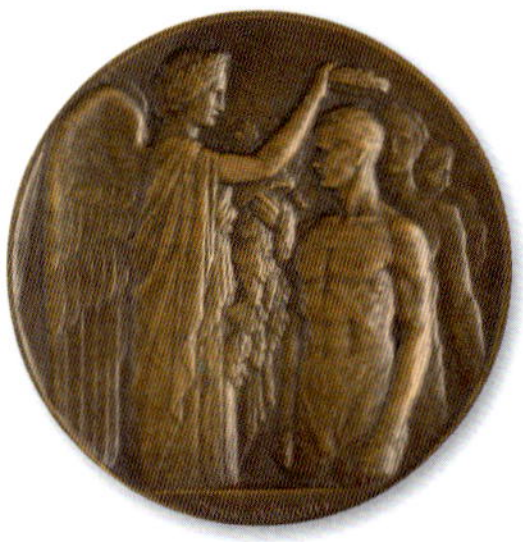

**32.** Raoul Bénard (1881–1961), designer;
Monnaie de Paris (founded 864), manufacturer
Participation medal, Paris 1924 Olympic Games, awarded to Sir Arthur Marshall (1903–2007), 1924
Bronze, 5.5 cm
Marshall of Cambridge
(Lower image taken from CM.639-2016)

In Paris in 1924, Cambridge University athletes won medals in 11 events. But winning was not everything. Every participating athlete and official received a medal with Paris on one side and a winged Victory figure crowning athletes on the other.

This medal belonged to Arthur Marshall, alumnus of the Perse School and Jesus College, Cambridge, who oddly had his name inscribed on it. He was reserve for the British relay team. After graduating with a first-class degree in Engineering, he made his home in the city, using family land to build Cambridge airport. He died on 16 March 2007, aged 103.

**33.** Elliott & Fry (founded 1863)
*Harold Abrahams* (1899–1978)
Modern print, 2002; from a half-plate glass copy negative, 1948; original negative 1930s
Black and white photograph, 20.5 × 15 cm
Lent by the National Portrait Gallery, London (X21178MP)

**34.** Harold Abrahams (1899–1978) interviewed by Rex Alston (1901–1994)
Extracts from a programme in the series *People Today*, broadcast 20 September 1963,
PRE: Band 1: 3'21"
BBC Archives

**35.** (fig. 32) Unrecorded photographer
Harold Abrahams (1899–1978) wins the 100-yard dash at the AAA Championships at Stamford Bridge, 1924
Black and white photograph, 25.4 × 20.2 cm
By permission of the Master and Fellows of Gonville and Caius College, Cambridge (PH: 1/50)

**36.** (fig. 33) Stearn & Sons, Cambridge (founded *c.* 1866)
*Caius College, Athletes 1922, Winners of Inter Collegiate Cup*, 1922
Black and white photograph mounted on board, pen and ink, metallic paint and coloured ink on applied paper, 36.6 × 43.2 cm
By permission of the Master and Fellows of Gonville and Caius College, Cambridge (PH.S.7.1922)

**37.** Stearn & Sons, Cambridge (founded *c.* 1866)
*Caius College Ball, May Term 1921*, 1921
Black and white photograph mounted on board, pen and ink, metallic paint and coloured ink on applied paper, 34.9 × 42.1 cm
By permission of the Master and Fellows of Gonville and Caius College, Cambridge (PH.B.15.3)

**38.** Stearn & Sons, Cambridge (founded *c.* 1866)
*Pembroke College Athletics Team*, 1923
Black and white photograph mounted on board, graphite, 26.5 × 33 cm
By permission of the Master and Fellows of Pembroke College, Cambridge (GBR/1058/col/9/1/2/1/1923)

**39.** Stearn & Sons, Cambridge (founded *c.* 1866)
*Pembroke College Football Team*, 1923–24
Black and white photograph mounted on board, graphite, 26.2 × 33 cm
By permission of the Master and Fellows of Pembroke College, Cambridge (GBR/1058/col/9/1/8/3/1923)

**40.** Douglas Lowe (1902–1981)
Application for admission to Pembroke College, 14 April 1921
Printing and pen and ink on paper, 27.6 × 22.5 × 3.8 cm
By permission of the Master and Fellows of Pembroke College, Cambridge (*Application for Admissions*, vol. 6)

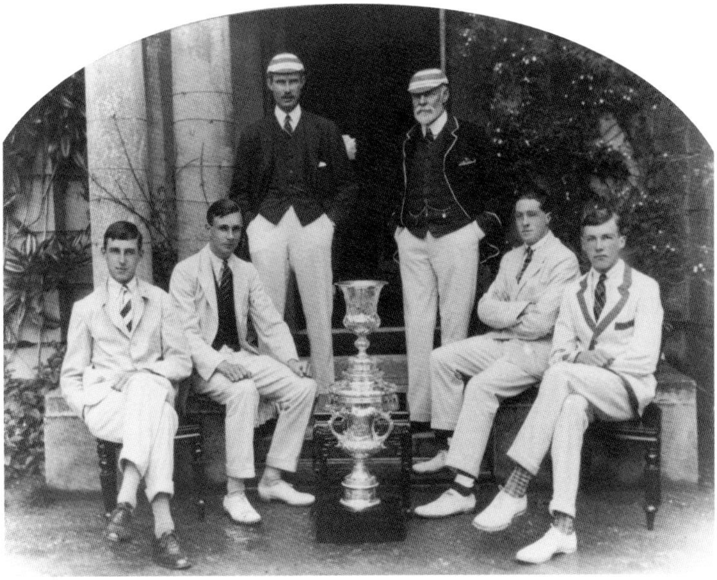

**45** ▲

**41.** Bernard Partridge (1861–1945), artist; Bradbury & Evans (founded 1830), printer
*Mr Douglas Lowe, Mr Punch's Personalities – LXXIX,* from *Punch, or the London Charivari*, 10 October 1928, loose sheet
Printed verse and reproduction of an original drawing, 27.6 × 20.5 cm
Private collection

**42.** Four menus for Oxford and Cambridge and Harvard and Yale Universities athletics team dinners, 9 July 1927; 9 July 1929; 13 July 1929
Printing, pen and ink and graphite on paper, 18 × 11.5 cm; 23 × 30.5 cm; 11.5 × 22.8 cm
Achilles Club

**43.** (fig. 39) Time Inc. (founded 1922)
*Time* magazine, vol. 4, no. 1 (7 July 1924), with cover photograph of 'Captain Rockefeller', James Stillman Rockefeller (1902–2004)
Printing on paper, 20.3 × 27.3 cm
Courtesy of Thomas E. Weil

**44.** (fig. 18) Unrecorded photographer
*Olympic Games of 1924, Rowing, the eight of the United States of America*
(A.N. Paris postcard series, no. 446), 1924
Black and white photograph
Comité International Olympique (CIO) (PHO11106794)
(Exhibition only)

**45.** Unrecorded photographer
James Alexander Macnabb (1901–1990), Charles Ryves Maxwell Eley (1902–1983), Robert Erskine Morrison (1902–1980) and Terence Robert Beaumont Sanders (1901–1985) seated with trophies won as a coxless four crew for Third Trinity, Cambridge and Eton Vikings at Royal Henley Regatta, 1922, from Robert Erskine Morrison's *Album of Rowing Photographs, both College and Boat Race Crews, 1921–1979, c.* 1922
Black and white photograph
Reproduced by kind permission of the Syndics of Cambridge University Library (GBR/0265/UA/OCBR.P3)

**46.** Metcalfe and Co. Limited, Cambridge (founded 1730)
*Metcalfe's Boat-Race Card*, June 1924
Printing on blue-coloured paper, 17 × 42.2 cm
By permission of the Master and Fellows of Trinity College, Cambridge (Rec. 34.9)

**47.** Unrecorded author (probably Robert Erskine Morrison (1902–1980))
Handwritten account of Third Trinity coxless four crew at the Paris 1924 Olympic Games, *Third Trinity Boat Club Minutes*, July 1924
Pen and ink on paper, 23 × 20.5 cm
By permission of the Master and Fellows of Trinity College, Cambridge (Rec. 31.2)

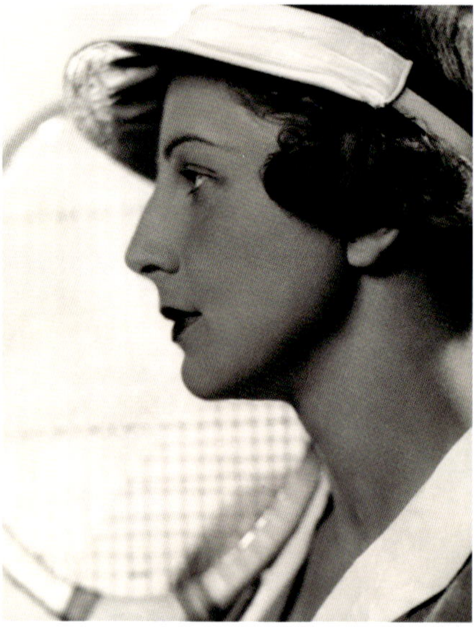

**52 ▲**

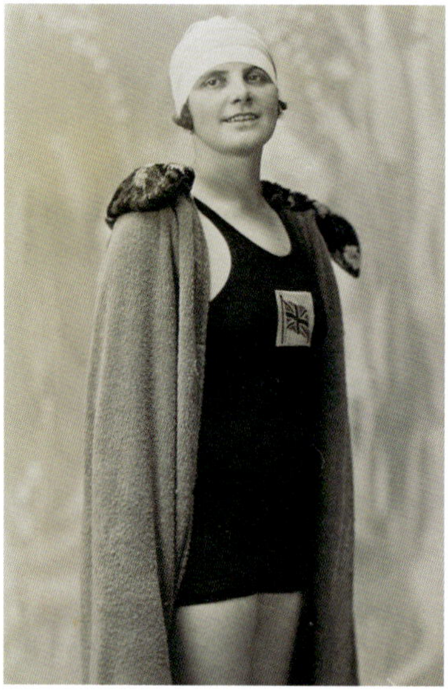

**53 ▲**

**48.** (fig. 30) Unrecorded maker
Illuminated trophy oar spoon celebrating the men's coxless four Olympic final and painted with the names of the four rowers, Charles Ryves Maxwell Eley (1902–1983), James Alexander Macnabb (1901–1990), Robert Erskine Morrison (1902–1980) and Terence Robert Beaumont Sanders (1901–1985), *c.* 1924
Wood, paint, gold leaf, 96.5 × 15.2 × 5.1 cm
The Macnab Memorial Trust

**49.** Unrecorded photographer
*Hubbard, Olympic Champion of the long jump*, postcard (A.N. Paris series, no. 387), 1924
Gelatin silver print on paper, 8.5 × 13.5 cm
Musée National du Sport, Nice, France (MNS IMG.1998.0040.0718)

**50.** (fig. 41) William DeHart Hubbard (1903–1976)
Letter written to his mother on board the SS *America* before sailing to Paris with the US Olympic Team, 16 June 1924
Pen and ink on paper with printed letterhead, 19 × 25.5 cm
On loan from Cincinnati Museum Center (MSS 1067)

**51.** (fig. 35) Sydney W. White (1870–1945)
*Kitty Godfree* (1896–1992), 1924
Oil on canvas, 86.5 × 69 cm
On loan from Wimbledon Lawn Tennis Museum (A2073)

**52.** Dorothy Wilding (1893–1978)
*Helen Wills Moody* (1905–1998), 1933
Bromide print, 21.8 × 17.4 cm
Lent by the National Portrait Gallery, London. Given by the photographer's sister, Susan Morton, 1976 (x21384)

**53.** John Capstack, Blackpool (1881–1967)
Lucy Morton (1898–1980) wearing her 1924 Olympic Games swimming costume, cap and robe, 1924
Black and white photograph, 13.7 × 8.6 cm
Showtown, Blackpool (BC.2023.1.2)

**54.** (fig. 36) Unrecorded photographer
Lucy Morton (1898–1980) competing in the women's 200m breaststroke at the 1924 Olympic Games, 1924
Black and white photograph, 21.4 × 16.7 cm
Showtown, Blackpool (BC.2023.1.22)

**55.** Unrecorded photographer
The British swimming team posing in front of the Musée du Louvre during the 1924 Olympic Games, in album
Black and white photograph, 34.7 × 44 cm
Showtown, Blackpool (BC.2023.1.24)

**56.** Unrecorded maker
Three FINA (*Fédération Internationale de Natation*) world-record badges, 1916 and 1920
Embroidered textile, 22.5 × 11.5 cm
Showtown, Blackpool (BC.2023.1.19; BC.2023.1.20; BC.2023.1.21)

**57.** Bernard Naudin (1876–1946), artist; unrecorded printer
Winner's certificate, Paris 1924 Olympic Games, awarded to Lucy Morton (1898–1980), 1924
Colour lithography on paper after an original drawing, 64 × 50 cm
Showtown, Blackpool (BC.2023.1.3)

Athletes in the 1924 Olympics received certificates designed by respected artist Bernard Naudin, who had graduated from Paris's School of Fine Arts and from military painting to a career in drawing and printmaking, much of it for the press. His design pays homage to classical antiquity: the goddess Nike (Victory) stands centre-stage between garlanded columns and other allegorical figures, one of them with a lyre.

Naudin's fears about the quality of the reproduction turned out to be baseless. The certificates are beautifully made and inscribed by a specially established calligraphy service – this one to Britain's Lucy Morton, 'Olympic Champion, 200m breaststroke'.

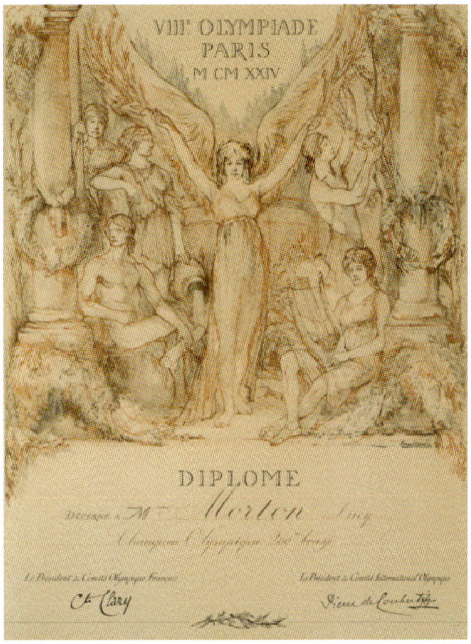


**58.** Laverne Studios Ltd, Blackpool (active 1916)
Lucy Morton (1898–1980) wearing a FINA world-record badge, *c.* 1916
Black and white photograph, 15.6 × 11 cm
Showtown, Blackpool (BC.2023.1.41)

**59.** Unrecorded photographer
Postcard with studio portrait of a young Lucy Morton (1898–1980), *c.* 1912
Black and white photograph on paper, 13.3 × 8.2 cm
Showtown, Blackpool (BC.2023.1.48)

**60.** André Adolphe Rivaud (1892–1951), designer; Monnaie de Paris (founded 864), manufacturer
Gold winner's medal, Paris Olympic Games, 1924, awarded to Lucy Morton (1898–1980) in the 200m women's breaststroke, 1924
Gilt silver, 5.5 cm
Showtown, Blackpool (BC.2023.1.1)

**61.** (fig. 38) Pach Brothers (active 1867–1993)
Johnny Weissmuller (1904–1984) posing for artist John Hubbard Rich (1876–1954), *c.* 1931
Gelatin silver print, 24.1 × 18.6 cm
National Portrait Gallery, Smithsonian Institution, Washington (S/NPG.93.388.39)

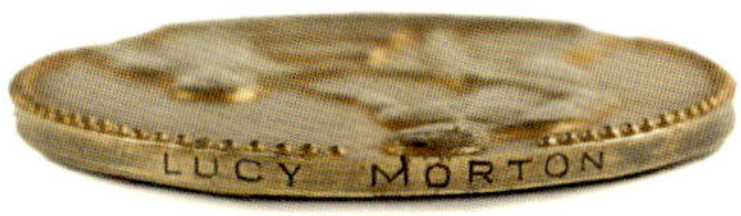


**60 ▲**

**62.** Emery Kelèn (1896–1964); unrecorded photographer
Johnny Weissmuller (1904–1984) with Arne Borg (Sweden) (1901–1987) and Andrew Murray 'Boy' Charlton (Australia) (1907–1975), caricature made *c.* 1924; photographed *c.* 1950
Gelatin silver print of an original drawing, 12 × 8 cm
Musée National du Sport, Nice, France (MNS 2005.136.7.1)

**63.** Emery Kelèn (1896–1964); unrecorded photographer
*John Weissmuller (U.S.A.)*, caricature made *c.* 1924; photographed *c.* 1950
Gelatin silver print of an original drawing, 13 × 9 cm
Musée National du Sport, Nice, France (MNS 2005.136.7.5)

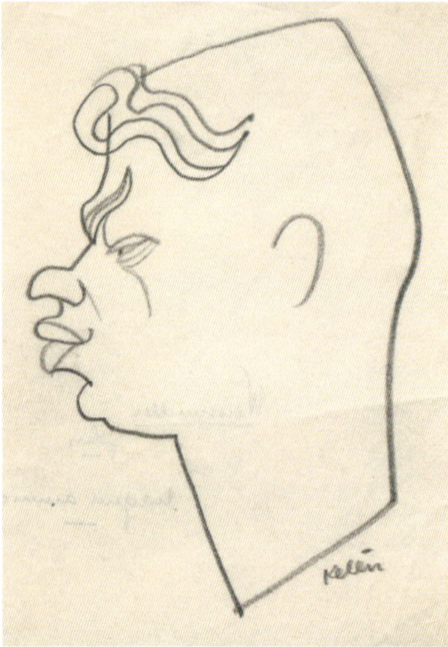


**64** ▲

**64.** Emery Kelèn (1896–1964)
*Weissmuller*, caricature of Johnny Weissmuller (1904–1984), *c.* 1924
Graphite on paper, 24.2 × 14.9 cm
Musée National du Sport, Nice, France (MNS 2005.136.8)

**65.** (fig. 47) Unrecorded photographer
*Olympic Games of 1924 – Football, the Team from Uruguay*, 1924
Black and white photograph
© 1924, Comité International Olympique (CIO) (PHO10005185)

**66.** (fig. 49) Stefan Strobl (active 1920s)
*Fotbolls Artisterna. Uruguay !!!; Les Artistes du Ballon Rond. Uruguay !!!; The Football Artists. Uruguay !!!*, in *1001 Champions, VIII Olympiade, Caricatures par Derso, Kelen, Strobl*, *c.* 1924
Lithograph with hand-colouring, in bound volume, 28.4 × 36 cm
Olympic Museum Collections, Lausanne (C-J01-1924/001)

**67.** (fig. 52) Unrecorded photographer
Footballers from the Uruguay football team pose as they prepare a barbeque at the team's Argenteuil base during competition in the football tournament at the 1924 summer Olympics in Paris, probably May 1924
Black and white photograph
Bob Thomas/Popperfoto/Getty Images

**68.** (fig. 50) Unrecorded photographer
Action in the quarter-final match between France and Uruguay, with Uruguay on the attack, at the 1924 Summer Olympics in the Stade Olympique in Colombes, near Paris, 1 June 1924
Black and white photograph
Bob Thomas/Popperfoto/Getty Images

**69.** (fig. 46) Unrecorded photographer
Reception of the victorious Uruguayan football team at the Plaza Cagancha in Montevideo following their return from the Paris Olympics, 18 July 1924
Gelatin silver print
Centro de Fotografía de Montevideo

**70.** (fig. 53) Unrecorded maker
Pair of football boots worn by José Leandro Andrade (1901–1957) in the match between Uruguay and Argentina in the final of the first FIFA (Fédération Internationale de Football Association) World Cup competition in 1930, *c.* 1930
Leather, textile, iron, 11.5 x 25.5 x 16 cm (shoe size 9)
Musée National du Sport, Nice, France (MNS 2007.7.53)

**71.** Louis Bonniot de Fleurac (1876–1965)
*Andrade*, 1924
Graphite and black crayon on paper, 26 × 23.7 cm
Musée National du Sport, Nice, France (MNS D.I.108)

**72.** (fig. 54) Unidentified artist, signed with initials *Ad.v.B*
*The Black Marvel*, caricature of José Leandro Andrade (1901–1957), 1924
Photograph of an original drawing
Bob Thomas/Popperfoto/Getty Images

**73.** (fig. 99) Renée Sintenis (1888–1965)
*The Athlete (Nurmi)*, 1926
Bronze, 41 × 34.5 × 16.5 cm
On loan from Leicester Museums and Galleries (Y.F1.2014.0.0)

**74.** (fig. 63) Unrecorded photographer
Paavo Nurmi (1897–1973) pictured during his training regime, 1925
Black and white photograph
Sports Museum of Finland

**75.** (fig. 97) Unrecorded photographer
Paris 1924 Olympic Games, Athletics, Paavo Nurmi (Fin) 1st in 1500m Men, 5000m Men, Team 3000m, Individual and Team Cross Country, 1924
Black and white photograph
© 1924, Comité International Olympique (CIO) (PHO10004733)

## 3. FASTER, HIGHER, STRONGER

The 'Roaring Twenties' were a fast-paced period of technological revolution. The Paris 1924 Olympics were the first to broadcast radio commentaries on events. Advances in training, clothing and equipment helped athletes break records. Beyond the Games, economic growth brought changes in lifestyle and fashion that encouraged everyone to be active.

Lifestyle changes could only do so much. The ideology and practice of eugenics were developing apace and underpinned by measuring the most successful sporting bodies. Eugenics opened up the more terrifying possibility of transforming and transcending human biology in a war-torn world still reeling from the lack of fitness of its pool of conscripts.

Artists too reimagined the relationship of man and machine. Already in 1909, poet Filippo Tommaso Marinetti had chosen Parisian newspaper *Le Figaro* to publicise his 'Futurist Manifesto', which urged artists to ditch tradition and the legacy of ancient Greece for the dynamism of modern life.

**76.** Unrecorded artist for Bardou, Savard & Co.
*Young people ...*, poster, 1901–33
Colour lithography on paper, 66 × 82 cm
Musée National du Sport, Nice, France (MNS MS 15199 b)

**77.** (fig. 56) Justin Marie Georges Dorival (1879–1968), artist; Georges Capon (1890–1980), artist; Atelier Dorival, Paris (active *c.* 1910–28), printer
*General Association for the War Disabled*, poster, 1917
Colour lithography on paper, 118.3 × 79.8 cm
IWM (Imperial War Museums)
(Art.IWM PST 11165)

**78.** (fig. 58) Robert Tait McKenzie (1867–1938), sculptor; cast at Roman Bronze Works, New York City (founded 1897)
*Sprinter*, 1902
Bronze, 22.3 × 29.1 × 15 cm
National Trust Collections, Anglesey Abbey (The Fairhaven Collection), Cambridgeshire
(NT 515040)

**79.** Robert Tait McKenzie (1867–1938)
*Sprinter*, plaster cast, 1902
Plaster, 23.2 × 30 × 15.5 cm
The Fitzwilliam Museum, Cambridge, bought from the sculptor, 4 March 1905 and received from Paris
(M.1-1905)

**80.** (fig. 55) Robert Tait McKenzie (1867–1938), sculptor; cast at Roman Bronze Works, New York City (founded 1897)
*The Athlete*, 1903
Bronze and marble, 43.3 × 13.2 × 13.5 cm
National Trust Collections, Anglesey Abbey (The Fairhaven Collection), Cambridgeshire
(NT 515046)

**81.** Robert Tait McKenzie (1867–1938)
*The Athlete*, plaster cast, 1903
Plaster, 43.3 × 13 × 17.8 cm
The Fitzwilliam Museum, Cambridge, bought from the sculptor, 4 March 1905 and received from Paris
(M.2-1905)

**82.** (fig. 9) George Grosz (1893–1959)
*The Gymnast*, *c.* 1922
Oil on canvas, 104.1 × 80 cm
Collection of the McNay Art Museum, Gift of Robert L.B. Tobin (1974.26)

**83.** (fig. 20) Gino Severini (1883–1966)
*Dancer no. 5*, 1915/16
Oil on canvas, 93.3 × 74 cm
Pallant House Gallery, Chichester, Kearley Bequest, through The Art Fund, 1989 (CHCPH 0594)

**84.** Le Corbusier
*Towards an architecture*, new edition, Paris: Flammarion, *c.* 2005 (first published Paris, 1923)
Printing on paper, covered boards, 23.2 × 15.2 cm
The Syndics of Cambridge University Library
(1:5.c.200.38)

**85.** (fig. 17) Agence Rol photographic agency (founded 1904)
Edmond Dehorter (1877–1965), prepares to broadcast at Colombes stadium from a tethered hot-air balloon, 9 June 1924
Glass-plate negative
Bibliothèque nationale de France, Paris
(Rol, 92780)

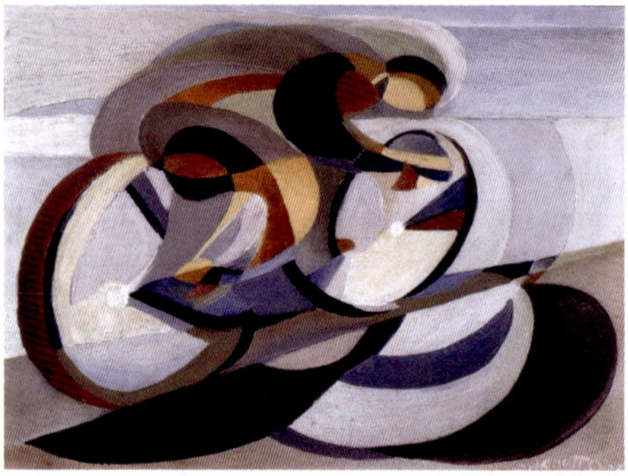

**86** ▲

**86.** Enzo Benedetto (1905–1993)
*Cyclist*, 1926
Oil on canvas, 28 × 38 cm
Courtesy Galleria Arte Centro, Milan

**87.** (fig. 13) George Grosz (1893–1959)
*The Cycle Race*, 1913
Chalk on tracing paper, 22 × 27.9 cm
The Fitzwilliam Museum, Cambridge, bought from d'Offay Couper Gallery, 1969 (PD.12-1969)

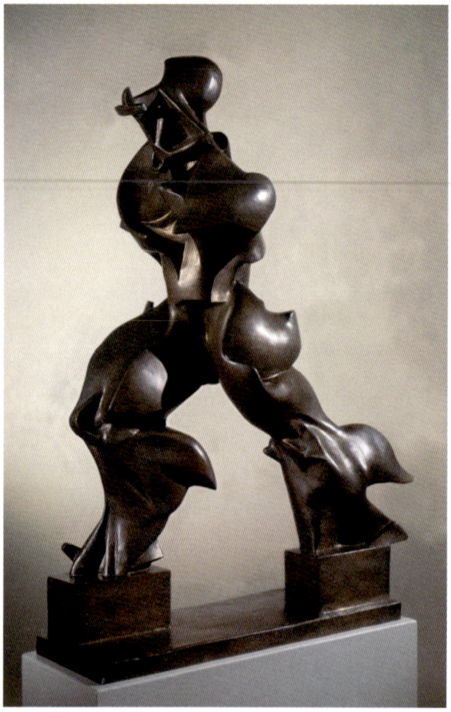

**88.** Umberto Boccioni (1882–1916)
*Unique Forms of Continuity in Space*, sculpted 1913, cast 1972
Bronze, 117.5 × 87.6 × 36.8 cm
Tate: Purchased 1972 (T01589)

'We affirm that the beauty of the world has been enriched by a new beauty: the beauty of speed' (Filippo Tommaso Marinetti, *Le Figaro*, 20 February 1909).

Boccioni's work lends flesh to Marinetti's Futurist vision. Supposedly inspired by a footballer in action, the sculpture was first cast in bronze by Marinetti in 1931. It leaves figurative form standing, fleeing convention to surge forwards. In the same year that he conceived the sculpture, Boccioni painted *Dynamism of a Soccer Player*, in which the body's materiality dissolves in movement.

Boccioni died young, in 1916, on a military exercise for the Italian army.

**89.** Jean de Rovéra (1898–1939), director;
Rapid Film, production company
Footage of the tandem-cycling event from *The Olympic Games in Paris 1924*, official film, 1924
© 2010, Comité International Olympique (CIO)

**90.** Jean de Rovéra (1898–1939), director;
Rapid Film, production company
Footage of the bobsleigh event from *The Olympic Games held at Chamonix in 1924*, official film, 1924
© 2010, Comité International Olympique (CIO)

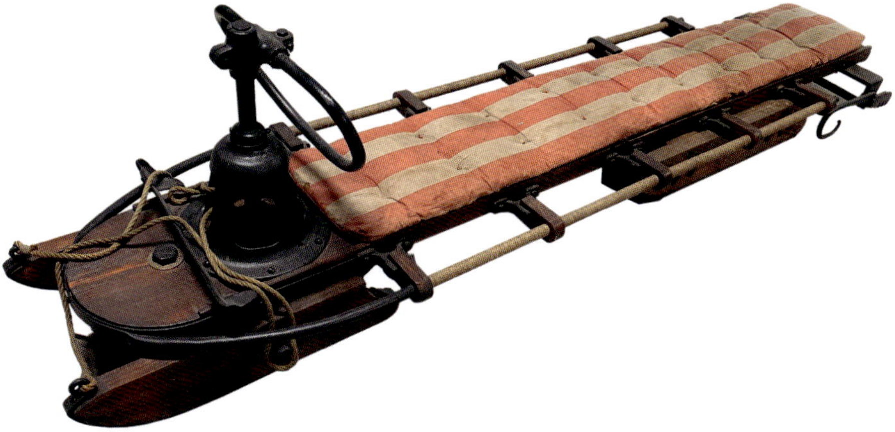

**91.** Unrecorded Swiss maker
Four-man bobsleigh, 1920s
Steel, wood, padded textile,
58 × 245 × 60 cm
Markus Osterwalder, Switzerland, Olympic historian and collector

The first Winter Olympics took place in 1924 in Chamonix, France, and featured bobsleigh. This 1920s sleigh is from Switzerland, which took gold.

Compared to today's aerodynamic sleighs, this one is cumbersome and exposed. In 1924, men competed without crash helmets on a 1,433m run with 18 turns. The Official Report of the British Team reflected that 'in spite of the skill possessed by the steerer and his crew', it had been impossible to negotiate 'at a fast speed without considerable danger'. In training, a British four took a bend too fast and overturned, leaving decorated war veteran Frederick 'Boy' Browning badly injured.

**92** ▶

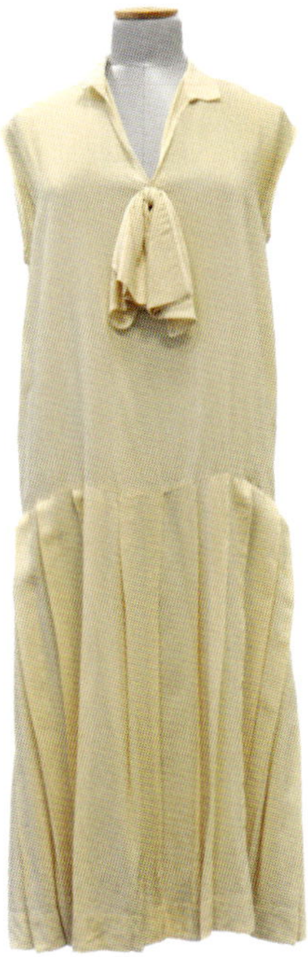

**92.** Unrecorded maker
Tennis dress, *c.* 1925
Silk, 110 × 49 × 7.5 cm
On loan from Wimbledon Lawn Tennis Museum (WTM:1993/447)

**93.** Probably J. Collinson & Co. (founded 1831, closed 1978)
Pair of women's tennis shoes with original box, 1920s
Buckskin, rubber, textile, metal; box: paper, 9.5 × 27.8 × 8.8 cm; 9.5 × 17.5 × 28.5 cm (box)
On loan from Wimbledon Lawn Tennis Museum (WTM:2002/22)

**94.** (fig. 21) André Lhote (1885–1962)
*Tennis Players*, 1917
Oil on canvas, 45.7 × 54.6 cm
On loan from Wimbledon Lawn Tennis Museum (WTM:1994/176)

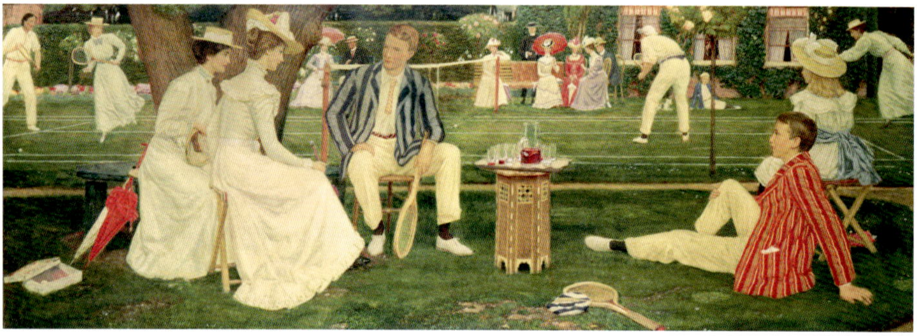

**95** ▲

**95.** Charles March Gere (1869–1957)
*The Tennis Party*, 1900
Oil on canvas, 39.3 × 107.4 cm
The Wilson, Cheltenham Trust, purchased with the assistance of the Museums and Galleries Commission Regional Purchase Grant Fund and donations from the All England Tennis Ground Ltd, the National-Art Collections Fund, the Friends of Cheltenham Art Gallery and Museums, the W.A. Cadbury Charitable Trust, the Orlando Oldham Charitable Trust, Cotswold Life Magazine, the Mercantile and General Re-Insurance Company, and Pillar Aluminium Ltd (1986.1136)

**96.** Unrecorded artist; Éditions d'art: Paris, publisher
'Two creations by Jean Patou', *Art-Taste-Beauty: Pages of Feminine Elegance*, no. 60 (August 1925)
Lithography with hand-coloured *pochoir* on paper, in bound volume, 33 × 24 cm
Victoria and Albert Museum (National Art Library), London (95.SS.17 )

**97.** Wright & Ditson (founded 1871)
'Challenge Cup' tennis racket, *c*. 1930
Wood frame (possibly ash), paint, fabric cord, synthetic strings, 69 × 24 × 3.5 cm
On loan from Wimbledon Lawn Tennis Museum (WTM:2014/190.1)

**98.** Allen West Company (founded 1910)
Steel lawn tennis racket, *c*. 1924
Steel frame and strings, wood handle, leather butt, painted enamel, 68 × 22 × 1 cm
On loan from Wimbledon Lawn Tennis Museum (WTM:1977/52)

**99.** (fig. 60) J.W. Foster & Sons (Athletic Shoes) Limited (founded 1895)
Running shoe, 1920–29
Leather, metal, textile, 9.5 × 25 × 9 cm
Reebok Brand Archive / © Reebok International Limited (RF-5233)

**100.** (fig. 61) Harold M. Abrahams (1899–1978); Dr Adolphe Abrahams (1883–1967)
*Training for Athletes*, George Bell and Sons Ltd, London, 1928
Printing on paper, covered boards (original book jacket), 19.3 × 29.3 cm
The Syndics of Cambridge University Library (9514.d.15)

**101.** (fig. 26) Robert Delaunay (1885–1941)
*The Runners*, *c*. 1924
Oil on canvas, 46 × 55 cm
The National Museum of Serbia (974)

**98** ▶

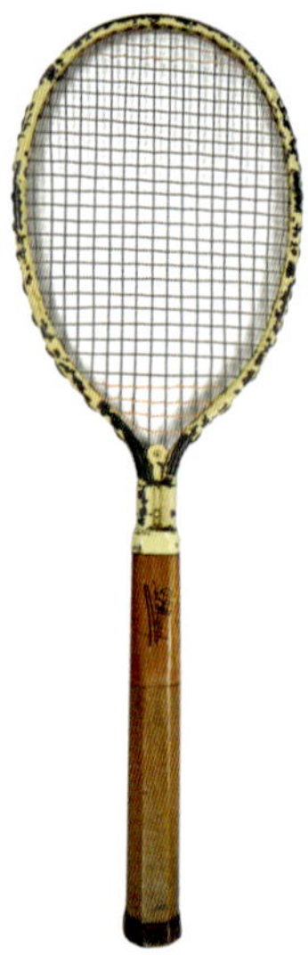

## 4. SPORT AS ART

In ancient Greece, contests in music, dance, theatre and athletics were a defining feature of public festivals. From 1912 to 1948, the modern Olympics included competitions in literature, music, architecture, painting and sculpture as well as sport. Entries had to be inspired by sporting activity. Ireland, competing for the first time as an independent nation, won its only medals in these events. France was over-represented, though even it could not convince the judges of the music competition to award any medals.

Music and dance were as defining of Paris as its fine arts. A supporting cultural programme ranged from performances of Greek tragedy and a new ballet with a tennis-playing lead to a costumed 'Olympic Ball', honouring the god Apollo.

Art and sport fed each other. When not winning gold in the 1924 singles and doubles, tennis player Helen Wills was sketching her opponents. She entered the 1932 Olympics in painting.

**102.** (fig. 87) Jean Jacoby (1891–1936)
*Corner*, from the *Sport Studies* triptych, 1924
Oil on canvas, 104 × 67 cm
Olympic Museum Collections, Lausanne (81598)

**103.** (fig. 88) Jean Jacoby (1891–1936)
*Rugby*, from the *Sport Studies* triptych, 1924
Oil on canvas, 99 × 59.5 cm
Olympic Museum Collections, Lausanne (81599)

**104.** (fig. 90) Unrecorded photographer
*Finnish Discus Thrower* by Kostas Dimitriadis (1879 or 1881–1943) seen in his Paris studio, *c.* 1924
Black and white photograph
Dimitriadis archive, Hellenic Literary and Historical Archive / National Bank of Greece Cultural Foundation

**105.** (fig. 91) Unrecorded photographer
Finnish Olympic discus thrower Armas Rudolf Taipale (1890–1976) poses in the Paris studio of Kostas Dimitriadis for the sculpture *Finnish Discus Thrower*, *c.* 1924
Black and white photograph
Dimitriadis archive, Hellenic Literary and Historical Archive / National Bank of Greece Cultural Foundation

**106.** (fig. 89) Jack Butler Yeats (1871–1957)
*The Liffey Swim*, 1923
Oil on canvas, 61 × 91 cm
On loan from the National Gallery of Ireland (NGI.941)

**107.** (fig. 83) André Adolphe Rivaud (1892–1951), designer; Monnaie de Paris (founded 864), manufacturer
Olympic silver winner's medal awarded to Jack Butler Yeats (1871–1957) in the Arts Competition, 1924
Silver, 5.5 cm
Yeats Archive, National Gallery of Ireland (IE NGI/YA/Y1/JY/10/2/2)

**108.** Raoul Bénard (1881–1961), designer; Monnaie de Paris (founded 864), manufacturer
1924 Olympics participation medal awarded to Jack Butler Yeats (1871–1957), 1924
Bronze, 5.5 cm
Yeats Archive, National Gallery of Ireland (IE NGI/YA/Y1/JY/10/2/3)

**109.** (fig. 85) Dorothy Margaret Stuart (1889–1963)
*Sword Songs*, with illustrations by Gerald Spencer Pryse, Methuen and Co.: London, 1925
Printing on paper, covered boards, 19 × 12.2 cm
The Syndics of Cambridge University Library (1925.7.4776)

**110.** Robert Tait McKenzie (1867–1938), sculptor; cast by Roman Bronze Works, New York City (founded 1897)
*The Javelin Cast*, 1923
Bronze, marble, 56.5 × 43.3 × 25.7 cm
National Trust Collections, Anglesey Abbey (The Fairhaven Collection), Cambridgeshire (NT 515038)

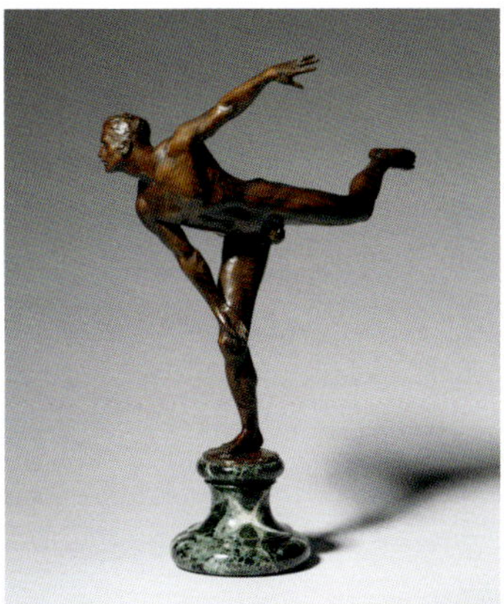

**110 ▲**

**111.** (fig. 82) Serge Youriévitch (1876–1969)
*The Dancer Nattova*, 1930
Bronze, marble, 41 × 25 × 20 cm
Northampton Museums and Art Gallery (2002.78.35)

**112.** (fig. 25) After Pablo Picasso (1881–1973); L'Union des Artistes Russes & François Bernouard: Paris
*Mercury: Study of a Dancer*, in *Olympic Ball, Real Sports Costume Ball*, programme, 1924
Printed illustration of an original drawing on heavy paper, 29 × 24.5 cm
Private collection

**113.** (fig. 23) After Pablo Picasso (1881–1973), Edouard Manet (1832–1883), Marie Vassilieff (1884–1957), Serge Fotinsky (1887–1971), Samuel Granovsky (1889–1942), Victor Barthe (1887–1954) and Boris Chatzman (1896–1938); L'Union des Artistes Russes & François Bernouard: Paris
*Olympic Ball, Real Sports Costume Ball*, programme, 1924
Printed text on heavy paper with illustrations of original drawings, 29 × 24.5 cm
Collection of the McNay Art Museum, Gift of Robert L.B. Tobin (TL1999.18.2)

**114.** (fig. 24) After Natalia Gontcharova (1881–1962)
*Costume Project for the Olympic Ball*, on double-sided flyer, 1924
Printed text on pink-coloured paper with illustration of an original drawing, 65.4 × 25.4 cm
Collection of the McNay Art Museum, Gift of Robert L. B. Tobin (TL1999.18.5)

**115.** (fig. 22) Pablo Picasso (1881–1973)
*Antique figures in profile*, Antibes, summer 1923
Ink on paper, *Excelsior*, Monday, 23 July 1923
33 × 35.5 cm
Musée national Picasso-Paris, given by Pablo Picasso, 1979 (MP984)

**116.** Darius Milhaud (1892–1974), composer
*The Blue Train: I. Choir of hens and gigolos*, performed by German Radio Saarbrücken-Kaiserslautern Philharmonic Orchestra, conducted by Robert Reimer, licensed courtesy of SWR Classic

**117.** (fig. 80) Henri Laurens (1885–1954)
*Head of a Boxer*, sculpted 1920, cast 1921
Painted terracotta, 24.2 × 23.8 × 2.5 cm
Tate: Bequeathed by Elly Kahnweiler 1991 to form part of the gift of Gustav and Elly Kahnweiler (T06833)

**118.** Attributed to Natalia Gontcharova (1881–1962); Myrbor, French fashion house (1922–36)
Opera cloak, *c.* 1924
Silk, metal thread (likely silver), fur (mink), 137 × 67 × 75 cm
Courtesy of Board of Trustees of National Museums Northern Ireland (BELUM.T2767)

An opera cloak was a statement piece in the art of dressing well in 1920s Paris. The motifs on this shining example are attributed to Natalia Gontcharova, the Russian-born costume-designer, painter and organiser of Paris's 'Olympic' or 'real sports costume ball' that coincided with the 1924 Games (figs 23 and 24).

As a painter, Gontcharova was inspired by Parisian modernism and Russian folk art, and keen on sporting themes – cycling, rowing, wrestling. As a designer, she honed her craft working for Paris's Ballets Russes and, like Picasso and Matisse, designed for Myrbor, a couture-house 'for the woman who seeks an expression of personality in her gowns'.

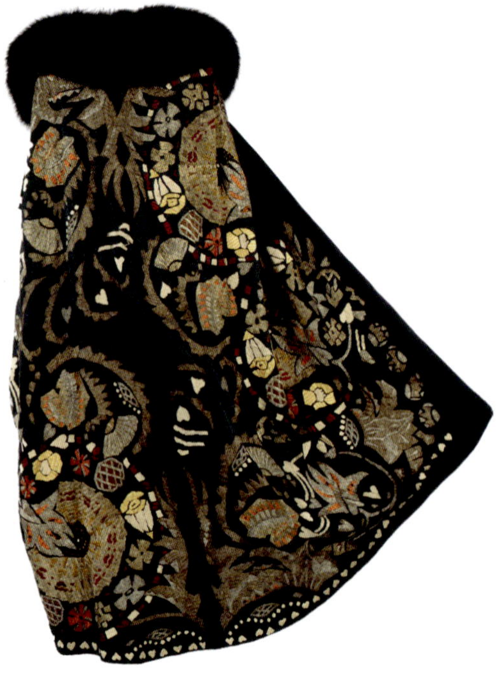

**119.** (fig. 44) Helen Wills (1905–1998), designer; Stehli Silks Corporation (founded 1837), manufacturer
*A Game of Tennis*, dressmaking fabric from the *Americana* series, 1926
Printed silk crepe, 51.4 × 98.7 cm
Allentown Art Museum, Gift of Kate Fowler Merle-Smith, 1978 (1978.26.165)

**120.** Helen Wills (1905–1998)
*Tennis*, with illustrations by the author, Scribner's Sons: New York and London, 1928
Printing on paper, covered boards, 23.2 × 15.2 cm
The Syndics of Cambridge University Library (9415.d.16)

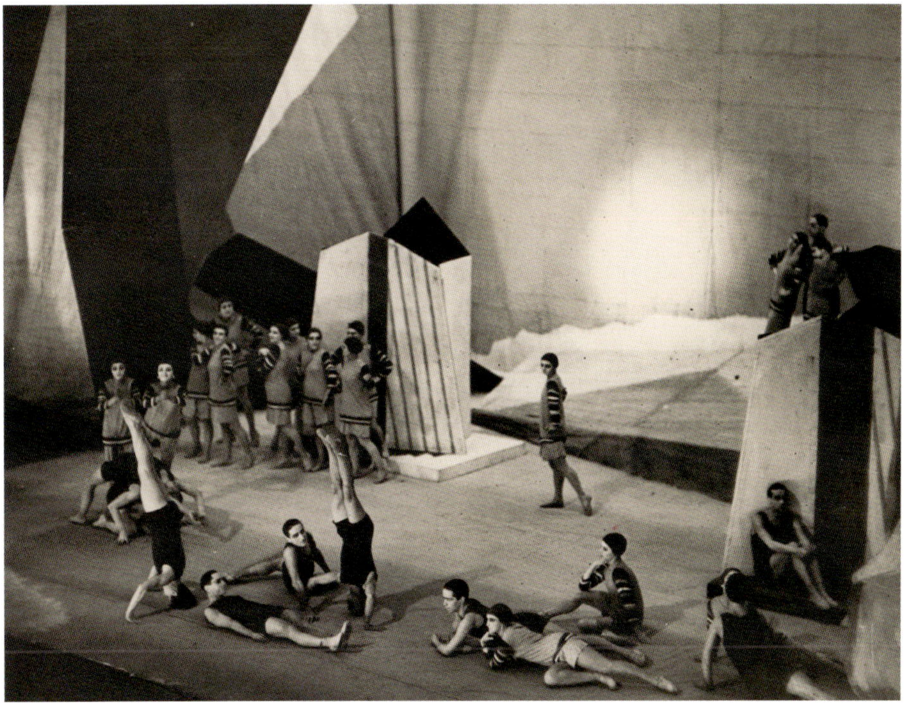

**121.** Unrecorded photographer
View of the stage with set by Henri Laurens (1885–1954) during a performance of the ballet *The Blue Train* at the Théâtre des Champs-Élysées, Paris, 20 June 1924
Black and white photograph
Library of Congress, Music Division.


With its libretto by artist Jean Cocteau, choreography by Bronislava Nijinska, costumes by Coco Chanel and curtain by Pablo Picasso, *The Blue Train* ballet could not have been more stylish.

Performed by the Ballets Russes in the 'Grand Season of Arts' accompanying the Paris 1924 Olympics, it was inspired by the luxury night-train that ferried passengers to the Riviera, and by the sports they played upon arrival. A tennis-playing heroine, based on Suzanne Lenglen, and a bathing beauty were joined by golfing and acrobatic men in Chanel costumes. The set with its neo-Cubist beach huts was designed by Henri Laurens (fig. 80).

## 5. SEX AND SPORT

Participation in sport made men stronger. Competing in sport at the Olympics paraded the masculinity of man and country to the world. Sport also made women stronger, challenging female passivity with a more active image. This agency spoke to women's fight for the vote and to 1920s Parisian fashion, which replaced the corset with freer flapper styles and boyish looks. Swimmers, tennis players and yachtswomen offered different ways of being a woman.

Olympic champions were also objects of the gaze. The mass dissemination of photographs and the advent of commercial cinema turned these men and women into sex-symbols. This made poster boys of even the strongest of strong men, appealing to an ancient Greek legacy that celebrated male beauty and male-male desire.

In 1924, same-sex desire and gender-nonconforming behaviour were still widely stigmatised, but Montmartre's salons and nightclubs gave a welcome home to a gay and lesbian subculture.

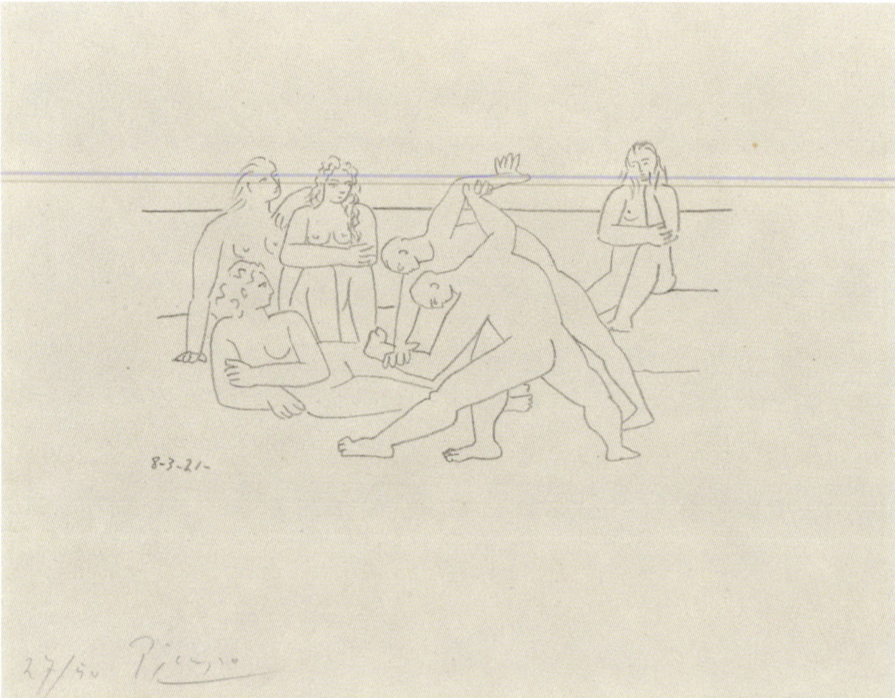


**122.** Pablo Picasso (1881–1973)
*The Wrestlers*, from the series
*Four Lithographs*, 8 March 1921
Lithography on paper,
11.3 × 19.5 cm, edition 27/50
The Fitzwilliam Museum, Cambridge,
given by Louis Colville Gray Clarke,
1940 (P.15-1940)

Some Olympic sports were considered manlier than others. Wrestling was one of those: it was as old as the Olympics itself, intensely physical, and sometimes violent.

Here, in one of a series of four lithographs, Picasso returns to wrestling's Greek roots by stripping his wrestlers bare and dwelling on the classical curves of their bodies. The spectating figures are also nude and condition the gaze as female and the physical contact of the men as erotic. They admire from different angles, reminding us of the ancient *Wrestlers* sculpture (cat. 3) that was designed to be viewed in the round.

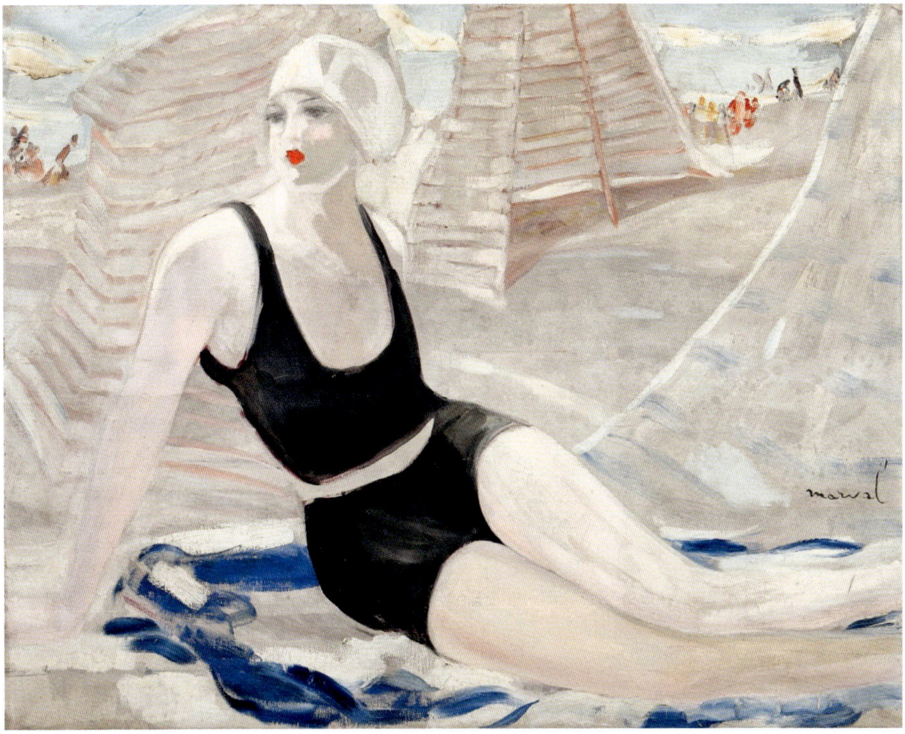

**123.** Jacqueline Marval (1866–1932)
*Bather in a Black Swimsuit*, 1920–23
Oil on canvas, 98 × 123 cm
Private collection, courtesy
Comité Jacqueline Marval, Paris

Women's swimwear was once about modesty. By the 1920s, however, it was skimpy and form-fitting like the men's (cat. 159).

Swimmers in the 1924 Olympics still had rules about what to wear, but the changes were liberating in the pool and out. Marval's painting plays with the art-historical tradition of reclining nudes to present the epitome of the modern woman in the latest wool swimsuit and bold lipstick.

Painted by a female artist, this modern woman oozes self-confidence. We are transported not to the Olympic stadium but to the beach and to the changes of lifestyle that came with economic prosperity.

**124.** Cast by unrecorded maker; after unrecorded Greek maker (National Archaeological Museum, Athens, *c.* 500 BCE, marble)
Plaster cast of a marble relief showing wrestling, one of six reliefs from the base of a Greek funerary monument, *c.* 1924
Plaster, 31 × 82 × 4 cm
Museum of Classical Archaeology, Cambridge (59a)

**125.** Jeanne Rij-Rousseau (1870–1956)
*The Wrestlers*, 1924
Ink wash drawing and graphite on paper, 67 × 51 cm
Private collection

**126.** (fig. 66) Jeanne Rij-Rousseau (1870–1956)
*The Wrestlers*, 1924
Ink and gouache on paper, 60 × 48 cm
Private collection

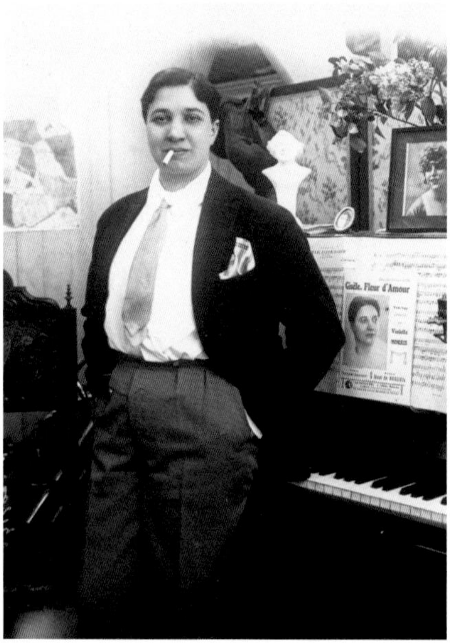

**130** ▲

**127.** (fig. 14) André Dunoyer de Segonzac (1884–1974)
*The Boxers*, *c*. 1910–14
Pen and ink on paper, 26 × 42.7 cm
The Fitzwilliam Museum, Cambridge, bequeathed by Louis Colville Gray Clarke, 1960, received 1961 (PD.104-1961)

**128.** (fig. 71) Jan Sluijters (1881–1957)
*The Boxer Rolf*, *c*. 1918
Oil on canvas, 143 × 104.5 cm
Collection Het Noordbrabants Museum, 's-Hertogenbosch (the Netherlands) (7762)

**129.** (fig. 69) Agence Rol photographic agency (founded 1904)
Violette Morris (1893–1944) boxing with a sparring partner, 1913
Glass-plate negative
Bibliothèque nationale de France, Paris (Rol, 33393)

**130.** Agence Meurisse, photographic agency (founded 1909)
Violette Morris (1893–1944) pictured around the time of her début as a singer in music halls, 1926
Glass-plate negative
Bibliothèque nationale de France, Paris (Meurisse, 31197 A)

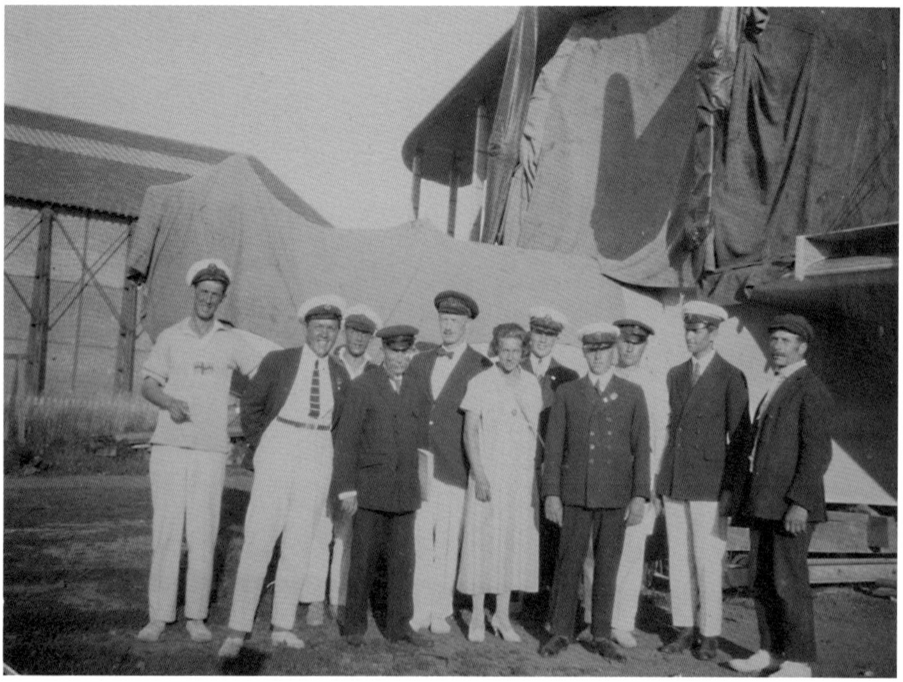

**131** ▲

135 ▼

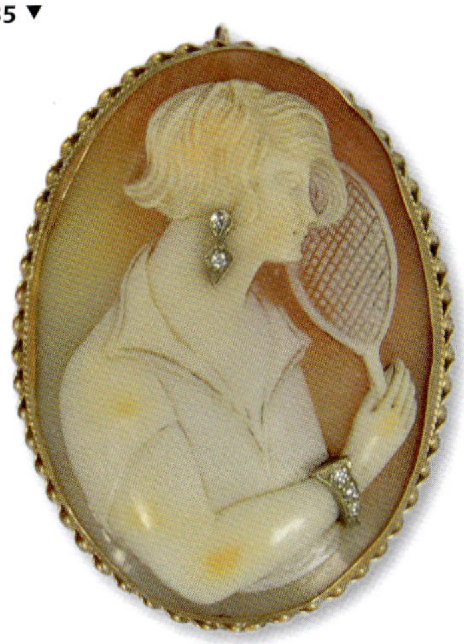

**131.** Unrecorded photographer
Ella Maillart (1903–1997) pictured at Meulan with sailing teams from Scandinavia, from her Paris 1924 Olympics scrapbook with handwritten caption, *Descendants of Vikings*, 1924
Black and white photograph
Succession Ella Maillart et Photo Elysée, Lausanne

**132.** (fig. 72) Marsden Hartley (1877–1943)
*The Strong Man*, *c.* 1923
Oil on canvas, 33 × 81.9 cm
The Jan T. and Marica Vilcek Collection, promised gift to The Vilcek Foundation (2006.03.05)

**133.** (fig. 64) Willi Baumeister (1889–1955)
*Female Runner II*, 1925
Oil on canvas, 119.5 × 80 cm
Staatsgalerie Stuttgart, acquired in 1968, Hugo Borst Collection (3042)

**134.** Unrecorded French maker
Beaded evening gown, *c.* 1925–28
Georgette, beading, glass, 106.5 × 101 cm
On loan from the Olive Matthews Collection, Chertsey Museum (MT.1410)

**135.** Unrecorded maker
Cameo brooch carved with a female tennis player holding a racket, *c.* 1930
Shell, diamonds, gold, 1.6 × 4.5 × 6 cm
On loan from Wimbledon Lawn Tennis Museum (WTM:2018/191)

**136.** Unrecorded maker, Birmingham
Powder bowl and cover decorated with a tennis racket and ball, *c.* 1924
Silver, mirror glass, 7 × 8.2 × 7.5 cm
On loan from Wimbledon Lawn Tennis Museum (WTM:2014/15)

**137.** (fig. 42) James Dixon & Sons (founded 1806); May Talbot (active 1930s), artist
Cigarette box, *c.* 1930
Pewter, wood, glass, oil paint, 5 × 18.9 × 10 cm
On loan from Wimbledon Lawn Tennis Museum (WTM:2000/29)

**138.** (fig. 43) Alexander Calder (1898–1976)
*Helen Wills*, 1927
Wire and wood, 33.6 × 43.2 × 20.3 cm
Calder Foundation, New York, Mary Calder Rower Bequest, 2011

**139.** (fig. 70) René Vincent (1879–1936)
*'Life on the Courts ... A Sports Star'*, *La Vie Parisienne*, vol. 59, no. 23 (4 June 1921), loose sheet
Colour lithography on paper, 33 × 24 cm
Private collection

**140.** Unrecorded artist
'Is Tennis a Graceful Game? The Answer of Wimbledon', *The Graphic*, 28 June 1924
Printing on paper, in bound volume, 38.6 × 26.9 cm
The Syndics of Cambridge University Library (NPR: Vols. 1–135)

## 6. SPORT SELLS

Winning or watching Olympic events was just the beginning. The 1924 Games inspired merchandise from figurines to paper fans and helped sell high-end Paris fashion. Medallists endorsed swimwear and tennis rackets and made an income from personal appearances, books and tours. The increasing power of Hollywood made film irresistible: one of the box office's biggest draws was five-times gold medallist Johnny Weissmuller.

These athletes became the faces and bodies of their nations, with an impact beyond sport or gender politics. In 1981, winning runners Eric Liddell and Harold Abrahams were immortalised in *Chariots of Fire*, a film that made their competition with each other a clash between Christianity and Judaism, and grossed $59 million at the box office.

When Weissmuller posed like a Greek statue of a discus thrower in photos advertising the 1932 Games, little did he know that Hitler, and Leni Riefenstahl's film of the Berlin Olympics, would soon use this statue to sell the Fascist fantasy of an Aryan master race.

**141.** (fig. 96) Unrecorded photographer / Hede Foto (Osvald 'Hede' Hedenström) (*c.* 1938–60s)
Czech long-distance runner Emil Zátopek (1922–2000) receiving a Paavo Nurmi statue from Ilmari Harki in Otaniemi, Espoo, during the 1952 Olympic Games in Helsinki, *c.* 1952
Black and white photograph

**142.** (fig. 95) Wäinö Aaltonen (1884–1966)
*Paavo Nurmi*, 1950–53
Metal (probably zinc), 44 × 41 × 13 cm
Finnish National Gallery,
State Art Deposit Collection
(SKOP-3740)

**143.** Still from the film *Chariots of Fire*, directed by Hugh Hudson, 1981
20th Century Studios, Inc.

**144.** The Parkstone Film Co. Ltd, Lytham (active 1920s)
*The Art of Tennis and How to Play It*, film poster, 1924
Colour printing on paper, 82.3 × 56.2 cm
On loan from Wimbledon Lawn Tennis Museum
(WTM:2022/143)

**145.** Unrecorded maker
*Suzanne Lenglen, North American Tour, Direction C.C. Pyle*, promotional leaflet, 1926
Colour printing on paper, 17.8 × 20.4 cm
On loan from Wimbledon Lawn Tennis Museum
(WTM:1995/53)

**146.** Unrecorded French maker
Souvenir handkerchief, 1924
Printed cotton, 21.7 × 22.5 cm
On loan from Wimbledon Lawn Tennis Museum
(WTM:2009/68)

**146 ▼**

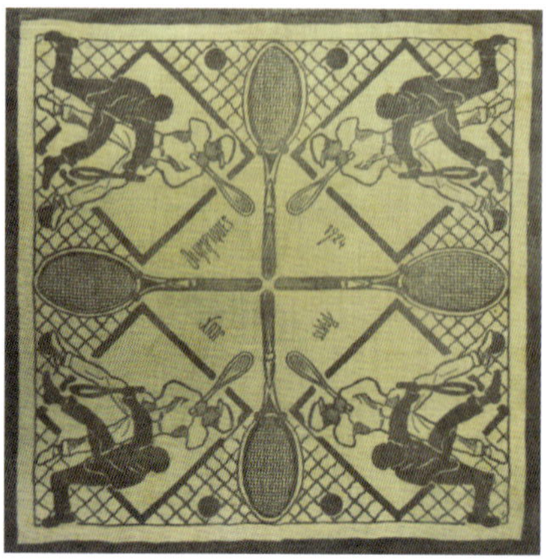

**148 ▼**

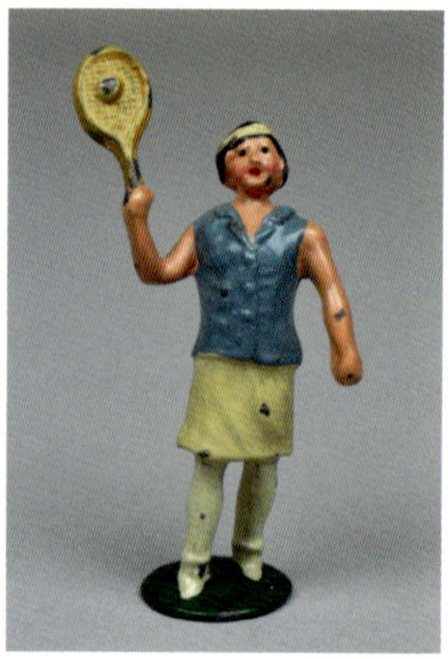

**147.** Fernand Coffin (d. 1946)
*Eighth Olympiad Paris 1924, Swimming,*
souvenir figurine, 1924
Plaster, paint, brass, 28 × 11.5 × 11 cm
Musée National du Sport, Nice, France
(MNS 2003.9.15)

This swimmer is part of a series of French figurines produced for the 1924 Olympics. The exhibition also includes a male runner, but there was a rugby player, footballer, boxer and female tennis player too, all of them with overly large heads and exaggerated expressions.

These plucky figures remind us that not all souvenirs or sculptures of the period were chic. Our swimmer stands, feet together and arms by her side, as though about to bend ready to dive. Is she holding her breath already? Like the other figures in the series, she invites the viewer to construct a narrative.

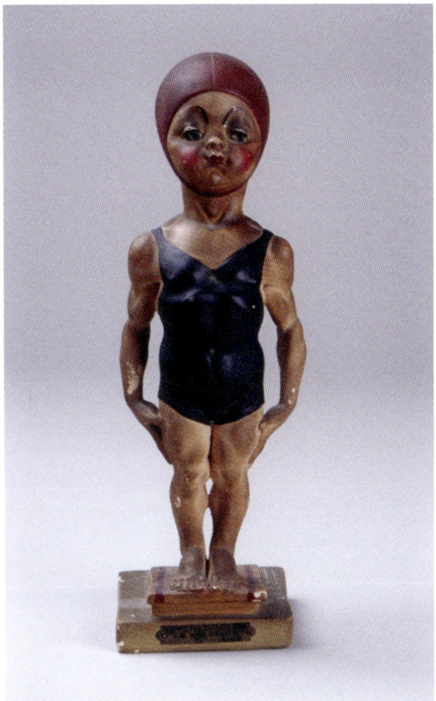

**148.** John Hill & Co. (Johillco) (founded 1898, closed 1960s)
Toy figure of a female tennis player, 1920s
Lead, paint, 6 × 3 × 1.5 cm
On loan from Wimbledon Lawn Tennis Museum
(WTM:2003/18)

**149.** Fernand Coffin (d. 1946)
*Eighth Olympiad Paris 1924, Running*, souvenir figurine, 1924
Plaster, paint, brass, 26.5 × 10 × 17 cm
Musée National du Sport, Nice, France (MNS 2003.9.10)

**150.** Benjamin Spock (1903–1988)
*The Common Sense Book of Baby and Child Care*,
Duell, Sloan and Pearce: New York, 1946
Printing on paper, covered boards, 21 × 16 cm
Newnham College Library (Parenting SPO 1 1946)

**151.** Unrecorded artist; Éditions d'art: Paris, publisher
*Art-Taste-Beauty: Pages of Feminine Elegance*,
no. 46 (15 June 1924), cover
Lithography with hand-coloured *pochoir* on paper, in bound volume, 33 × 24 cm
Victoria and Albert Museum (National Art Library), London (95.SS.16)

**152.** (fig. 10) Unrecorded artist; Éditions d'art: Paris, publisher
*Art-Taste-Beauty: Pages of Feminine Elegance*, no. 46 (15 June 1924), centre spread
Lithography with hand-coloured *pochoir* on paper, paper covers, 33 × 24 cm
Private collection

**153.** (fig. 109) Affiches Gaillard, Paris, Amiens (active 1920s)
*School of Mermaids*, film poster, *c.* 1927
Colour lithography on paper, 162.5 × 236 cm
Musée National du Sport, Nice, France
(MNS 1993.38.8)

**154.** (fig. 45) Unrecorded photographer
Grease-coated Olympic swimmer Gertrude Ederle (1906–2003) wades into the sea in France on her way to becoming the first woman to swim the English Channel, 6 August 1926
Black and white photograph
New York Daily News Archive/Getty Images

**155.** Réné Préjelan (1877–1968)
Advertising fan for *Volt* perfume by
L.T. Piver, Paris, *c.* 1924
Paper, wood, metal, 25 × 29.5 × 17 cm
The Fan Museum, Greenwich
(LDFAN2007.9.HA)

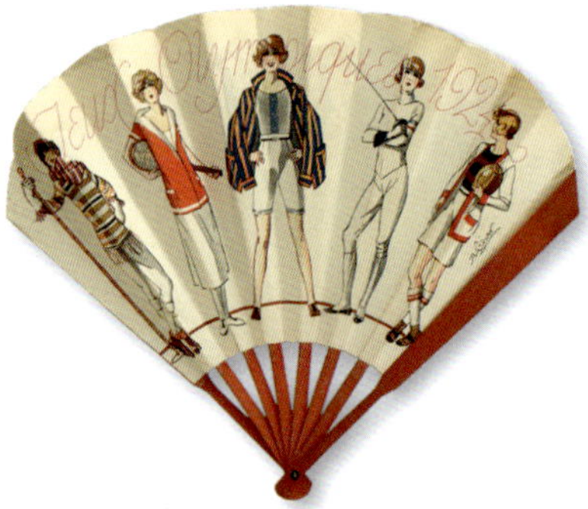

The fan uses the 1924 Games to advertise the French perfume Volt. On the same side as the Olympic slogan, women are dressed for summer and winter sports, only two of which (tennis and fencing) were open to female competitors. The fencer favours the trouser suit of her male counterparts over the skirt that women normally wore in competition; she is as iconoclastic as she is active. On the other side, in a style inspired by ancient Greece, is a laurel wreath, sword and helmet.

The fan was originally doused in scent. This scent sells itself as avant-garde and classic.

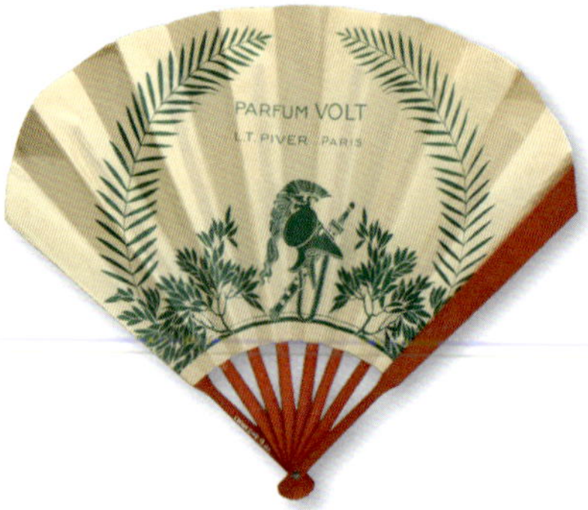


**156.** Unrecorded author
'Is this the World's Perfect Male?', *Movie Mirror*,
vol. 2, no. 2 (June 1932), p. 39
Printing on paper
Library of Congress, MBRS, Moving Image Research
Center, Washington

**157.** (fig. 110) Enzo Nistri (1923–2008), artist;
A.G.A.F, Firenze (active 1940s–60s)
*Tarzan and the Mermaids* (Italian release),
film poster, *c.* 1948
Colour lithography on paper, 192.2 x 134.6 cm
Musée National du Sport, Nice, France (MNS 84.6.7)

**158.** (fig. 40) Unrecorded photographer
Johnny Weissmuller (1904–1984) and Duke
Kahanamoku (1890–1968) at the Paris 1924
Olympic Games, 1924
Black and white photograph
Gamma-Keystone/Getty Images

**159.** Jantzen (founded 1916)
Men's swimsuit, *c.* 1925–35
Rib-knitted wool, 60 × 37 cm
On loan from the Olive Matthews Collection,
Chertsey Museum (M.2001.22)

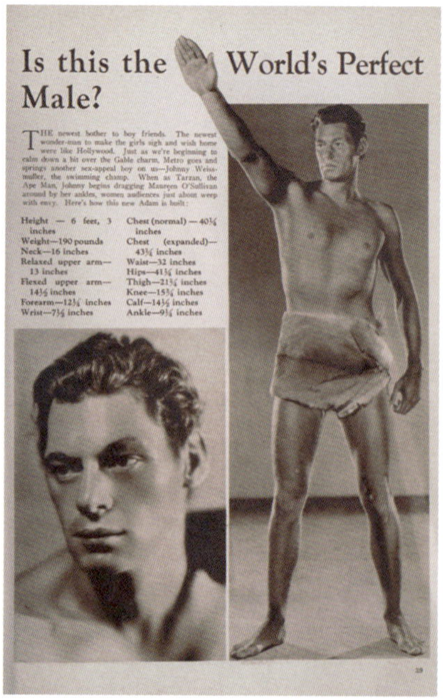

Is this the World's Perfect Male?

THE newest bother to boy friends. The newest wonder-man to make the girls sigh and wish home were like Hollywood. Just as we're beginning to calm down a bit over the Gable charm, Metro goes and springs another sex-appeal boy on us—Johnny Weissmuller, the swimming champ. When as Tarzan, the Ape Man, Johnny begins dragging Maureen O'Sullivan around by her ankles, women audiences just about weep with envy. Here's how this new Adam is built:

Height — 6 feet, 3 inches
Weight—190 pounds
Neck—16 inches
Relaxed upper arm—13 inches
Flexed upper arm—14½ inches
Forearm—12¼ inches
Wrist—7½ inches
Chest (normal)—40¼ inches
Chest (expanded)—43¼ inches
Waist—32 inches
Hips—41¼ inches
Thigh—21¼ inches
Knee—15¾ inches
Calf—14½ inches
Ankle—9¼ inches

**156** ▲

**160.** National Cycle & Novelty Company, Los Angeles (active 1920s)
*Betty*, car hood ornament, 1924
Steel, chrome-plating, paint, 13.3 × 9.1 × 6.7 cm
On loan from John Giannini

**161.** The Blackpool Tower Co. Ltd (founded 1890)
*Tower, Palace and Grand Souvenir Programme*, week of 9 April 1928
Colour printing on paper, 24.7 × 15.5 cm
Showtown, Blackpool (BC.2023.1.144)

**162.** The Blackpool Tower Co. Ltd (founded 1890)
*Memorandum of Agreement between The Blackpool Tower Co. Ltd and Miss Lucy Morton*, 25 March 1927
Typescript on paper, 33.2 × 20.3 cm
Showtown, Blackpool (BC.2023.1.154)

**163.** (fig. 37) Unrecorded photographer
Lucy Morton (1898–1980) performing her swimming classes at the Blackpool Tower Circus, 1928
Black and white photograph, 15.8 × 21.0 cm
Showtown, Blackpool (BC.2023.1.152)

**164.** (fig. 74) Diego Rivera (1886–1957)
*Mrs Helen Wills Moody*, 1930
Pastel on paper, 227.7 × 160.2 cm
Tate: Presented by the Earl of Huntingdon 1958 (T00200)

**165.** (fig. 76) Domenico Brucciani and Co., London (1841–1900s); after unrecorded Roman maker (British Museum, London, Townley Collection, 117–38 CE, marble); after Myron (bronze, now lost, *c.* 460–450 BCE)
*Discus Thrower*, *c.* 1880
Plaster, metal, paint, 176 × 58 × 115 cm
Museum of Classical Archaeology, Cambridge (118)

**166.** (fig. 75) George Hurrell (1904–1992)
Actor and Olympian Johnny Weissmuller poses as the *Discus Thrower* for the 1932 Los Angeles Olympic Games, 1932
Black and white photograph
John Springer Collection/Corbis via Getty Images

**167.** (fig. 103) Willy Zielke (1902–1989)
Production still from the prologue to Leni Riefenstahl's (1902–2003) film *Olympia* (Germany, 1938)
Black and white photograph
Album / Alamy Stock Photo

**168.** (fig. 79) Walter Herz (1909–1965), artist; McCorquodale & Co. Ltd (1846–1937), printer
Official poster for the 1948 London Olympic Games, 1948
Colour lithography on paper, 100.5 × 62.5 cm
Olympic Museum Collections, Lausanne (81722)

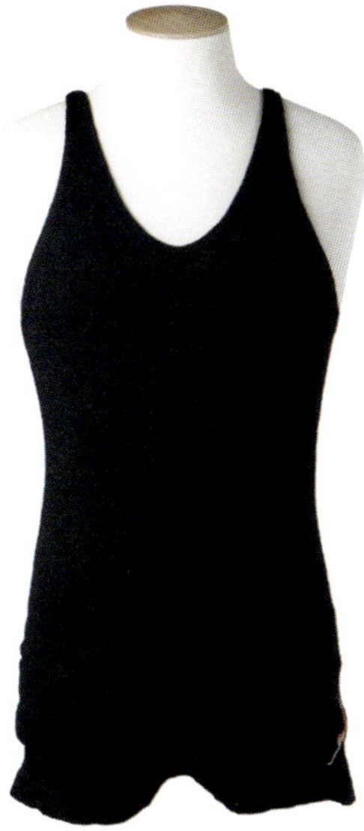

**159** ▲

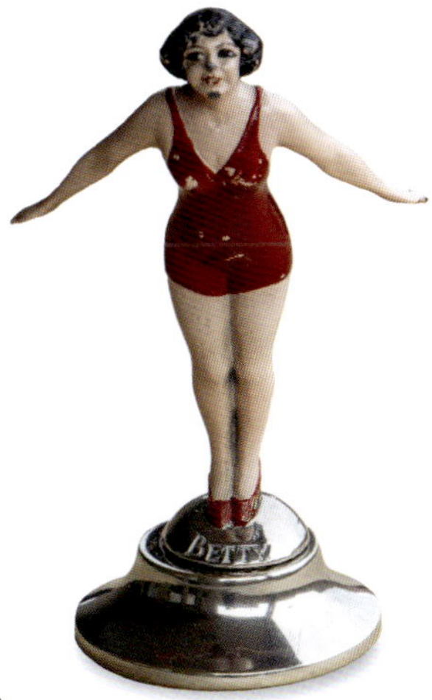


**160** ▲

**169.** Joaquin Jimenez (b. 1956); Monnaie de Paris (founded 864)
*Olympic Games Paris 2024 10 Euro Silver Hexagonal Coin – Genius*, 2022
Silver, 3.2 cm
Private collection

# FURTHER READING AND NOTES

## Introduction

### Further reading


Bouvet, Vincent and Gérard Durozol, *Paris Between the Wars: Art, Style and Glamour in the Crazy Years*, London 2010

Camps Y Wilant, Natalia, 'Charles de Coubertin's "Sports Allegory/The Crowning of the Athletes": New Insights', *Diagoras: International Academic Journal on Olympic Studies*, 1 (2017), pp. 209–28

Comité Olympique Français, *Rapport Officiel des Jeux de la VIIIe Olympiade, Paris 1924*, Paris 1924

Coubertin, Pierre de, *Mémoires Olympiques*, Paris 2016 (first published 1931)

Eiben, Jörn and Olaf Stieglitz (eds), *Visualities – Sports, Bodies, and Visual Sources*, special issue of *Historical Social Research*, 43, no. 2 (2018)

Fairlie, Francis Gerard Luis (for the British Olympic Association), *The Official Report of the VIIIth Olympiad, Paris, 1924*, London 1925

Guttmann, Allen, *The Olympics: A History of the Modern Games*, Champaign, IL 1992

Hobermann, John, 'Toward a Theory of Olympic Internationalism', *Journal of Sport History*, 22, no. 1 (1995), pp. 1–27

Holt, Richard, *Sport and Society in Modern France*, London 1981

Kramer, Bernhard, *Die olympischen Kunstwettbewerbe von 1912 bis 1948: Ergebnisse einer Spurensuche*, Munich 2004

Llewellyn, Matthew P. and John Gleaves, *The Rise and Fall of Olympic Amateurism*, Champaign, IL 2016

MacAloon, John J., *This Great Symbol: Pierre de Coubertin and the Origins of the Modern Olympic Games*, Chicago and London 1981

Müller, Norbert (ed.), *Pierre de Coubertin (1863–1937): Selected Writings*, Lausanne 2000

O'Mahony, Mike, *Olympic Visions: Images of the Games Through History*, London 2012

Osterwalder, Markus, *Olympic Games: The Design History of the Olympic Games since Athens 1896*, 2 vols, Salenstein 2020

Roche, Maurice, *Mega-Events and Modernity: Olympics and Expos in the Growth of Global Culture*, London and New York 2000

Stanton, Richard, *The Forgotten Olympic Art Competitions: The Story of the Olympic Art Competitions of the 20th Century*, Victoria, BC 2000

Terret, Thierry (ed.), *Les Paris des Jeux Olympiques de 1924*, 4 vols, Biarritz 2008

Thompson, Robert M. (for the American Olympic Association), *Report on VIII Olympiad, Paris, France, 1924*, no place 1924

Tumblety, Joan, *Remaking the Male Body: Masculinity and the Uses of Physical Culture in Interwar Vichy France*, Oxford 2013

Vere, Bernard, *Sport and Modernism in the Visual Arts in Europe, c. 1909–39*, Manchester 2018

Young, David C., *The Modern Olympics: A Struggle for Revival*, Baltimore 1996

Young, Christopher, 'Sport in West and North Europe', in Robert Edelman and Wayne Wilson (eds), *The Oxford Handbook of Sports History*, Oxford 2017, pp. 331–46


### Notes

1 Pierre de Coubertin, *Souvenirs d'Oxford et de Cambridge*, Paris 1887, unpaginated.

2 MacAloon, p. 168.

3 Don Anthony, 'The Remarkable Waldstein', *Journal of Olympic History*, 5, no. 1 (1997), p. 19.

4 Stefan Wassong, *Pierre de Coubertins US-amerikanische Studien und ihre Bedeutung für die Analyse seiner frühen Erziehungskampagne*, Würzburg 2002, p. 213.

5 Roche, p. 1.

6 Eric Hobsbawm, 'Mass-Producing Traditions: Europe, 1870–1914', in Eric Hobsbawm and Terence Ranger (eds), *The Invention of Tradition*, Cambridge 1992, p. 303.

7 MacAloon, pp. 132–8.

8 Ulrich Köhler, *Gedächtnissrede auf Ernst Curtius*, Berlin 1897.

9 'Les Jeux Olympiques à Olympie', in *Rapport Officiel*, pp. 13–19.

10 Ansgar Molzberger, *Die Olympischen Spiele 1912 in Stockholm: Zwischen Patriotismus und Internationlität*, Sankt Augustin 2012.

11 Ben Bennison, *London Daily Telegraph*, 7 July 1924, p. 12.

12 All quotations here are from the British Olympic Association (Fairlie, p. 87), who are themselves unable to resist the language of empire in noting that 'The teams of the Dominions also looked well' and in qualifying the similarity between the British and American team, whose women were distinct in being all in white.

13 Fairlie, p. 85.

14 Samuel T. Williamson, *The New York Times*, 20 July 1924, p. XX 5. See also Harold M. Abrahams and Adolphe Abrahams, *Training for Athletes*, London 1928, p. 178.

15 Montague Shearman, 'International Athletics', *Badminton Magazine*, 1 (1895), p. 389.

16 Abrahams and Abrahams, pp. 3, 24, 31, 32 and 172–8 on specialisation.

17 Ian Stone, *Alec Nelson and British Athletics Prior to World War Two*, Cambridge 2023.

18 Christopher Young, '"A Victory for the Olympic Idea": Berlin 1936 in its Sporting and Socio-Cultural Contexts', *Stadion*, 32 (2006), p. 167.

19 Jennifer Hargreaves, *Sporting Females: Critical Issues in the History and Sociology of Women's Sports*, London 1994, pp. 130–3; Florence Carpentier and Jean-Pierre Lefèvre, 'The Modern Olympic Movement, Women's Sport and the Social Order during the Inter-War Period', *The International Journal of the History of Sport*, 23, no. 7 (2006), pp. 1112–27.

20 Fairlie, pp. ix–x.

21 Olympics webpage, https://olympics.com/ioc/news/paris-2024-ticket-draw-registration-now-open (accessed 17 January 2024) and Robert W. Lewis, *The Stadium Century: Sport, Spectatorship and Mass Society in Modern France*, Manchester 2017, p. 35.

22 *Legacy 2012: Understanding the Impact of the Olympic Games*, https://www.sportsthinktank.com/uploads/legacy-2012---understanding-the-impact-of-the-olympic-games-(1).pdf (accessed 17 January 2024), and, on Paris 1924, Lewis 2017, p. 16.

23 Fairlie, pp. 43–4.
24 *L'Auto*, 26 July 1924, pp. 4 and 1.
25 Hans Joachim Teichler, 'Coubertin und Hitler', *Stadion*, 46, no. 1 (2022), pp. 6–21.
26 Coubertin, pp. 208–9 and 233–4.
27 'The Olympic Games Doomed', *The Times*, 22 July 1924, p. 14.

## 1. City of Sport

### Further reading


Holt, Richard, *Sport and Society in Modern France*, London 1981
Lewis, Robert, *The Stadium Century: Sport, Spectatorship and Mass Society in Modern France*, Manchester 2017
Pizzorni Itié, Florence (ed.), *Les Yeux du stade: Colombes, temple du sport*, Thonon-les-Bains 1993
Pointu, Raymond, *Paris Olympique*, Paris 2005
Schut, Pierre-Olaf, Sandie Beaudouin and Marion Philippe, 'Interaction Between Olympism and Host Cities: The Example of Paris', *International Journal of the History of Sport*, 37, no. 14 (2020), pp. 1443–65
Terret, Thierry (ed.), *Les Paris des Jeux Olympiques de 1924*, 4 vols, Biarritz 2008


### Notes

1 Available online at https://www.paris2024.org/en/competition-venue-concept/ (accessed 8 January 2023).
2 Jean Boggs, *Degas at the Races*, New Haven, CT 1998, p. 82. The broader concept applied here was delineated by Guy Debord in *La Société du spectacle*, Paris 1967.
3 Patrick Clastres has argued persuasively that the modern Olympic Games should not be regarded as a revival as such, but rather as 'a qualitatively new combination of competition and diplomacy ... the sporting expression of the patriotic and liberal pacifism specific to the Western elites of the Belle Époque' (my translation of the original French here and elsewhere); see Patrick Clastres, 'La renaissance des Jeux Olympiques, une invention diplomatique', *Outre-Terre*, 8, no. 3 (2004), p. 291.
4 Comité Olympique Français, *Rapport Officiel des Jeux de la VIIIe Olympiade, Paris 1924*, Paris 1924, p. 54. Available online through the LA84 Foundation, https://digital.la84.org/digital/collection/p17103coll8/id/13498/ (accessed 8 January 2023).
5 Catherine Palmer, '"We Close Towns for a Living": Spatial Transformation and the Tour de France', *Social & Cultural Geography*, 11, no. 8 (2010), pp. 865–81. On the Tour's cultural resonance more broadly, see Hugh Dauncey and Geoff Hare, 'The Tour de France: A Pre-Modern Contest in a Post-Modern Context', in Hugh Dauncey and Geoff Hare (eds), *The Tour de France, 1903–2003: A Century of Sporting Structures, Meanings and Values*, London 2003, pp. 175–202.
6 The venue was to gain lasting notoriety during the Occupation. As Colin Jones observes: 'the building is most famous for being infamous: as the holding place in which Parisian Jews were incarcerated following a major round-up in 1942, before being deported to death camps'; see Colin Jones, *Paris: Biography of a City*, London 2004, p. 483. See also Liliane Grunwald and Claude Cattaert, *Le Vel' D'Hiv', 1903–1959*, Paris 1979, pp. 78–81.
7 Paul Morand, *Ouvert la nuit*, Paris 1922; Ernest Hemingway, *A Moveable Feast*, New York 1964. See also Thomas Bauer, 'Paris in the 1920s: Hemingway's City of Sport', *Sport in History*, 39, no. 3 (2019), pp. 254–69.
8 For an overview of professional boxing in Paris in this period, see André Rauch, *Boxe, Violence du XXe siècle*, Paris 1992.
9 Claude Meunier, *Ring noir: Quand Apollinaire, Cendrars et Picabia découvraient les boxeurs nègres*, Paris 1992, p. 13.
10 Meunier, *passim*.
11 Élisabeth Lê-Germain and Philippe Tétart, 'Naissance et développement du spectacle sportif (1880–1939)', in Philippe Tétart (ed.), *Histoire du sport en France*, vol. 1, *Du Second Empire au régime de Vichy*, Paris 2007, pp. 227–59.
12 Cited in Richard Holt, *Sport and Society in Modern France*, London 1981, p. 145.
13 Racing 92, the professional rugby union franchise that is heir to the legacy of the Racing Club de France, announced in July 2021 that it had launched a women's team, combining this highly symbolic news with the rather more mundane information that it was changing its kit supplier. *L'Équipe*, 'Le Racing 92 crée une équipe féminine et change d'équipementier', 5 July 2021, https://www.lequipe.fr/Rugby/Actualites/Le-racing-92-cree-une-equipe-feminine-et-change-d-equipementier/1267986 (accessed 8 January 2024).
14 The game took place in the grounds of the former Château de Bagatelle, also in the Bois de Boulogne. This venue would subsequently be used, together with the nearby racecourses at Auteuil and Saint-Cloud, for a variety of equestrian competitions at the 1924 Games.
15 Robert Lewis, *The Stadium Century: Sport, Spectatorship and Mass Society in Modern France*, Manchester 2017, p. 24.
16 Ibid., pp. 43–5.
17 Ibid., p. 36.
18 For details of the Colombes Stadium's transformation, see Agnès Delannoy, 'Les Jeux Olympiques de 1924 et l'architecture: La construction du stade athlétique', in Pizzorni Itié, pp. 60–97.
19 See Julien Sorez, *Le Football dans Paris et ses banlieues: Un sport devenu spectacle*, Rennes 2013.
20 Lewis, pp. 15–16.
21 Raymond Pointu, Paris Olympique, Paris 2005, pp. 112–15. See also Centre d'Études Olympiques, 'Paris 1924: Stade nautique des Tourelles', in *Les Piscines olympiques des Jeux d'Été de Londres 1908 à Tokyo 2020*, Lausanne 2021, pp. 12–14. Available online through the Olympic Studies Centre's Olympic World Library at https://library.olympics.com/ (accessed 9 January 2024).
22 Antoine Le Bas, 'Des piscines et des villes: genèse et développement d'un équipement de loisir', *Histoire urbaine*, 1 (2000), pp. 145–62.

## 2. City of Art

### Further reading


Davis, Mary E., *Classic Chic: Music, Fashion and Modernism*, Berkeley, CA 2006
Dyer, Angela (ed.), *On Classic Ground: Picasso, Léger, de Chirico and the New Classicism, 1910–1930*, London 1990
Green, Christopher, *Cubism and its Enemies: Modern Movements and Reaction in French Art, 1916–1928*, New Haven, CT 1987
Green, Christopher, *Art in France, 1900–1940*, New Haven, CT 2000

O'Mahony, Mike, *Olympic Visions: Images of the Games Through History*, London 2012

Silver, Kenneth E., *Esprit de Corps: The Art of the Parisian Avant-Garde and the First World War, 1924–1925*, London 1989

Vere, Bernard, *Sport and Modernism in the Visual Arts in Europe, c. 1909–1939*, Manchester 2018

### Notes

1 Amédée Ozenfant and Charles-Edouard Jeanneret [Le Corbusier], 'After Cubism', trans. John Goodman, in Carol S. Eliel (ed.), *L'Esprit Nouveau: Purism in Paris, 1918–1925*, Los Angeles 2001, p. 137.

2 Guillaume Apollinaire, 'Through the Salon des Indépendants', in LeRoy C. Breuning (ed.), *Apollinaire on Art: Essays and Reviews, 1902–1918*, trans. Susan Sulieman, Boston 2001, p. 293.

3 Robert Delaunay, 'Notes on the Development of Robert Delaunay's Painting (1939–1940)', trans. David Shapiro and Arthur A. Cohen, in Arthur A. Cohen (ed.), *The New Art of Color: The Writings of Robert and Sonia Delaunay*, New York 1978, p. 18. The Heim provenance for the Troyes painting is given at *POP: La Plateforme Ouverte du Patrimoine*, https://www.pop.culture.gouv.fr/notice/joconde/000PE028453 (accessed 17 January 2024).

4 Guy Habasque, *Robert Delaunay (1885–1941)*, Paris 1941. That the entry for the Heim/Troyes painting does not mention its exhibition at the 1925 Indépendants is unsurprising: it was exhibited under a different title and it is unlikely that Delaunay possessed the kind of photograph of the work in the form that it was exhibited then that would have led Habasque to deduce, or Sonia Delaunay-Terk to recall, that it was the same work.

5 Filippo Tommaso Marinetti, 'Destruction of Syntax – Untrammeled Imagination – Words-in-Freedom', in Günter Berghaus (ed.), *Marinetti: Critical Writings*, trans. Doug Thompson, New York 2006, p. 122.

## 3. Cambridge, Britain and the 1924 Olympics

### Further reading

Guttmann, Allen, *The Olympics: A History of the Modern Games*, Champaign, IL 1992

Hamilton, Duncan, *For the Glory: The Life of Eric Liddell From Olympic Hero to Modern Martyr*, London 2016

Jeffreys, Kevin, *The British Olympic Association: A History*, London 2014

Llewellyn, Matthew P. and John Gleaves, *The Rise and Fall of Olympic Amateurism*, Champaign, IL 2016

Polley, Martin, *The British Olympics: Britain's Olympic Heritage 1612–2012*, Swindon 2011

Ryan, Mark, *Running with Fire: The True Story of 'Chariots of Fire' Hero*, London 2011

Stone, Ian, *Alec Nelson and British Athletics Prior to World War Two*, Cambridge 2023

### Notes

1 Neil Duncanson and Patrick Collins, *Tales of Gold*, London 1992; also Ian Buchanan, *British Olympians: A Hundred Years of Gold Medallists*, London 1991.

2 Polley, pp. 100–26.

3 Francis Gerard Luis Fairlie (for the British Olympic Association), *The Official Report of the VIIIth Olympiad, Paris, 1924*, London 1925, pp. 26–7.

4 Ian Stone, 'Alec Nelson: Professional Runner, Athletics Coach and Entrepreneur-Client', in Dave Day (ed.), *Sporting Lives*, Manchester 2010, pp. 88–111.

5 W.R. Seagrave et al., *Notes on Athletics by Members of the Cambridge University Athletics Team*, Cambridge 1922, p. 60.

6 *The Observer*, 23 March 1924, cited in Stone 2010, note 50.

7 Hamilton, pp. 121–7.

8 Duncanson and Collins, pp. 40–1.

9 *The Caian: The Magazine of Gonville and Caius College*, 28 (1920), pp. 22–3; 31 (1923), pp. 31 and 52. See also David Dee, *Sport and British Jewry: Integration, Ethnicity and Anti-Semitism*, Manchester 2013, pp. 53–69.

10 Duncanson and Collins, pp. 24–6.

11 Buchanan, p. 24.

12 Duncanson and Collins, pp. 83–4; see also David Horspool, *More than a Game: A History of How Sport Made Britain*, London 2023, pp. 193–4.

13 *Lucy Morton: A Presentation of her Life and Experiences*, unpublished personal memoir (Family Archive of the Late Lucy Morton), 2012.

14 Hugh Hudson, dir., *Chariots of Fire*, 1981.

## 4. The USA, the Sporting Superpower

### Further reading

Boddy, Kasia, 'American Girl: The Iconographies of Helen Wills', *Historical Social Research*, 43, no. 2 (2018), pp. 109–28

Bower, Brooke L., *Becoming Americans in Paris: Transatlantic Politics and Culture Between the World Wars*, Oxford 2011

Cherry, Jeanne, *Helen Wills: Tennis, Art, Life*, Wimbledon 2018

Davis, David, *Waterman: The Life and Times of Duke Kahanamoku*, Nebraska 2015

Dyreson, Mark, *Making the American Team: Sport, Culture and the American Experience*, Champaign, IL 1998

Dyreson, Mark, 'Scripting the American Olympic Story-Telling Formula: The 1924 Paris Olympic Games and the American Media', *Olympika*, 5 (1996), pp. 55–80

Gunby, Phil, 'Oarsman No. 7 Recalls 1924 Glory Days', *JAMA: The Journal of the American Medical Association*, 236, no. 2 (1976), pp. 170–2

Osmond, Gary, 'Myth-Making in Australian Sport History: Re-evaluating Duke Kahanamoku's Contribution to Surfing', *Australian Historical Studies*, 42, no. 2 (2011), pp. 260–76

Pope, Steven W., *Patriotic Games: Sporting Traditions in the American Imagination, 1876–1926*, New York and Oxford 1997

Roger, Philippe, *The American Enemy: The History of French Anti-Americanism*, Chicago 2005

Stout, Glen, *Young Woman and the Sea: How Trudy Erdele Conquered the English Channel and Inspired the World*, Boston, MA 2009

Tadie, Alexis, 'Understanding Competitive Tennis through Literature and the Visual Arts', in Robert J. Lake (ed.), *Routledge Handbook of Tennis: History, Culture and Politics*, Abingdon 2019

### Notes

1 *The New York Times*, 'U.S. STARS CLINCH ALL-AROUND TITLE', 22 July 1924, p. 10.

2 Robert M. Thompson (for the American Olympic Association), *Report on VIII Olympiad Paris, France, 1924*, no place 1924, p. 5.

3 Ibid., p. 14.
4 Ibid., p. 6.
5 John A. Lucas, 'Setting the Foundation and Governance of the American Olympics Association: The Efforts of Robert Means Thompson, 1911–19 and 1922–26', *Journal of Sport History*, 29, no. 3 (2002), p. 461.
6 Pope, p. 40.
7 *The New York Times*, 'SPORT WORLD SET FOR GREATEST OLYMPICS', 20 April 1924, section XX, p. 5.
8 *The Philadelphia Inquirer*, 23 January 1951, p. 1.
9 *The New York Times*, 'U.S. TEAM IS HISSED BY FRENCH WHEN IT WINS OLYMPIC TITLE', 19 May 1924, p. 1.
10 David Davis, *Waterman: The Life and Times of Duke Kahanamoku*, Lincoln 2015, p. 157.
11 Helena Huntington Smith, 'Another Glorified Girl', *The New Yorker*, 27 August 1927, p. 16.
12 Boddy, p. 121.

## 5. Uruguay, Football and Global Stardom

### Further reading


Campomar, Andreas, *¡Golazo! A History of Latin American Football*, London 2014

Da Cruz, Martin, *From Beauty to Duty: A Footballing History of Uruguay 1878–1917*, Chichester 2022

Galeano, Eduardo, *Football in Sun and Shadow*, London 2018

Giulianotti, Richard, 'Built by the Two Varelas: The Rise and Fall of Football Culture and National Identity in Uruguay', *Culture, Sport, Society*, 2, no. 3 (1999), pp. 134–54

Goldblatt, David, *The Ball is Round*, London 2007

Oddone, Juan, 'The Formation of Modern Uruguay, *c.* 1870–1930', in Leslie Bethell (ed.), *The Cambridge History of Latin America*, Cambridge 1986, pp. 453–74

Oliver, Brian, 'Before Pelé there was Andrade', *The Guardian*, 24 May 2014, https://www.theguardian.com/football/2014/may/24/before-pele-there-was-andrade (accessed 17 January 2024)

Williams, Adam, 'Faster, Higher, Stronger: How Uruguay Lifted the First Three Global Football Tournaments', *These Football Times*, 11 August 2020, https://thesefootballtimes.co/2020/08/11/faster-higher-stronger-how-uruguay-lifted-the-first-three-global-football-tournaments (accessed 17 January 2023)


### Notes

1 *L'Auto*, 1 June 1924, p. 1.
2 Franklin Morales, *Literatura y fútbol*, Montevideo 1969, p. 658.
3 *Chicago Daily Tribune*, 3 June 1924, p. 8.
4 Peter Winn, 'British Informal Empire in Uruguay in the Nineteenth Century', *Past & Present*, 73 (1976), p. 110.
5 Joshua Nadel, *Fútbol! Why Soccer Matters in Latin America*, Gainesville 2014, p. 23.
6 See Luis Bértola and José Antonio Ocampo, *The Economic Development of Latin America Since Independence*, Oxford 2012.
7 Oddone, p. 453.
8 Letter by José Batlle y Ordoñez to Domingo Arena and Pedro Manini Ríos, dated 7 February 1908, cited in Milton Vanger, *Uruguay's José Batlle y Ordoñez: The Determined Visionary, 1915–1917*, Boulder, CO 2010, p. 3.
9 Cited in Alejandro Giménez Rodríguez, *Sangre de campeones. Una historia del fútbol uruguayo*, Montevideo 2022, p. 5.
10 Bernard Joy, 'The Olympic Games', in A.H. Fabian and Geoffrey Green (eds), *Association Football*, vol. 4, London 1960, p. 457.
11 *Mundo Deportivo*, 16 April 1924, p. 2.
12 *Le Figaro*, 9 June 1924, p. 5.
13 *Aire Libre*, 17 June 1924.
14 Comité Olympique Français, *Rapport Officiel des Jeux de la VIIIe Olympiade, Paris 1924*, Paris 1924, p. 68.
15 Asociación Uruguaya de Football, *Uruguay campeón de football mundial: La Olímpiada de París de 1924*, Montevideo 1925, p. 47.
16 Willy Meisl, *Die Olympischen Spiele 1924 in Wort, Bild, Statistik*, Oldenburg 1924, p. 24.
17 *Mundo Uruguayo*, 13 September 1928, pp. 12–13.
18 Galeano, p. 46.
19 *Sporting*, 11 June 1924, p. 3783.
20 *L'Auto*, 27 May 1924, p. 4.
21 Florencia Faccio and Stefan Rinke, 'La globalización del fútbol durante la crisis de 1930: Uruguay y la primera Copa del Mundo', in Diego Armus and Stefan Rinke (eds), *Del football al fútbol/futebol: Historias argentinas, brasileras y uruguayas en el siglo xx*, Madrid 2014, p. 73.
22 Enrique Buero, *Negociaciones internacionales*, Brussels 1932, p. 25.
23 *El Día*, 31 July 1924, p. 8.

## 6. Sport, Science, Public Health

### Further reading


Berryman, Jack W. and Roberta J. Park (eds), *Sport and Exercise Science: Essays in the History of Sports Medicine*, Champaign, IL 1992

Heggie, Vanessa, *A History of British Sports Medicine*, Manchester 2011

Hoberman, John M., *Mortal Engines: The Science of Performance and the Dehumanization of Sport*, Caldwell, NJ 2001

Lo, Vivienne (ed.), *Perfect Bodies: Sports, Medicine and Immortality*, London 2012

Massengale, John D. and Richard A. Swanson (eds), *The History of Exercise and Sport Science*, Champaign, IL 1997

Rabinbach, Anson, *The Human Motor: Energy, Fatigue and the Origins of Modernity*, Berkeley, CA 1992

Séguillon, Didier, 'The Origins and Consequences of the First World Games for the Deaf: Paris, 1924', *The International Journal of the History of Sport*, 19, no. 1 (2002), pp. 119–36

Tumblety, Joan, *Remaking the Male Body: Masculinity and the Uses of Physical Culture in Interwar and Vichy France*, Oxford 2012

Welshman, John, 'Only Connect: The History of Sport, Medicine and Society', *International Journal of the History of Sport*, 15, no. 2 (1998) pp. 1–21


### Notes

1 Vanessa Heggie, 'Bodies, Sport and Science in the Nineteenth Century', *Past & Present*, 231 (May 2016), pp. 169–200.
2 John M. Hoberman, 'The Early Development of Sports Medicine in Germany', in Berryman and Park, pp. 233–81.

3 Ivan Waddington, 'The Development of Sports Medicine', *Sociology of Sport Journal*, 13 (1996), pp. 176–96.
4 Séguillon, pp. 119–36.
5 Brandon Moblo, 'Failed Men: The Postwar Crisis of Masculinity in France 1918–1930', *Student Summer Scholars Manuscripts*, 7 (2008), unpaginated.
6 Joanna Bourke, *Dismembering the Male: Men's Bodies, Britain and the Great War*, London and Chicago 1996.
7 Coreen McGuire, *Measuring Difference, Numbering Normal: Setting the Standards for Disability in the Interwar Period*, Manchester 2020.
8 Greg Reid and Ian F. Jobling. 'R. Tait McKenzie: Inspirational Sculptor and a Pioneer Advocate of Physical Activity for People with Disabilities', *International Journal of Disability, Development and Education*, 59 (2012), pp. 231–42.
9 Ana Carden-Coyne, *Reconstructing the Body: Classicism, Modernism, and the First World War*, Oxford 2009.
10 Vanessa Heggie, 'Testing Sex and Gender in Sports; Reinventing, Reimagining and Reconstructing Histories', *Endeavour*, 34 (December 2010), pp. 157–63.
11 The one exception is his last memorial work, the *Jane Delano Memorial* (1933) which honours nurses. See Fred Mason, 'Sculpting Soldiers and Reclaiming the Maimed: R. Tait McKenzie's Work in the First World War Period', *Canadian Bulletin of Medical History*, 27 (2010), pp. 363–83.
12 Heggie 2011.
13 Harold M. Abrahams and Adolphe Abrahams, *Training for Athletes*, London 1928.
14 Phil Gunby, 'Oarsman no. 7 Recalls 1924 Glory Days', *JAMA: The Journal of the American Medical Association*, 236, no. 2 (1976), pp. 170–2.
15 Hoberman; Robin Wolfe Scheffler, 'The Fate of a Progressive Science: The Harvard Fatigue Laboratory, Athletes, the Science of Work and the Politics of Reform', *Endeavour*, 35, nos 2–3 (2011), pp. 48–54.
16 Marta Braun, *Picturing Time: The Work of Etienne-Jules Marey*, Chicago 1992.
17 Mark L. Dyreson, 'Scripting the American Olympic Story-Telling Formula: The 1924 Paris Olympic Games and the American Media', *Olympika: The International Journal of Olympic Studies*, 5 (1996), pp. 45–80; George Trevor, 'Nurmi May Be Pressed by Ray in Millrose Meet', *The Brooklyn Daily Eagle*, 25 January 1925, p. 5.
18 Vanessa Heggie, 'A Century of Cardiomythology: Exercise and the Heart c.1880–1980', *Social History of Medicine*, 23, no. 2 (2009), pp. 280–98.
19 Adolphe Abrahams, 'Exercise and Cardiac Hypertrophy', *The Lancet*, 248, no. 6425 (1946), pp. 565–6.
20 Autio Veli-Matti, 'Nurmi, Paavo (1897–1973)', *The National Biography of Finland/Finnish Literature Society*, https://kansallisbiografia.fi/kansallisbiografia/henkilo/1786 (accessed 17 January 2024). Note that the English translation of this site by Fletcher Roderick renders this as 'nervous debility' but it is the more obvious *neurasteenikko* in the original Finnish; see 'Nurmi, Paavo (1897–1973)', *The National Biography of Finland/Finnish Literature Society*, https://kansallisbiografia.fi/english/person/1786 (accessed 17 January 2023).
21 Robert A. Nye, 'Degeneration, Neurasthenia and the Culture of Sport in Belle Époque France', *Journal of Contemporary History*, 17, no. 1 (1982), pp. 51–68.
22 Other traumas are less well studied by historians, see Lynsey Shaw Cobden, 'The Nervous Flyer: Nerves, Flying and the First World War', *British Journal for Military History*, 4, no. 2 (2018), pp. 121–42.

## 7. Sex, Gender, Body Image

### Further reading


Burstyn, Varda, *The Rites of Men: Manhood, Politics, and the Culture of Sport*, Toronto 1999

Cahn, Susan, K., *Coming on Strong: Gender and Sexuality in Twentieth-Century Women's Sport*, New York 1994

Dyreson, Mark, 'Icons of Liberty or Objects of Desire? American Women Olympians and the Politics of Consumption', *Journal of Contemporary History*, 38, no. 3, *Sport and Politics* (2003), pp. 435–60

Englemann, Larry, *The Goddess and the American Girl: The Story of Susanne Lenglen and Helen Wills*, Oxford 1988

Latimer, Tirza True, *Women Together/Women Apart: Portraits of Lesbian Paris*, New Brunswick, NJ 2005

Merrick, Jeffrey, 'Natalism, Homosexuality and the Controversy over *Corydon*', in Jeffrey Merrick and Bryant T. Ragan (eds), *Homosexuality in Modern France*, Studies in the History of Sexuality, New York 1996, pp. 202–4

Potvin, John, *Deco Dandy: Designing Masculinity in 1920s Paris*, Manchester 2020

Roberts, Mary Louise, *Civilization Without Sexes: Reconstructing Gender in Post War France, 1917–1927*, Chicago 1994

Schultz, Jaime, *Qualifying Times: Points of Change in U.S. Women's Sport*, Urbana, IL 2014

Tumblety, Joan, *Remaking the Male Body: Masculinity and the Uses of Physical Culture in Interwar and Vichy France*, Oxford 2012


### Notes

1 Young girls may have been able to attend as well as a priestess of Demeter, see David C. Young, *A Brief History of the Olympic Games*, Malden, MA 2004, pp. 119–21. For women admiring a victor in a race in armour, see the fifth-century BCE Greek poet Pindar, *Pythian Ode*, 9.97–100.
2 Dio Chrysostom (born c. 40 CE), *Discourses* 28.3, trans. James W. Cohoon.
3 1925 print advertisement from *The Saturday Evening Post*.
4 *The Saturday Evening Post*, 28 May 1932, p. 29.
5 'OLYMPIC GAMES HELP TO DOOM CORSET: Paris Dictators Say That New Lines Must Follow Lines of the Body', *The New York Times*, 16 June 1924, p. 17.
6 Cited in Engelmann, p. 302.
7 *Montana Herald*, 24 April 1925, cited in Caroline Evans, 'Jean Patou's American Mannequins: Early Fashion Shows and Modernism', *Modernism/modernity*, 15, no. 2 (2008), pp. 243–63.
8 Walter Camp in *Home Companion*, 49 (November 1922), p. 10.
9 See Austin Hancock, 'Queering Modernism's Masculine Arena: In the Boxing Ring with Claude Cahun and Marcel Moore', *Modernism/modernity*, 28, no. 4 (2021), pp. 735–59.
10 See Florys Castan-Vicente, Anaïs Bohuon and Lucie Pallesi, '"Ni de seins, ni de règlement": L'Athlète Violette Morris ou le procès de l'identité sexuée de l'entre-deux-guerres', 20 & 21. *Revue d'histoire*, 152, no. 4 (2021), pp. 87–105.
11 Ella K. Maillart, *The Cruel Way*, London 1986 (first published 1947), p. 117. The book is dedicated to 'Christina', Maillart's name for the late Schwarzenbach.
12 Suzanne Lenglen, *Lawn Tennis for Girls*, E.E. White (ed.), New

York 1920, p. 99. Also the front page of *The Illustrated London News*, 28 June 1924, which describes her as 'The Great "Gate" Attraction for Wimbledon'.

13 '"Decidedly Unconquerable" is Mlle. Lenglen, Tennis Champion', *Literary Digest*, 62 (13 September 1919), p. 80.

14 Henry de Montherlant, 'Mademoiselle de Plémeur: Championne du "Trois Cents"', *Première Olympique: Le Paradis à l'ombre des épées*, Paris 1924, pp. 139–40; translation adapted from that of John Weightman, see Henry de Montherlant, *Selected Essays by Henry de Montherlant*, Peter Quinnell (ed.), trans. John Weightman, London 1967, pp. 34–5.

15 A.G. Spalding and Bros. advertised their Mary K. Browne 'Top-Flite' model, complete with her signature, in these terms. Browne was in the world top-ten rankings in 1924.

16 'Aquatic Champions', *Current Opinion*, 73 (1922), p. 333.

17 *Los Angeles Times*, 13 April 1924, cited in Elsa Devienne, 'Spectacular Bodies: Los Angeles Beach Cultures and the Making of the "California Look" (1900s–1960s)', *European Journal of American Studies*, 14, no. 4 (2019), pp. 1–25.

18 'Paris and Hollywood Pick Men for Beauty', *Life*, 11 (October 1937), p. 107.

19 Daniel Guérin, *Le Feu du sang: Autobiographie politique et charnelle*, Paris 1977, p. 57.

20 See Julie Gaucher, 'Black Males in the Stadium: All "Bad Niggers"? French Literature, Sport and Masculinity from the 1920s to the 1950s', *The International Journal of the History of Sport*, 26 (2009), pp. 1171–86.

21 Justin Lawrence, 'Emma Raducanu's Incredible 12-Month Body Transformation Has Tennis Fans in Awe', *Daily Star*, 19 March 2023, https://www.dailystar.co.uk/sport/other-sports/raducanu-body-transformation-stuns-fans-29496100 (accessed 7 January 2024).

22 Angelique Chrisafis, 'Paris Olympic and Paralympic Games Mascots Likened to "Clitoris in Trainers"', *The Guardian*, 15 November 2022, https://www.theguardian.com/sport/2022/nov/15/mascot-paris-olympic-games-2024-likened-to-clitoris-in-trainers-phryges#:~:text=France's%20mascots%20for%20the%202024,symbol%20of%20the%20Eiffel%20Tower (accessed 7 January 2024).

## 8. The Olympics, Nationhood and the Rise of Fascism

### Further reading

Bancel, Nicolas, Pascal Blanchard, Gilles Boëtsch, Daphné Bolz, Yvan Gastaud, Sandrine Lemaire and Stéphane Mourlane (eds), *Une histoire mondiale de l'Olympisme*, Limoges 2023

Beck, Peter, 'Politics and the Olympics: The Lesson of 1924', *History Today*, 30, no. 7 (1980), pp. 7–9

Bolz, Daphné, 'Sport and Fascism', in Alan Bairner, John Kelly and Jung Woo Lee (eds), *Routledge Handbook of Sport and Politics*, London 2016, pp. 55–65

Carpentier, Florence, 'Henri de Baillet-Latour: Globalising the Olympic Movement', in Emmanuel Bayle and Patrick Clastres (eds), *Global Sports Leaders: A Biographical Analysis of International Sport Management*, Basingstoke 2018, pp. 107–23

Guttmann, Allen, *The Olympics: A History of the Modern Games*, 2nd edn, Champaign, IL 2002

Keys, Barbara J., *Globalizing Sport: National Rivalry and International Community in the 1930s*, Cambridge, MA 2006

Large, David Clay, *Nazi Games: The Olympics of 1936*, New York and London 2007

Llewellyn, Matthew P. and John Gleaves, *The Rise and Fall of Olympic Amateurism*, Champaign, IL 2016

Martin, Simon, *Sport Italia: The Italian Love Affair with Sport*, London 2011

Renson, Roland, 'War is Over, Sport is King: The Political Climate During the 1920 Olympic Games of Antwerp', *Stadion*, 21/22 (1995/1996), pp. 193–209

Torres, Cesar R., 'The Latin American "Olympic Explosion" of the 1920s: Causes and Consequences', *The International Journal of the History of Sport*, 23, no. 7 (2006), pp. 1088–111

### Notes

1 Alan Bairner, *Sport, Nationalism, and Globalization: European and North American Perspectives*, New York 2001, pp. 1–20.

2 Guttmann, p. 43.

3 Joris Vincent, 'La dernière aventure du rugby', in Thierry Terret (ed.), *Les Paris des Jeux Olympiques de 1924*, vol. 2, *Les Paris sportifs*, Biarritz 2008, pp. 421–44.

4 Fabrice Auger, 'Le Comité International Olympique face aux rivalités franco-allemandes (1918–1928)', in Pierre Milza, François Jéquier and Philippe Tétart (eds), *Le Pouvoir des anneaux: Les Jeux Olympiques à la lumière de la politique, 1896–2004*, Paris 2004, p. 111.

5 Thierry Terret, 'Les affaires du "Jury d'honneur"', in Thierry Terret (ed.), *Les Paris des Jeux Olympiques de 1924*, vol. 1, *Les Paris de la candidature et de l'organisation*, Biarritz 2008, p. 271.

6 Timothée Jobert, 'La boxe aux JO de 1924. Paris à sang et aux feux des épreuves olympiques?', in Terret, vol. 2, pp. 587–601.

7 *The Times*, London, 22 June 1924, p. 14.

8 *The New York Times*, 22 July 1924, p. 10.

9 Daphné Bolz, 'Rabaisser, dénoncer et dépasser: la réception des Jeux olympiques de 1924 dans la presse allemande', in Thierry Terret (ed.), *Les Paris des Jeux Olympiques de 1924*, vol. 3, *Paris politique, Paris médiatiques*, Biarritz 2008, pp. 773–801.

10 Alan Tomlinson and Christopher Young, 'Culture, Politics, and Spectacle in the Global Sports Event – An Introduction', in Alan Tomlinson and Christopher Young (eds), *National Identity and Global Sports Events: Culture, Politics and Spectacle in the Olympics and the Football World Cup*, New York 2006, pp. 1–9.

11 Pierre de Coubertin, *Mémoires olympiques*, Paris 1996 (first published 1931), pp. 177–88.

12 Carpentier, pp. 107–23.

13 Cesar R. Torres, 'Spreading the Olympic Idea to Latin American: The IOC-YMCA Partnership and the 1922 Latin American Games', *Journal of Olympic History*, 16, no. 1 (2008), pp. 16–24.

14 Carpentier, pp. 118–19.

## 9. Paris and the Olympic Arts Competition

### Further reading

Bateman, Anthony, 'Ludus Tonalis: Sport and Musical Modernisms 1910–1938', in Anthony Bateman and John Bale (eds), *Sporting Sounds: Relationships Between Sport and Music*, London 2009, pp. 145–63

Callède, Jean-Paul, 'Textes et écrivains français à l'heure olympique! Les concours littéraires des Jeux olympiques (1912–1948). 1re Partie: de Stockholm (1912) à Berlin (1936)', *Revue française d'histoire du livre*, 133 (2012), pp. 199–226

Charreton, Pierre, *Les fêtes du corps: Histoire et tendances de la littérature à thème sportif en France, 1870–1970*, Saint-Etienne 1985

Culleton, Claire A., 'Competing Concepts of Culture: Irish Art at the 1924 Paris Olympic Games', *Estudios Irlandeses*, 9 (2014), pp. 24–34

Guillain, Jean-Yves, *Art et Olympisme: Histoire du concours de peinture*, Biarritz 2004

Guillain, Jean-Yves, 'Quand la capitale des Arts et des Lettres accueille la troisième édition des concours d'art olympiques', in Thierry Terret (ed.), *Les Paris des Jeux Olympiques de 1924*, vol. 4, *Les Paris culturels*, Biarritz 2008, pp. 993–1029

Stanton, Richard, *The Forgotten Olympic Art Competitions: The Story of the Olympic Art Competitions of the 20th Century*, Victoria 2000

### Notes

1 Pierre de Coubertin, 'Discours d'ouverture (du 23 mai 1906) de la Conférence consultative des arts, lettres et sports', in Norbert Müller (ed.), *Textes Choisis*, vol. 2, *Olympisme*, Zurich 1986, pp. 483–4. My translation.

2 'Olympic Competitions in Painting, Sculpture and Architecture for 1908', *Revue Olympique*, 2, no. 22 (1907), pp. 344–5.

3 'Rapport sur les concours artistiques et littéraires de la Ve Olympiade', *Revue Olympique*, no. 79, July 1912, pp. 102–7.

4 *Olympic Games Antwerp 1920: Official Report*, Brussels 1957, p. 80.

5 'De Polignac Dies; Noted Sportsman', *The New York Times*, 12 December 1950; André de Fouquières, 'Concerning Americans in Paris', *The Spur*, 34, 1 July 1924, p. 56.

6 Melchior de Polignac, letters to Godefroy de Blonay, 5 March 1923 and 23 April 1923; Melchior de Polignac, *Correspondence*, Olympic Studies Centre, International Olympic Committee, Lausanne; Comité Olympique Français, *Rapport Officiel des Jeux de la VIIIe Olympiade, Paris 1924*, Paris 1924, p. 603.

7 Ibid., p. 603.

8 Ibid.

9 *Contests of Art: VIIIe Olympiade – Paris 1924*, Paris 1923, pp. 7–11.

10 Ibid., pp. 14, 18, 20, 22 and 27.

11 Jean Giraudoux, 'L'Olympiade de 1924' (first published 1920), in *Cahiers Jean Giraudoux*, vol. 12, Paris 1983, pp. 171–3.

12 Jean Giraudoux, 'Le Champion' (first published 1932), in *Cahiers*, pp. 189–91.

13 Jean de Pierrefeu, 'L'Art et le Sport', *L'Illustration*, 4250, 16 August 1924, pp. 131–4.

14 Ibid.

15 See *General Regulations for the Art Competition: IXth Olympiad Amsterdam 1928*, Amsterdam *c.* 1928, pp. 12, 17, 20 and 24.

16 See Adolphe Deville, 'L'Œuvre de Jean Jacoby', in Pierre Gricius (ed.), *Médaillés luxembourgeois aux Concours Artistiques des Jeux Olympiques: Jean Jacoby et Frantz Heldenstein. Exposition à l'Espace Royal-Monterey de la Fortis Banque Luxembourg*, Luxembourg 2008, pp. 27–34.

17 The reproduction of *Corner* in the Comité Olympique Français's *Rapport Officiel*, p. 608, raises doubts as to whether it is the same painting as in the Fitzwilliam Museum's show. Investigation by the Olympic Museum at Lausanne, however, has uncovered the label for the Paris 1924 Arts Competition. Any differences are presumably due to changes made to the painting by Jacoby after the competition.

18 Bruce Arnold, *Jack Yeats*, New Haven, CT 1998, pp. 220–1 and 227; Hilary Pyle, *Jack B. Yeats: A Catalogue Raisonné of the Oil Paintings*, vol. 1, London 1992, pp. 184–5.

19 Nikoleta Tzani, *Costas Dimitriadis: La Carrière européenne d'un sculpteur grec*, Strasbourg 2012, pp. 235–6.

20 Ibid., p. 240.

21 Ibid.

22 Pierrefeu, p. 133.

23 Guy Hickok, 'The Amazing Serge Yourievitch', *The Brooklyn Eagle*, 22 March 1925; author unattributed, 'Yourievitch, Serge (Prince)', *Benezit Dictionary of Artists*, Oxford 2023.

24 See Charles F. Hynes, 'The Presentation Field', *The Film Daily*, 22 May 1927, p. 7. See also Sidney Harris, 'Fox's Academy, N.Y.', *Billboard*, 7 December 1929, p. 18.

25 Florence Heywood, 'Notes from Paris', *The American Magazine of Art*, 15, no. 1 (1924), p. 738.

26 See '1923. c. 386 – Acquisitions et Commandes d'oeuvres d'art', Article 3, *Bulletin municipal officiel de la Ville de Paris*, 26 March 1924, p. 1693. See also 'Demain, Vernissage du salon d'Art Olympique', *L'Auto*, 15 May 1924, p. 3.

27 Géo-Charles, *Jeux Olympiques*, Paris 1925, pp. 12 and 74.

## 10. Paavo Nurmi in Prose, Poetry and Sculpture

### Further reading

Buhlmann, Britta E., *Renée Sintenis: Werkmonographie der Skulpturen*, Darmstadt 1987

Culture PL (Poland), https://culture.pl/en (accessed 8 January 2024)

Guttmann, Allen, '*Le Plaisir du Sport*: French Writers of the 1920s', *Arete*, 1 (1983), pp. 113–24

Karikko, Paavo and Mauno Koski, *Legendary Runner: A Biography of Paavo Nurmi*, trans. John O. Virtanen and Christopher Grapes, Helsinki 2006

*Kazimierz Wierzyński, Selected Poems*, Clark Mills and Ludwik Krzyżanowksi (eds), introduction Donald Davie, New York 1959

Keane, Barry, *Skamander: The Poets and their Poetry, 1918–1929*, Warsaw 2004

Kettelhake, Silke, *Renée Sintenis: Berlin, Boheme und Ringelnatz*, Berlin 2010

Kirby, David, *A Concise History of Finland*, Cambridge 2006

Lovesey, Peter, *The Kings of Distance: A Study of Five Great Runners*, London 1968

Nathan, Daniel A., '"The Nonpareil, the Runner of the Ages": Paavo Nurmi and his 1925 American Exhibition Tour', *Sport History Review*, 43 (2012), pp. 43–71

O'Byrne, Darren and Christopher Young, *Willy Meisl 'King of the Sports Journalists': A Jewish Career in Times of Change. A Critical Edition of his Writings*, Berlin forthcoming

*Renée Sintenis: Das Plastische Werk*, Ursel Berger and Günter Ladwig (eds), exh. cat., Berlin 2013

### Notes

1 John Bale, *Running Cultures: Racing in Time and Space*, London and New York 2004, p. 31.

2 Nigel Spivey, *The Ancient Olympics*, 2nd edn, Oxford 2012, p. 159.

3 Gabriel Hanot in *Le Miroir des sports*, 1924, cited in *Paavo Nurmi: The Official Site of the Flying Finn*, https://paavonurmi.fi/en/quotes (accessed 8 January 2024).

4 Daphné Bolz, 'Rebaisser, dénoncer et dépasser: la réception des Jeux olympiques de 1924 dans la presse allemande', in Thierry Terret (ed.), *Les Paris des Jeux Olympiques de 1924*, vol. 3, *Paris politiques, Paris médiatiques*, Biarritz 2004, pp. 773–801.

5 See Erik Eggers, 'Willy Meisl: Der König der Sportjournalisten', in Dietrich Schulze-Marmeling (ed.), *Davidstern und Lederball:*

Die Geschichte der Juden im deutschen und internationalen Fußball, Göttingen 2003, pp. 288–99; Kay Schiller, 'Willy Meisl's "German Football Nation": Internationalism, Austrian Patriotism, and Jewish Pride in Interwar Sports Writing', in Rebeccah Dawson, Baston Heinsohn, Oliver Knabe and Alan McDougall (eds), *Football Nation: The Playing Fields of German History, Culture and Society*, New York and Oxford, pp. 83–101.
6 Willy Meisl, *Olympische Spiele 1924 in Wort, Bild, Statistik*, Oldenburg 1924.
7 Anke Hilbrenner and Britta Lenz, 'European Sports from an Eastern European Perspective: Football in the Multiethnic Polish Territories', *European Review*, 19, no. 4 (2011), pp. 595–610.
8 Davie in *Kazimierz Wierzyński, Selected Poems*, p. 6; next quotation, p. 7.
9 Keane, p. 147. The following quotations also, pp. 147–51; on the metaphysical, Davie, p. 6.
10 The translation by Ludwik Krzyżanowksi in Mills and Krzyżanowksi, p. 30, reduces the poem from six to four stanzas and is therefore a highly marked interpretation. I am grateful to Anna Cieslik for her assistance with this literal translation. The original can be read in *Laur olimpijski: w 90-lecie zdobycia złotego medalu na Olimpiadzie w Amsterdamie*, Krzysztof Zuchora (ed.), Warsaw 2018, p. 19.
11 Natalia Camps Y Wilant, 'Der Flechteim Zirkel: Eine Inspirationsquelle für Sportmotive bei Künstlern der Weimarer Republik', in Martin Ehlers, Markus Friedrich, Helga Holz and Lothar Wieser (eds), *Kunst – Sport – Literatur*, Hildesheim 2019, pp. 116–26; also Natalia Camps Y Wilant, 'A Female Medallist at the 1928 Olympic Art Competitions', *International Journal of the History of Sport*, 33, no. 13 (2016), pp. 1483–8.
12 *Sport: 52. Ausstellung der Berliner Secession*, exh. cat., Berliner Secession in collaboration with the Museum für Leibesübungen, Berlin 1927.
13 *German Painting and Sculpture*, exh. cat., Museum of Modern Art, New York 1931, p. 43.
14 Hanna Kiel, *Renée Sintenis*, Berlin 1935, p. 31.
15 Ibid., p. 37.
16 Stephanie Barron, 'Einführung', in Stephanie Barron (ed.), *Skulptur des Expressionismus*, Munich 1984, pp. 11–26; and, in the same volume, Stella Paul, 'Renée Sintenis', pp. 186–7.
17 René Crevel and Georg Biermann, *Renée Sintenis*, Berlin 1930, pp. 10–11.
18 Buhlmann, p. 52.
19 Hans Siemsen, 'Renée Sintenis', *Veröffentlichungen des Kunstarchivs*, 27/28, Berlin 1926–27, pp. 10–14; cited here after *Renée Sintenis: Plastiken, Zeichnungen, Druckgraphiken*, exh. cat., Georg-Kolbe-Museum, Berlin 1984, pp. 121–2.
20 Crevel and Biermann, p. 14.
21 From Ron Clarke and Norman Harris, *The Lonely Breed*, London 1967, cited in *Paavo Nurmi: The Official Site of the Flying Finn*.

## 11. Cinema and the Sporting Body

### Further reading

Downing, Taylor, *Olympia*, London 2012
Kasson, John F., *Houdini, Tarzan, and the Perfect Man: The White Male Body and the Challenge of Modernity in America*, New York 2001
McKernan, Luke, 'Sports Films', in Richard Abel (ed.), *Encyclopedia of Early Cinema*, London 2005, pp. 875–6
McKernan, Luke, 'Rituals and Records: The Films of the 1924 and 1928 Olympic Games', *European Review*, 19, no. 4 (2011) pp. 563–77
Rippey, Theodore F., 'The Body in Time: Wilhelm Prager's *Wege zu Kraft und Schönheit* (1925)', in Christian Rogowski (ed.), *The Many Faces of Weimar Cinema: Rediscovering Germany's Filmic Legacy*, Rochester, NY 2010, pp. 182–97

### Notes

1 McKernan 2005, p. 875.
2 Quote from McKernan 2005, p. 876. On film and the Olympic Games before 1924, see McKernan 2011, pp. 564–7.
3 *100 Years of Olympic Films: 1912–2012*, The Criterion Collection, 2017, available on DVD, Blu-Ray and via The Criterion Channel.
4 Comité Olympique Français, *Rapport Officiel des Jeux de la VIIIe Olympiade, Paris 1924*, Paris 1924, p. 797.
5 See, for instance, the footage of cultural events around the Olympics collected in the documentary *Paris Jeux t'aime* (2005); women divers practising for the Olympics in Devon, UK, no title, 1924, https://www.britishpathe.com/asset/56072/ (accessed 10 January 2024); athletes arriving in Ireland for the Tailteann Games, *WORLD'S GREATEST ATHLETES AND RECORD-BREAKER AT THE OLYMPIC GAMES arrive for Aonac Tailteann and are welcomed by the Director Mr. J.J. Walsh*, 1924, https://www.britishpathe.com/asset/50851/ (accessed 10 January 2024); and the finals at Wimbledon, *Lawn Tennis Finals at Wimbledon*, 1924, https://www.britishpathe.com/asset/168758/ (accessed 10 January 2024).
6 Downing, p. 18.
7 Ibid.
8 The sources are collected in McKernan 2011, pp. 567 and 576.
9 See further Pantelis Michelakis, 'The Antelope and the Lioness: Ancient Greece in the Prologue of Leni Riefenstahl's *Olympia*', *Fascism: Journal of Comparative Fascist Studies*, 12, no. 2 (2023), pp. 228–53.
10 Rippey, p. 187.
11 Andreas Huyssen, *After the Great Divide: Modernism, Mass Culture, Postmodernism*, Bloomington, IN 1986, p. 79.
12 Thomas Elsaesser, 'Innocence Restored: Reading and Re-Reading a Classic', in Michael Minden and Holger Bachmann (eds), *Fritz Lang's 'Metropolis': Cinematic Visions of Technology and Fear*, Rochester 2000, p. 132.
13 Rippey, p. 192.
14 Ibid.
15 The film is held in the British Film Institute. The film's full title is *Running – A Sport That Creates Both Bodily and Mental Health (1924): Juvenile Races at a Country Sports Meeting, and Scenes from the 1924 Olympics with W.M. Cotterell, Harold Abrahams, E.H. Liddell, D.G. Lowe, H.B. Stallard, G.M. Butler and D. McLeod Wright*. The film was part of the series *Sporting Life and What Not to Do but How to Do It*, made by Stoll Film Company.
16 Quotation from S. Kay Tombs, *Handbook of Phenomenology and Medicine*, Dordrecht 2001, p. 44.
17 Shelley Stamp, 'Women's Movement: USA', in Richard Abel (ed.), *Encyclopedia of Early Cinema*, London 2005, p. 1008.
18 Kasson, p. 222.
19 See Bolz's essay in this volume.

# PICTURE CREDITS

Page 2 © AELTC / Wimbledon Lawn Tennis Museum. © ADAGP, Paris and DACS, London 2024; 1 © 1924 / Comité International Olympique (CIO); 2 Museum of Classical Archaeology, University of Cambridge. Photo by Michael Webb, Photography and Reprographics, Yusuf Hamied Department of Chemistry, University of Cambridge; 3 © Olympic archive Markus Osterwalder, Switzerland; 4, 5 © 1924 / Comité International Olympique (CIO); 6 Churchill Archives Centre, Papers of Sir Arthur Marshall; 7 © Victoria and Albert Museum, London; 8 © The Trustees of the British Museum; 9 Collection of the McNay Art Museum, Gift of Robert L. B. Tobin, 1974.26. © Estate of George Grosz, Princeton, N.J. / DACS 2024; 10, page 26 Private Collection; 11, 12 © 1924 / Comité International Olympique (CIO); 13 © The Fitzwilliam Museum, Cambridge. © Estate of George Grosz, Princeton, N.J. / DACS 2024; 14 © The Fitzwilliam Museum, Cambridge. © ADAGP, Paris and DACS, London 2024; 15, 16 © 1924 / Comité International Olympique (CIO); 17 Bibliothèque nationale de France; 18 Courtesy of Thomas E. Weil; 19 © 1924 / Comité International Olympique (CIO) / United Archives; 20 Pallant House Gallery / Kearley Bequest through The Art Fund (1989) / Bridgeman Images. © ADAGP, Paris and DACS, London 2024; 21 © AELTC / Wimbledon Lawn Tennis Museum. © ADAGP, Paris and DACS, London 2024; 22 RMN-Grand Palais / Photo Tony Querrec / RMN-GP / Dist. Photo SCALA, Florence. © Succession Picasso/DACS, London 2024; 23 Collection of the McNay Art Museum, Gift of Robert L. B. Tobin, TL1999.18.2; 24 Collection of the McNay Art Museum, Gift of Robert L. B. Tobin, TL1999.18.5; 25 Librairie Le Feu Follet – Edition-Originale.com. © Succession Picasso/DACS, London 2024; 26 National Museum of Serbia; 27 RMN-Grand Palais / Photo Gérard Blot/ Dist. Photo SCALA, Florence; 28 Bibliothèque nationale de France; Page 54 akg-images / ullstein bild; 29 The Burghley House Collection; 30 Courtesy Jamie Macnab of Macnab; 31 Hulton-Deutsch Collection/ Corbis via Getty Images; 32 By permission of the Master and Fellows of Gonville and Caius College, Cambridge. Photo © Keystone/Getty Images; 33 By permission of the Master and Fellows of Gonville and Caius College, Cambridge. Photo © Lafayette Photography Ltd; 34 PA Images / Alamy Stock Photo; 35 © AELTC / Wimbledon Lawn Tennis Museum; 36 akg-images / ullstein bild; 37 Showtown Blackpool; 38 National Portrait Gallery, Smithsonian Institution, Washington; 39 Courtesy of Thomas E Weil; 40 Gamma-Keystone / Getty Images; 41 DeHart Hubbard Collection, Mss 1067, Cincinnati Museum Center; 42 © AELTC / Wimbledon Lawn Tennis Museum; 43 Photo courtesy of Calder Foundation, New York / Art Resource, New York. © 2024 Calder Foundation, New York / DACS, London; 44 Allentown Art Museum, Gift of Kate Fowler Merle-Smith, 1978. (1978.26.165); 45 New York Daily News Archive / Getty Images; 46 Centro de Fotografía de Montevideo; 47 © 1924 / Comité International Olympique (CIO) / United Archives; 48 Homecrowd.io; 49 © 1924 / Comité International Olympique (CIO); 50 Bob Thomas / Popperfoto / Getty Images; 51 Paul Popper / Popperfoto / Getty Images; 52 Bob Thomas / Popperfoto / Getty Images; 53 © Collections Musée National du Sport, France; 54 Bob Thomas / Popperfoto / Getty Images; Page 92 Private collection, courtesy Comité Jacqueline Marval Paris. © Nicolas Rouxdit Buisson; 55 National Trust Images. Photo Jaron James; 56 © Imperial War Museum (Art.IWM PST11165) © ADAGP, Paris and DACS, London 2024; 57 *Exercise in Education and Medicine*, by R. Tait McKenzie, 1915. Photograph by Pennsylvania Institution for the Instruction of the Blind; 58 National Trust Images. Photo Jaron James; 59 charistoone-images / Alamy Stock Photo; 60 Reebok Brand Archive / © Reebok International Limited; 61 Reproduced by kind permission of the Syndics of Cambridge University Library; 62 Courtesy of The Cadbury Research Library, University of Birmingham. MS935/2; 63 Sports Museum of Finland; 64 Photo Scala, Florence/bpk, Bildagentur für Kunst, Kultur und Geschichte, Berlin. © DACS 2024; 65 Bibliothèque nationale de France; 66 Private collection ; 67 mycomicshop.com; 68, 69 Bibliothèque nationale de France; 70 Private Collection; 71 Collection Het Noordbrabants Museum, 's-Hertogenbosch. © DACS 2024; 72 The Jan T. and Marica Vilcek Collection, Promised gift to The Vilcek Foundation; 73 Museum of Classical Archaeology, University of Cambridge. Photo by Michael Webb, Photography and Reprographics, Yusuf Hamied Department of Chemistry, University of Cambridge; 74 Presented by the Earl of Huntingdon 1958. © Banco de México Diego Rivera Frida Kahlo Museums Trust, Mexico, D.F. / DACS 2024. Photo Tate; 75 John Springer Collection / Corbis / Getty Images; 76 Museum of Classical Archaeology, University of Cambridge. Photo by Michael Webb, Photography and Reprographics, Yusuf Hamied Department of Chemistry, University of Cambridge; 77 CBW / Alamy Stock Photo; 78 © Victoria and Albert Museum, London; 79 © 1924 / Comité International Olympique (CIO); 80 Photo © Tate. © ADAGP, Paris and DACS, London 2024; 81 INTERFOTO / Alamy Stock Photo; Page 130 © 1924 / Comité International Olympique (CIO); 82 Photograph reproduced with the kind permission of Northampton Museums and Art Gallery; 83 Photo © National Gallery of Ireland; 84 © 1924 / Comité International Olympique (CIO); 85 Reproduced by kind permission of the Syndics of Cambridge University Library; 86 Chronicle / Alamy Stock Photo; 87, 88 © 1924 / Comité International Olympique (CIO); 89 Photo © National Gallery of Ireland. © Estate of Jack B Yeats. All rights reserved, DACS 2024; 90, 91 Dimitriadis archive, Hellenic Literary and Historical Archive / National Bank of Greece Cultural Foundation; 92 Michel Euler / Associated Press / Alamy Stock Photo; 93 Olaf Protze / Alamy Stock Photo; 94 © 1924 / Comité International Olympique (CIO); 95 Finnish National Gallery / State Art Deposit Collection. Photo Finnish National Gallery / Museokuva. © DACS 2024; 96 Hede Foto (Osvald 'Hede' Hedenström); 97, 98 © 1924 / Comité International Olympique (CIO); 99 Leicester Museums and Galleries. © DACS 2024; 100 Photo Scala, Florence/bpk, Bildagentur für Kunst, Kultur und Geschichte, Berlin. © DACS 2024; 101 © Collection Kröller-Müller Museum, Otterlo, the Netherlands. Photo by Tom Haartsen. © DACS 2024; 102 Comité International Olympique (CIO); 103 Album / Alamy Stock Photo; 104 akg-images / ullstein bild; 105 *Metropolis*, Fritz Lang, 1927; 106 *Barnyard Olympics*, from the series *Aesop's Fables*, Paul Terry, 1924; 107 Comité International Olympique (CIO); 108 Wellcome Collection, London; 109, 110 © Collections Musée National du Sport, France; Page 170 © National Portrait Gallery, London; Cat. 3 Museum of Classical Archaeology, University of Cambridge. Photo by Michael Webb, Photography and Reprographics, Yusuf Hamied Department of Chemistry, University of Cambridge; Cat. 6 © The Trustees of the British Museum, London; Cat. 7 © Olympic archive Markus Osterwalder, Switzerland; Cat. 8 © Collections Musée National du Sport, France; Cat. 10 © Collections Musée National du Sport, France; Cats 13, 14 © AELTC / Wimbledon Lawn Tennis Museum; Cat. 19 © Olympic archive Markus Osterwalder, Switzerland; Cat. 29 © National Portrait Gallery, London; Cat. 32 Churchill Archives Centre, Papers of Sir Arthur Marshall; Cat. 45 Reproduced by kind permission of the Syndics of Cambridge University Library; Cat. 52 © National Portrait Gallery, London; Cats 53, 57, 60 Showtown, Blackpool; Cat. 64 © Collections Musée National du Sport, France; Cat. 86 Private collection / Album / Alamy Stock Photo; Cat. 88 Photo © Tate; Cat. 91 © Olympic archive Markus Osterwalder, Switzerland; Cat. 92 © AELTC / Wimbledon Lawn Tennis Museum; Cat. 95 The Wilson collection © the artist's estate; Cat. 98 © AELTC / Wimbledon Lawn Tennis Museum; Cat. 110 National Trust Images. Photo Jaron James; Cat. 118 Courtesy of National Museums Northern Ireland; Cat. 121 Library of Congress, Music Division. © ADAGP, Paris and DACS, London 2024; Cat. 122 © The Fitzwilliam Museum, Cambridge. © Succession Picasso/DACS, London 2024; Cat. 123 Private collection, courtesy Comité Jacqueline Marval Paris. © Nicolas Rouxdit Buisson; Cat. 130 Bibliothèque nationale de France; Cat. 131 Succession Ella Maillart and Photo Elysée, Lausanne; Cats 135, 146, 148 © AELTC / Wimbledon Lawn Tennis Museum; Cat. 147 © Collections Musée National du Sport, France; Cat. 155 The Fan Museum, Greenwich; Cat. 156 Library of Congress, MBRS, Moving Image Research Center; Cat. 159 © The Olive Matthews Collection, Chertsey Museum. Photo by John Chase Photography; Cat. 160 Courtesy of John Giannini.

# ACKNOWLEDGEMENTS

This exhibition has had a long gestation, starting with the spark of an idea in 2019 and spanning and surviving the pandemic. It is our pleasure to thank the many people who helped in the various phases of its development. At the Fitzwilliam, Luke Syson deserves much credit for showing real enthusiasm for a show that lay beyond his personal sphere of interest; Jo Vine and David Evans provided indispensable support at the concept stage. Beyond the Fitzwilliam, Robin Osborne was a sounding board throughout, and academic colleagues Richard Holt and Mike Cronin lent their expertise with typical generosity as we submitted an application to the Cambridge Humanities Research Grant Scheme for the exploratory workshops from which all else flowed. Our thanks to the Isaac Newton Trust and the School of Arts and Humanities for providing the underlying funding for these.

We count ourselves fortunate indeed to have worked with Rebecca Virág and Sophia Patel at the Fitzwilliam. Rebecca is more than an Exhibitions Research Assistant. Her attention to detail and grasp of the bigger picture are impressive, her ability to identify loans superb, and her tenacity in chasing them down – when all appears lost – unsurpassed. Rebecca put heart and soul into this exhibition from the start and we consider her a third curator. Sophia brought calm, order and direction to the project in autumn 2023, just when we needed it most. Her skill in persuading those around her to contemplate, then achieve the impossible is remarkable. Without the close bonds we formed with Rebecca and Sophia, the labour required to put on a show of such complexity would have been scarcely imaginable. We are delighted to call them friends.

It is our pleasant duty to record special thanks to other colleagues at the Fitzwilliam. Alex Fairhead helped keep the project on track. Elena Saggers did an outstanding job in securing loans from around the world. Susanna Pancaldo dealt with the conservation of very diverse objects, always explaining her reasoning with compelling clarity. Natasha Lawson inspired confidence in everything she said and did in collection matters. Nadine Langford brought her experience to bear on the narrative, showing much patience over many months. Our thanks also go to: Claire Alfrey, Natalie Duff, Jennifer Grindley, Karen Livingstone, Carey Robinson, Emma Shaw, Neal Spencer at the Fitzwilliam; and to the whole team at Nissen Richards Studio for the exhibition design, Sam Talbot for PR and Kellenberger-White for marketing.

The ideas that underpin such a wide-ranging exhibition require input from many perspectives. We convened two virtual workshops, in May and December 2020, at the height of the first and second lockdowns, and are enormously grateful to colleagues who joined us from near and far and gave so freely and creatively at a time of global anxiety: Kristi Bain, Tricia Beer, Daphné Bolz, Hannah Brown, (the sorely missed) Jane Brown Grimes, Diana Caulfield, Paul Cartledge, Mike Cronin, Philip Dine, Erica Emond, Vanessa Heggie, Richard Holt, Vince Hunt, Randy Kaufman, Manfred Lämmer, Paul Lawrence, Amanda Lightstone, Luke McKernan, Kevin Moore, Jane Munro, Darren O'Byrne, Miles Osgood, Mark Purcell, Miranda Stearn, Bernard Vere, Derek Wilson, Wayne Wilson, Peter Young.

We are indebted to the colleagues who worked with us on this catalogue. At an in-person workshop in November 2023, our authors brought their specific expertise to bear in working with and speaking to each other in ways we have rarely witnessed before. They produced draft essays in record time, and met our requests and suggestions over several iterations with openness and flexibility. We are grateful to them all for entering into the spirit of true collaboration, and we trust this has left a palpable trace for our readers. Our internal copy editor, Orsolya Petocz, brought incredible precision to a challenging manuscript, often thinking and working beyond her immediate remit, always to great effect. To her, we owe a great debt of gratitude, as we do also to the photographers at the Fitzwilliam: Mike Jones, Amy Jugg, Katie Young and Elaine Holder. Our thanks too to Jo Walton, who did sterling work as image researcher; Susannah Lawson and Mary Scott for editorial consultancy; and all at Paul Holberton Publishing.

Last but not least, the list of lenders to this exhibition, from both public and private collections, is a very long one and although we cannot list them all here, we would like to extend our heartfelt gratitude to each and every one. This exhibition simply could not have happened without their generous support.

**Caroline Vout and Christopher Young**

First published in 2024 to accompany the exhibition
*Paris 1924: Sport, Art and the Body*
at the Fitzwilliam Museum,
University of Cambridge, 19 July 2024 – 3 November 2024



ISBN 978-1-913645-60-1
British Library Cataloguing in Publication Data
A catalogue record for this book is available from the British Library

Produced by Paul Holberton Publishing
www.paulholberton.com

Designed by Paul Sloman
Printing by Gomer UK



This publication has been generously supported by The Fitzwilliam Museum Development Trust